D1168364

QUEST FOR REFUGE

*The Mormon Flight from
American Pluralism*

QUEST FOR REFUGE
The Mormon Flight from American Pluralism

Marvin S. Hill

Signature Books
Salt Lake City
1989

© 1989 by Signature Books, Inc. All rights reserved
Signature Books is a registered trademark of Signature Books, Inc.
Printed in the United States of America
96 95 94 93 92 91 90 89   6 5 4 3 2 1

Library of Congress Cataloging-in-Publication Data

Hill, Marvin S.
   Quest for refuge : the Mormon flight from American Pluralism
  Marvin S. Hill.
     p.   cm.
   Includes index.
   ISBN 0-941214-70-2
   1. Mormon Church—Northeastern States—History—19th century.
2. Mormon Church—Northwest, Old—History—19th century.   3. Smith,
Joseph, 1805-1844.   4. Northeastern States—Church history.
5. Northwest, Old—Church history,   6. Church of Jesus Christ of
Latter-Day Saints—Northeastern States—History—19th century.
7. Church of Jesus Christ of Latter-Day Saints—Northwest, Old—
History—19th century.   I. Title.
BX8615.NG9H55   1989
289.3'09'034—dc19

                                          88-30213
                                          CIP

ON THE HALF-TITLE PAGE: ORIGINAL RENDERING OF THE WEATHER VANE ON THE NAUVOO TEMPLE BY WILLIAM WEEKS, CIRCA 1843

Contents

Acknowledgements

Because this study began as a Ph.D. dissertation more than twenty-five years ago at the University of Chicago, the number of scholars and others to whom I am indebted is long and there is risk that I may unintentionally overlook some who helped. If so, here is my expression of thanks. Among those who are remembered are Sidney E. Mead, then professor of American Christianity at the Chicago Divinity School, whose classes on American religious history first called my attention to a significant relationship between American pluralism and the rise of Mormonism. Mead left the university before I began research or writing. The rough draft was read and criticized constructively by Martin E. Marty, also of the divinity school, and to him I owe a special thanks. I also am deeply in debt to Daniel J. Boorstin, professor of American intellectual history, who offered in classes and out special encouragement and insight, read the manuscript, and made important suggestions. Although I have made some substantial alterations, in the narrative of the dissertation much of the material remains the same. So too does my gratitude to these three superb historians who inspired and refined the original work.

I owe much to Don Schmidt and Earl Olson, formerly of the Historical Department of the Church of Jesus Christ of Latter-day Saints in Salt Lake City, who allowed me free access to a great deal of material not otherwise accessible, as well as to James Kimball who helped me to locate much of these then-unorganized sources. Without their generous cooperation this study would be devoid of a great deal of rich documentation. I am also indebted to Richard P. Howard, of the History Commission of the Reorganized Church of Jesus Christ of Latter Day Saints in Independence, Missouri, for access to important sources. Many archivists and librarians at several other institutions made similar contributions. Included are those at the University of Chicago, the Chicago Historical Society, the Newberry Library, and the Illinois State Historical Society, as well as Professor Stanley B. Kimball of Southern Illinois University who has collected important material at Edwardsville. I also visited the Western Reserve Historical Society in Cleveland and the library of the University of Wisconsin at Madison. In Missouri several institutions and their staffs contributed, including the Missouri Historical Society at St. Louis, the Missouri State Historical Society at Columbia, and in the same city the University of Missouri with its Western Manuscripts Collection.

I made use of newspapers at the Library of Congress and found other sources there of value. The Huntington Library at San Marino, California, granted me and my sister, Donna Hill, a stipend and access to their rich resources on Mormonism in connection with another work. The Department of History at Yale University offered me a research fellowship for a year to make use of their valuable sources in the Beinecke Library and also to take classes from Sidney B. Ahlstrom and Daniel Howe.

As important as any are archivists and librarians at the Harold B. Lee Library, Brigham Young University, Provo, Utah, who have gathered what I consider to be one of the finest collections of Mormon materials in the country. Special Collections administrator Chad Flake and the curator of the Archives of the Mormon Experience, David Whittaker, assisted me on innumerable occasions, the latter going far beyond the routine help that archivists provide in keeping me informed of new sources. Harvard Heath, archivist of Utah and the American West, was also helpful.

There are many others to whom I am indebted. Richard Hughes of Pepperdine University read my dissertation and made suggestions that helped me to eliminate certain superfluous material. Colleagues in the history department at Brigham Young University provided insights and helped me to find material, as well as generated an atmosphere where inquiry into Mormon history is valued. These include James Allen, Thomas Alexander, Ronald Walker, Michael Quinn, and Malcolm Thorp. Several department chairmen over the years— Eugene Campbell, DeLamar Jensen, Ted Warner, James Allen, and Paul Pixton—granted me time free from classes to pursue research and writing. Two deans of the College of Family and Social Sciences—Martin Hickman and Stanley Albrecht—also helped in this way, as did Leonard Arrington and Ronald Esplin of the Joseph Fielding Smith Institute for Church History.

I owe something special to many family members, including Bob, Donna, Lila (who contributed more than she or I can fully appreciate), Steven who helped with some research, and Leslie who helped with the index. Dallin Oaks, formerly president of Brigham Young University and a friend at Chicago who co-authored a previous book with me, contributed great insight into the trial of the murderers of Joseph Smith.

To the staff at Signature Books—Gary Bergera, Brent Corcoran, Connie Disney, Jani Fleet, and Ronald Priddis—many thanks for encouraging me to revise and update the dissertation and for their editorial efforts which saved errors and ineffectual writing.

To all I express thanks. Yet the ideas and arguments presented here are my own, gleaned from my reading of original sources and the works of other specialists in the field of Mormon history. Not they but I alone am responsible for what follows.

Introduction

When the Mormon prophet Joseph Smith, Jr., recalled the beginnings of his movement in a history published in 1842, he noted that a revival he attended in the area around Palmyra, New York, had initially created "unusual excitement" among the people but then divided them, with "priest contending against priest, and convert against convert." Whatever good will had flourished among his neighbors was soon "lost in a strife of words and a contest about opinions." In another version of his experiences, Smith concluded that "if God had a church, it would not be split up into factions." Thus the prophet spoke of the deep Mormon aversion to religious institutional diversity, which I term here religious pluralism. But in 1834 Oliver Cowdery, Smith's close friend and co-worker in the Mormon kingdom, remembered in the young church's *Messenger and Advocate* that this antipathy extended beyond sectarian rivalry to all voluntary associations in America and predicted their impending doom: "Certain the Gentile world, with all its parties, sects, denominations, reformations, revivals of religion, societies and associations, are devoted to destruction."[1]

The Latter-day Saints saw the maelstrom of competing faiths and social institutions as evidence of social upheaval and found confirmation in the rioting and violence that characterized Jacksonian America. One nationally recognized scholar has noted that there was reason for concern, for America was experiencing a degree of social disintegration "unequalled in American history" due to rapid westward expansion and the resulting breakdown of family, church, and community ties.[2]

Yet as Alexis de Tocqueville perceived, the voluntary reform, religious, and other associations which littered the American landscape were institutional means by which the individualistic, democratic society preserved social cooperation and purpose. If Americans "never acquired the habit of forming associations in ordinary life," de Tocqueville wrote, "civilization itself would be endangered. A people among whom individuals lost the power of achieving great things single-handed, without acquiring the means of producing them by united exertions, would soon relapse into barbarism."[3] In opposing voluntary associations the Saints were repudiating some of the fundamental ways in which the developing democratic society functioned. Recognition of that attitude and its implications cuts far deeper, I believe, than most historians have realized.

The Latter-day Saints were influenced in their social theory by their unique scripture, the Book of Mormon, which Joseph Smith said was translated in 1829 from golden plates buried in the earth for more than fourteen hundred years. The text described a society of ancient Americans faced with social disintegration, brought on by religious disbelief, rampant materialism, indifference toward the poor, political corruption, and war, all of which threatened their survival. Book of Mormon society was divided into two main factions: Nephites who were true Christians and who established a theocratic government to offset social disintegration, and Lamanites who were atheists and who waged a war of extermination on God's elect. The scripture describes a thousand years of such warfare between the two groups, until the Nephites succumbed to materialism, declining faith, and destruction. Nephite society thrived only at times when prophet-statesmen controlled the government and sustained the support of the faithful. Thus Nephite society was anti-pluralistic, for dissent and diversity were always atheistic and destructive.[4]

Despite this, Nephites believed in individual freedom—freedom to choose between two opposites, faith and disbelief, good and evil. Thus the Nephite concept of freedom fell far short of the religious freedom being advanced in the United States in 1830. Reminiscent in some ways of the beliefs of early Massachusetts Bay Puritans, Nephites wanted freedom mainly to preserve their own true religion but were reluctant to allow others the might to oppose it. Although one Book of Mormon prophet recorded that laws were passed to allow disbelievers to hold their own opinions without sanctions by church or state, false prophets were nonetheless punished and judged for wrong thinking. It is unlikely that dissenters were truly free to express their opinions openly. One of these preached his views for a time but was confronted by ecclesiastical and civil authorities, banned from the society, and subsequently killed. Thus the true faith was preserved.[5] The dominant message of the Book of Mormon is not merely that the nation must believe in the true gospel of Jesus Christ to survive, but that godly men must rule. When they do not society is imperiled.

In the years prior to 1830 when the Book of Mormon was published and the Mormon church organized, some Americans had argued for an exclusively Christian nation, but the founding fathers through the Constitution had established a society based on different principles.[6] Instead of concentrating power in the hands of a single religious or political group, they created a government which diffused such power through a network of checks and balances between the states and the branches of the national government. Certainly the new Constitution licensed a stronger central government than had the Articles of Confederation. But according to James Madison of Virginia, this new institutional power would be moderated by the expanse of the nation and by the greater diversity of peoples and interests competing within its boundaries. No single interest group or "faction" would be able to dominate.[7] Thus pluralism would help preserve American freedom. Madison's argument was effective in helping to get the new Constitution adopted, because the American people were suspicious of power held in the hands of a few individuals.

The founding fathers abandoned the idea predominant in Europe of an established church supported by state taxes and favored by the government. America's founders introduced a concept of religious freedom which left every person free to choose a denomination or to choose none and believe none. No religious requirements were to be imposed on those seeking public office.[8] Madison and Thomas Jefferson best articulated this principle. Jefferson first advanced his ideas in Virginia in 1776, arguing that religion is a personal matter between God and the individual and that the state should not intrude. He stated his beliefs in Virginia's famous Bill for Religious Freedom adopted in 1785:

> No man shall be compelled to frequent or support any religious worship, place, or ministry whatsoever, nor shall be enforced, restrained, molested, or burdened in his body or goods, or shall otherwise suffer, on account of his religious opinions or belief;

> but that all men shall be free to profess, and by argument to
> maintain, their opinions in matters of religion, and that the same
> shall in no wise diminish, enlarge, or affect their civil capa-
> cities.

Jefferson believed that people are molded by experience and that
each mind is therefore unique. To coerce conscience is to create hyp-
ocrites. Clearly Jefferson did not want religious groups to have special political prerogatives, although he would leave them free to promote their cause.[9]

The founding fathers adopted Jefferson's perspective in the Constitutional Convention but largely from necessity. They could not
agree whether an established church was necessary or which church
to establish.[10] The eventual disestablishment of religion in America
created a society that was potentially religious should people voluntarily support the churches but also potentially secular should they
not do so. Jefferson held that religion if true would prevail in the
open market. Such a belief encouraged the multiplication of sects
and, inevitably, conflict among them, but it also guaranteed that no
one denomination would gain national political dominance.

Most nineteenth-century Americans supported this enshrine-
ment of religious pluralism in the Constitution. Their ideal national
government consisted of civilians governing a diverse, competitive,
secular society, where no religious group had priority.[11] Mormons
with their ideal of a society in which the godly ruled over a unified,
religious people stood in sharp contrast. Ideally, the Mormon
"kingdom" was an all-inclusive community with social, economic,
religious, and political aspects. The political dimension was certainly
its most controversial aspect and perhaps its most significant.

Until recently Mormon writers, with rare exceptions, have maintained that the Latter-day Saints were first and foremost loyal citizens of the United States, holding no other political allegiance.[12]
Non-Mormons from the mid-nineteenth century to the early twenti-
eth century usually held otherwise.[13] Although the ideals of gathering to a central kingdom have since died, in the early part of the
nineteenth century Mormons were evolving toward what sociologist
Thomas F. O'Dea termed "incipient nationality."[14] As a result, they
vacillated between two strong and conflicting loyalties.

Mormon political ambitions grew out of millennial expectations
and a desire for sovereignty, and were reinforced by the persecutions their ideals engendered. Still, the ideals came first and were

more important than some have supposed.[15] Within the vast territorial expanse which engulfed Americans during this period (and which had much to do with fostering two American nations between 1861 and 1865), Mormons—uprooted and on the move—dreamed of an empire in the West where they could have both a home and home-rule, a chance to perfect their institutions. Many other Americans shared such visions of a new society,[16] and Mormon expectations were one variation on a popular theme.

By the 1840s the Mormon dream of a kingdom had become such a concrete social and political entity in Illinois that notable Americans including Thomas Ford,[17] Josiah Quincy,[18] and even the itinerant preacher Peter Cartwright remarked upon the unusually ambitious temporal designs of the Mormons and their prophet. Cartwright maintained that in 1839 Joseph Smith said, "I will raise up a government in these United States which will overturn the present government and I will raise up a new religion that will overturn every other form of religion in the country."[19]

Six years later, on 6 April 1845, less than a year after the prophet's death, Brigham Young announced that the divine government envisioned by Joseph Smith had been established. The proclamation, addressed to "All the Kings of the World, to the President of the United States of America, to the Governors of the Several States, and to the Rulers and Peoples of All Nations," maintained that "the Kingdom of God has come, as has been predicted by the ancient prophets . . . even that Kingdom which shall fill the whole earth and stand forever." The decree went on to warn the world leaders: "You cannot . . . stand idle and disinterested spectators of the scenes and events which are calculated, in their very nature, to reduce all nations and creeds to *one* political and religious standard, and thus put an end to Babel forms and names and to strife and war."[20]

According to Young, this theocratic empire would provide a single political and religious standard for absorbing the multitude of societies and groups which had emerged in the nineteenth century under the aegis of "Freedom's Ferment." In an article about the Millennium written for the Mormons' first newspaper, *The Evening and the Morning Star*, in 1834, the author viewed with nostalgia the theocratic kingdom of God which he believed had existed anciently among the Jews. With inspired prophets to allay every disagreement, the ancient Hebrews "put an end to all strife" and were "of one heart and one mind."[21]

For a time, recently, scholars showed a renewed interest in the Mormon kingdom and studied its economic, social, and political aspects,[22] but there has been little effort to relate these aspects to religious ideals.[23] Klaus J. Hansen's 1967 study, *Quest for Empire*, is the most able attempt to date.[24] Hansen shows that the Saints indeed formed an independent government by 1844,[25] but by focusing too much on the role of the secret Council of Fifty, the governing body of the Mormon political system,[26] and not enough on the complex origin and nature of Mormon ideals, he tends to see the political conception of the kingdom as a late development in Smith's mind. Hansen argues that only in 1844 did the kingdom take on political ramifications.[27]

More recently, D. Michael Quinn has criticized Hansen and others in what he terms the "kingdom school" for the "confusion of symbol and substance" in their "failure to separate the temporal realities of the Mormon Kingdom of God from its unachieved millennial anticipations." Quinn insists that the Council of Fifty was "most often not functioning and was only a symbolic formality when it was functioning," that it did not meet from the time of the prophet's death in June 1844 until February 1845 and only sporadically thereafter. He admits, however, that it planned and carried out Smith's campaign for the presidency of the United States in 1844 and much of the exodus from Nauvoo to the Rocky Mountains. Whether the Council of Fifty was central, mere symbol, or a revolutionary government, it came as the culmination of a long period of church political involvement in which the Saints sought to have the political balance of power.[28]

It may be that the Mormon quest for political power came not from a rising estimation of man's capabilities to usher in his own millennium, as Hansen supposed, but rather from a terrible fear that the people could not govern themselves without divine direction.[29] In 1842 Smith affirmed publicly that human beings are incapable of self-government and that all must yield to "the Government of God." Behind the prophet's political theory was a Calvinistic-like skepticism.

> The great and wise of ancient days have failed in all their attempts to promote eternal power, peace, and happiness. Their nations have crumbled to pieces, their thrones have been cast down in their turn; and their cities and their mightiest works of art, have been annihilated. . . . They proclaim as with a voice of

thunder, those imperishable truths—that man's strength is a weakness, his wisdom is folly, his glory is his shame.

Monarchical, aristocratic, and republican forms of government, of their various kinds and grades, have in their turn been raised to dignity and prostrated in the dust. The plans of the greatest politicians, the wisest senators, and the most profound statesman have been exploded.

The only solution to humanity's uniform failure to govern justly is to establish the government of God. It has been, Smith explained,

> the design of Jehovah, from the commencement of the world, and his purpose now, to regulate the affairs of the world in his own time; to stand as the head of the universe, and take the reigns of government into his own hand. When that is done judgment will be administered in righteousness; anarchy and confusion will be destroyed, and "nations will learn war no more." It is for want of this great governing principle that all this confusion has existed; "for it is not in man that walketh to direct his steps."[30]

Eight years earlier in 1834, the prophet had written a long letter to the elders of the church which argued that the true members of Christ's kingdom must obey the laws of God. If they would do so, they would reign on the earth with Christ during the Millennium. He summarized his discourse by promising the brethren that "there is to be a day when all will be judged of their works, and rewarded according to the same; that those who have kept the faith will be crowned with a crown of righteousness; be clothed in white raiment; be admitted to the marriage feast; be free from every affliction, and reign with Christ on the earth, where, according to the ancient promise, they will partake of the fruit of the vine new in the glorious kingdom with Him."[31]

This kingdom was clearly a millennial one; there is no indication here that Joseph Smith expected the Saints to rule before that time. (Such may have been anticipated, however, for one Mormon suggested in 1834 that "previous to the Millennium there must be great changes take place in the world, both political and religious . . . to prepare the way for the Son of Man."[32]) By 1840 the prophet had come to the view that the task of administering the millennial kingdom was to be left mostly to the Saints. The editor of the *Quincy Whig* quoted the prophet in answer to his question whether Mormons believed in Christ's personal reign on earth during the Millennium: "I believe that Christ will descend, but will immediately return to heaven. Some of our elders, before I had found time to instruct them better, have unadvisedly propagated some such opinion; but I tell my people it is absurd."[33]

Thus the Saints believed from early on that they would be responsible to govern, and it made little practical difference to them whether the kingdom was the church or a distinct political organization. Benjamin Winchester, a Mormon elder who edited the *Gospel Reflector* in New York in 1841, identified the kingdom as "the church militant" and held that "when we speak of the kingdom of God . . . we mean to be understood as speaking of an organized government on earth."[34] According to his view, Christ would be the king and all earthly empires would be swept from the earth "just prior to the millennium."[35]

Speaking at a church conference in 1844, Sidney Rigdon, a former Campbellite minister, remembered that when he joined the Mormons in 1830, the political side of their apocalyptic expectations was already well developed. He described his visit to the Mormons in Waterloo, New York, in 1830.

> I met the whole church of Christ in a little log house about 20 feet square . . . and we began to talk about the kingdom of God as if we had the world at our command; we talked with great confidence, and talked big things, although we were not many people, we had big feelings; we knew fourteen years ago that the church would become as large as it is to-day; we were as big then, as we shall ever be; we began to talk like men in authority and power—we looked upon men of the earth as grasshoppers; if we did not see this people, we saw by vision, the church of God, a thousand times larger; and when men would come in, they would say we wanted to upset the government, although we were not enough to well man a farm. . . . And if we had talked in public they would have ridiculed us more than we were, the world being entirely ignorant of the testimony of the prophets, and without knowledge of what God was about to do . . . we talked about the people coming as doves to the windows, that all nations should flock unto it; that they should come bending to the standard of Jesus, saying our fathers have taught falsehood and things in which there is no profit; and of whole nations being born in one day; we talked such big things that men could not bear them.[36]

Rigdon indicated that they had expected Old and New Testament prophecies regarding the ultimate triumph of God's elect to have been fulfilled very soon. According to the editor of the

Painesville Telegraph, Book of Mormon scribe Martin Harris similarly predicted in 1832:

> Within four years there will not be one wicked person left in the United States; . . . the righteous will be gathered to Zion, . . . and there will be no President over these United States, after that time.
>
> I do hereby assert and declare that in four years from the date thereof [September] every sectarian and religious denomination in the United States will be broken down, and every Christian shall be gathered unto the Mormonites, and the rest of the human race shall perish.[37]

By 1837 or 1838 it seems likely that the notion that the Latter-day Saints were soon to rule on the earth had become a widely accepted principle among them. In a popular Mormon pamphlet, *A Voice of Warning*,[38] which according to its author, Mormon apostle Parley P. Pratt, sold over forty thousand copies by the mid-1850s,[39] attention centered on the kingdom of God as foreseen by the prophet Daniel.[40] Pratt proclaimed in his work that sectarians had misapplied the text of chapter 7, thinking that it symbolized the churchly kingdom as established by Christ. Pratt insisted that Christ's kingdom had been "prevailed against" and had fallen due to apostasy. The kingdom envisioned by Daniel, however, would never falter but would "break all others into pieces."[41] This kingdom would constitute God's "organized government on earth" and would be composed of a king, commissioned officers, a divine code of laws, and lawful subjects.[42]

As Pratt foresaw it, no sectarian effort could establish such a kingdom, which would require a manifestation of divine power. The kingdom would come "without the aid of human institutions or the precepts of men."[43] This did not mean that God's authorized servants would not have a part to play in the divine drama. They would gather the elect from the scattered tribes of Israel into a city, Zion, or the New Jerusalem, which they would soon build.[44] Most of the actual work would be accomplished by the American Indians, the "seed of Joseph." In fact, even now the U.S. government was helping to fulfill prophecy by gathering the Indians to the western frontier where the city and God's temple would be erected.[45] The New Jerusalem would provide an asylum for the weary, the humble, and the poor in spirit who harkened to God's commands. An ensign to the nations, all the righteous would soon be gathered there to hide from God's wrath, for those who would not "serve the city" would perish.[46]

In a subsequent pamphlet written in 1838, a year after his *Voice of Warning*, Apostle Pratt made certain implications of his prophetic views clearer. He wrote that the Book of Mormon was intended as an ensign to prepare the people for the gathering. The Mormon scripture

> set the time for the overthrow of our government and all other Gentile governments on the American continent, but the way and means of this utter destruction are clearly foretold, namely the remnant of Jacob [the Indians] will go through among the Gentiles and tear them to pieces, like a lion among the flocks of sheep. . . . This destruction includes an utter overthrow, and desolation of all our cities, Forts, and Strong Holds—an entire annihilation of our race, except such as embrace the covenant, and are numbered among Israel.

Pratt added, "I will state as a prophecy, that there will not be an unbelieving Gentile upon this continent 50 years hence; and if they are not greatly scourged, and in a great measure overthrown, within five or ten years of this date, then the Book of Mormon will have proved itself false."[47]

Pratt's interpretation of scriptural prophecy had something in common with the apocalypticism of Alexander Campbell. According to Disciples of Christ historian Amos Hayden, in the Western Reserve in 1830

> the restoration of the ancient gospel was looked upon as the initiatory movement, which, it was thought, would spread so rapidly that existing denominations would almost immediately be reorganized; that the true people of whom it was believed that Christ had a remnant among the sects, would at once embrace them, and thus form the union so long prayed for; and so would establish the Kingdom of Jesus, in form, as well as fact. . . . All the powers in array against this newly established kingdom . . . would soon surrender at the demand of the king of kings.[48]

Mormons juxtaposed such millenarian beliefs, including the conviction that they themselves must build and establish the kingdom,[49] with the notion that the Millennium would come instantaneously through the unsheathed sword of the great Jehovah.[50] They were not always clear in their own minds how the power of God would be applied, sometimes holding that he would employ a human agent to effect his destruction of the wicked. The Mormons thus not only combined a do-it-yourself psychology with a very literalistic interpretation of prophetic judgment, but they also formulated a precise scheme of interpretation as to the sequence in which the pre-millennial events would occur. They believed that the "ensign to the nations" had come in the form of a new scripture, published in 1830, and that the gathering, commencing just at that time, would bring the elect to their specifically designated place of refuge, Zion, in Missouri. God's time-table allowed for the building of the city and its temple by the Indians who were just then gathering, and this task must be accomplished before the Lord would appear. In the minds of many Saints a divine blueprint of events could be matched neatly with the unfolding affairs of everyday life. As Parley P. Pratt put it, "The predictions of the prophets can be clearly understood as much as the Almanac."[51]

These apocalyptic views were doctrinaire, revolutionary, at times hostile in implication and suggest that the Saints' reaction to religious pluralism was much sharper than anything experienced by the Campbellites. What saved the Saints, perhaps, from acting upon these views with reckless and destructive abandon was that the blueprint was incomplete until they could first build the Holy City. Although Martin Harris, Parley P. Pratt, and presumably others were certain of the imminence of the ultimate consummation, the Mormon prophet generally[52] pushed the terminal day into the distant future so that tendencies toward unusually radical behavior were somewhat diverted. Thus in 1835 Smith predicted that "the coming of the Lord was nigh" but added "fifty-six years should wind up the scene."[53]

In April 1843 Smith was no less certain that more time must elapse before the Millennium would begin. Willard Richards noted his saying,

> Were I going to prophecy I would prophecy the end will not come in 1844 or 5 or 6 or 40 years ["more" deleted] there are those of the rising generation who shall not taste of death till christ comes. I was once praying earnestly upon this subject, and a voice said unto me. My son, if thou livest till thou are 85 years of age, thou shalt see the face of the son of man.—I was left to draw my own conclusions concerning this & took the liberty to conclude that if I did live till that time ["Jesus" deleted] he would make his appearance.—but I do not say whether he will make his appear[a]nce or I shall go where he is.—

> I prophecy in the name of the Lord God.—& let it be writ-
> ten that the Son of Man will not come in the heavens till I am 85
> years old 48 years hence or about 1890 . . .
>   Jerusalem must be rebuilt.—& Judah return, must return
> & the temple water come out from under the temple—the waters
> of the dead sea be healed.—it will take some time to build the
> walls & the Temple. &c & all this must be done before the Son of
> Man will make his appearance; wars & rumors of wars.[54]

This postponement of the consummate day became necessary
as day-by-day events seemed to frustrate the initial ideal. Postponement allowed the Saints an opportunity to focus their immediate
attention on the task of building the kingdom in preparation for
that day. This responsibility would temper the raw thrust of their
chiliastic expectations and divert their idealism into constructive
channels. Nonetheless, the Saints understood that the time for the
establishment of the government of God on earth was at hand and
that they were to effect it. This provided a strong stimulus to the collective political activity that would be resented by other Americans.

The point of the study that follows is not that the Mormons were
the only religious people to fear pluralism and its consequences but
that they may have comprised the denomination upon which this
reaction has had its most power influence.[55]

QUEST FOR REFUGE

CHAPTER 1

Wanted: A Refuge for the Unconverted, Religiously Disoriented, and Poor

When Joseph Smith, Sr., and his wife, Lucy Mack, emigrated from New England to western New York in 1816, they numbered among the socially disinherited. They had drifted from town to town during their twenty years together, and by the time of their departure they had moved seven times and had lived in five different villages.[1] Much of this was due to discouraging financial difficulties. They had tried farming and merchandising without much success. Lucy later remembered that they owned a farm when they began their marriage, but the evidence for this is conflicting.[2]

Tenancy explains much of the Smiths' uprootedness. When those without land rented and the rented farms were resold, the renters were often forced to move on.[3] During this period, Joseph Sr. lost heavily when he tried to circumvent the middle man in a ginseng operation and was defrauded by his business associate. Afterward he rented a farm from his father-in-law but again experienced misfortune. Three successive crop failures ruined his hopes for future wealth[4] and may have driven him to excessive drinking,[5] a habit he apparently retained until his conversion to Mormonism many years later.[6] Despondent, the Smiths made plans following the end of the

War of 1812 to migrate to western New York, where hundreds suffering a similar fate had already immigrated, drawn by reports of rich
farm land in the Genessee country.[7]

When they migrated the Smiths had eight children, and it was
the mother who led them westward. They settled in the town of
Palmyra, a thriving village located in the middle of a rich valley. They
squatted on vacant land and took odd jobs[8] for two years before moving to Manchester, two miles south. The village was small when they
arrived but grew to 2,851 in 1830 and by then boasted three mills, an
academy, and a library of six hundred volumes.[9] The region where
they settled, according to one scholar, was a "more vigorous and cos-
mopolitan community"[10] than that which they had left behind in
Vermont.

The Smiths struggled to pay for a one-hundred-acre farm and
built a small log house for their large family. William Smith, the
fourth son, recalled proudly some sixty years later how strenuously
they had worked to make the enterprise pay: "We cleared sixty acres
of the heaviest timber I ever saw. . . . We also had on it from twelve to
fifteen hundred sugar trees, and to gather sap and make sugar and
molasses from that number of trees was no lazy job." Even the third
son, Joseph Jr., born in 1805, labored hard to help the family, remembered William. "Whenever the neighbors wanted a good day's work
done they knew where they could get a good hand and they were not
particular to take any of the other boys before Joseph either."[11]
William's contention that the family worked hard is supported by at
least one neighbor, Orlando Saunders, who told William Kelley in
1884 that "they all worked for me many a day; they were very good
people; young Joseph . . . had worked for me, and he was a very good
worker; they all were."[12]

Despite their hard work, the Smiths lived on the edge of poverty much of the time and eventually lost their farm just before the
last payment was due.[13] It may be that they had been required to pay
too high a price for their land in the first place.[14] Their frustration
was compounded by the fact that they had not been able to convince
most of their middle-class neighbors that they belonged. Because of
their poverty and enthusiasm for what many neighbors perceived as
"get-rich-quick schemes," they were viewed as lazy and socially infe-
rior. This was so despite the fact that many of their neighbors had
been as poor as the Smiths on coming to western New York.[15]

A former resident of Palmyra revealed many years afterward
the general attitude of many citizens when he commented, "I knew

the Smiths but did not associate with them for they were too low to associate with." In a public statement many Palmyrans maintained that the family was "without influence in the community." The people of Manchester affirmed, "We are glad to dispense with their society."[16] Most of this hostility probably developed after family members emerged as founders of a new religious movement. According to William Smith: "We never knew we were bad folks until Joseph told of his vision. We were considered respectable till then, but at once people began to circulate falsehoods and stories in wonderful ways."[17]

Antagonism toward the Smiths comes from some of the earliest sources now extant and reaches back to within two weeks of Mormonism's founding in April 1830. Obadiah Dogberry, a liberal village newspaper editor, described Joseph Jr. as "that spindle shanked ignoramus," "idle and slothful," and his followers as "ill-bred," "ignorant wretches." The following year Dogberry wrote, "We have never been able to learn that any of the family were ever noted for much else than ignorance and stupidity."[18]

Despite Dogberry's assertions, several of the Smith family, including Lucy, had been admitted to the Presbyterian church in 1824 and had remained active for several years.[19] No attempt was made during this time to exclude them for reasons of depravity. There were other factors which contributed to the general distrust in Palmyra. Dogberry belittled the Smiths because of the family's involvement in money digging,[20] a common form of folk magic practiced primarily by the poor and itinerant in New England and western New York during the early nineteenth century and usually opposed by middle- and upper-class Americans.

Lucy Mack Smith admitted candidly in the original dictated manuscript of her history that the family was involved in this and other forms of folk magic:

> Let not my reader suppose that because I shall pursue another topic for a season that we stopt our labor and went at trying to win the faculty of Abrac drawing magic circles or sooth saying to the neglect of all kinds of business we never during our lives suffered one important interest to swallow up every other obligation but whilst we worked with our hands we endeavored to remember the service of & the welfare of our souls.[21]

The "other topic" to which Lucy turned her attention was the coming forth of the Book of Mormon, the activity she wanted read-ers to understand did not take up their whole time or keep them from working. In her mind magic circles, sooth saying, and other magical arts were one with her religious activities. Similarly her son Joseph Jr. in a revelation delivered to his close friend Oliver Cowdery in April 1829 endorsed magical practices, commending Cowdery's own gift of "working with the [divining] rod" prior to becoming a Mormon as "the work of God." Smith pronounced, "There is no other power save God that can cause this rod of nature to work in your hands."[22] Hyrum Smith, the future prophet's older brother, believed that seerstones (crystal gazing) would be "as true as preaching" so long as evil spirits did not interfere with their proper functioning. He reportedly said he thought the time would come when there would be no such interference.[23]

Some historians, including Fawn Brodie, have tended to view a belief in magic in much the same way that Obediah Dogberry did, as chicanery and fraud—proof that Smith's religious claims were not genuine.[24] A more temperate view has recently emerged among schol-ars of religion, and it is now clear that magic is but one means peo-ple employ in efforts to make contact with the divine.[25] Belief in magic was not at odds with the Smith family's religious attitudes and can be seen instead as evidence of them.

In both their religious and business affairs the Smiths were rest-less, dissatisfied, itinerant. Joseph Sr. and Lucy came to maturity in New England at a time when the domination of the Calvinistic Con-gregationalists was diminishing and new sects such as the Baptists, Methodists, and Universalists were gaining influence. The latter two particularly challenged the negative view of humanity inherent in Calvinism and came to stress free will and one's ability to influence his or her own salvation.[26] But everywhere there was a rampaging revolt against Calvinistic orthodoxy, as the career of the Yale divine Nathaniel William Taylor shows.[27] In an atmosphere of conflict and reevaluation of old theological positions, many people drifted away from the churches, not finding a comfortable social or religious niche into which they could settle. Frequently uprooted, the Smiths were among those who had periods of intense religious concern but had not decided upon any single denomination. They were seekers, two among thousands in New England and western New York who were searching for the right place and the right church.[28]

Lucy records that her religious searching began a few years after her marriage. In 1802 during a near fatal illness, she pleaded with God to spare her life so that she could raise her family. She pledged that "if he would let me live I would endeavor to get that religion that would enable me to serve him." She then heard a voice telling her to "let your heart be comforted." At that point she began to recover. When her health fully returned she began going "from place to place to seek information or find if possible some congenial spirit who might enter into my feelings and sympathize with me." She said she learned that "one noted for his piety" was to preach in the Presbyterian church that Sunday, but when she attended "all was emptiness vanity vexation of spirit." The experience did not "satisfy the craving hunger of the soul." In "almost total . . . despair" she returned home to continue her quest by studying the "word of God."

Lucy reports that she continued this course for several years and then found a minister who would baptize her without requiring that she join a church. She remained in this state until her oldest son reached his twenty-second year,[29] which would be 1820, although her later recollections contradict this date.

Lucy says little about her husband's religious attitudes during these early years, suggesting there may have been a difference of opinion between them on this point. We know from other sources that Joseph Sr. joined the Universalists in Vermont in 1797 at the same time his father Asael did.[30] William Smith wrote that his father's belief in universal restoration brought him into conflict with those who believed in endless punishment, showing that he was more than a casual convert.[31] When Lucy first mentions her husband's religious attitudes it is in connection with her attempt to get him to attend Methodist meetings in Tunbridge, Vermont, in 1808. She says that she became concerned about her promises made to the Lord during her illness six years before. But her husband showed little enthusiasm despite her pleadings. He attended on a few occasions "to gratify me for he had so little faith in the doctrines taught by them that my feelings were the only inducement for him to go."

Joseph's occasional accommodation to Lucy's wishes vanished when his father Asael, long a champion of Universalist doctrines, grew upset. Lucy recalls that Asael was "much displeased" and that one day he appeared at the door and "threw Tom Paine's *Age of Reason* into the house and angrily told him that he ought not to let his wife go to the meetings and it would be better for him to stop going."

Joseph agreed and told Lucy that they must comply to save their family from "such disagreeable feelings." Lucy later confessed that she was "very much hurt by this."[32] But she records in her history that she remained unchurched for years. Evidently her husband's will prevailed. No doubt this caused her anguish in light of her earlier promise to the Lord that she would "get religion." She would have been a rare individual if she had avoided guilt and even resentment against her husband for the stand he took against her. These lingering feelings would overwhelm her following the death of her oldest son in 1823.

Lucy says in her history that between 1811 and 1816 her husband began to show more concern for religion. If he did he was still unwilling to join any church. Her recollection thirty years later of her husband's religiously oriented dreams may have reflected her own anxiety as much as his. She says that in the first of these dreams Joseph was moving in a barren field, where nothing living appeared, accompanied by a spirit which told him that the field was the world "which lies inanimate & dumb as to the things pertaining to true religion." Joseph was instructed to move on until he found a box whose contents if consumed would make him wise. As he found the box and was ready to eat, wild beasts came at him menacingly. He dropped the box and ran. When he then awoke from the dream, he was "trembling with terror." The wild beasts who disrupted his quest for true religion may have been Asael and Joseph's brother Jessee, who no doubt appeared bestial to Lucy.

In another dream Joseph reportedly saw many people rushing toward an impressive meeting house "from every direction and pressing with great anxiety." He felt "careless and easy" and took his time getting to the church door. When he arrived an angel blocked his way and told him that he would have to "plead the merits of Jesus."[33] Again, Joseph was seen as being outside the congregation and careless about his salvation. But these attitudes may better reflect the concerns of Lucy than of her husband, who apparently was comfortable as a seeker. When conversion came to the Smiths it was Lucy who experienced it. Joseph remained outside the fold of a church.

The latter dream was reported to have occurred in 1816, apparently after the family had come to Palmyra. At this time the town was alive with religious ferment and a year later experienced a major revival with hundreds joining the churches.[34] The region was the special target of a host of preachers, missionaries, and Sunday School and Tract Society enthusiasts, who were determined to save the west from infidelity.[35] But, as Charles G. Finney reported, much of the region was already "burned out," having experienced too much religious excitement over a long period of time, beginning with the Second Great Awakening in the early 1790s.[36] Most of the settlers were from New England, but a greater diversity of people and opinions prevailed in New York and made for a sharp clash of religious views. For example, the secretary to the American Home Missionary Society commented in 1827 that throughout western New York the people "are much divided in regard to their religious sentiments."[37] A Disciples of Christ historian, reporting on much the same thing further west in Ohio, later observed that the coming together of many different people from New England and elsewhere, "was a powerful stimulus" to the study of the Bible.[38]

Political conflict was also intense, and often political and religious issues intermingled. Almost every dispute was heralded as having religious import, so that it was difficult to escape an overburdening religious orientation. Such controversial issues as anti-Masonry, the removal by the government of the Indians to a reserve in the west, and the circulation of the mails were each portrayed as religiously significant.[39] Old-line church ministers warned their congregations that the battle against infidelity was not over, and a sense of crisis rested upon those in the churches.[40] In this spiritually charged atmosphere many people talked about the coming Millennium. The editor of the *Wayne Sentinel* in Palmyra wrote that "everyone looked for some ingenious application of the revelations to the peculiar situation in the present century."[41] Some sought to give themselves totally to God and to reach a state of religious perfection and sinlessness.[42]

The revivals were a potent force compelling thousands of people to reexamine their religious state. But not everyone approved of the fierce emotional intensities the revivals engendered. For example, Willard Richards, later a Mormon convert, disapproved of the emotional traumas and the "new measures" which Charles Finney employed.[43] Finney set western New York afire with religious excitement and anxiety, shutting down whole towns for days during his protracted meetings.[44] Richards complained that the revivals "stirred up the imagination exciting unnecessary fears and torture[d] the mind."[45]

A recent scholar has discovered that many revivalists deliberately focused their attention upon the "youth" whose life style was

not yet set, employing strong peer pressures to compel youthful hear-
ers to make a religious commitment. Those who did often found
peace of mind in an old-line church, but those who could not under-
went severe mental anguish.[46] Sectarian competition, demands for
conversion, and anticipations of a millennium placed many Americans under great pressure, leaving them guilt ridden, confused, frus-
trated, even disillusioned. One man who had fled sectarian claims
confessed, "I was at first a Baptist, then a kind of New Light [Chris-
tian], afterward a Congregationalist; now my only creed is *God be mer-
ciful to me a sinner*."[47]

Another disillusioned casualty of sectarianism was Asa Wild, a
resident of New Amsterdam, New York, who turned away from organized religion to his Bible and his God, receiving a revelation that
the Lord would soon overthrow all of the churches made by men. As
reported in the Palmyra newspaper of 1823, Wild claimed:

> Having a number of months enjoyed an unusual degree of the
> light of God's countenance . . . the Lord in his boundless good-
> ness was pleased to communicate the following revelation. . . .
> He told me that the Millennial state of the world is about to take
> place; that in seven years literally [1830], there would scarce a
> sinner be found on earth; that the earth itself, as well as the souls
> and bodies of its inhabitants, should be redeemed, as before the
> fall, and become as the garden of Eden. He told me that all of
> the most dreadful and terrible judgments spoken in the blessed
> scriptures were to be executed within that time, that more than
> two thirds of the inhabitants of the world would be destroyed
> by these judgments; some of which are the following—wars,
> massacres, famine, pestilence, earthquakes, civil, political and
> ecclesiastical commotions; and above all, various and dreadful
> judgments executed immediately by God, through the instru-
> mentality of the Ministers of the Millennial Dispensation which
> is to exceed in glory every other dispensation. . . . He also told
> me that every denomination of professing christians had become
> extremely corrupt; many of which had never had any true faith
> at all; but are guided only by depraved reason, refusing the teach-
> ing of the spirit . . . which alone can teach us the true meaning
> of the [scriptures]. . . . He told me further, that he had raised
> up, and was now raising up, that class of persons signified
> by the angel mentioned by the Revelator XIV. 6, 7, which flew
> in the midst of heaven; having the everlasting gospel to
> preach, that these persons are of an inferior [social] class, and
> small learning; that they were rejected by every denomination
> as a body; but soon, God will open their way, by miracles, judg-
> ments, &c. that they will have higher authority, greater power,

superior inspiration, and a greater degree of holiness than was ever experienced before. . . . Furthermore he said that all the different denominations of professing christians constituted the New Testament Babylon . . . that he is about to call out all his sincere children who are mourning in Zion, from oppression and tyranny of the mother of harlots; and that the severest judgments will be inflicted on the false and fallen professors of religion.[48]

It was from this maelstrom of religious ferment that Joseph Smith, Jr., as prophet emerged. Religious commitment was encouraged at revivals occurring intermittently throughout western New York from 1800 onward. In his official history of Mormonism Joseph Smith acknowledged that revivals had a compelling, if in some ways negative, influence on him. In 1838 when he was the leader and prophet of a growing and controversial religious society, Smith dictated to a church scribe that it was during a revival in Palmyra in 1820 that he first turned to God to ask which church among so many was right to join, the results of which came to be known among Mormons as the first vision.

Recently, scholars have learned that as early as 1832 Smith partly wrote and partly dictated another account of this first vision, which made no mention of revivals.[49] In this earliest account Smith said that at the age of twelve he began to be concerned for the salvation of his soul and searched the scriptures. He said he was already very familiar with the existing denominations but believed that they "did not adorn their profession with a holy walk." He went to the Lord in his sixteenth year to learn if he was accepted of him and was told that his sins were forgiven. The messenger who came to him said, "I am the Lord of glory I was crucifyed for the world." No mention was made of any other personage appearing. The messenger continued that the "world lieth in sin at this time and none doeth good." Smith said that for many days afterward he felt great joy but then fell into transgression. This account, as some Mormon scholars have noted, is similar to others of the period[50] and reveals the sort of religious experience that was expected of youth who were exposed to intense proselyting.

When Smith dictated a more polished version in 1838, it was altered in many details and more elaborate. He said he was in his fifteenth year when his family, except for his father and brother William, were converted at a revival by the Presbyterians. He said he kept himself aloof after attending a few meetings. He described

"unusual excitement" in the neighborhood on the subject of religion with multitudes joining the churches. He admitted that his
"mind at different times was greatly excited" amidst the "war of words
and tumult of opinion." He wondered "who of all these parties are
right? Or are they all wrong together?" He said two personages visited him and that he was told specifically that he should join none of
the churches "for they are all wrong."[51]

Considerable controversy has been generated by the various
accounts of Smith's vision. One early scholar contended that little
was said about the first vision at the time it supposedly occurred and
that there are significant differences in details among several
accounts, including a recital drafted by church historian Oliver
Cowdery in 1834.[52] Other scholars have since claimed that there was
no major revival in Palmyra in 1820, the year Smith would have been
fifteen years old, again contradicting the traditional account.[53]

Smith may have had difficulty remembering the exact year of
his vision. His mother indicates in her published narrative that the
vision came four years after they arrived in Palmyra, making it 1820
as Mormon tradition holds. But her preliminary manuscript com-
bines her son's first vision with subsequent visions to present her
own account bearing little resemblance to any of Smith's own recit-
als. And it is hard to establish a major revival in Palmyra in 1820,
although there was one in late 1823 and early 1824,[54] the time when
Lucy and others in the family evidently joined the Presbyterian
church. Lucy says that they joined after the death of her oldest son
Alvin, who died in the fall of 1823. Her grieving for Alvin was one
reason Lucy sought out the Presbyterians.[55] Burdened with guilt
because of her unfulfilled promise to find a church, she found release
for her pent-up emotions by conversion at the revival. Very likely
then, since Smith does not mention revivals in his 1832 account, there
was no great revival in Palmyra itself which precipitated his teenage
conversion in 1820.

Still, it is evident that Joseph Smith was later moved to religious
questions when Alvin died and his family, except principally his
father and brother William, joined the Presbyterians. He recalled in
1844 that he wanted to "feel and shout" with the rest of his family
but could "feel nothing."[56] Conceivably he was made numb by the
enduring tension between his mother and his father regarding religion.[57] Joseph Sr. had been deeply offended at Alvin's funeral when
the Presbyterian minister said publicly that Alvin had gone to hell[58]
and would have nothing to do with the church. Yet, as William

recalled, his mother "continued her importunities and exertions to interest us in the importance of seeking for the salvation of our immortal souls, until almost all of the family became either converted or seriously inclined."[59] The tension in the family must have been considerable for Joseph to have had "deep and often poignant" feelings at this time and yet been unable to yield to the revivalist's message and his mother's pleas.

Despite its inaccuracies and omissions, Joseph Smith's 1838 account is important because it provides Smith's recollection of those forces which brought his religious movement into being. It was the excitement of the revivals with their appeal for Christian conversion which stirred him and the war among contending sects which repelled him. Pluralism caused the young prophet-to-be great anxiety. Lucy explained in her history the torture of deciding among several churches. Describing the time of her first awakening, she wrote, "If I remain a member of no church, all religious people will say I am of the world; and if I join some of the different denominations, all the rest will say I am in error. This makes them witness against each other; and how can I decide?"[60]

Lucy perceived what others recognized at the time, that a religious decision of this sort had more than religious consequences. Such commitment established one's friends and life style. Barton W. Stone, later a Christian, was influenced by a series of revivals conducted by James McReady in 1790-91 but was tormented when it came to making a decision whether to accept the revivalists' message: "Shall I embrace religion or not: If I embrace religion, I must incur the displeasure of my dear relatives, lose the favor and company of my companions—become the object of scorn and ridicule. . . . Are you willing to make this sacrifice to religion? No, no, was the answer of my heart. Then the certain alternative is you must be damned."[61]

For Joseph Smith the anguish that normally accompanied such a decision was accentuated in his early mature years. He had associated with his father in the money-digging business and had established some close friendships. But he experienced shame in connection with money digging in 1826 when he was brought to trial as a "glass looker" in Bainbridge, New York. Some of his friends and associates in the enterprise were interrogated as to his personal character, which no doubt brought him personal humiliation. Existing accounts differ as to the charges against him, witnesses and testimony given, and even the final verdict. Nonetheless, it is clear that a trial did take place and that at issue was Joseph Jr.'s money digging. One

account indicates that Joseph Sr. said he and his son were "morti-
fied that this wonderful gift which God had so miraculously given . . .
should be used only in search of filthy lucre," showing that father
and son were very sensitive to the public censure they experienced.[62]

Perhaps the embarrassment of the trial was a turning point for
young Smith, but no doubt his increasing attraction to Emma Hale,
whom he had met during his treasure hunting in Pennsylvania, also
had considerable influence. Emma and her father Isaac were devout
Methodists and increasingly opposed to Smith's money digging. Isaac
was unwilling to give his approval for a marriage, so Joseph and
Emma eloped in February 1827. Hale then pressured Smith to give
up money digging and exacted pledges on the matter from his new
son-in-law. Joseph and Emma moved to a house on Isaac's property
in 1828,[63] suggesting that this arrangement may have figured in the
promise made by Smith. It was after this that Smith began attending
Methodist meetings held in individual homes in Harmony, Pennsylvania. He sought membership after a time, and his name was added
to the class role. But Emma's cousin, Joseph Lewis, bitterly opposed
his membership due to his treasure hunting. Smith was asked to make
a public confession but could never bring himself to do so.[64] The
chagrin which he doubtless felt may have finally dissolved any attraction which the old-line churches had for him. He made no comment
about this episode in his history, except to note that at one point he
was attracted to the Methodists.[65]

From this point on Smith had little good to say about Protestant denominations generally, and his calling as prophet rather than
money digger became increasingly important to him. To satisfy his
own developing religious conscience, to escape the contending Protestant denominations, particularly the Methodists at Harmony, to reconcile his mother's and father's differences on religion, to please his
new bride, he had to find a church that he could accept and that
would accept him. Joseph Smith at this point became a religious
seeker. But he began with a much stronger sense of alienation from
society than most of the other seekers of his day. His poverty, his
much disparaged career as a money digger, his court trial, and his
expulsion from the Methodist church left him outside the usual religious and social circles. He would of necessity have to pursue a course
radically different from that of the ordinary seeker.

When Smith began his translation of the Book of Mormon in
1828 and initiated a new religious movement, there were hundreds

in western New York like himself, at odds with the religious establishment for various reasons. Many were struggling to break free of
Calvinism or revivalism and the associated demand for spiritual conversion. Others were unchurched and despised the professional
clergy. All were disgusted with sectarian opinion and conflict. They
required a new start, a faith based on something more than divergent biblical interpretations, a religion which would again manifest
the power of God on earth.

Many had been adversely affected by Calvinism and revivalism.
George A. Smith, a cousin of the prophet, remembered that his father
was alienated from his Congregational church because he was baptized before experiencing a change of heart. George himself attended
Congregational revivals in 1831 and became a "seeker after religion
night and day." He was unconverted despite his diligence and was
"sealed up to damnation."[66] Willard Richards attended revivals at
his Congregational parish but experienced no change of heart and
was denied membership although his friends were admitted. He
reported that his efforts were all to "no purpose" and he lost all
hope.[67] Parley P. Pratt also admitted that he never believed himself
a sinner and could "experience no great change."[68] Calvinistic
requirements made no sense to him. George Laub began attending
Methodist meetings and sat on the mourner's bench "to pray to have
my sins forgiven. I did this in three evenings in succession but found
no deliverance." On the third evening, Laub recalled, "the priest
told me to believe I had it and then I would have it. I told him I could
not believe that I had a thing when I knew it was not so. I said if this
is religion there is none for me."[69] George Whitaker said that at age
seventeen he thought a lot about heaven and hell but did not think
God showed much love or mercy if he was going to send most people to "an endless hell."[70] Even Lucy Mack Smith wrote to a relative
in 1831 that she rejected the format of conversion. "Peter did not tell
them to go away and mourn over their sins weeks and months, and
receive a remission of them and then come and be baptized."[71]

Similarly, Warren Foote said he "often went to the Methodist
revival meetings to see them jump and hear them sing and when
they all got to praying, shouting and singing at once it was fun to
hear them." But, he added, "I could not see anything in such proceedings like the gospel."[72] Lewis Shurtliff drifted from the Baptists
to the Campbellites but had no conversion experience and did not
feel saved. He said that by 1836 he was "fast approaching a state of
infidelity and had little confidence in anything and believed

nothing."[73] Lorenzo Dow Young, a younger brother of Brigham Young, attended a Methodist revival where everyone but himself experienced a change of heart. He recalled, "When I failed to come to the 'anxious seat' Elder Gilmore told me I had sinned away the day of grace and my damnation was sure."[74]

All of these and other future Mormons participated in a general break with Calvinism. They were casualties of revivalism and its powerful pressures. In his *Lectures on Revivals of Religion*, which he published after his whirlwind campaign in western New York, Charles Finney described his methods. He told young converts that they must be religious in "every department of life and in all that they do." He accentuated his point by saying, "If they do not aim at this, they should understand that they have no religion at all," and added, "Obedience to God consists in the state of the heart. It is being willing to obey God; willing that God should rule in all things."[75] Finney's protracted meetings and anxious bench were psychologically oriented tools for compelling members of his audience to face the choices he insisted that they make.

For those future Mormons who were shut out from the saving graces and from saved congregations, the effect could be devastating. Cast adrift, they desperately needed to bring God into their lives, to allow him to rule in all things. They wanted a society that would exclude unnecessary choices and would exclude pluralism. Above all, they wanted to diminish the secular influences that pluralism engendered.

Sociologist Peter L. Berger has described how pluralism promoted secularization.[76] He argues that religious impotence in today's world began to develop rapidly after the Reformation as the church became less and less involved in day-to-day matters. As a result, men and women today face choices about where to live, where to work, where and what to worship, and whom to have as friends. Such choices did not exist in the medieval world, where the social order was set and sustained a unified, religious world view. However, Protestantism promoted secular tendencies by diminishing the role of miracles, magic, sacraments, and ceremonies, which brought God into the everyday life of average men and women. Protestants depended solely upon the conversion experience to make God manifest. Cast loose into a sectarian world, the unconverted could become confused and uncertain as to whether God was manifest in any of the competing denominations.

Hosea Stout was one of many Mormon converts who demonstrate this pattern. He attended a revival in 1829 and found many of
his friends joining the "Cumberlands." Yet he disliked the sectarian
rivalry which resulted: "I soon discovered a hostile spirit between
them and the Methodists which I thought was uncalled for. It threw
me much in the back grounds to hear preachers slander each other
because of small differences of opinion in 'non-essentials,' so called."
Stout added that the "perpetual quarrel" between the sects "nearly
extinguished my religious fire."[77]

Edward Hunter, another early Mormon convert and later a
bishop in Illinois, said that in the 1830s he was "watching sectarian
strife, waiting to see what he could make of it."[78] Martin Harris, a
witness to the Book of Mormon, recalled that in 1818 he felt inspired
"that I should not join Eny church although I was anxiously sought
for By Meny Sectarians. . . . I might just as well plunge myself into
the water as to have any one of the Sects baptize me."[79] Sarah Leavitt,
daughter of a Presbyterian deacon, had a vision of the "damned spirits in hell" and was filled with horror. She was visited by many sects
but after studying her Bible found none to her satisfaction.[80] John
Murdock traveled in many parts of New York but waited before
becoming a Dutch Lutheran. Then he left them and joined the
"Seceder Church." Moving to Ohio he joined the Baptists, the
Campbellites, and finally the Mormons.[81] Laban Morrill, a black-
smith, reported that he was sought after by many churches but was
skeptical of them all.[82] And Lewis Barney said that before joining
the Mormons he had decided that "all religion [is] a hoax and that
preachers were hypocrits, that they preached for money and
popularity."[83]

Oliver Cowdery, another Book of Mormon witness, touched
upon a sensitive point when he wrote, "There is so great a resemblance between all the religious sects of the day, that one who stands
aloof from all of them is astonished why there should be so much
strife and contention from among them; for all the difference there
is between them consists of opinion."[84] Isaac Haight, who became a
Baptist at age eighteen, decided three years later that all the churches
had departed from "primitive purity."[85] Oliver Granger started as a
Methodist but then "stood aloof from all sects and all creeds."[86]
Wandle Mace in New York was reared by parents who were Bible
readers but would join no church. He went into the grocery business, acquired two stores, and then lost both of them when his friends
soon disassociated themselves. Mace lamented what he termed "the

hollowness of so-called society." After this he joined the New School Presbyterians but argued with the elders over the christening of infants. He withdrew and joined a seeker society, only to once more feel out of place. He met Parley P. Pratt in 1837 and joined the Mormons.[87]

Class-oriented antagonisms were another reason many looked outside the old-line churches for religious solace. The revivals were aimed at the American middle class, which flocked to the churches. But W. W. Phelps wrote that they did not seem suitable for the poor: "It may be worthwhile for the humble disciple of the meek and lowly Jesus to notice how the rich, the great and noble, are flattered and honored, and even excused from acts of sin . . . how the Christians, as they style themselves, following the changing fashions of the day, to the most extravagant extremes. . . . All sects are striving for the uppermost rooms at feasts, and for the chief seats in the synagogues."[88]

The Book of Mormon, in passages addressed to Americans in the 1830s, likewise expressed the view that the churches were accommodating the wealthy but slighting the poor: "Because of pride, and because of false teachers, and false doctrine, their churches have become corrupted; and their churches are lifted up; because of pride they are puffed up. They rob the poor, because of their fine clothing; and they persecute the meek, and the poor in heart; because in their pride they are puffed up."[89] According to another passage, the modern churches were too worldly and too caught up in their own learning, too given to division and strife: "And the Gentiles are lifted up in the pride of their eyes, and have stumbled, . . . that they have built up many churches; nevertheless they put down the power and the miracles of God; and preach up unto themselves, their own wisdom, and their own learning, that they may get gain, and grind the face of the poor; and there are many churches built up which causeth envyings, and strifes, and malice."[90]

There is a good deal of evidence that many, if not most, early Mormons were men and women of modest means and little formal education. Such notables as Brigham Young, Wilford Woodruff, John Taylor, Lorenzo Snow, Parley P. Pratt, and Lyman Wight were poor farmers or artisans barely finding the funds to meet their needs in 1830. Young was a carpenter and jack-of-all trades, Woodruff a miller, Taylor an apprentice to a cooper, Snow a "sufer" of hardships in his youth, Wight a participant in Sidney Rigdon's pre-Mormon communal experiment.[91] These findings compare favorably with Orson

Spencer's assertion in 1842 that "our people are mostly the working class."[92] They undoubtedly felt ill at ease in middle-class churches, as Brigham Young's sojourn in the Methodist Reformed church suggests. Yet there is no evidence, as anthropologist Mark P. Leone has asserted,[93] that the industrial revolution affected them directly. There was an anti-capitalistic quality to the early Mormon movement, but this had more to do with the divisive, pluralistic character of capitalism than to permanent ideological objections to it.

A degree of class consciousness among early Mormons seems evident too in their involvement with treasure hunting and its associated pre-Reformation style of religion, which had largely died out among the middle classes but continued to thrive in the early nineteenth century among the destitute and downtrodden. Many of the common people brought the miraculous into their lives by using forked sticks to find water or magic stones to find lost articles and hidden treasures. It was no accident that such peoples were millennialists looking for the New Jerusalem and a new social order.[94]

Joseph Smith, the Mormon prophet, sought to revitalize this magical world view, combine it with elements of more traditional Christianity, and establish a theocratic society where the unconverted, the poor, and the socially and religiously alienated could gather and find a refuge from the competing sects and the uncertainties they engendered. His efforts to do so would bring him into conflict with leaders and others of the established order who were otherwise-minded.

CHAPTER 2

"A Principle Means
in the Hands of God"

While translating the Book of Mormon, Joseph Smith and his
new wife, Emma, were completely destitute, living on handouts from
sympathetic neighbors like Joseph Knight, Martin Harris, and others.[1] Lucy and Joseph Smith, Sr., who had lost their farm in 1825,
were also in economic straits.[2] Joseph the prophet hoped that the
publication of the Book of Mormon would provide the income his
family so desperately needed.

When Martin Harris, however, lost the first 116 pages of the translation in 1828, Joseph was in total despair. Emma, sick and pregnant,
had just lost her baby. Joseph wondered if he dared tell his still grieving wife of the loss of the manuscript.[3] After several months Joseph
again began to translate and prospects brightened. Joseph Capron
wrote that Smith hoped his volume would "relieve the family from
all pecuniary embarrassment."[4] There is evidence from Mormon
sources to confirm Capron's recollections. Smith himself admitted
in his unpublished history that "he sought the plates to obtain
riches."[5] Hyrum Smith wrote to his grandfather, Asael, that he
believed that service to the Lord would bring the family their long-
awaited prosperity.[6] In October 1829, Joseph wrote excitedly to Oliver

Cowdery that Josiah Stowell had a chance to obtain five or six hundred dollars and that he was going to buy copies of the Book of Mormon.[7] Lucy Mack Smith said that when it was finally published in March 1830 the family had to sell copies of the book to buy food.[8]

The economic situation of the Smith families was so desperate at this time that Joseph tried to sell the copyright of the Book of Mormon. Hiram Page wrote with bitterness years later that the prophet heard he could sell the copyright of any useful book in Canada and that he then received a revelation that "this would be a good opportunity to get a handsome sum." Page explained that once expenses were met the profits were to be "for the exclusive benefit of the Smith family and was to be at the disposal of Joseph." Page indicated that they hoped to get $8,000 for the copyright and that they traveled to Canada covertly to prevent Martin Harris from sharing in the dividend. Smith evidently believed that Harris was well enough off while his own family was destitute. When Page, Cowdery, and Knight arrived at Kingston, Ontario, they found no buyer. Page concluded that some revelations were not beneficial.[9] Martin Harris apparently learned of what was done, and Joseph guaranteed him in writing that he would share in any profits made from the subsequent sales of the book.[10] In the spring of 1830 Harris walked the streets of Palmyra, trying to sell as many copies of the new scripture as he could. Shortly after Joseph Smith and Jesse Knight saw him in the road with books in his hand, he told them "the books will not sell for nobody wants them."[11]

A failure financially, the Book of Mormon was nonetheless the catalyst which placed Joseph Smith at the head of a revitalized religious movement with certain roots in magic. A. W. Benton reported that as early as 1826 Smith had several followers in Chenango County with money digging interests,[12] while David Whitmer said that Smith had established a fully functioning church by 1829 before the Book of Mormon was published.[13]

In any case, there was certainly more continuity between the money-digging religious culture and the early Mormon movement than some historians have recognized.[14] Joseph Smith began receiving revelations as a prophet in 1823,[15] and thus began assuming the role central to his religious movement long before he abandoned his money digging in 1827.

Unlike church leaders today, Smith had no model established for him as prophet and seer in a church, except what he had learned

as a village seer. At times afterward he showed a degree of uncertainty as to the proper limits of his role.[16] Yet his experience with
magic provided some guidelines. The traditional magician in Europe
and America searched for buried treasure, healed the sick, interpreted dreams, forecast the future, and translated ancient hiero-
glyphics.[17] Joseph carried these functions with him into his role as
church prophet. His primary innovation came in publishing his revelations as scripture.

The Book of Mormon was a history of ancient America, but its
primary purpose was to warn Americans in the 1830s. Its message
appealed to common men with sectarian or money-digging back-
grounds. It was a jeremiad addressed to the American Indians, part
of the House of Israel, and affirmed that these chosen people were
to take part in the building of the New Jerusalem in preparation for
the coming Millennium.[18] It warned that "many churches [were] built
up which causeth envyings, and strife and malice, and it denounced
the self-serving professional clergy who were to blame.[19] It warned
against contentions that tore society asunder, where people are "dis-
tinguished by ranks, according to their riches and their chances for
learning."[20] It testified to the unchurched and disbelieving that Jesus
is the Messiah soon to return to earth. It informed Americans that
the best way to prepare for these momentous events is to accept the
modern day prophet who voiced these warnings.[21] It reminded Americans that the ancient inhabitants of the promised land had destroyed
themselves through love of worldly things and disregard for the message of the prophets.

Theologically the Book of Mormon was a mediating text standing between orthodox Calvinists and emerging Arminians. Its mediatory tendencies are best illustrated in a passage where the prophet
Lehi tells his son Joseph that the Book of Mormon along with the
Bible "shall grow together, unto the confounding of false doctrine
and laying down of contentions, and establishing peace among the
fruit of thy loins." The scripture was to provide a second witness to
a disbelieving world. Nephi was told by an angel that his records
"shall establish the truth of the first, which is of the Twelve Apostles
of the Lamb, [the New Testament] and shall make known the plain
and precious things which have been taken away from them; and
shall make known to all kindreds, tongues, and people, that the Lamb
of God is the Eternal Father and Saviour of the world."[22]

Mediation seems evident in the ambivalent position on the trinity. George Arbaugh maintained that the Book of Mormon is Unitarian, with a "monism which completely identified the persons of the Trinity with one another."[23] It is true that some passages blur the distinctions between the Father and the Son, but in other passages the distinction seems clear,[24] and the Holy Ghost appears to be distinct as well.[25] Rather than being Unitarian, the text may simply be ambiguous.

Another category where the treatment seems mediatory is the scripture's view of man and mortality. At one point the text sounds Calvinistic. The prophet Helaman laments: "O how foolish, and how vain, and how evil, and devilish and how quick to do iniquity, and how slow to do good, are the children of men. . . . O how great is the nothingness of the children of men; yea, even they are less than the dust of the earth."[26] According to the Book of Mormon salvation comes only through grace. Nephi admonishes the people to "reconcile yourselves to the will of God, that it is only in and through the grace of God that ye are saved."[27] In another passage an apostate, Korihor, attacks the idea of the Fall and that the children are guilty of the transgression of their parents, making it apparent that the true faith includes this doctrine.[28]

Despite their sinfulness, men and women are capable of faith and repentance and have the will to believe.[29] Ultimately, they are to be rewarded according to their works.[30] No coercion will be employed if they choose not to believe,[31] but they are doomed to everlasting torment.[32] Thus sociologist Thomas F. O'Dea exaggerated in concluding that the Book of Mormon is Arminian throughout.[33] Passages which are strongly anti-Universalist suggest once again the Calvinistic inclinations in the text,[34] while others speak against the doctrine of election.[35] Mediation rather than Arminianism seems evident here.

The scripture warns Americans in the 1830s of their peril. During his post-resurrection visit to America, Jesus tells the Nephites that the Indians may be set loose against the wicked:

> But if they will repent, and hearken unto my words, and harden
> not their hearts, I will establish my church among them . . . and
> they [the Gentiles] shall assist my people, the remant [sic] of
> Jacob; and also, as many of the house of Israel as shall come,
> that they may build a city, which shall be called the New
> Jerusalem; and then shall they assist my people that they may
> be gathered in, which are scattered upon all the face of the land,

in unto the New Jerusalem. And then shall the power of heaven come down among them; and I shall be in their midst.[36]

Like an angelic trumpet the Book of Mormon called the nation to repentance for the time was short. The elect must heed the solemn sound and gather to the holy city. The sword of judgment hung heavily over the land and soon only those within the confines of the city would be safe.

Those who found that the Book of Mormon spoke to their hopes and fears remembered long afterward the shattering impact it had upon their lives. Apostle Parley P. Pratt was converted by reading the book before even meeting a Mormon. He recalled that it was "the principle means, in the hands of God, of directing the entire course of my future life." It was first given to him by a Baptist deacon, and he "read it all day; eating was a burden, . . . [he] preferred reading to sleep." As he read "the spirit of the Lord was upon me and I knew and comprehended that the book was true."[37] Sidney Rigdon's son recalled that his father also "got so engaged in [the book] that it was hard for him to quit long enough to eat his meals. He read it both day and night."[38] William W. Phelps, who became the church's first newspaper editor, said the book "produces an earthquake in this generation. It explains the Bible; it opens the vision of the prophets; it unravels the mystery who first settled this country, and it shows the old paths wherein if a man walk he shall live."[39] More pointedly, Brigham Young reported that the Book of Mormon and the Bible "will save you and me and the whole world."[40]

Of course, not everyone reacted positively to the new scripture. Those who rejected it saw it as the work of an impish and impious youth, Joseph Smith.[41] However, when the Mormons moved to Ohio in early 1831, adding hundreds to church rolls, some began to take the work more seriously. Alexander Campbell wrote the first major critique of the book in the fall of 1831,[42] when the Saints were making inroads into his and other congregations in and around Kirtland, Ohio.[43] He declared that the work contradicted the Bible and that it was written by Joseph Smith.[44] Despite this Mormonism spread,[45] and Campbellites and other denominations became increasingly alarmed.[46]

In this context a new theory as to the origin of the Book of Mormon emerged, the so-called Spaulding theory. Just how this theory first took shape is uncertain.[47] Mormons charged that it originated with Philastus Hurlbut, a Mormon apostate who collaborated with

Eber D. Howe, editor of Ohio's *Painesville Telegraph*, to produce in 1834 the influential expose, *Mormonism Unvailed*. Hurlbut collected important documents for Howe, who authored the bulk of the text. Some Mormons have contended that Hurlbut actually wrote the book but that Howe's name appears on the cover due to Hurlbut's unsavory reputation. This greatly exaggerates Hurlbut's role, however.[48] There is no doubt that Hurlbut went to New York in 1833 to learn about the origins of Mormonism[49] and that he received funding from several people in New Salem (Conneaut), Ohio, and elsewhere.[50] In any case, *Mormonism Unvailed* succeeded in establishing the Spaulding theory as the most widely accepted explanation of the origin of the Book of Mormon among non-Mormon writers. In fact, by 1914 one such writer termed it "the impregnable rock upon which the anti-Mormon forces have taken their stand."[51]

According to the theory, Joseph Smith was far too ignorant to write a volume as intricate and scriptural as the Book of Mormon, and was assisted by someone better prepared.[52] The logical choice at the time seemed to be Sidney Rigdon, a former Baptist preacher who had joined the Campbellites but disagreed with Alexander Campbell over such matters as the gathering of Israel, latter-day miracles, the Millennium,[53] and the desirability of having all property held in common among modern Christians.[54] In the view of some writers, eventually including Campbell himself,[55] Rigdon conspired with Joseph Smith to write the text and launch his own religious movement.[56] It was said that the ideas which went into the narrative had come from a novel written by Solomon Spaulding, a would-be author who wrote the "Manuscript Found," which allegedly told of the immigration to America of early Israelitish tribes.[57] To this romantic base Rigdon was said to have added doctrinal and other religious material. Thus alleged similarities between Campbellite and Mormon doctrine could be accounted for.[58]

Despite able criticism of the Spaulding theory in 1902, 1931, 1945, and 1977,[59] the theory still retains a few adherents, although Fawn M. Brodie dealt it a heavy blow in 1945 in her biography of the Mormon prophet. She argued that the Book of Mormon was written by Joseph Smith himself, unaided, except that he borrowed ideas from Ethan Smith's *View of the Hebrews*, a religious text written in the early 1820s which argued that the American Indians were the lost tribes of Israel.[60] Although Brodie has had her critics,[61] her version of the origin of the Book of Mormon has remained the most widely accepted one in non-Mormon scholarly circles during the past forty-four years.

Whatever the origins of the Book of Mormon, when it was trans-lated, probably in June 1829, newspaper editors in Vermont, New York, and Ohio began to take notice of the book,[62] and the curiosity of many was aroused.[63] Inquiries led to converts in Palmyra (although not many) and in southern New York, and the prophet had to give more thought to the organization of a church. These concerns were reflected in the revelations which he continued to receive.[64] Six elders were ordained in June 1830,[65] and a revelation to David Whitmer and Oliver Cowdery commanded the choosing of twelve disciples.[66] Under what priesthood authority this was done is still a subject of controversy.

Church tradition holds that Aaronic and Melchizedek priest-hoods were conferred on Smith in 1829, a year before the church was formally organized. Conflict regarding the time sequence largely revolves around the higher or Melchizedek Priesthood. Some years ago historian Kent Fielding argued that the higher priesthood was not conferred on the elders until a conference in Ohio in June 1831.[67] Considerable testimony supports this view. Several men prominent in the early church stated that this priesthood was not introduced until that time, among them David Whitmer, Oliver Cowdery, John Whitmer, William E. McLellin, John Corrill, J. C. Brewster, the prophet's brother, William, and Brigham Young.[68] Even those who compiled the official history after the prophet's death quoted him as saying that in 1831 the "authority of the Melchizedek Priesthood was manifest and conferred for the first time upon several of the elders."[69] None of Joseph Smith's contemporaries indicate that the higher priesthood was restored in 1829.

Parley P. Pratt, who joined the Mormons in 1830, affirmed what he believed on the matter very emphatically. He wrote that at the conference in June 1831 "several were selected by revelation, through President Joseph Smith, and ordained to the high priesthood after the holy order of the Son of God; which is after the order of Melchizedek. This is the first occasion in which this priesthood had been revealed and conferred upon the Elders in this dispensation." Pratt said, "The office of the Elder is the same in a certain degree, but not in the fullness." Pratt had been an elder for nine months prior to the conference of 1831.[70] David Whitmer insisted that the idea of a higher priesthood was an afterthought, which had come from Sidney Rigdon.[71] William Smith said that in Ohio "Elders, Priests, Teachers and Deacons received some general instructions from the Church concerning the Priesthood of Melchizedek, to which they had not as yet been ordained for they had not attained to all the power of their ministry."[72] Brigham Young explained the circumstances of the bestowal of the higher priesthood in detail at a meeting in Utah. He said that when Joseph received this priesthood "he received . . . [a] revelation, Peter, James and John came to him in Kirtland" in 1831.[73]

B. H. Roberts argued at the turn of the century that the problem was one of terminology, that Joseph and others spoke of the office of high priest when they talked about the high priesthood being restored in 1831.[74] Roberts is correct that there was initial confusion concerning the office and its relationship to other offices such as that of the seventy. But this contention hardly accounts for the very explicit statements of Brigham Young and others that the priesthood itself was restored in 1831.

Despite such testimony, it is possible that the "lesser" or Aaronic priesthood was conferred in 1829 and that the position of elder was initially included under this authority.[75] Oliver Cowdery wrote in the *Messenger and Advocate* in 1834 that the "angel of God" had appeared in 1829 and that "we received under his hand the holy Priesthood."[76] This phraseology suggests the lesser priesthood.

However, the Book of Mormon, which Joseph Smith with Cowdery's assistance was translating at this time, mentions no priesthood while recounting the ordaining of teachers and priests by the twelve disciples.[77] The scripture does speak of priesthood elsewhere, however, explaining that the "high priesthood . . . [was] after the order of his son, which order was from the foundation of the world." This priesthood is mentioned briefly during the administration of the prophet Alma, some eighty years before the birth of Jesus.[78] As David Whitmer contended, nothing is said of it after the appearance of Jesus to the Nephites.[79]

Whatever the status of priesthood in the first year or so of church organization, great stress was placed on the idea that special authority had been given the new dispensation. E. D. Howe, writing in the *Painesville Telegraph* reported that when Oliver Cowdery first visited Ohio in November 1830 he proclaimed that "he and his associates are the only persons on earth who are qualified to administer in his name."[80] If ideas and institutional procedures which eventually assumed central importance in the tradition were not firmly established in the first months, this may only suggest that this was a religious movement that was first experienced and then afterward reflected upon and systematized.

It was in keeping with the primitive gospel ideals of early Mormonism[81] that laymen were called to preach and administer the ordinances of the new church. Frequently they were converted and baptized one day and sent out as missionaries the next, returning to their families and friends to spread the good news.[82] By April 1830, when the church was officially organized, there were already between thirty to seventy members,[83] and meetings were being held at several locations.[84] To govern the new church officers were given New Testament titles.[85] Joseph Smith was designated the "first elder," perhaps indicating his preeminence over the whole church.[86] Later he was named "seer, translator, a prophet, and an apostle of Jesus Christ."[87] Oliver Cowdery was termed "second elder" and an apostle.[88]

Joseph and Oliver were commanded to "ordain other elders, priests, teachers, and deacons" and to "administer bread and wine" and to "teach, expound, exhort, baptize . . . and to take the lead in all meetings."[89] The elders in the local branches were to take charge of their meetings. The priests were to preach, exhort, baptize, administer the sacrament, and visit the homes of members. Teachers were to "watch the church always and be with them and strengthen them and see that there is no iniquity in the church."[90] Teachers and elders were to hold periodic conferences.[91] No one was to be baptized who did not understand the principles of the gospel.[92]

Between April 1830 and January 1831 when the Saints left New York for Ohio the church grew slowly but encountered increasing opposition among Gentiles.[93] In September Joseph Smith was brought to trial for disturbing the peace, and his father was jailed for thirty days for failing to pay a small debt.[94] With outside pressure mounting, the Saints were told by revelation that the time of the Second Coming was near and that they must gather and make ready.[95]

Joseph Smith was ordained "prophet and seer" in April 1830,[96] but in July Oliver Cowdery and the Whitmers objected to one of his revelations.[97] As the months passed more of the Saints were on the verge of open rebellion. Opposition to Joseph came from the followers of Hyrum Page, who had a peepstone and had received a handful of revelations of his own.[98] About this time, Smith had ceased to rely heavily upon his own seerstone for inspiration, and the change was disturbing to Cowdery and the Whitmers.[99] They expressed their disenchantment by meeting secretly with Page,[100] and Cowdery began to write down Page's and possibly his own revelations.[101] It required a divine rebuke through Joseph Smith to remind these

elders that only he was to receive revelations for the church.[102] The
Page affair marked an initial turning point for Joseph Smith, as he
discontinued some aspects of his role as magician and discounte-
nanced it to some degree for his church members. There was to be
but one seer governing the church.

During this crisis the Saints were reminded that they must
gather to escape the judgments.[103] In September 1830 four missionaries, including the reconciled Cowdery, were sent to the Indian
tribes in the western part of Missouri to gather this branch of Israel
and to solicit their help in building the Holy City.[104] The Saints were
told that they would soon have a land of inheritance in the West.[105]
They were instructed to flee to Ohio,[106] where they would receive
the laws of the kingdom and become a "righteous people, without
spot and blameless."[107] They were informed that in the promised
land their property would be gathered into the "bosom of the
church."[108] The office of bishop was established to administer what
would be designated the "law of consecration"[109]—the basis for the
communal order which would exist in the kingdom of God on earth.

The message which the Mormon missionaries now preached
with a sense of urgency—door to door, street corner to street corner, assembly hall to assembly hall, in the towns and cities of the
eastern half of the United States—was revolutionary.[110] Orson Pratt,
an apostle, affirmed that the people should "utterly reject both the
Popish and Protestant ministry, together with all the churches which
have been built up by them or that sprung up from them, as being
entirely destitute of authority."[111] This affirmation thus challenged
some of the basic assumptions of American religious pluralism.[112]
In self defense the other churches fought back. Both the prophet
and his mother recount vigorous opposition from ministers of other
denominations between 1827 and 1831. One of the occasions they
describe involved Joseph's trial for "being a disorderly person," for
"setting the country in an uproar by preaching the Book of
Mormon."[113] A letter from a resident of South Bainbridge in 1831
confirms Smith's charge that religious intolerance was involved. "A.
W. B." explained to the editors of the *Evangelical Magazine and Gospel
Advocate*:

> In order to check the progress of delusion, and open the eyes
> and understandings of those who blindly followed him, . . . he
> was again arraigned before a bar of Justice, during the last sum-
> mer, to answer to a charge of misdemeanor. This trial lead to an

investigation of his character and conduct, which clearly evinced
to the unprejudiced, whence the spirit came which dictated his
inspirations. During the trial it was shown that the Book of Mormon was brought to light by the same magic power by which he
pretended to tell fortunes, discover hidden treasures, &c.[114]

The trial was remembered long afterward by John S. Reid, a
friend of Joseph Knight. Reid served as Smith's lawyer during the
hearing and said the trial was brought on by sectarians who "uniting their efforts, roared against him." Reid recalled that "their cry
of 'False Prophet! False Prophet!' was sounded from village to village, and every foul epithet that malice and wicked ingenuity could
invent were heaped upon him."[115]

This antagonism to the prophet and his movement was thus
sectarian in nature, but there was opposition from other sources as
well. Many people whether members of other denominations or not
were indignant at the charge that they were among the damned unless
they joined with the new movement. When Sidney Rigdon came to
Waterloo, New York, in December 1830 he pronounced judgments
against the Gentiles in the city. According to a correspondent of the
Palmyra Register, Rigdon delivered a discourse at the courthouse,
"wherein he depicted in strong language, the want of charity and
brotherly love among the prevailing sects and denominations. . . .
After denouncing dreadful vengeance on the whole state of New York,
and this village in particular, and recommending to all such as wish
to flee from 'the wrath to come,' to follow him beyond the 'western
waters,' he took his leave."[116]

Previous to this, Hyrum Smith, the prophet's older brother,
warned of judgments against those who opposed the Book of Mormon. An outraged citizen voiced his indignation to the *Palmyra
Reflector*: "Please advise hyrum smith and some of his ill-bred associates, not to be quite so impertinent, when decent people denounce
the imposition of the "GOLD bible," the anathemas of such ignorant wretches, although not feared are not quite so well relished by
some people—apostles should keep cool."[117] The Mormons irritated,
among others, Obadiah Dogberry with their jeremiads. He protested
that Joseph Smith and his followers "go from place to place disturbing, to a greater or lesser degree, the peace of the community—
denouncing dire damnation on such as may hold approbation from
the world's most ridiculous impostures."[118]

Another Mormon custom during this early period which won them no favor was the holding of secret meetings.[119] Sidney Rigdon explained that it was due to fear of persecution that the Saints met in seclusion.

> We knew the whole world would laugh at us, so we con-
> cealed ourselves; and there was much excitement about our meet-
> ings, charging us with designs against the government, and with
> laying plans to get money &c, which never existed in the heads
> of any one else, and if we talked in public, we should have been
> ridiculed more than we were, the world being entirely ignorant
> of the testimony of the prophets. . . . So we were obliged to retire
> to our secret chambers, and commune ourself with God.

Rigdon felt bolder in Nauvoo, Illinois, in 1844 than he did in New York in 1830 and described why the secret meetings were necessary.

> The time is now come to tell why we held secret meetings. We
> were maturing plans fourteen years ago which we can now tell;
> were we maturing plans to corrupt the world, to destroy the peace
> of society? Let fourteen years of the experience of the church
> tell the story. The church would have never been here, if we had
> not done as we did in secret. The cry of false prophet, and
> imposter rolled upon us . . . There was no evil concocted when
> we first held secret meetings.[120]

The Mormons were planning no coup d'etat to seize the reins of government, but already they were set upon separating themselves from American society and awaiting the destruction of all governments that would precede their own rise to power.

CHAPTER 3

"I Say Unto You, Be One"—Social Unity and Economic Equality

The Book of Mormon convinced Mormons that God could reveal his will to them through their prophet-seer and that thereby they could achieve a godly life in their social, economic, and political affairs. Behind the resulting experimentalism was a quest for cultural unity erected upon a religious base.[1] The meager sources of early Mormonism in New York reveal little of the depth and breadth in the Mormon search for social seamlessness which would later become so apparent. It is clear, however, that some of the Mormon emigrants who fled New York for Kirtland, Ohio, pooled their material wealth on the eve of departure. A resident of Waterloo indicated that not everyone was cooperative: "Two of the most responsible Mormonites . . . demurred to the divine command . . . requiring them to sell their property and put into the common fund. . . . A requisition of *twelve* hundred dollars, in cash, it is said was made upon one of these gentlemen . . . the Lord having need of it."[2] The injunction in question, given in January, had commanded the church to "Be one, and if ye are not one, ye are not mine."[3] What was in New York a command to fill a temporary economic need would become in Ohio,

Missouri, and Illinois a fundamental preoccupation expressing the most basic attitudes of the Mormon people.

The first Mormons in Ohio were Oliver Cowdery and three other missionaries sent westward to convert the American Indians. Eber D. Howe, editor of the *Painesville Telegraph*, took notice of them in November 1830, writing that they were "bound for the regions beyond the Mississippi, where [Joseph Smith] contemplates founding a 'City of Refuge' for his followers, and converting the Indians under his prophetic authority."[4]

Cowdery and company had already visited Sidney Rigdon at Mentor, Ohio, and converted him and some of his Campbellite followers.[5] They then went to Kirtland and baptized twenty or thirty more.[6] Travelling to New York, Rigdon succeeded in persuading Joseph Smith that the Ohio region would be a fertile missionary field. He was right, for by February 1831 several hundred new members had been added there.[7]

Parley P. Pratt, one of the four missionaries, described this phenomenal success which they initially enjoyed:

> The interest and excitement now became general in Kirtland, and in all the region round about. The people thronged to us night and day, insomuch that we had no time for rest and retirement. Meetings were convened in different neighborhoods, and multitudes came together soliciting our attendance; while thousands flocked about us daily; some to be taught, some for curiosity, some to obey the gospel, and some to dispute or resist it.[8]

The reasons for the unusual success in the Western Reserve of Ohio were many. Pratt's determination to see his old mentor, Rigdon, provided the missionaries with an unusually receptive audience.[9] Most northern Ohioans were originally from New England and had endured a heavy barrage of revivalistic preaching before and after they moved west.[10] Millennialist expectations were pervasive, and sectarian discord in the region had likewise been strong. Many were dissatisfied with the aftereffects.[11] The Disciples of Christ had made significant progress in spreading restorationism in the area before the Mormons came, and the rich religious soil became even more fertile for the planting of Mormonism.[12]

What set Mormons apart was their announcement of new revelation from heaven through a prophet and seer, the promise of impending fulfillment of prophecy, and of miracles as signs of the Millennium which would surely follow.[13] Rigdon found the prophetic

theme especially convincing: "The Scriptures informed us of peril-
ous and distressing times, great judgments that should come in the
last days, and destructions upon the wicked: and now God had sent
along his servants to inform us of the time."[14] John Corrill, who
joined the Mormon church in January 1831, said that what persuaded
him, aside from Rigdon's baptism, was that in "every age (according
to the scriptures) God continued to send prophets to the people."[15]

Mormon teachings seemed in harmony with the Bible. According to Corrill,

> The Mormons believe in the same God, and in the same
> Saviour, and the same Gospel that other professors do, and they
> believe as firmly in the Scripture of the Old Testaments as any
> other people. They look upon their new revelations only as bring-
> ing about the fulfillment of the Bible. The main difference
> between them and other professors of the Gospel is, that they
> believe rather more firmly in the promises of God, especially
> those that require great faith for their fulfillment.[16]

One observer who attended the first Mormon meetings in
Kirtland said they took place in the schoolhouse or at different res-
idences and that the initial prayer meetings were "generally decently
conducted" but rather informal. But, he continued, once the spiritual power came, bedlam broke out.[17] Enthusiasm among the
Kirtland converts for prophecies and other spiritual gifts quickly
reached a high pitch.[18] After the missionaries departed and Rigdon
went to New York, the excitement intensified. One writer observed:

> A scene of the wildest enthusiasm was exhibited, chiefly, how-
> ever, among the young people: they would fall, as without
> strength, roll upon the floor, and, so mad were they that even
> the females were seen in a cold winter day, lying under the bare
> canopy of heaven with no couch or pillow but the fleecy snow.
> At other times they exhibited all the apish actions imaginable,
> making grimaces both horrid and ridiculous. . . . At other times
> they are taken with a fit of jabbering which they neither under-
> stood themselves nor any body else, and this they call speaking
> foreign languages by divine inspiration.[19]

Another witness added, "Young men and women would rush to the
corner, fall in a promiscuous heap, others laid on bed[s] indiscriminately, others talked Indian."[20]

Franklin D. Richards, who was first contacted by Mormons in
the East in 1831, recalled the experience of speaking in tongues:

> You have sometimes been impressed with overwhelming Emotions upon you and attempt to say something and could not, that is just the way the spirit works, you say something even if you do not know anything about it and find out that it was something that ought to be proper and right. . . . If a man goes out to preach and not had a good education, he naturally feels backward and diffident as if he could not,—then by faith the Spirit comes upon him, he talks things he never knew of before both edifying and profitable to people. . . . The ways of the spirit are not as mens ways it is wonderful [and] marvelously singular.[21]

For some Saints, the passion they felt for their new faith was greater than their ability to express. There was, however, an uneasiness among many that the spiritual manifestations had gotten out of control.[22]

Philo Dibble described Joseph Smith's reaction when he arrived in Kirtland in February 1831. "When the prophet . . . saw the false spirits which caused jumping, shouting, falling down, he said, 'God has sent me here, and the devil must leave, or I will.' "[23] In late March, Smith wrote to his brother Hyrum that "the devil had made many attempts to overthrow them, it has been a serious job but the Lord is with us."[24]

The gift of prophecy which appeared frequently also concerned Smith.[25] Some so endowed seemed to threaten the emerging hierarchical order in the church. Among these was a woman named Hubble, who professed to be a prophetess "and to have many revelations and knew that the Book of Mormon was true; and that she would become a teacher in the Church of Christ. She appeared very sanctimonious and deceived some, who were not able to detect her in her hypocrisy."[26] Hubble's manifestations caused the prophet to remind the Saints through a revelation that "there is none other [but Joseph Smith] appointed unto you to receive commandments and revelations." Should the prophet err, the revelation continued, "he shall not have power except to appoint another in his stead."[27]

Yet the spiritual excesses and the frequent appearance of aspiring prophets in the mold of village seers continued, and the fundamental unity of the church was endangered. In May the prophet finally took steps to curb these tendencies. He informed through revelation that whatever "doth not edify is not of God, and is darkness."[28] Spiritual manifestations must match the mind and mood of the priesthood or be rejected. The prophet explained, "If you behold a spirit manifested that you cannot understand, and you receive not that spirit, ye shall ask of the Father in the name of Jesus; and if he not give unto you that spirit, then you may know that it is not of God."[29]

Some of the brethren who had formulated their own style of spiritual enlightenment and were now censured left the church. George Albert Smith recalled that "among the number was Wycom Clark; he got a revelation that he was to be a prophet—that he was the true revelator; and himself, Northrop Sweet and four other individuals retired from the Church, and organized the 'Pure Church of Christ.' . . . John Noah, another of this class, assumed to be prophet, and in consequence thereof was expelled from the church."[30] But Mormons did not easily lose their fervor for spiritual gifts nor their faith in itinerant prophets. They still longed for a great bestowal of the power of God, even though the prophet had placed limits on the mode of expression a manifestation might assume, and spontaneous seers were disapproved. In time, however, the antipluralism of the Saints would override their passion for spontaneous spirituality and village prophets. Their spiritual modes would become standardized and limited within an increasingly organized and hierarchical institution.

In 1854 LDS apostle Orson Pratt explained how important the matter of social harmony was to Latter-day Saints. "The command to 'Be one,' " he said, "embraces all other commands. There is no law, statute, ordinance, covenant, nor blessing, but what was instituted to make the Saints one."[31] His statement came after years of persecution and hardship endured by Mormons in Missouri, Illinois, and early Utah, although in the beginning years in Ohio the search for communal unity and homogeneity was already absorbing Mormon interests. In fleeing New York the Saints were not only escaping persecution but also a divided and wicked Babylon.[32] They were convinced that to escape the debilitating secularizing tendencies of sectarian pluralism, they must live apart from the Gentiles.[33] In so doing they did not intend to take flight from the world permanently but to inherit it eventually as their own.[34] First, however, they would have to dedicate themselves totally to God's will and God's law.[35]

Even this early they believed that to achieve complete commitment to God, they must have a theocratic government. Before they left New York the Lord had promised, "In time ye shall have no king nor ruler, for I will be your king and watch over you—wherefore, hear my voice and follow me, and ye shall be a free people, and ye shall have no laws but my laws, when I come."[36] Expecting that the

time was near, in February 1831 twelve elders assembled as commanded in Ohio, and there the law that was to govern the Saints in
the New Jerusalem was given.[37] The law provided a number of moral
imperatives similar to the Ten Commandments and instructed that
those who would not obey the law were to be cast out.[38] But the Lord
cautioned, "Thou shalt observe to keep the mysteries of the kingdom unto thyself."[39] The new millennial precepts outlined by the
Lord included what became known as the "Law of Consecration and
Stewardship":[40]

> And behold, thou shalt consecrate all thy properties, that which
> thou hast unto me, with a covenant and a deed which can not be
> broken; and they shall be laid before the bishop of my church. . . .
>   And it shall come to pass, that the bishop of my church,
> after he has received the properties of my church, that it can
> not be taken from the church, he shall appoint every man a stew-
> ard over his own property, or that which he has received, inas-
> much as it [is] sufficient for himself and family:
>   And the residue shall be kept to administer to him who
> has not, that every man may receive according as he stands in
> need:
>   And the residue shall be kept in my storehouse, to admin-
> ister to the poor and needy . . . and for the purpose of purchas-
> ing lands, and the building up of the New Jerusalem.[41]

The Law of Consecration was partly a result of the Mormon
attempt to recreate the New Testament church.[42] Orson Pratt
explained that in the ancient church the Saints had consecrated all
to the Lord and were equal temporally. The "same order of things
must exist in the Zion of the latter-days," he said, "or else the inhabitants thereof never will be one."[43] In Pratt's view, the ultimate purpose was unity. Thus the Saints' experiment in communitarianism
was closely related to their flight from sectarian conflict and the pluralism which engendered it. Pratt made this clear by insisting that
"an inequality in property is the root and foundation of innumerable evils, it tends to division, and to keep asunder the social
feelings."[44] He added emphatically, "It is the great barrier erected
by the devil to prevent that unity and oneness which the Gospel
requires."[45]

Consecration had a practical purpose. It required church members already in Kirtland to share their land with immigrants coming from New York and provided funds for more land.[46] As a result,
the New Yorkers were able to settle on a farm at Thompson[47] called

"the church farm," the land being partly donated by church members.[48] The Saints at Thompson had instituted their own community of goods, but this arrangement was subsequently forbidden in favor of deeding property to the church in return for a lease.[49] When one of the Thompson members who had consecrated a large amount of land withdrew and took legal action to recover his property, most of the New York Saints packed up and headed for Missouri.[50]

The bishop was to determine in consultation with each member how much property should be leased to each member. The residue of property went into a common storehouse to care for the poor or finance church business, including the needs of church officials.[51] The embarrassment of having a "hireling clergy" was thus avoided.[52] As historian Leonard J. Arrington notes, this law curbed unequal accumulation among the Saints, yet allowed room for individual initiative and responsibility.[53] The Law of Consecration then was not so much opposed to individual enterprise as it was to social cleavages which accompany the unequal distribution of wealth. Social cohesiveness was the intent of the law, but securing the Saints' complete cooperation was difficult.

Bishop Edward Partridge went from branch to branch in Ohio, trying to persuade members that consecration was the Lord's way. But not all congregations would receive the law. John Whitmer said that one of the difficulties was that the Saints outside Kirtland were too widely scattered and too few in number. Further, many converts had come into the church too hastily. They anticipated having common ownership but little understood the demands of individual responsibility imposed.[54] And those who did have property were not always willing to part with it.

This was the case with some new converts at Hiram, twenty miles south of Kirtland. The prophet went to live among these members in September 1831.[55] Many had been attracted by Smith's prophetic calling and by a miracle he had performed in curing the lame arm of a Mrs. Johnson.[56] But most were unprepared for the demands made upon them by consecration. According to Symonds Ryder, a Campbellite converted by witnessing the fulfillment of Mormon prophecy,[57] they were told in a revelation that they were to sell their farms and give the proceeds to the church. "This was too much for the Hiramites," Ryder commented, "and they left the Mormonites faster than they had ever joined them."[58]

In October a storehouse-commissary was established under the direction of Newel K. Whitney.[59] Meanwhile Joseph Smith was readying his revelations for publication, anticipating that under the stewardship principle the profits would pay for maintaining his family as well as those of Oliver Cowdery, Rigdon, and several of the Whitmers.[60] Even the lowliest church officials, including the teachers, priests, and elders, were to have access to the storehouse when they were in the Lord's service.[61] The job of maintaining the storehouse quickly became a burdensome one, and in 1832 the management of the storehouse and the whole consecration system was put under a central board composed of several men, including Joseph Smith, Sidney Rigdon, Martin Harris, and Oliver Cowdery.[62] The new board would manage consecration matters simultaneously in Missouri as well as Kirtland.[63] They also formed the United Firm, which used funds to purchase a steam sawmill, a tannery, a printing press, and more land. Most of these enterprises proved to be unprofitable, and the firm would not be a financial success.[64] After the Mormons were driven out of Jackson County, Missouri, the firm was dissolved in 1834.[65]

Smith first proposed the United Firm in a revelation given in March 1832. This revelation explained the reason behind this consolidation of church funds: "That ye may be equal in the bonds of heavenly things, and earthly things also, for the obtaining of heavenly things. For if ye are not equal in earthly things ye cannot be equal in obtaining heavenly things."[66] The intent was to promote equality, but hopefully the church also would be made "independent above all other creatures beneath the celestial world."[67] Arrington indicates that in Geauga County and Missouri the Mormons attempted to eliminate all trade with the Gentiles but were only partially successful.[68]

When the United Firm was dissolved those who had contributed to it were given a stewardship over an individual piece of property.[69] Under the new arrangement the brethren were to pool their funds into two treasuries, one made up of funds earned from the publication of Smith's revelations and the other of profits coming from new individual stewardships. Although the consecration of property was discontinued for a time among the membership after 1834,[70] church leaders were apparently still to share their capital in an effort to build up the finances of the kingdom.

After the United Order was discontinued, many Saints still expected church leaders to provide for them generously regardless

of whether or not it was economically feasible. Brigham Young
recalled an incident in Kirtland, where Joseph served as a storekeeper:

> Joseph goes to New York and buys $20,000 worth of goods,
> comes into Kirtland and commences to trade. In comes one of
> the brethren. "Brother Joseph, let me have a frock pattern for
> my wife." What if Joseph says, "No, I cannot without money."
> The consequence would be, "He is no Prophet," says James.
> Pretty soon Thomas walks in. "Brother Joseph, will you trust me
> for a pair of boots?" "No, I cannot let them go without money."
> "Well," says Thomas, "Brother Joseph is no Prophet; I have found
> *that* out and I am glad of it." After a while in comes Bill and Sis-
> ter Susan. Says Bill, "Brother Joseph, I want a shawl. I have not
> got any money, but I wish you to trust me a week or a fortnight."
> Well, Brother Joseph thinks the others have gone and aposta-
> tized, and he don't know but these goods will make the whole
> church do the same, so he lets Bill have a shawl. Bill walks off
> with it and meets a brother. "Well," says he, "what do you think
> of Brother Joseph?" O, he is a first rate fellow with them all the
> time, provided he never would ask them to pay him.[71]

Being a prophet and a storekeeper at the same time was symptom-
atic of certain difficulties which occurred when sacred and secular
roles were homogenized within the Mormon theocratic kingdom.

Under Mormon theocratic ideals no distinction was drawn
between religious and secular aspects of life. There was only one
world and that was the Lord's. The children of the kingdom could
build a tannery or a temple with equal zest and equal assurance that
they were following God's commands. Or, when their new zion in
Missouri was threatened in 1833 by rioting and mobbing, they could
organize an army in Ohio called "Zion's Camp" and invade the state
to redeem their promised land. To be sure, they were assured before
they left Kirtland that the state militia would be there to escort those
who had been forced to flee back to their farms, but this did not nec-
essarily mean that the governor wanted armed forces coming in from
outside the state, a course which the Mormons chose to take. Thus
the quest for a kingdom and refuge on earth could lead down strange
paths and tempt a usually peace-loving people to militaristic aggression. Zion's Camp was a portent of things to come.

The Saints had begun to settle on the far western border of Missouri in 1831. They were drawn there after the proposed Indian mission failed, the elders having been driven away by a federal agent

and hostile Protestant preachers.[72] Undaunted, the missionaries had gone to preach in Independence, in Jackson County, Missouri, and had sent Parley Pratt back to Ohio to report their reverses. Pratt informed the prophet of good prospects for a Mormon gathering in the region, and soon preparations were made to migrate.[73] Among these were the Colesville, New York, Saints whose sojourn at Thompson had come to an end.

To spread the gospel and to seek out an inheritance for themselves, the prophet and all the elders journeyed west in the summer of 1831.[74] They began filtering into Independence in July.[75] Smith acted quickly to establish the United Order among the new immigrants, naming Bishop Edward Partridge to manage economic affairs. Partridge was instructed to buy land, build a storehouse, and set up a printing press.[76] It was revealed that Independence would be the central gathering place for the New Jerusalem, or Zion, and the Saints were commanded to buy all the additional land possible from Independence to the western border of the state.[77] In August the promised land was dedicated in a simple ceremony,[78] and Smith, shunning the primitive life on the frontier, returned to Ohio.[79]

During the next year Zion grew slowly, and there was no overt hostility between the incoming strangers and the old Missourians.[80] However, a feeling of uneasiness developed among some who calculated that Mormons would soon acquire all the desirable grazing land.[81] Others began to fear the political potential of the Saints' slow but steady growth, even though the Mormons had not yet involved themselves in politics.[82] As the number of Mormons grew, tension between the two groups increased.[83] Some Gentiles came forward, offering to sell their lands to the Saints and leave, but the newcomers lacked the capital.[84] Many Mormons in their conversations with "Gentiles" were outspoken, freely voicing eschatological expectations of inheritance and dominion.[85] The Mormon newspaper, *The Evening and the Morning Star*, was widely read but was "very distasteful" to members of other denominations.[86]

Sectarian opposition to the Saints appeared at the very first and caused antagonism.[87] Squatters who had exercised their rights in a traditionally American fashion were afraid that Mormons might purchase their claims at auction,[88] and land speculators feared that the Mormon presence would depreciate the available land.[89] Also, Gentile merchants disliked the exclusive economic policies of the Saints.[90] An assortment of "old timers" thus objected to Mormon intrusions. One opponent later admitted as much when he said that non-Mormons had first settled western Missouri, thereby giving them prior rights under "natural law" in organizing and governing the region.[91]

Such were the sources of anxiety when a group in Jackson County met in March 1832 to discuss extra-legal ways of ridding themselves of the uninvited. But an Indian sub-agent discouraged them and they dispersed.[92] In the fall came some haystack burning and bitter name-calling,[93] and the following March the Missourians met again in an abortive effort to form a united front to oust the Saints.[94] At this point, in July 1833, W. W. Phelps, editor of *The Evening and the Morning Star*, alienated nearly all the Missourians in Jackson County. Phelps, for reasons which became the subject of much controversy, provided explicit instructions about legal requirements for free Negroes immigrating to the state.[95] Slavery, which was widespread in western Missouri,[96] seemed endangered by possible free Negro infiltration,[97] and many leading citizens of Jackson County now became hostile toward the Mormons.[98]

On 20 July, four hundred to five hundred Missourians massed at the Independence courthouse to insist that the Mormons leave the county immediately or suffer the consequences.[99] When the Mormons demurred, the mob destroyed their press and beat two elders.[100] Mormon leaders at Independence finally promised to evacuate by the following January but did not act on this, believing that the agreement made under duress was not binding. Following Smith's advice, they sought through legal process to have their property damages paid.[101] But they were unable to persuade any civil official in the county to execute the law against the earlier settlers.[102] In desperation they petitioned the governor, who replied that if no local officer would serve a writ upon Mormon persecutors, he would intervene.[103]

Many Missourians resumed their persecution, and Mormons began to arm themselves in self-defense, determined to remain in their promised land whatever the cost.[104] But in early November, a series of skirmishes left some Saints and Missourians dead. The old settlers secured assistance from outside the county, and the Mormons were outnumbered[105] and fled, having been disarmed by the local militia and then harassed by angry mobs. Their best remaining hope was the possible intervention of Governor Dunklin.

At first the governor seemed to promise significant help. Through his letters Dunklin informed the Mormons that they were entitled to reinstatement on their lands and that they could be

escorted en route by a detachment of state militia. He did not believe
that the situation justified his placing a body of troops permanently
in Jackson County, but the resident Saints were free to arm themselves in defense of their lives and property, and state arms could be
made available for this purpose. He indicated that he was anxious
that a court of inquiry search out the guilty and guarantee protection to any Mormons willing to return to Jackson County to testify.[106] But legal justice would have to be administered in Jackson
County, where public opinion was overwhelmingly against the Mormons.

   In February preparations were made for a public investigation,
and several Mormon witnesses were marched into Independence
under the protection of a contingent of the state militia commanded
by David Atchison, a friend of the Mormons. The state's attorney
reported after a short inquiry that no criminal prosecution was possible.[107] The discouraged Mormons were told that public feeling in
Jackson County was too intense, that any conviction would bring no
more than a five-dollar fine, and that most jury members were also
mobocrats.[108] It was obvious to all that no legal process in the county
would restore Mormon rights or property. The local Saints had given
up any expectation of immediate help from the state and were determined to await help from their eastern brethren.[109]

   The dilemma facing the Mormons was explained by Oliver
Cowdery: "You will undoubtedly see that it is of but *little* consequence
to proclaim the everlasting gospel to men, and warn them to flee to
Zion for refuge, when there is no Zion, but that which is in possession of the wicked. Lo, Zion must be redeemed, and then the Saints
can have a place to flee to for safety."[110] The ensuing paramilitary
expedition seemed the only course.[111] E. D. Howe described the elaborate preparations and eventual departure from Kirtland in May 1834:

> Gen. Joe Smith took his line of march from this county on Mon-
> day last, with a large party of his fanatical followers, for the seat
> of the [Missouri] war.—This expedition has been a long time in
> active preparation . . . last November . . . the prophet here sent
> forth his general orders, which he pretended was a revelation
> from God, for all his able bodied men to repair to the scene of
> difficulty. His preachers were sent forth to all parts of the coun-
> try among their proselytes, with a printed copy of the revelation
> in their pockets, reiterating and magnifying all the tales of woe
> which had befallen "the church" in the "promised land." . . .
> For several months past they have been collecting munitions of

war for the crusade. Dirks, knives, swords, pistols, guns, power-horns, &c. &c. have been in good command in this vicinity.[112]

The Mormon army, one hundred fifty strong, marched from Kirtland to Missouri with high millennial hopes. The previous December after the Missouri Saints had been driven from Zion, the Lord had commanded:

> Go and gather together the residue of my servants; and take all the strength of mine house, which are my warriors, my young men, and they that are of middle age also . . . and go ye straightway into the land of my vineyard, and redeem my vineyard, for it is mine, I have bought it with money. Therefore get ye straightway unto my land; break down the walls of mine enemies; throw down their tower, and scatter their watchmen; and inasmuch as they gather together against you, avenge me of mine enemies; that by and by, I may come with the residue of mine house and possess the land.[113]

Use of military force was thus suggested in the revelation. It indicated, however, that a call to arms was to be a last resort: "Let them importune at the feet of the Judge; and if he heed them not, let them importune at the feet of the governor; and if the governor heed them not, let them importune at the feet of the President; and if the President heed them not, then will the Lord arise and come forth out of his hiding place, and in his fury vex the nation."[114]

Hoping to avoid stirring excitement,[115] the elders traveled in small groups, confident that if they were unified no one would be harmed in the campaign.[116] They took special care not to advertise that they were en route to Jackson County,[117] but if they expected to catch the Missourians asleep, the hope was vain. Two Ohioans had already written the postmaster at Independence warning of the Mormon invasion. On 7 June the *Missouri Intelligencer and Boon's Lick Advertizer* announced the coming of Zion's army: "ANOTHER MORMON WAR THREATENED."[118] When the editor first heard the rumor that the Mormons were invading he was skeptical, but a week later he confirmed the report: "The last Springfield, Ill. Journal announces the passage through that place of a company of Mormons, 250 or 300 strong—composed of able bodied men. . . . They appeared to be generally armed."[119]

By 4 June the elders had reached the Mississippi River, still expecting that the governor would assist them once they reached the borders of Jackson County. Smith had left Kirtland dismayed because he had not been able to raise sufficient funds for provisions and because his military force was not large enough to adequately protect the Saints.[120] He wrote his wife Emma to this effect on 4 June: "Our numbers and means are altogether too small for the accomplishment of such a great enterprise, . . . our only hope is that whilst we deter the enemy, and terrify them for a little season (for we learn by means of some spies we send out for that purpose that they are greatly terrified) notwithstanding they are endeavoring to make a formidable stand." Smith hoped that more church elders would yet rally to the cause and "come to our relief."[121]

Meanwhile, Governor Dunklin was wavering in his resolve to intervene in behalf of the resident Saints. On 6 June he wrote to James Thornton that he had determined to await the course of events. The Mormons had an undeniable right to return to their lands but might yet be persuaded to forfeit that right in view of the difficulties. His first advice would be for them to sell out if they could get a fair price. Another possibility would be to give both groups separate territories. If that failed, he might have to intervene. But he warned that the coming of armed Mormons or Missourians into Jackson County would be illegal,[122] thus expressing his opposition to the intrusion either of Zion's Camp or of armed Missourians from other counties. Already Missourians from adjoining counties were planning an armed intervention of their own if the Mormon army tried to enter Jackson County.[123]

Unaware of Dunklin's position, Smith sent Apostles Orson Hyde and Parley Pratt to Jefferson City on 12 June to ask for the governor's protection. Two days later they returned with the message that Dunklin refused to act. The governor had said that "if he sought to execute the laws in that respect" it would "deluge the whole country in civil war and bloodshed."[124] Nonetheless, after counseling together, the camp decided "that we should go on armed and equiped."[125]

Evidently Smith determined at this point to make a show of force, despite Dunklin's counsel to the contrary. Otherwise it is difficult to explain why the camp did not disband and why so many camp members were furious when Smith determined later to negotiate for peace. Benjamin Winchester, who was with the camp, insisted that force had always been considered a viable option. The camp was "effected with the understanding that they were to fight their way, if necessary."[126] Hosea Stout assumed he was marching to Zion "to fight for their lost inheritances."[127] This was no doubt a widely held expectation. According to Nathan Tanner, when a revelation later came that their offering was sufficient and they need not fight, "sum of the camp be came angry & said they had rather die than return with out a fite."[128] Harrison Burgess added that "some individuals of the Camp felt to murmer at this decree and wanted to fight the enemies of God."[129] However, in the circular Oliver Cowdery and Sidney Rigdon sent to the churches immediately after the camp's departure from Kirtland, it was said that if the camp were large enough "the mob will either flee the country or remain inoffensive."[130] Thus, intimidation rather than war may have been initially intended by church leaders, as suggested in Joseph Smith's 4 June letter to Emma.[131]

Perhaps with this intimidation in mind, the camp continued toward Clay County, where most of the Saints expelled from Jackson County had relocated. When camp members reached Fishing River, as recorded by Heber C. Kimball, they stopped for the night. But then, "five men rode into the camp, and told us we should see hell before morning. . . . They told us that sixty men were coming from Richmond, Ray County, who had sworn to destroy us, also, seventy more were coming from Clay County, to assist in our destruction. These men were armed with guns, and the whole country was in a rage against us, and nothing but the power of God could save us."[132]

For the moment, the power of God did not fail. A storm blew up over the Fishing River, and the water level rose "forty feet."[133] The Missourians, hastening to engage the Lord's anointed, were stalled, and the lull gave the Mormons further time to reconsider. During this time W. W. Phelps, the embattled editor of the newspaper which the Jackson County settlers had destroyed, came to camp with John Corrill and told the prophet that the Gentiles were determined either to drive the Mormons out or to exterminate them.[134] At this, church leaders decided to capitulate.[135] When Colonel Searcy of Ray County came into camp to test Mormon intentions, Smith appealed to his sense of decency, recounted the sufferings of the Saints in Jackson County, and insisted that they had come merely to provision the sufferers and to see them reinstated through legal process. Force would be employed only as a last resort.[136] After this, a peace conference was held at Liberty, Missouri. Propositions were made that the Mormons or the Missourians buy the other out. Smith lacked the means to purchase the land and was unwilling to have the Saints sell their holdings. At the meeting Judge Ryland warned the Mormons that should they defeat the citizens of Jackson County

in battle, they would face Missourians from adjoining counties.[137]
This was apparently a deterrent to those still wishing to redeem the
promised land by force. In addition, the Mormons had become devastated by cholera. Smith sought peace. On 21 June a letter was sent
by several of the brethren in Clay County to the Missourians, which
explained that they had no intention of invading Jackson County
and would make every sacrifice to find an honorable adjustment of
their differences.[138]

The prophet now disbanded the camp, but the protest against
returning to Kirtland without restoring the Saints to their
"inheritances" became so violent among camp members that Smith
had to promise that Zion would be redeemed once the Saints had
sufficient militia in Missouri. He pledged that within three years the
Saints would come to Jackson County with a mighty army and "there
would not be a dog to open his mouth against them."[139] In a revelation at Fishing River, the elders were told that they failed to redeem
Zion because they had neither made Zion's army sufficiently
strong[140] nor been united "according to the union required by the
laws of the celestial kingdom."[141] The Lord told them that they must
no longer speak of judgments but say to the Missourians, "redress us
of our wrongs,"[142] thereby buying time "until the army of Israel
becomes very great."[143] The Saints were to raise funds to buy additional land in the vicinity of Jackson County, and then "I will hold
the armies of Israel guiltless in taking possession of their own
lands . . . and of throwing down the towers of mine enemies."[144] In
the meantime,

> let my army become very great, and let it be sanctified before
> me, that it may become fair as the sun, and clear as the moon,
> and that her banners may be terrible unto all nations;
>   That the kingdoms of this world may be constrained to
> acknowledge that the kingdom of Zion is in very deed the king-
> dom of our God and his Christ; therefore, let us become subject
> unto her laws.[145]

By June 1834 Zion had begun to take on a quasi-nationalistic and
militaristic dimension.

Before Smith departed from Missouri, he organized a high council and named David Whitmer the president of Zion.[146] Back in
Kirtland, he urged the new council "to be in readiness to move into
Jackson County in two years from the eleventh of September next,
which is appointed time for the redemption of Zion. If—verily I say

unto you—if the Church with one united effort perform their duties."[147] Every man was to have his "tent, his horses, his chariot, his armory, his cattle, his family, and his whole substance in readiness against the time when it shall be said: To your tents, O Israel!"[148]

It was this turn of events which afterward caused Apostle William E. McLellin to depict the entire camp expedition as a fiasco which raised in the church "the spirit of war."[149] Martin Harris also said that at this time the church was changed from "a peaceful company to that of a warrior band."[150] The disillusionment felt by these brethren spread from Missouri to Kirtland.

When Smith returned the town was torn apart for several weeks as his prophetic claims were openly challenged.[151] People began to doubt the Book of Mormon. The most vocal critics shouted that Smith had prophesied lies in the name of the Lord.[152] To assuage the discontented Smith announced that twelve apostles would be chosen to direct missionary efforts abroad and that seventy elders would assist them. The new apostles, chosen from among those who had journeyed to Missouri, were told to gather the elect for the Millennium. Several of the twelve were promised that they would personally complete the gathering and live to witness the advent of Christ. One was also promised that "the nations of the earth shall acknowledge that God has sent him."[153] But the anger that was engendered over Zion's Camp was not pacified, and the prophet was soon forced to act on his pledge to redeem his land of refuge.

Some of the most fundamental aspects of Mormon doctrine and theology were shaped during this crisis. According to one student, as Joseph Smith's position in Kirtland was deteriorating, he formulated what amounted to a new direction in doctrine.[154] This overstates and ignores both the continuity of Mormon thought and the gradual way in which new concepts were incorporated into the average Mormon's mind.[155] Rather than advocating completely new principles, Smith usually reshaped old ones. But it was not disturbing to most Mormons when some initial ideas were brushed aside, and the Saints were generally more concerned that the process of revelation continue than that old ideas be harmonized with the new. Only a few Saints felt otherwise.

Biblicism provided a base for theological development in Kirtland, and the broad revolt against Calvinism provided a framework from which to view the Old and New Testaments. In his early

theological insights Smith often sought to reconcile the Presbyterian Calvinism of his mother with the more liberal Universalism of
his father. His inclination to harmonize divergent ideologies was not
altogether unrecognized. Smith explained his purpose in 1843: "If
by the principles of truth I succeed in uniting men of all denominations in the bonds of love, shall I not have attained a good object? . . .
Christians should cease wrangling and contending with each other,
and cultivate the principles of union and friendship in their midst;
and they will do it before the millennium can be ushered in and
Christ take possession of his Kingdom."[156]

The theological blending occurred slowly, and ecumenicalism
was not realized at all. Initial theological changes came in the form
of a new doctrine of salvation. According to the new understanding,
all but the most rebellious—the sons of perdition—would eventually gain salvation.[157] In February 1832 God revealed that the dual-
ism preached by the revivalists was in error. Humanity was not
resigned to eternal bliss or everlasting burning but would gain salvation based on individual merit. The existence of three heavenly
degrees was announced, with the Saints who were true inheriting
the highest reward in the celestial kingdom, where God himself
dwells.[158] In keeping with Mormon eschatological thought, the celestial kingdom was to be established on the earth after it had been
purified by fire. Thus the Saints would literally inherit the earth for
all eternity.[159] Such ideas were advanced early in the Kirtland period,
but they did not take hold rapidly, and most Latter-day Saints still
spoke of the saved and the damned in opposing categories. The Book
of Mormon does not address the issue of humankind's ultimate destiny in these terms, and it was not until they reached Nauvoo, Illinois, when Smith further elaborated his ideas, that the more liberal
view of salvation began to take hold.[160]

In Smith's evolving theology anyone who did not live the Mormon law or who died without knowledge of Jesus Christ but lived an
honorable life would inherit in the next life a heavenly glory termed
the terrestrial kingdom.[161] A third glory, the equivalent of the usual
Protestant version of hell where the soul would suffer endless
remorse, was the "telestial" kingdom, saved for those who had lived
immoral lives—the murderers, adulterers, liars, and whoremong-
ers.[162] A final status, devoid of glory, was preserved for those few
who betrayed Jesus after having received a testimony of him. They
would be sons of perdition doomed to everlasting torment. This concept of perdition retained only a vestige of the earlier Calvinism.

It was during this same period that the Mormon doctrine of deity began to take on a distinctive shape. Whereas in the Book of Mormon the relationship between the members of the godhead was unclear, now some Saints began to accept the principle that God and Jesus were two distinct persons, God being a personage of spirit and Jesus having bodily form.[163]

The development of a more positive view of man was a fundamental alteration in Mormon beliefs which directly affected both of the above principles. The Book of Mormon had seen humans as God's creatures, contingent and sinful, but some of the Saints in the early 1830s began to see them as children of God, whose essence was uncreated and co-eternal with God. In 1833 Joseph Smith received a revelation to this effect, which explained that human "intelligence," their innermost self or reality, was neither created nor made but existed through all eternity.[164] God, the father of spirits, gave his children a spiritual body, much like their early, "intelligence" form but of a finer substance.[165] Men and women were indeed God's children but partook of divinity by existing in their original state entirely independent of his will.[166]

One of the ideas which was circulating widely in Smith's intellectual environment in the 1830s was that of a plurality of worlds. Thomas Paine had argued in his *Age of Reason* that plurality was incompatible with orthodox Christianity, but several writers had countered Paine in attempting to reconcile revealed and natural religion.[167] One of these writers was Thomas Dick, a Christian naturalist whose reaction to Paine was widely read in western New York. His *Philosophy of a Future State* was read by Mormon leaders in Kirtland in the mid-1830s and may have been read by and/or discussed in the presence of Joseph Smith. Dick envisioned a divine cosmos much like that of the Mormons[168] and tied Christian theology to a material universe, where in the afterlife worthy souls would dwell on some distant planet and progress toward perfection. He even speculated on the possibility of degrees of glory in the eternal world.[169]

Although there is no reliable evidence that Dick directly influenced Smith's thinking, by the end of 1834 Smith had revealed a universe similar to Dick's, peopled with intelligences progressing toward perfection.[170] Smith was no mere copier of other men's ideas, however, for he had begun to work out his own materialistic cosmology as early as 1830. In what became his Book of Moses, a series of biblical revelations he received, he outlined a universe of multiple worlds:

> And were it possible that man could number the particles
> of the earth, yea, millions of earths like this, it would not be a
> beginning to the number of thy creations; . . .
>   Wherefore, I can stretch forth mine hands and hold all
> the creations which I have made; and mine eye can pierce them
> also, and among all the workmanship of mine hands there has
> not been so great wickedness as among thy brethren.[171]

Smith thus believed in multiple worlds inhabited by beings capable
of wickedness. Yet the prophet's thought had not fully matured. For
example, he had not yet contended that the basic element of the universe was a form of matter.[172] This did not come until the Saints
were in Nauvoo, but Smith was moving in this direction. He recounted
in a Kirtland, Ohio, revelation that the elements of the universe were
eternal.[173]

To many in the early nineteenth century, a materialistic universe made good sense. Thomas Jefferson had affirmed that "to say
that the human soul, angels, God, are immaterial is to say that they
are nothing, or there is no God, no angels, no soul. I cannot reason
otherwise."[174]

In 1849 Orson Pratt, while defending Mormonism in the Brit-
ish Isles, argued much the same way: "There are two classes of Atheists in the world. One class denies the existence of God in the most
positive language; the other denies his existence in duration or space.
One says, 'There is no God,' the other says 'God is not *here* or *there*,
any more than he exists *now* and *then*.' The infidel says, 'God does
not exist anywhere.' The immaterialist says, 'He exists No-
where.' "[175]

Thus Mormons met the challenge of a materialistic and secular world view by incorporating some of it into their own theology.
Mormons were mindful of the dangers of infidelity in doing so[176]
but generally felt they could extract a greater truth by harmonizing
divergent views. Such a quest structured not only their economic but
also their intellectual life, although the thrust toward inclusiveness
could at times foster discord within the church itself.

One area of Mormon life which could not remain permanently
excluded from the enveloping reaches of the theocratic kingdom
was marriage. Although no revelation exists on the subject dating
this early, rumors that some form of polygamy was practiced by
Joseph Smith in Kirtland in 1835 circulated widely.[177] Church leaders responded with a denial in the Doctrine and Covenants. "We
believe," they said, "that one man should have one wife, and one

woman but one husband."[178] Nonetheless, enamored with the theocracy of the ancient Hebrews and the career of the patriarch
Abraham, Smith and his Saints could have hardly overlooked Old
Testament marital institutions. Mormons believed that before the
final day of millennial consummation all the truths practiced by the
ancient prophets would be restored,[179] and it was inevitable that the
"Patriarchal Order of Marriage"[180] would be one of these. According to W. W. Phelps, as early as January 1831, Smith told certain of
the elders in Missouri that in time the Lord wanted them to take
additional wives among the Indians. In 1834 Smith reportedly
explained to Phelps that this would be done as it had been by the
ancient Hebrews—by divine revelation.[181] According to another
church member, Smith told Lyman R. Sherman in 1835 that the
ancient order of plural marriage would again be restored to the
church.[182]

For the Mormons to introduce plural marriage relationships
in America where monogamy was universally revered was, at the very
least, risky. Emma Smith wrote that her husband told her when
rumors regarding polygamous practices were circulating among the
Saints that "such a system might be, if everybody agreed to it, and
would behave as they should."[183] But the prophet added that he did
not think such would be the case. Nonetheless, with Smith himself
being charged with polygamous inclinations, some of his seventies
evidently soon initiated the practice.[184] Uriah and Lydia Hawkins
were tried by the high council on 7 September 1836 for "unlawful
matrimony." Jared Carter said at the trial that there was a tendency
of "countenancing such practices in our midst."[185] With growing
numbers practicing plurality and potential strife attending it, Smith
avoided any effort to incorporate the principle into the official doctrine of the church.[186] He had to await a time when the kingdom
seemed more secure than it was in Ohio.

In Kirtland following the failure of Zion's Camp, Smith endeav-
ored to rally the discordant elements in the village by hastening the
building of the temple.[187] He told the elders that they would receive
a special endowment of spiritual power once the work was finished.[188] They required a period of study and preparation in the
meantime to enable them to preach the gospel abroad, to gather the
elect, and to return to Zion.[189] The Saints now worked with a will to
finish the structure so that the promised endowment would come.
Sacrifice was the order of the day, according to Heber C. Kimball:

> Our women were engaged in spinning and knitting in order to
> clothe those who were laboring at the building. . . . My wife toiled
> all summer in lending her aid towards its accomplishment. She
> had a hundred pounds of wool, which, with the assistance of a
> girl, she spun in order to furnish clothing for those engaged in
> the building . . . and although she had the privilege of keeping
> half the quantity of wool for herself . . . she did not reserve even
> so much as would make her a pair of stockings.[190]

Church leaders and common elders made an extra effort to raise
the walls of the Lord's house: "The whole church united in this under-
taking and every man lent a helping hand. Those who had no teams
went to work in the stone quarry and prepared the stones for drawing to the house, President Joseph Smith Jr. being our foreman in
the quarry. The Presidency, High Priests, and Elders all alike
assisting."[191]

The building of the temple helped the Kirtland economy, and
some of the poor were fed by the temple committee in exchange for
their labor.[192] To finance the purchase of supplies and to pay other
costs associated with the building, Smith borrowed heavily everywhere he could.[193] He received generous assistance from one new
member, a merchant, who loaned Smith $2,000 to pay the mortgage
on his farm, loaned the temple committee $13,000 in goods, and
signed a note which enabled Smith to purchase $30,000 worth of
additional merchandise for the temple in New York. This generosity
kept the temple storehouse operating and thereby provided for many
laboring on the Lord's house.

The Kirtland economy felt some strains from the rapidly growing population, and by the summer of 1835 there were from 1,700 to
1,800 Saints in the city. As the temple neared completion, it was difficult to find work for everyone.[194] To keep pace with the rapidly
expanding population, Smith bought land and resold it to the Saints.
He also maintained the operation of his store, which increased the
amount of debt he was forced to carry.[195] One of the difficulties for
the Kirtland economy was the critical shortage of liquid capital
throughout 1835.[196] Prices seemed high for mere necessities. In May
W. W. Phelps wrote to his wife living in Missouri: "It is hard living
here; flour costs from $6.00 to $7.00 a barrel and cows from $20.00
to $30.00 a head. It is a happy thing that I did not move back, for
everything here is so dear. Our brethren are so poor and hard run
for money that it would have been more than I could have done to
maintain my family."[197]

Phelps's general picture may have been overdrawn, because the Kirtland economy probably was typical for the region and not without prospects for stability and growth.[198] But for those who found it hard going there was also the expectation that soon they would be marching to Missouri. From late summer 1835 through the following April, the prophet's history is filled with comments on the approaching migration. In September he met with the Kirtland High Council "to take into consideration the redemption of Zion." The elders pledged "that we [will] go next season, to live or die on our own lands, which we have purchased in Jackson County." They enrolled the names of those anxious to migrate, and the prophet commented, "I ask God in the name of Jesus that we may obtain eight hundred or one thousand emigrants."[199] In October he counseled with the twelve and "told them that it was the will of God they should take their families to Missouri next season."[200] During the following March the church presidency and twelve "resolved to emigrate on or before the 15th of May next, if kind Providence smiles upon us."[201] At the end of the month Smith informed the seventies they were "at liberty" to go to Zion and urged them to send all the strength of the Lord's house. The brethren then made a covenant "that if any more of our brethren are slain or driven from their lands in Missouri, by the mob, we will give ourselves no rest, until we are avenged of our enemies to the uttermost."[202]

In the meantime, Smith secretly organized the Army of Israel. John Whitmer recorded that on 24 September 1835 "we met in counsel at the house of J. Smith, Jr., the seer, where we according to a previous commandment given, appointed David Whitmer captain of the Lord's Host." Smith was made head of the "war department," and several other church leaders were given high ranking military posts.[203] This was a fateful turn of events which would have unforeseen consequences in the years to come.

The long-planned-for invasion of Missouri was launched in 1836 in a less dramatic manner than Zion's Camp. In May a Missouri newspaper at Independence described how some 1,500 to 2,000 men were making their way into the country "in detached parties."[204] The same newspaper contained an account of a resident of Kirtland, identified as "O.P.Q.," who explained the new Mormon policy of infiltration: "Their object as I learn from them is to settle in any part of the State . . . as contiguous to Jackson County as circumstances will permit . . . they expect in a few years to fill up the counties on the north side of the River, so as to control the elections, and they expect to be able to raise a force sufficient to conquer Jackson County."[205] The editor of *The Far West* did not like what was happening and promised that Jackson County citizens would be ready when the elders arrived.[206]

In Clay County, where most of the Saints had immigrated, the old citizens had become greatly disturbed by the trend of events and gathered in a public meeting on 29 June to invite all Mormons to leave the county. They affirmed "that at this moment the clouds of civil war are rolling up their fearful masses." The major cause of the difficulty was the "rapid and increasing emigration of that people commonly called Mormons during the last few months."[207] The citizens warned that if the Mormons "persist in the blind course they have heretofore followed in flooding the country with their people, that we fear and firmly believe that an immediate civil war is the inevitable consequence."[208]

After this show of united opposition to the Saints, nothing remained but for Smith to call off the massive migration. He wrote to the Missouri Saints that they should avoid any aggression and that if their enemies would permit dispose of their property and go in peace.[209] Within a few months the members began to gather at Shoal Creek, in the northern part of Ray County.[210] Here too they began to encounter opposition to their gathering.[211] At this point Alexander Doniphan led an effort in the state legislature to have a separate county set apart for Mormons north of Ray County but, according to Doniphan,[212] with the strict understanding that they would remain within the bounds of their new district. Certainly the Missourians in the region understood this to be a condition.[213] Later an editor of a Missouri newspaper would protest the harsh terms imposed on the Mormons by this agreement, but by then it was too late.[214]

Within six months the Mormons were gathering rapidly to the county and filling political offices.[215] Before long they began to look for new areas to settle. But the combination of Mormon politics and the massive gathering did not bode well for lasting peace between the Saints and western Missourians. Meanwhile Smith began making plans to build up Kirtland as an alternative gathering place.[216] But deep resentment among some Mormons over the failures of Zion's Camp, the increasingly militaristic posture of the church, and its expanding theocratic involvement in economic affairs stirred the smoldering embers of rebellion within the ranks of the Kirtland elect.

CHAPTER 4

Establishing a
Theocratic Government

According to early Mormon convert Benjamin Winchester, Joseph Smith in the 1830s "received a revelation especially concerning Kirtland": "It was to be the great center of the world. Kings and Queens were to come there from foreign lands to pay homage to the Saints. It was to be the great commercial point of the universe."[1] Joseph Young, brother of Brigham Young, predicted that the city would prosper and that no other in the United States "will for some years increase like Kirtland."[2] Wilford Woodruff wrote in November 1836 that already Kirtland was a beehive of activity and enterprise: "The noise of the axe and the hammer, and their bank and market, and especially the House of God speak in language as loud as thunder that the Saints will have a city in spite of the false prophets of Baal."[3]

The whole Mormon community was caught up in the boosterism shown by Young and Woodruff. Many of the poorer Saints began to flock into the city, and large scale borrowing, merchandising, land sales, and construction followed.[4] In fact, some historians have seen this period as one of excessive speculation and spending,[5] although

new evidence suggests that land values rose naturally as the population increased and that Joseph Smith and his associates had acquired
significant amounts of wealth in land against which they were able
to borrow to expand the Kirtland community.[6]

As Kirtland grew in population there was an increasing shortage of liquid capital. To meet the cash shortage Smith planned to
secure a charter for a local bank. On 2 November 1836, a "constitution" was written for a bank called the Kirtland Safety Society.
Apostle Orson Hyde was sent to Columbus to seek a corporate charter from the legislature. Smith was to be bank cashier and Sidney
Rigdon president.[7] Oliver Cowdery traveled to Philadelphia to purchase engraved plates for the bank notes, since the bank was expected
to open shortly. But on 1 January Hyde returned to Kirtland with
news that the charter would not be granted.[8]

The Mormons, who voted Democratic and were sympathetic to
the soft money faction of the party, found themselves thwarted by a
new Whig administration which blocked Democratic-sponsored bank
legislation.[9] The *Cleveland Daily Gazette*, a forum for the soft money
forces in the state, warned that if "the legislature refuses to grant the
necessary bank charters, and thus refuses to do away with the monop-
oly that exists, they must expect the people will take care of their
own interest."[10] Apparently Mormons were thinking along similar
lines, because when they learned of the legislature's negative
response, they immediately met on 2 January, wrote new "Articles of
Agreement" to establish the "Kirtland Safety Society Anti-banking
Company," and issued their first notes on 5 January. Acting on what
may have been bad legal counsel,[11] they assumed that they could
assign banking functions to a private business corporation. During
January the bank's managers issued a total of over $15,000 in notes[12]
but only had enough cash on hand to redeem these notes during the
first two weeks of operation. By 23 January they resorted to backing
the notes with property.[13] Newspapers in Cleveland and adjoining
towns attacked the "Mormon bank" and warned that its notes were
of dubious value.[14] L. L. Rice of the *Cleveland Daily Gazette* said that
the only security backing the notes was the word of the untrustworthy
Mormon leaders.[15] Nonetheless, during the next two months the new
bank managers issued at least $70,000 more of the depreciating cur-
rency.[16]

Smith himself began to invest heavily in the bank in an attempt
to save it.[17] As late as 6 April he apparently believed his banking
project might work: "If the elders will remember the Kirtland Safety

Society and do as they should Kirtland will become a great city." But three days later his mood changed for he warned the Saints that "severe judgments awaited those characters that professed to be his friends & friends to . . . the Kirtland Safety Society but had turned traitors and opposed the currency."[18] Despite Smith's efforts, confidence in the bank waned and few Saints would take its notes.[19] Certain elders, trying to cut their losses, rode into the countryside to exchange bank notes for whatever they could get.[20] Smith had to denounce them in the press to stop the practice.[21] By October he and Sidney Rigdon were brought to trial for violating an 1816 anti-banking law and were fined $1,000 each.[22] Finally, in November, the bank closed its doors forever.[23]

The failure of the banking firm convinced many Mormons, including some of its highest ranking leaders, that something was wrong at Kirtland. The festering discontent that had resided just beneath the surface since the days of Zion's Camp finally erupted, and a storm of denunciation was hurled against the prophet.

Among the leading dissenters in Kirtland in 1836 and 1837, nine had been members of Zion's Camp: Frederick G. Williams, Parley P. Pratt, Luke and Lyman Johnson, Martin Harris, Roger Orton, Warren Parrish, Leonard Rich, and Sylvester Smith. Another dissenter, Oliver Cowdery, had sent the circular letter urging that the elders enlist in the camp. When Warren Parrish published a critique of the prophet's policies in the newspaper in 1838, he began by denouncing the camp. Several dissenters agreed with his assessment.[24]

Apostle William E. McLellin was an articulate leader for the discontented who saw the camp and the bank as part of a general pattern. McLellin said that Zion's Camp was an expensive failure and that it produced "a different spirit [which] . . . seized almost the whole ranks of the church." He maintained that "their practice was in 1834 to proclaim war and gather up a troop, and travel to Clay Co. Mo., with arms and munitions of war."[25] He lamented the massive merchandizing in Kirtland, the heavy indebtedness, land speculation, and the pretense of a bank. He said that the leaders were enamored of worldly riches, thereby bringing "ruin, inevitable ruin upon thousands."[26] They became obsessed with power, "grasping like the Popes of Rome both the spiritual and temporal powers of the church."[27] In their financial speculations and establishment of an unlawful bank, he concluded, "they seemed to think that everything must bow at their nod."[28]

The bank failure was a deep disappointment and imposed economic hardship on some. Oliver Cowdery invested and lost $197, a substantial portion of his annual income. Parley Pratt lost $102, Leonard Rich $50, and Luke Johnson $46.[29] There is no way to tell how much Mormons lost when they took the depreciating currency of the bank. But financial losses alone do not account for the degree of discontent. More significant was the fact that many of the Saints believed that the bank was established by divine revelation and that it could not fail. Apostle John F. Boynton spoke for these Saints when he remembered Joseph Smith declaring that "the audible voice of God instructed him to establish a Banking-Anti-banking institution, which like Aaron's rod should swallow up all other banks . . . and grow and flourish and spread . . . and survive when all others should be laid in ruins."[30]

Actually, Smith qualified his prophecy regarding the bank. Wilford Woodruff recorded his statement the day it was made and reported Smith saying he had received the word of the Lord on the bank that morning, 6 January: "if we would give heed to the commandments of the Lord . . . all would be well."[31] It is unclear which commandments were here being referred to or whether they were being observed, but for Mormons like Apostle Boynton who expected literal fulfillment for every aspiration spoken by the prophet, the bank failure was shattering.

Apostle Parley Pratt, one of the more ardent defenders of the Mormon faith, was, like McLellin, more concerned with the expanding powers the prophet seemed to be assuming. He wrote an angry letter on 23 May 1837, telling Smith that he had wronged him in turning his personal notes for debt over to a bank. Pratt said Smith was "taking advantage of your brother by undue religious influence" and thus attacked the theocratic concept. Pratt said he was certain that "the whole scheme of speculation in which we have been engaged, is of the devil." He insisted it had given rise to "lying, deceiving, and taking advantage of one's neighbor." Thus Smith and Rigdon "have been the principle means in leading this people astray . . . by false prophesying and preaching." Pratt threatened to bring church charges against Smith,[32] but six days later it was his brother, Orson, and Apostle Lyman Johnson who brought charges before a bishop's court condemning Smith for "lying and misrepresentation—also for extortion—and for speaking disrespectfully against his brethren behind their backs."[33]

According to Mary Fielding in a letter written 15 June 1837, two successive Sundays were consumed by internal dissension. Warren Parrish and others denounced Smith in these meetings. Their initial attack was so devastating that Smith took sick and was "near death" and could not defend himself. Parley Pratt presided on the second Sunday and continued the attack. He charged that virtually the entire church had departed from the ways of the Lord and that the prophet had committed "great sins." Alluding in his address to an apology made by Smith, Pratt said this was not sufficient because the prophet must confess to those who were aware of his wrong doing. Pratt said he would retract none of the charges he had made in his letters to Smith regarding financial transactions. The plural marriage issue then was raised, and Pratt said he had not broken the "matrimonial covenant." Sidney Rigdon followed and said that he shared the reproach heaped upon the prophet and if there was any more fault finding, he would leave the meeting. Shortly thereafter he and several others marched out.[34]

Brigham Young later recalled that at this time the discontented gathered in a room of the temple to voice their protests and to propose that Smith be removed as prophet and that David Whitmer be named his successor. Vigorous opposition to this by Brigham Young, Heber C. Kimball, and John Smith (the prophet's uncle) prevented immediate action, but many left the meeting determined that Smith must be replaced. Young said that shortly after this an attempt was made on the prophet's life.[35]

Hoping to free himself from some of his apostolic critics, Smith announced in the later part of June that the twelve would be sent to England to open the church's first European mission. Heber Kimball and Orson Hyde were called to head the first overseas outpost.[36] But other apostles like Parley Pratt, Boynton, and Luke and Lyman Johnson were not so easily reconciled.[37]

For many Saints at Kirtland there was more at stake than the failures of Zion's Camp and the bank. The church was undergoing substantial growth and change, and power was concentrating at the top. At Kirtland, for the first time, Smith was sustained as head of the entire church, including Missouri.[38] Besides assuming management of the Kirtland economy, Smith also attempted to martial a unified Mormon vote to give the church power in local politics.[39] And it was at Kirtland that he first moved beyond the bounds of civil law in performing a marriage under divine authority without being duly authorized by the state. When he married Lydia and Newell

Knight on 23 November 1835, he told the congregation that it was done "by the authority of the priesthood which he had received from God and not from man and further Said he the gentile law shall not have power to hurt me for it as I have done as God hath required at my hand and he will bear me out and eventually bring me off conquorer over all my adversaries for his kingdom shall prevail."[40] When John Whitmer and Benjamin Winchester complained of Smith's intimacy with a lady in the congregation, the prophet again appealed to higher law: "He was authorized by God Almighty to establish His Kingdom—that he was God's prophet and God's agent and that he could do whatever he should choose to do, therefore the Church had NO RIGHT TO CALL INTO QUESTION anything he did, or to censure him for the reason that he was responsible to God Almighty alone."[41] Winchester said this "created a great sensation" and some of the best talent in the church left.

It seemed to critics like David Whitmer, who eventually left the church, that Smith had fallen from grace, no longer exemplifying the humility of earlier years, now claiming infallibility, changing revelations to suit his mood and attempting to redeem Zion before the proper time.[42] John Whitmer found fault with Smith and Rigdon, saying that they had become "lifted up in pride, and lusted after forbidden things of God, such as covetousness . . . secret combinations, [and] spiritual wife doctrine."[43] He said this brought division and distrust. It also brought bitterness and violence.

Lucy Mack Smith relates a confrontation in the temple at this time. She says that the prophet's father went to the stand and publicly criticized Warren Parrish, an outspoken dissenter. Parrish, however, pushed his way to the stand and tried to remove the old patriarch bodily. The senior Smith appealed to Cowdery for help but to no avail. Then William Smith, his youngest son, moved in only to have John Boynton menace William with a drawn sword.

Lucy also indicates that David Whitmer, Frederick G. Williams, Jared Carter, and others began holding secret meetings at Whitmer's home. At one such meeting a young woman with a black seer stone prophesied that one third of the church would turn against the prophet.[44] Some were beginning to revert to other sources of authority as their confidence in Joseph Smith waned.

But it was the Cowdery brothers, Oliver and Warren, who best described what most troubled many Saints in Kirtland. Oliver had written to another of his brothers, Lyman, in January 1834, that there was a "certain sect in our land" which was moving toward a union of church and state. Oliver said that if this happened then "adieu to our hard won liberty." He wanted to be "uncontrolled and unshackled" in his politics, since "pure republicanism" was the foundation of his political beliefs.[45] In July 1837 Warren Cowdery, editor of the *LDS Messenger and Advocate*, made his similar objection clear when he attacked the idea that one man should dictate in religious and secular affairs. Warren feared the church was becoming despotic:

> If we give all our privileges to one man, we virtually give him our money and our liberties, and make him a monarch, absolute and despotic, and ourselves abject slaves or fawning sycophants. . . . Whenever a people have unlimited confidence in a civil or ecclesiastical ruler or rulers, who are but men like themselves, and begin to think they can do no wrong, they increase their tyranny and oppression and establish a principle that man, poor frail lump of mortality like themselves, is infallible. Who does not see a principle of popery and religious tyranny involved in such an order of things? . . . Intelligence of the people is the only guarantee against encroachments upon their liberties, whether those encroachments are from the civil or ecclesiastical power.[46]

Despite growing discontent, not all Kirtland Saints were dissatisfied with Joseph Smith. Mary Fielding was among a diminishing number who still believed him to be a prophet of God. She pondered in her letter of 15 June "what the Lord will have to do with his church before it will submit to be governed by the Head but I fully believe we shall have no prosperity till this is the case."[47] Smith said little in his published history about developments in Kirtland during the next month, but a sister of Elias Smith, "M. J.," wrote in August that she believed "times are growing better here. There is some prospect of peace being restored." She said that the prophet's brother had returned from Far West, Missouri, with David Patten and Thomas B. Marsh and had made confession of his own opposition to Joseph. She said Orson Pratt was now "in fellowship with the Church" and that Parley Pratt had "made a partial confession for what he had spoken against Joseph." She noted, however, that Smith and Rigdon had left, probably for Canada.[48]

In September, Smith and Rigdon hurried to Missouri to forestall a possible rebellion. They found leaders in Zion sharply divided over the administration of town plots in the growing community at Far West. Two assistant presidents, John Whitmer and W. W. Phelps, had held exclusive control of land sales and had stirred opposition from the high council and the two apostles who resided there. To smooth over these differences, Smith announced that the proceeds from the sale of lots would be shared by "poor and bleeding zion."[49] He said that it was now the Lord's will that all the Saints should gather to Far West and organize new stakes there. The time was short, for the Lord had said in revelation, "peace shall soon be taken from the earth . . . for a lying spirit has gone out upon all the face of the earth and shall perplex the nations and stir them to anger against one another: for behold saith the Lord, very fierce and very terrible war is near at hand, even at your doors."[50]

Smith said that he would bring his family as soon as circumstances would allow,[51] thus indicating that Far West was now to become the central gathering place and headquarters for the church. The announcement pleased most Saints at Far West, but some leaders were not so delighted. Oliver Cowdery, who had learned of a plural marriage relationship between the prophet and Fanny Alger, believed the church leader guilty of adultery and had fled to Far West.[52] He began to doubt the imminence of the Millennium, to which Smith had repeatedly alluded in justifying his actions, and was dissatisfied with the Law of Consecration. He was not certain that the Saints should have to make sacrifices to uphold the practice. John and David Whitmer also had expressed discontent. But when Smith arrived he patched up differences with Cowdery, the two men shaking hands and agreeing to forget past differences.[53] Smith quickly solidified his leadership and was named head of the church in Missouri as well as in Kirtland.[54] He left Missouri confident that he had full support of the Missouri Saints.

While Smith was away, Warren Parrish and others in Kirtland had organized a new Church of Christ. They said they adhered to the "Old Standard," protesting the current name of the church, the Church of the Latter Day Saints, and its enlarged role in economic affairs.[55] George A. Smith remembered that Parrish had thirty followers in Kirtland, but they were probably stronger than this because they soon gained control over considerable church property, including the temple and printing office.[56]

In Missouri, it was not long before Oliver Cowdery and others had begun corresponding with leaders of the "Old Standard." On 30 January Cowdery met with David, John, and Jacob Whitmer, Frederick G. Williams, Lyman Johnson, and W. W. Phelps "to take into consideration the state of the Church." They said they were opposed to the manner in which "some of the Authorities of the . . .

[church] have for the time past, and are still, endeavoring to unite ecclesiastical and civil authority, and force men under the pretense of incurring the displeasure of heaven to use their earthly substance contrary to their interest and privilege." Cowdery said local author-ities were "endeavoring to make it a rule of faith for said church to uphold a certain man or men right or wrong." He and his friends were determined to separate themselves from such a society and find a new place to gather where they could "live in peace."[57]

Meanwhile, after returning to Kirtland, Smith and Rigdon sought to rally support among the remaining faithful, fearing that they may have lost complete control of their Kirtland stronghold.[58] But by 12 January 1838, Smith received a revelation to abandon Kirtland and head west:

> Let the presidency of my church take their families as soon as it is practical and a door is open for them and move to the West as fast as the way is made plain . . . Verily I say unto you the time has come that your labors are finished in this place for a season. Therefore rise and get yourselves into a land which I shall show you, even a land flowing with milk and honey. You are clean before the Lord of this people, and wo unto them who have become your enemies who have professed my name, saith the Lord for their judgement lingereth not and their damnation slumbereth not.

On the same day Smith received another revelation warning church leaders in Kirtland that no court action could be taken against the presidency there. Charges leading to their removal, he was told, would have to be made in Missouri by three unimpeachable witnesses, and a verdict would have to be sustained by a majority vote in both states.[59] Thus the Saints in Kirtland had no voice in the matter, and if Smith and Rigdon could rally a majority in Zion, their position would remain secure.

Shortly afterwards, Smith and Rigdon with their families headed west, dodging angry dissenters and creditors as they went. They con-templated the lessons of Kirtland and determined not to tolerate dis-sent at Far West. In Missouri they would adopt more drastic mea-sures to assure the unity of the Saints.

It is ironic that Mormon leaders were compelled to leave Ohio by internal critics rather than by outsiders, although lawsuits filed by non-Mormons added to the pressures on Smith and Rigdon.[60] Hepsebah Richards noted in February 1838 that the elect had been "driven out of this place . . . by persecution, chiefly from the dissenters."[61] For much of the time, compared with Missouri or Illinois afterward, Mormon relations with Gentile neighbors in Ohio had been relatively tolerable. There was little violence, although once the prophet was mobbed and on occasion one or two members threatened.[62] This usually peaceful antipathy can be explained to some extent by the fact that only limited aspects of the kingdom developed at Kirtland.

There was sectarian antagonism at Kirtland initially.[63] E. D. Howe gave generous space in his newspaper to Mormon matters, insisting that it was "the business of an Editor to collect and lay before his readers, whatever seems to agitate the public mind."[64] In December he ran a piece from the *Milan Free Press* warning northern Ohioans to "BEWARE OF IMPOSTORS."[65] On 15 February 1831, he printed a submission from "M.S.C." of Mentor, who recounted how after the "four pretended prophets" left Kirtland, the Mormons broke into a rash of spiritual excesses.[66] The same issue reproduced Thomas Campbell's open letter to Sidney Rigdon, challenging him to a public debate. Howe justified his continued departure from neutrality by maintaining that the subject of Mormonism had "become a matter of general inquiry and conversation through the whole community." His newspaper was now open, he said, to the "investigation of the divine pretentions of the Book of Mormon and its 'Author and Proprietor,' Joseph Smith." Howe noted at this time that the Mormons numbered several hundred in the area.[67]

A barrage of criticism appeared in the *Telegraph* from 1831 through January 1835, but the amount of space Howe devoted to Mormon issues diminished after 1831.[68] Sectarian opposition declined as Mormon missionary successes among the Campbellites and other denominations slowed.[69]

Sectarian antagonism may have dwindled, but politically oriented antipathy increased.[70] As early as March 1831, Howe took occasion to disagree with those who held that Mormonism was the "Anti-Masonic religion." He pointed out that there were also many "republican jacks" among them.[71] As yet he made no complaints about their bloc voting.

Mormons believed that they had destiny manifest to govern themselves and ultimately the nation and the world. But these ambitions were tied to their millennial expectations and may not have demanded immediate involvement in politics in Ohio. But after the expulsion of the Saints from Jackson County the prophet came out publicly for the Jacksonian political party. He urged the elders in Missouri to "print a paper in favor of the government as you know we are all friends to the Constitution yea true friends to that Country."[72] In December 1833 he wrote to Bishop Partridge that the Saints would undertake a similar course in Kirtland:

> The inhabitants of this country threaten our destruction, and we know not how soon they may be permitted to follow the example of the Missourians; . . . We are now distributing the type, and calculate to commence setting today, and issue a paper the last of this week, or beginning of next. . . . We expect shortly to publish a political paper, weekly, in favor of the present administration; the influential men of that party have offered a liberal patronage to us, and we hope to succeed, for thereby we can show the public the purity of our intention in supporting the government under which we live.[73]

But Mormon activity in local politics could bring quick repercussions. The *Anti-Masonic Telegraph*, published at Norwich, New York, maintained in 1833 that the Masonic candidate for the assembly had been making overtures toward the Mormons. The paper charged that the aspirant's favorable comments regarding the Saints and his willingness to have a missionary preach in the town were politically motivated. The allegation precipitated a sharp argument with the *Chenango Journal*.[74] The Mormons were of no importance politically in Chenango County during these years, but the flare-up at Norwich was a portent of what was to come in Ohio.

Mormons did not become objects of political diatribe in Ohio until the following year, when they became involved in a local political issue, the removal of the county seat from Chardon to Painesville, a move which they initially advocated. When the issue was lost the editor of the *Chardon Spectator and Geauga Gazette* exulted that the "Removealists," Mormons included, had come in a poor third in the election.[75]

In February 1835, Oliver Cowdery began editing at Kirtland *The Northern Times*, a champion of Jacksonian causes, which he published weekly for a year.[76] In one of the few issues extant, Cowdery warned that the election in Geauga County in 1835 would be one of the "most important . . . ever held. The opposition wishes to control all offices, credit, money to flatter their own ambition." He feared the people would be "subjected to live in the society of men who ride over us in gilded coaches."[77]

Although Mormons were politically weak in Geauga County, the strident claims of Rigdon that the Saints would soon control all of the county offices caused some alarm.[78] In Kirtland township, where the Saints held a near majority, there was a mass political alert. A non-Mormon in Kirtland wrote in April 1835 that the Saints had "entered *pell mell* into the arena of political controvercies." The Mormons, he reported,

> are ready to harness in with any party that is willing to degrade themselves by asking their assistance. They now carry nearly a majority of this township, and every man votes as directed by the prophet and his elder. Previous to the recent township election here, it was generally understood that the Mormons and Jacksonians had agreed to share the spoils equally, in consequence of which the other citizens thought it useless to attend the polls. This brought out an entire Mormon ticket which they calculated to smuggle in, independent of the Democrats not under orders of the prophet. This caused the citizens to rally and make an effort, which by a small majority, saved the township from being governed by *revelation* for the year to come.[79]

The reaction to Mormon bloc voting in Geauga County typified the response of other Americans afterward in states to the west.

Some negative comments about Mormon politicking continued to appear in northern Ohio newspapers through 1836 and 1837[80] and were a source of concern to non-members. The dissatisfaction was minimized by the fact that the Saints were too few in number to make much difference outside their own township.

The most hostile press coverage in Ohio since 1831 came six years later when their banking experiment was launched. Most Cleveland newspapers viewed the circulation of the Kirtland Safety Society's notes with alarm, charging that it was an attempt by Mormons to defraud the public. In addition, the passing of the notes outside Kirtland placed the Saints in the middle of a political conflict between the Whig party and the Jacksonians on the banking issue. This becomes clear in the criticism of L. L. Rice, a Whig, who wrote:

> It is not possible for us to be neutral. If it is fraud on the community, a duty rests upon us to expose it. . . . With the religion we have nothing to do, except as connected with this pecuniary matter and illustrative of their character and honesty. . . . Here is [Kirtland Anti-Banking] paper finding its way into the pockets of our citizens, of whose credit the majority not only do not know any thing, but have the public statutes of the country open

before them . . . that is a legal nullity, and its circulation prohib-
ited by penalty.[81]

The bank's failure brought embittered resentment toward Mormon
leaders. One reader of the *Cleveland Herald* recommended vigilante
actions against Smith and Rigdon.[82] Most outsiders lumped all Mormons together and held them all equally responsible for the bank's
failure, which they tended to view as a moral issue.[83]

Despite the criticism of Mormon doctrines and practices in the
Ohio press, there was surprisingly minimal name calling or demand
for Mormon blood, especially compared to what would later come
in Missouri and Illinois. An additional reason for the difference may
be that most Ohioans, like many Mormons, were from New England.
In Missouri the Mormons would come up against Southern tradition,
which would not yield to Mormon experimentalism.[84]

It should also be remembered that in Ohio Mormons were a
distinct minority and offered little threat to the social and political
status quo. They were considered a nuisance, not dangerous political upstarts. In western Missouri, where population was sparse and
Indians menacing, and in Illinois, where the Saints grew to be a size-
able political bloc, the situation would be different. There was no
fear of land monopolization in Ohio; as late as August 1836 the Saints'
holdings were small, and this was well known.[85] The Kingdom of
God was not as well organized or as powerful in Ohio as it would be
later.

The Saints fled westward, convinced that they had failed due
to lack of church unity and Gentile wickedness.[86] They never perceived that their quest for social and political control might have
influenced others negatively. In their minds the strife and contention that pluralism had engendered imperiled not only Kirtland but
the nation as well. According to one of the departing Saints, the consequence of their failure would be that Roman Catholics would soon
seize political control. Then "there will be a chance for the Lamanites
[i.e., American Indians] to finish it." Kirtland, once sanctified as a
gathering place and great metropolis, would be the first city destroyed
by the Lord, according to the departing Mormons.[87] The Mormon
mind was a millennial mind, longing for peace and tranquility but
convinced that war and destruction would come first. The Latter-
day Saints would seek their place of refuge westward, where their
prophet would tell them what the Lord would have them do to prepare for the tribulations ahead.

"In a Military Spirit"

Years later, in turn-of-the-century Utah, Mormon patriarch Benjamin F. Johnson would write that during the church's early days in Missouri, "the Prophet Joseph laid the foundation of our church in a military spirit, and as the Master taught his disciples so he taught us to 'sell our coats and buy swords.' " Johnson reflected that the sword never fully prevailed among the Saints and acknowledged that later, when the federal government took their arms away, they became more secure.[1]

This was a lesson that could only be learned by experience. Mormon militarism was a strange mixture of the American revolutionary idea of the defense of natural rights and a millennialism that drew heavily upon Old Testament and Book of Mormon models of warrior-saints.[2] Since the days of Zion's Camp the belief had gained ground that the elders would be justified in arming themselves to take the kingdom by force.[3] These feelings of aggression, born of fear, frustration, and a sense of millennial destiny, could be easily stirred in Missouri, where the Saints believed that the great events of the last days were soon to unfold. Continued harassment by old citizens, wherever the Saints settled in Missouri, seemed to invoke bitter memories of Jackson County and fed the martial spirit. The desire for refuge from pluralism and the uncertainty of choice in a free society encouraged a quest to eliminate opposition both within and without the church through intimidation and, when necessary, violence.

Such tendencies began when Joseph Smith and Sidney Rigdon came to Far West in the fall of 1837 to strengthen their hold on the church in Missouri. Regimentation swept through the city, and demands were made that the Saints obey the entire law of God,[4] including the dietary proscriptions of the Word of Wisdom[5] and the Law of Consecration.[6] Initiated by Apostle Thomas B. Marsh, oaths of allegiance were demanded of the elders.[7] Those critical of the prophet were counted disloyal.[8] Oliver Cowdery lamented the "radical principles taught by the church leaders," saying they "have given loose to the enthusiastik." Fearing that the liberties of the entire church would be subverted, Cowdery wrote that he would not be dictated to when deciding what to eat and drink when he was sick.[9]

John Whitmer, a Book of Mormon witness, and William W. Phelps, a former editor of *The Evening and the Morning Star* in Independence, Missouri, were also critical. Plagued by creditors[10] and perhaps disillusioned with any possibility of redeeming Zion in the foreseeable future, these two men had sold their land in Jackson County. Although Mormons were still unwelcome in Jackson County, most refugees had refused to relinquish title to their property. In the eyes of the high council in Far West the sale of property in Independence constituted a denial of the faith.[11] Consequently, Phelps and John Whitmer were rejected as presidents in Zion, as was David Whitmer, another of the three witnesses of the Book of Mormon. Apostles Thomas B. Marsh and David W. Patten were named as acting presidents until the arrival of Joseph Smith.[12]

Cleansing the divided house at Far West had only begun. In March, a month after being removed from the presidency, John Whitmer and Phelps were charged with "unChristian-like conduct" and excommunicated.[13] As justification the high council rehearsed an old issue between themselves and the former presidency concerning the proper disposition of $2,000 in personal contributions given by Phelps and Whitmer, who had initially offered to help finance construction of a temple in Far West but later demanded that the bishop return the money.[14] Phelps and Whitmer maintained that these funds were rightly theirs since others had been allowed to with-

draw their subscriptions.[15] But Marsh, who presided at the excommunication, wrote that the money belonged to the church and that,
in addition, the membership was dissatisfied with "many things" the
former presidents had done.[16] On reviewing the matter Joseph Smith
said that the council had acted "judiciously."[17]

When Smith reached the outskirts of Far West on 13 March, internal problems seemed of small concern, for he was greeted "by an
escort of brethren" who "welcomed us to their bosoms." Once rested,
he met with some of the elders and gave vent to his feelings. He said
that the motto of the church was the Constitution "formed by the
fathers of liberty peace and good order of society," and, reflecting a
certain anti-democratic bias, "aristarchy [government by the best peo-
ple] live forever." He proclaimed "woe to tyrants, mobs, aristocracy,
anarchy and toryism, and all those who invent or seek unrighteous
and vexatious lawsuits under the pretext or color of law or office
either religious or political."[18] Smith was determined to be free of
lawsuits similar to those filed in Kirtland which had driven him away.
But the measures he would initiate to prevent recurring lawsuits
would contribute to rising militancy in the church and retaliation
by Missourians.

At the end of the month, however, Smith wrote to followers still
in Kirtland that "the Saints are at this time in union" and that "peace
and love prevail throughout."[19] This jubilation was premature.
Within two weeks Smith testified against Lyman Johnson, David
Whitmer, and Oliver Cowdery,[20] who were excommunicated for
bringing "vexatious lawsuits" against church leaders and for seeking to lessen his influence among the Saints.[21] An additional charge
of counterfeiting was levied against Cowdery for attempting to produce a bogus scrip.[22] Cowdery's criticism of the prophet's sexual conduct was denounced, as was his sale of Missouri land.[23]

Lyman Johnson was excluded from fellowship for assaulting
Phineas Young and for threatening to appeal the case to a court outside Caldwell County, the county seat set aside by the state legislature for Mormons. It was affirmed that Johnson was bringing discredit
to the county.[24] To this accusation Johnson replied that he would
not "condescend to put [his] constitutional rights at issue on so dis-
respectful a point." He said that the church had no business telling
him where he could appeal his case.[25] Smith and Rigdon told the
Saints in April that "they meant to have the words of the Presidency . . . to be as good and as undisputed as the words of God."[26]

Action was also taken against David Whitmer for joining the dissenters and neglecting church meetings.[27] It was clear that he had disassociated himself from the main church body. On 12 April he wrote a letter to this effect, adding that he did not believe the church council which removed him as president in Missouri had proper jurisdiction.[28]

Oliver Cowdery summarized the feelings of most of the dissenters in Far West in a letter to the high council. He said he would not be governed in temporal affairs by an ecclesiastical tribunal, that if he wished to sell his lands in Jackson County it was his legal right to do so. For the church to claim authority in this matter, he wrote, is

> an attempt to set up a kind of petty government, controlled and dictated by ecclesiastical influence, in the midst of this national and state government. You will, no doubt, say this is not correct; but the bare notice of these charges over which you assume a right to decide, is, in my opinion, a direct attempt to make the secular power subservient to Church direction—to the correctness of which I cannot in conscience subscribe—I believe that principle never did fail to produce anarchy and confusion.[29]

But the prophet was disinclined to pay heed to such criticism. After he settled himself and his family in Far West and had for the moment disposed of dissenters, he looked out with satisfaction on the more than one hundred fifty houses and several stores already constructed[30] and on the open spaces that surrounded him. He wrote that "no part of the world can produce a [view] superior to Caldwell County." Having assumed the editorship of the *Elders' Journal*, he commented in his first editorial that "to all appearance the country is healthy, and the farming interest is equal to that in any part of the world." The prospects for expansion seemed good, and he wrote that "from this to the territorial line on the north is from eighty to one-hundred miles, and to the line on the west twenty-five or upwards." He exuded confidence in the future saying, "The Saints are at perfect peace with all the surrounding inhabitants, and persecution is not so much as once named among them."[31]

Another wave of millennial optimism now swept over the Saints. In the July issue of the *Elders' Journal*, Alanson Ripley wrote to the missionaries abroad to rejoice for "the Lord our God is about to establish a Kingdom, which cannot be thrown down, neither can the gates of hell prevail against it."[32] Appropriate to this end, Smith received a revelation near the end of April in which Far West was declared to be "a holy and consecrated land," where members were encouraged to gather "for a defense and a refuge from the storm."[33] They were also commanded to build "a house unto me, for the gathering together of my Saints, that they may worship me." Smith and Rigdon were informed that they were not to go into debt, as they had in Kirtland, in order to erect the sanctuary. A new method for financing the project would be made known.[34]

Despite these steps to reconfirm Smith's prophetic leadership, there was still murmuring among many faithful who were rankled at the financial losses they had sustained in the Kirtland banking fiasco. Responding to such dissatisfaction, Smith preached to the congregation in May, warning them "against men who came amongst them whining and growling about their money . . . I cautioned the Saints to beware of such, for they were throwing out insinuations here and there, to level a dart at the best interests of the Church, and if possible destroy the character of its Presidency."[35]

Smith's attempt to quiet those in financial distress was not entirely successful, since some members believed that the presidency had used church funds for their own purposes.[36] Determined to avoid such criticism in the future, Smith and Rigdon went to the high council in May to request financial support, maintaining that "we have for eight years [spent] our time, talents, and property, in the service of the Church." With only one dissenting vote, the council decided to grant each man an eighty-acre lot from the property of the church. It was also agreed that they should receive $1,000 apiece, "not for preaching, or for receiving the word of God by revelation, . . . but for services rendered in the printing establishment, in translating the ancient records, etc. etc."[37] When word of the transaction reached the church members, Ebenezer Robinson recalled, they opposed it "almost to a man."[38] The resolution was quickly rescinded, but Ebenezer Robinson reported that shortly after this the revelation on tithing was received.[39] Thus debts the presidency incurred building Zion and constructing the temple were to be paid with tithing funds.[40]

A few days later Smith and a company of other elders left Far West to search the northern countryside for potential locations for the hundreds of Saints who were flocking into Missouri. The prophet found an area that seemed ideal. It was situated twenty-five miles north of Far West, outside of the Mormon county, on "an elevated piece of ground" overlooking the Grand River in Daviess County.

Lyman Wight said Smith commenced laying off town lots and looking for adjacent government land that might be purchased by the
Saints. He told them that the new settlement would be called Adam-
ondi-Ahman because this was where Adam, the "Ancient of Days,"
would visit prior to the second coming of Christ.[41] When refugees
from Kirtland arrived in Far West in June, Smith directed them to
the new settlement. Wight said that floods of immigrants came each
day during the summer, and by October two hundred houses had
been built. Joseph McFee said that Adam-ondi Ahman grew so fast
that it had five hundred people before Gallatin, the county seat, had
five houses.[42] In June Smith organized the settlement into a stake,
with his uncle, John Smith, as president.[43] Not long afterward the
number of Mormons in the county nearly equaled the number of
non-Mormons.[44]

During the same month another settlement was located south
of Far West at DeWitt in Carroll County, where Mormons hoped to
secure a port on the confluence of the Missouri and Grand rivers.[45]
The choice of DeWitt as a gathering place had been persistently urged
by three land speculators who had contacted Sidney Rigdon when
he first passed through in March.[46] But the expansion of the Saints
into counties adjoining Caldwell stirred opposition among politicians, religious leaders, and land speculators. Before such opposition could crystalize, however, events in Caldwell County itself were
moving rapidly toward a climactic clash between dissenters and
church leaders. The issue which divided them was the nature and
authority of civil law inside Caldwell. Word was spreading outside
the county that the Saints were unwilling to obey the laws of the state.

Sidney Rigdon protested angrily in June that after David
Whitmer and Oliver Cowdery came to Far West, they "set up a nasty,
dirty, pettifoggers office, pretending to be judges of the law." In
addressing a farewell epistle to these ex-brethren, Rigdon complained:

> You began to interfere with all the business of the place, trying
> to destroy the character of our merchants, and bringing their
> creditors upon them, and break them up. In addition to this,
> you stirred up men of weak minds to prosecute one another, for
> the vile purpose of getting a fee for pettifogging for one of them.
> You have also been threatening continually to enter into a gen-
> eral system of prosecution determined, as you said, to pick a
> flaw in the titles of those who have bought city lots and built
> upon them.[47]

The dissenters were not the only ones who threatened legal action. In 1837 Reed Peck noted that the Mormons in Far West had borrowed heavily from non-Mormons to finance several merchandising stores,[48] and a year later in November 1838, a letter to the *Missouri Argus* commented that the Saints were still "largely in debt to various citizens in neighboring counties."[49] Threat of court action was alarming to those who remembered being driven from Kirtland in just such a manner. John Whitmer affirmed that in April Joseph Smith publicly asserted that "he did not intend in [the] future to have any process served on him, and the officer who attempted it should die; that any person who spoke or acted against the presidency or the church should leave the country or die."[50] Sidney Rigdon was similarly disposed and told the Saints that "he would suffer no process of law to be served on him hereafter."[51] According to John Corrill, through the remainder of the spring, Smith and Rigdon continued to preach that "they were fed up with dissenter criticism, and with being harassed to death, that God would protect them henceforth from all enemies if the Saints would 'become one,' and be perfectly united in all things."[52]

The desired unanimity did not come.[53] Some elders began to talk of the need for a body of enforcers who would sustain church leaders without question and harry the critical minded out of their midst.[54] John Whitmer said the elders "began to form themselves into a secret society which they termed the brother of Gideon, in the which society they took oaths that they would support a brother right or wrong, even to the shedding of blood."[55] Samson Avard was credited with organizing the possible successor to this group, known as the "Danites," but George W. Robinson, Smith's personal scribe and Rigdon's son-in-law, was also involved in the founding.[56] In recruiting new members Avard addressed the captains of tens, fifties, and hundreds of the Armies of Israel that Smith organized in 1834 to redeem Zion.[57] Avard told them, "You have been chosen to be our leading men, or captains to rule over this last kingdom of Jesus Christ."[58] But in a short time the designation "Danite" was applied to all soldiers of the Armies of Israel, not just the officers. This was how Albert P. Rockwood used the term in his letters written in October as did Anson Call years later.[59] In its strictest meaning, however, Danites were those of the inner circle who had been initiated into the secret fraternity. Rockwood said that the Danites were established by divine revelation, which indicates that he thought the idea had come from the prophet. Oliver B. Huntington referred to the order as a "divine brotherly union."[60]

According to later court testimony, in June when they were organized, the Danite society was bound together by a series of oaths through which they swore unqualified allegiance to the church presidency and to "stand by each other right or wrong." The terms of their agreement were subscribed to in a "constitution," in which they promised to be "governed by such laws as shall perpetuate these high privileges [and rights] of which we know ourselves to be the rightful possessors." The order was to have a "Secretary of War," a legislative assembly, and several military officers responsible to the president of the society, who was declared to be Joseph Smith. Members pledged that they would resist all tyranny "whether it would be in kings or in the people."[61]

Apparently Smith did not have much to do with the Danites initially,[62] keeping a discrete distance but voicing support for the disposing of dissenters and demanding absolute loyalty. John Corrill said, however, that the church presidency would attend Danite meetings from time to time and sanction their plans in person.[63] John Cleminson said that Smith told a meeting of Danites that the organization was according to the will of God.[64] And another loyal Latter-day Saint said it was established by revelation. It is difficult to believe that an organization dedicated to upholding the presidency right or wrong could have advocated actions of which members of the presidency themselves did not generally approve. To do so would have caught the society in contradictions that would have led to its immediate exposure.[65]

John Corrill said that Avard did not inform the church presidency about everything he did.[66] But many close to Smith, including his Uncle John, Apostle Orson Hyde, and Thomas B. Marsh, president of the Quorum of the Twelve Apostles, knew of Danite extravagances.[67] It does not seem likely that in a town made up of Mormons, where Smith's word was law, the Danites could have done very much without Smith hearing about it from one of these men. George Robinson, Smith's scribe, wrote in the prophet's "Scriptory Book" that "We have a company of Danites in these times [27 July 1838], to put right [physically?] that which is not right, and to cleanse the Church of every [very?] great evil[s?] which has hitherto existed among us inasmuch as they cannot be put to right [-] by teachings and [persuasyons?]."[68] If Smith dictated or proofread this journal, he would have known of Danite intentions to drive the dissenters out of Far West by force.

The Danites now met secretly to consider how dissenters could be driven from Far West. Speaking for those who preferred to see the non-conformists cast out of the city by force, Rigdon informed a large congregation on 17 June that "when men embrace the gospel and afterward lose their faith, it is the duty of the Saints to trample them under their feet. . . . [Rigdon] called on the people to rise en masse and rid the country of such a nuisance."[69] Excitement spread rapidly through the community, and threats of violence were leveled against the undesirables.[70] Rigdon himself composed an ultimatum to Cowdery and the others signed by eighty-three Mormons, warning them to flee from the city in three days or suffer the consequences.[71]

Justifying his demand that dissenters depart from their midst, Rigdon commented afterward that "when the country, or body or people have individuals among them with whom they do not wish to associate, and a public expression is taken against their remaining among them, and such individuals do not remove, it is the principle of Republicanism itself that gives that community the right to expel them forcibly, and no law can prevent it."[72] This kind of reasoning with its appeal to popular sovereignty and higher law would soon bear bitter fruit as Mormons were increasingly viewed as the undesirable minority in western Missouri.

Within a few days four of the leading dissenters, Oliver Cowdery, Lyman Johnson, and the two Whitmers fled to Richmond.[73] David Whitmer wrote that he had been required to take an oath of loyalty to the presidency and had refused, thus necessitating his flight from Danite wrath.[74]

After the expulsion of the dissenters, a wave of apocalyptic fervor rolled through Far West sweeping the Saints toward even more rash measures. Apostle David Patten wrote in the July issue of the *Elders' Journal* that members should be "prepared for the grand assembly, . . . [to] sit there with the Ancient of Days, even Adam, our father, who shall come to prepare you for the coming of Jesus Christ, our Lord; for the time is at hand."[75]

It was in such a mood of millennial exuberance, as well as anger and frustration, that Rigdon addressed a mixed gathering of Mormons and Missourians at Far West on 4 July—a speech that would have fateful consequences. He announced with ringing protest that the Mormon people would suffer persecutions no more. "If on this day," Rigdon began, "the fathers of our nation, pledged their fortunes, their lives, and their sacred honor, to one another, . . . to be *free*, . . . so ought we to follow their example." The rights of the Saints are so identified with the welfare of the country, Rigdon declared, "that to deprive us of them, will be to doom the nation to ruin, and the Union to dissolution." The Mormons would lay the foundation for their temple and make themselves ready for the distress of the nations that was shortly to come. The Saints had warned the Gentiles by precept and by example of the calamitous days ahead, and their words would yet be fulfilled.

Turning to the matter of current Mormon-non-Mormon relations, Rigdon proclaimed, "Our cheeks have been given to the smiters, and our heads to those who have plucked off the hair. We have not only when smitten on one cheek turned the other, but we have done it, again and again, until we are wearied of being smitten, and tired of being trampled upon." Rigdon warned friend and foe

> in the name of Jesus Christ, to come on us no more forever, for from this hour we will bear it no more, our rights shall no more be trampled on with impunity. The man or set of men, who attempt to, does it at the expense of their lives. And that mob that comes on us to disturb us; it shall be between us and them a war of extermination, for we will follow them, till the last drop of their blood is spilled, or else they will have to exterminate us; for we will carry the seat of war to their own houses, and their own families, and one party or the other shall be destroyed. Remember it then all MEN.

"We will never be the aggressors," Rigdon asserted, but

> no man shall be at liberty to come into our streets, to threaten us with mobs, for if he does, he shall atone for it before he leaves the place. We therefore . . . proclaim our liberty on this day, as did our fathers. And we pledge . . . our fortunes, our lives and our sacred honors, to be delivered from the persecutions which we have had to endure, for the last nine years, or nearly that. Neither will we indulge any man, or set of men, instituting vexatious law suits against us, to cheat us of our just rights, if they attempt it we say unto them we this day proclaim ourselves free, with a purpose and a determination, that can never be broken, no never! no never!! NO NEVER!!![76]

Rigdon thus announced that the Saints would not tolerate further legal or violent measures without retaliation.

When Rigdon finished, "three loud and long cheers and amens" shook the air of Far West. The old settlers were justifiably alarmed, and Emily Austin remembered that a "very great excitement" was created among them. At this point, she said, "Rigdon's life could not have been insured for five coppers [pennies]."[77]

The speech had been carefully prepared. W. W. Phelps said that a few days before the 4th he heard David Patten say that Rigdon was writing a declaration to proclaim the church independent.[78] Joseph Smith wrote in the *Elders' Journal* in August that all the Saints should have a copy for their families to read and that they could obtain it in pamphlet form. He reaffirmed his approval of its central point, that the Saints were determined to retaliate against further persecution: "We are absolutely determined no longer to bear [mobbing] come life or come death for to be mob[b]ed any more without taking vengeance, we will not."[79]

Rigdon's speech stirred lasting enmity among the Missourians. A citizen of Liberty, in Clay County, commented in the *Western Star*: "Until July 4th, we heard no threats being made against them in any quarters. The people had all become reconciled to let them remain where they are. . . . But one Sidney Rigdon, in order to show himself a great man, collected them all together in the town of Far West, on the 4th of July, and there delivered a speech containing the essence of, if not treason itself."[80]

There is considerable evidence that Rigdon's speech was, in fact, the turning point in Mormon-Gentile relations in western Missouri.[81] Smith himself said there was no persecution through May, and a recent study confirms this was true into July.[82] To Missourians it seemed that Mormons had declared themselves above the law. The editor of the *Missouri Argus* said as much: "If this is not a manifestation to prevent the force of law we do not know what it is."[83] Soon vigilante forces would be gathering against the Mormons, affirming that they would not honor the law.

Unfortunately, Rigdon's proclamation that "vexatious" lawsuits must cease in Caldwell County was not mere bombast. A resident of Richmond wrote to the *Missouri Republican* on 13 November 1838 that the Danites had been organized to prevent any collection of debts owed by those within the Mormon community. Recalling Rigdon's declaration, he charged that "the Courts of Justice in Caldwell county were closed, no debts could be collected, the Justices, Constables, and Juries, Clerks and Sheriffs, refused or neglected to do their duties." This writer's accusation is substantiated by a statement of a circuit court judge in Caldwell, John Cleminson. He remembered that Smith told him that a certain writ was not to be issued and that he felt "intimidated and in danger, if I issued it, knowing the regulation of the Danite band."[84] W. W. Phelps, who was a justice in the county court, said that in early July he was forbidden by the prophet to issue any legal process against him.[85] Citizens of Ray County also said that the Mormons would "not indite one another in Caldwell."[86] Later Rigdon, while still in the First Presidency in Nauvoo, Illinois, acknowledged that the reason the Saints were harassed in Missouri was that they would not have anything to do with the laws—"we did not break them we were above them."[87]

Even after they left Far West the feeling was strong among the Saints that any appeal to a civil court was wrong. In a high council report in Nauvoo in 1842, it was noted that certain elders "were going to law with [their] brother for trivial causes which we consider a great evil and altogether unjustifiable, except in extreme cases, and then not before the world."[88] Years later the wife of Apostle Franklin D. Richards told an inquirer that "it is a shame to go to law before the ungodly."[89] Moved by apocalyptic fervor, the Saints assumed a status of sovereignty above the laws of Missouri, reserving to themselves the right to determine which lawsuits to allow. John Cleminson indicated that Smith exercised this responsibility when the judge himself would not.[90] This amounted to legal nullification so far as dissenters and non-Mormons in the county were concerned and left Missourians with no recourse but an appeal to arms when involved in disputes with the Saints.

Mormons justified preventing legal process by maintaining that the Kingdom of God had been established and that its laws superceded those of the state. When John Whitmer protested after Rigdon's declaration of independence that state laws should be obeyed, Alanson Ripley retorted that "as to the technical niceties of the law of the land, he did not intend to regard them; that the kingdom spoken of by the prophet Daniel had been set up, and that it was necessary every kingdom should be governed by its own laws."

George Robinson, the prophet's personal scribe, informed Whitmer at this time, "when God spoke he must be obeyed, whether his word came in contact with the laws of the land or not; and that, as the kingdom spoken of by Daniel has been set up, its laws must be obeyed."[91] A few days before this W. W. Phelps warned David Patten that to create a government within a government might be treason, but Patten shrugged and said, "It would not be treasonable if they would maintain it, or fight till they died."[92]

Rigdon's 4th of July oration was a calculated declaration of independence from legal process in Caldwell County, an appeal to higher law—the natural right to self defense legally and militarily. Appeals to higher law could be traced to the American revolutionary tradition, although revolutionaries had not claimed prophetic powers to determine divine law. Mormon higher law justified the establishment of theocratic rule, which the Saints believed was the only law that would protect their rights. Rigdon in his address went a step further, saying that should Gentiles violate those rights again, the elders would carry the war to their houses and families and wage a war of extermination. Rigdon believed that millennial forces were at work, that the vexation of nations had begun. In this context a divinely sponsored war to protect the Saints and their kingdom was fully justified. It is clear since Smith approved the address that these were his beliefs also.[93] There was more to Rigdon's speech than religious fervor and 4th of July rhetoric. It was tactical. John Corrill said that for several weeks many feared saying anything against these policies,[94] thus precluding a voice of caution. Smith and Rigdon had given an ultimatum and the issue of peace or war consequently rested on actions of non-Mormon vigilante leaders in Carroll and Daviess counties. There events moved rapidly toward a military solution.

On the same day that Rigdon declared the legal independence of the kingdom, efforts were underway to make the Saints economically self-sufficient. Smith preached that all the Saints everywhere were required to sell their property to raise funds for buying land around Far West.[95] Special groups were to buy land from the federal government and deed it to the church. A tract would then be set aside for each family, its size depending upon the number of family members. In this way, Smith said, Zion might be redeemed without the shedding of blood. Rigdon added that the Saints must be united in temporal and spiritual matters or they would never be accepted as children of God.[96] A few days after this Rigdon elaborated on his theme: "We are soon to commence building the Lord's house in Far West, which will enhance the value of property ten fold in its vicinity, and such proprietors as will not consecrate the whole amount of that increase for the building of the house and other uses, shall be delivered over to the brother of Gideon and be sent bounding over the prairies as the dissenters were."[97] Despite these threats, not all of the Saints were willing to part with their property.[98] Many "felt like Ananias and Sapphira" and entered land in their own names at the land office, afterward "forcing the poor Saints to pay them large advances for every acre."[99]

A program was established for the newcomers who were flooding into Far West in Caldwell County and Adam-ondi-Ahman to the north in Daviess County. Luman Shirtliff wrote in his journal that when he arrived in Far West in June without funds, he gave all that he possessed into a "cooperative firm" organized into companies of ten men, each with an appointed president.[100] John Smith recorded that when he came to Adam-ondi-Ahman he joined a similar unit.[101] By October some of these were nearly set up, and leaders had high hopes for their success. Albert Rockwood described with enthusiasm how

> permanent arrangements are now makeing for constant employ-
> ment for both male and female by the operations of Church
> firms, which are . . . being . . . verry extensively established. The
> members lease all their Real Estate, save the city lots to the firm
> to which they belong, for a term of years from 10 to 99, without
> any consideration or interest. . . . Every member that joins is to
> put in all he has over and above his needs and wants for his pri-
> vate stewardship in all cases each person is bound to pay his
> honest debts before leasing. The Calculation is for the brethren
> to dwell in the cities and cultivate the lands in the vicinity, in
> fields many miles in extent.

Rockwood further explained that city plots were provided for cooperative workers by the bishop until they could be purchased as private stewardships. All kinds of commodities, farm and manufac-tured, were produced by these cooperatives. Already they were giv-ing "constant employ . . . [to] all who join them and pay $1.00 per day for a man's work—any surplus that may remain, after paying the demands of the firm is to be divided according to the needs and wants, not according to property invested, to each family annu[al]ly or [more] often if needed."[102]

A large crop of wheat had been planted, and now the coopera-tive members began building new houses. For a man to secure one, he had to work seventy to eighty days for the firm. Rockwood pre-dicted enthusiastically that "arrangements will soon be made that a person can get every necessity to eat, drink and live on and to wear at the store house of the firm and the best of it is they want no better pay than labour arrangements." Thus Rockwood was pleased with the prospect of economic independence, maintaining that there would be "no necessity of purchasing of our enemies."[103] The kingdom was to be economically as well as legally independent.

Despite this buoyant optimism in Far West in the fall of 1838, there was also a note of foreboding expressed in Rockwood's letter to his father. He explained that October, a "time of union and peace in the church," was also one of "rob, mob and plunder without."[104] The truth was that in the three months since Rigdon's 4th of July speech, Mormon-non-Mormon relations had deteriorated in Daviess and Carroll counties. When they first moved into Daviess, Mormons had encountered little protest from the old residents,[105] although Peter H. Burnett said the old citizens were "rather rude and ungovernable" and "opposed to the Mormons extending their settlement" into the county.[106] But protest was quick to be voiced when the newcomers made pre-emptive claims on public land surrounding Adam-ondi-Ahman. It was broadcast among the Missourians that this was an attempt to "take advantage of the [old] citizens in the approaching land sales." Public land auctions were a popular means of acquiring assets cheaply and profit later. There would be less land available to buy because of the influx of Mormon squatters.[107]

If collective monopolization of the land by Mormons in Daviess County stirred Missourian hostility, Mormon group politicking prompted greater antagonism. A state election was due in August, and the politically ambitious began to court the Mormon vote. In May a Democratic candidate for state senator, Judge Morin, spent the day with the prophet, and General Wilson, a Whig aspirant, also visited Far West. Afterward, Rigdon, "assisted by the Spirit of God," stood up in the school house and delivered to his mixed audience an "impartial review of both sides of the question."[108]

One of the politicos who frequented Far West was William Penniston, who initially opposed the Saints expanding beyond Caldwell County into Daviess County.[109] During the campaign, he visited the Mormon meetings and affirmed that they were "first rate citizens."[110] But like most of the old settlers, Penniston was a Whig and had small chance to win favor with the Mormons, who were uniformly committed to the Democratic party.[111] Fearing that there might be enough new Mormon settlers in Daviess County to swing the election for the Democrats,[112] Penniston led Daviess County Whigs in a determined effort to keep Mormons from exercising their political power.[113] In July he told supporters in the outlying area of

.e county to vote early on the first day of balloting and then rush to Gallatin to keep the Saints from voting.[114] Judge Morin warned the elders of this threat, and on the first morning of the election several brethren, deciding not "to be deprived of their liberty and rights, . . . determined to go and put in their vote."[115] With this in mind, eight to ten elders arrived in Gallatin early on the morning of 6 August, where Penniston had mounted a whiskey barrel and "harrangued the electors for the purpose of exciting them against the Mormons."[116] John Butler remembered that Penniston told the crowd "he had headed a company to order the Mormons off of their farms and possessions, stating at the same time that he did not consider the Mormons had any more right to vote than the niggers."[117]

As Missourians gathered around the Mormons and tried to bully them from casting their ballots, fighting erupted. Lyman Wight said that he was "followed to the polls by three ruffians with stones in their hands, swearing they would kill me if I voted."[118] John Butler was initially a spectator, but when he saw several Missourians ganging up on one elder, he grabbed a large chunk of oak and entered lustily into the melee: "When I got in reach of them, I commenced to call out loud for peace and at the same time making my stick to move to my own utter astonishment, tapping them as I thought light, but they fell as dead men."[119] The fight lasted only a few minutes, but perhaps as many as thirty men were wounded "with bloody heads and some of them badly hurt."[120] According to Vinson Knight, armed non-Mormons came to Gallatin the next morning to see to it that no more Mormons voted.[121] The reason for the Whig party's fear of Mormons is shown in the Caldwell County vote for the congressional representative. There were 337 votes for the Democratic candidate, and 2 for the Whig.[122] Mormons in Missouri voted en bloc, a circumstance that invariably brought opposition.

Judge Morin, who was elected to the state senate, informed the Mormons that some of their elders were dead and left unburied on the ground at Gallatin.[123] Angry and determined to right a sacrilege, Smith and Rigdon rounded up fifteen to twenty armed men, with "General" Higbee, "General" Avard and "Colonel" George Robinson among them, his duty being "to command one regiment." As this contingent of the Armies of Israel left Far West, they were joined by "the brethren from all parts of the county"[124] until there were at least 100 men in their force.[125] Robinson said that when they arrived at Lyman Wight's house, they found that some of the brethren were "badly wounded" from the election fight. He said that certain Missourians were also badly hurt, "some of their sculls cracked."[126]

They soon learned that the story of the uninterred dead was untrue, but rather than return to Far West they rode the next day to the house of local justice of the peace, Adam Black. According to Robinson, he was "an enemy of ours for the evidences were before us that he did, last summer, unite himself to a band of robbers to drive our brethren from the county."[127] Given Black's hostility, surrounding his house with a band of militia was a provocative act. When some of the elders entered the house, they inquired "whether he justified the course of conduct at the state election." Black said he did not.[128] The elders then demanded "that he confess to the wrong he had done them," insisting that in working to drive them from the county he had violated the demands of his office. Of course, the question of whether Mormons, in the first place, were violating the conditions of their agreement with Missouri legislators by settling outside of Caldwell County blurred an otherwise straightforward issue. When the elders "required him to give us some satisfaction so that we might know whether he was our friend or enemy and whether he would administer the laws of our country or not," and that he sign an article of peace, he refused. He would agree to sign a statement of his own composition only. This document apparently affirmed that he would not molest Mormons.[130]

The next day church leaders met at Adam-ondi-Ahman with non-Mormon leaders, including Senator Morin, to agree to a "covenant of peace . . . to preserve each other's rights and stand in their defense." The agreement provided that if any did wrong they would not be kept from justice in the courts. The agreement seemingly assured non-Mormons that none of the elders would stand above the law, but it also seemed in some respects a mutual defense pact. George Robinson wrote that when the elders returned to Far West at midnight they thought that all was well.[131] They could not have been more wrong.

Before the returning elders settled in Far West, Adam Black made a deposition before a justice of the peace in Daviess County on 9 August, stating that about 154 Mormons surrounded his house and demanded that he sign a peace pledge that he would either not molest the Mormons or suffer "instant death." Black alleged that the Mormons said they would not "submit to the laws."[132] The next day

...iam Penniston swore before Judge Austin A. King in Ray County
...nat Mormons had threatened Adam Black's life and that they
intended to drive all the old citizens out of the county and seize their
land.[133]

The Black affair was a boon to those who were hostile to the
Mormon advance into Daviess County. Penniston's affidavit forced
civil authorities to take action, and a sheriff went to Far West to bring
Joseph Smith and Lyman Wight to trial. The pair was reluctant to be
tried in Gallatin, and Wight unadvisedly boasted that he could not
be taken into custody even if the whole state of Missouri wanted him.
His words spread through the western part of the state,[134] and the
response was prompt. In Ray County on 9 August a group of citizens
organized a committee of vigilance and sent a delegation of three to
investigate.[135] Three days later a contingent from Livingston County
prepared to march to Black's home. They wrote to Carroll County
that additional assistance might soon be needed.[136]

Events already underway in Carroll added more supporters to
the anti-Mormon cause. Two such meetings were held in Carrollton,
the county seat, during early July[137] and a third on 30 July. There the
old citizens passed resolutions requesting that the Mormons at DeWitt
leave the county.[138] Some of the Saints replied emphatically that they
would not be driven out, and Henry Root, who had first encouraged
the Saints to settle there, hastily retorted that if the citizens of
Carroll attempted to expel them they would "apply to Far West for
assistance and . . . [the Missourians] would have to abide the
consequences."[139] On 7 August the people of Carrollton met once
more to correspond with nearby counties and to request aid "to
remove Mormons, abolitionists, and other disorderly persons from
our county."[140]

In response to the appeals from Daviess and Carroll county residents, bands of armed men began to collect around Adam-ondi-
Ahman and DeWitt in mid-August.[141] At the end of the month, Governor Lilburn W. Boggs was sufficiently alarmed by the likelihood
of violence that he ordered General David R. Atchison, Commander
of the 3rd Missouri Division, to ride with four hundred men to the
scene.[142] Joseph Smith also had become fearful of the legions clus-
tering around the Mormon settlements, but he and the other members of the First Presidency resolved that "our rights and our liberties shall not be taken from us, and we peaceably submit to it . . . we
will avenge ourselves of our enemies, inasmuch as they will not let
us alone."[143]

This statement, recorded by Robinson, indicated again that Smith and Rigdon were in agreement on retaliation against the marauding Missourians should they cause harm to people or property. Smith wrote to Judge Austin King that government assistance was needed in "putting down and scattering the mob in Daviess county." Smith requested that General Atchison of the state militia visit Far West and advise him as to how to "put a stop to hostilities in Daviess county."[144] When Atchison arrived on the evening of 3 September, he urged Smith to submit to trial before the circuit court. Smith agreed and met Judge King on the 7th at a secluded farmhouse in a wooded area in Daviess, just over the county line.[145] He was accompanied by General Atchison. Quite a few Missourians heard of the secret proceedings and appeared there to threaten Smith. Atchison frightened them off by warning, "If you fire the first gun there will not be one of you left."[146] Although Smith and Wight were held over for probable cause, the *Western Star* reported at Liberty that the hearing had shown that "Adam Black had misrepresented Mormon intentions."[147]

Minute men who had gathered from adjoining counties still lingered in the area to harass the Latter-day Saints. On the 7th a Daviess County committee wrote to citizens of Howard County to come to their rescue since many of their people had already fled. The committee affirmed that Mormons were in rebellion against the laws and that war was inevitable.[148] When General Atchison returned to the area on 15 September, he found two to three hundred men from Livingston, Carroll, and Saline counties marshaled under William W. Austin of Carroll County. Many of the citizens of Daviess had already abandoned their farms and joined the troops at "camp ground," while the Saints too had fled their homes and assumed a defensive position at Adam-ondi-Ahman.[149] The editor of the *Western Star* wrote that the Gentiles in Daviess County wanted to keep the Mormons away from the free land remaining in the county.[150]

An attempt was made to end hostilities. General Atchison ordered Mormons and Missourians to return home, and when most did so he departed, leaving a token force to keep the peace.[151] General Parks, in charge of the remaining contingent, wrote on 25 September that those in Daviess County were yet determined to "drive the Mormons with powder and lead," unless one or the other party would buy their opponents out. He said the Mormons at this point "have shown no disposition to resist the laws, or of hostile intentions."[152]

On 26 September the opposing groups met, and it was proposed that the Saints purchase the land of Missourians still remaining in the county. Elders were sent out to solicit financial aid from the Saints in the south and east.[153] Generals Atchison and Parks believed that the situation had stabilized; Atchison wrote to Governor Boggs on the 27th that the Mormons "are not to be feared."[154] But a few days later Albert P. Rockwood reflected a different mood among the Saints, writing that "very great fear rests on the Missourians"; they are "selling their property verry low to the Brethren, in many cases they sell their Real Estate with their houses and crops on the ground, for less than the crop is worth." Rockwood said, "Davies[s] County is now in the possession of the Brethren," and noted with satisfaction, "thus the Lord is preparing a way for his children."[155] But the course of events was to prove that Rockwood and the Saints had badly misjudged the signs of the times.

During the latter half of September the situation in Carroll County had become more war-like. There had been a brief lull while William Austin had gone to Daviess to help intimidate the Saints there,[156] but when he returned to DeWitt on 20 September, he brought additional troops from Saline County. Mormons were given until 1 October to depart.[157] Within the next few days more anti-Mormon troops began to arrive from Ray, Howard, and Clay counties, and after they formed themselves into military companies,[158] they surrounded DeWitt, leaving only the road northward to Far West open for the Saints' departure.[159] In the first days of October the two hostile groups began shooting at each other.[160]

Meanwhile, Missourians in the more populous areas of the state were growing anxious over the continuing threat of Mormon-Gentile conflict in the north. The editor of the *Jeffersonian Republican* lamented on 22 September: "Our ploughshares have been turned into swords in this quarter, and the Mormon war is the all engrossing topic of conversation. Even politics is submerged in the deafening sound of the drum and the din of arms." General Samuel D. Lucas, on the scene with a body of state militia, revealed his own and others' bitter hostility toward Mormons in a letter to the governor in which he stated that if a confrontation occurred, "it will create excitement in the whole upper Missouri, and those base and degraded beings will be exterminated from the face of the earth. If one of the citizens of Carroll should be killed, before five days I believe that there will be from four to five thousand volunteers in the field against the Mormons, and nothing but their blood will satisfy them."[161]

The editor of *The Far West* maintained that "both parties are in the wrong," regretting that some "contentious and quarrelsome disposed persons can throw a whole community into commotion."[162] Another editor maintained that the war was "alike disgraceful to all parties concerned."[163] A fourth writer took a more belligerent tone, insisting that the situation "will not be settled without a fight, and the quicker they have it the better for the peace and quiet of the county."[164]

For a time greater patience prevailed among some in Howard and Chariton counties, where William F. Dunnica formed a committee to find a compromise between the warring parties. A proposition was made by non-Mormons to pay the Saints for their property with 10 percent interest, but the committee was told that the Mormons had been driven enough and preferred to "die on the ground."[165] Mormon determination had been bolstered by the arrival from Far West of Lyman Wight and a company of armed defenders.[166] The Missourians responded by making a plea for more military support from their neighbors: "the people ought to take the execution of justice into their own hands."[167]

A small force of militia under General Parks came to DeWitt to keep the peace but was ineffective in preventing skirmishes.[168] Mormons, therefore, appealed desperately to the governor for his intervention, sending a Mr. Caldwell personally to ask for assistance. Boggs claimed to be out of town at the time, but the editor of the *Missouri Republican* said Boggs believed that the expense of sending more troops was too great.[169] Caldwell reported back to the Mormons that the governor had said they would have to fight it out with their enemies.[170] The Saints at DeWitt chose not to fight and loaded their wagons and departed for Far West on 11 October,[171] agreeing to accept compensation for their property.[172] William Dunnica, who had helped to arrange the final settlement, commented that the Saints made their departure on the very day the Missourians were ready to attack.[173]

If the Saints who fled DeWitt hoped they would escape their tormentors, they hoped in vain. Sashiel Woods urged the troops who had surrounded the town to hurry to Daviess County, because the pre-empted lands would soon go on sale and must be secured by Missourians.[174] Samuel Bogart, a non-Mormon from Ray County, noted to Governor Boggs on 15 October that volunteers from

Livingston and other counties were on their way to Daviess to prevent the exiled Saints from returning there. He warned the governor that great excitement prevailed in his county and Daviess and
concluded his letter with the terse observation that "you may rest
assured times grow worse and worse here. [Things are] desperate in
the extreme. . . . You will soon be called on. I hope you will take steps
to make a final settlement of this matter, if not soon our country will
be ruined."[175]

General David Atchison wrote to Boggs a day later, 16 October,
saying that troops from Carroll County were on their way to Daviess
to play "the same lawless game." He urged "strong measures to put
down the spirit of mob and misrule, or to permit them to fight it
out." Atchison pleaded that Boggs himself come to the scene, but
the governor apparently decided to let the contending parties settle
their differences themselves, for he did nothing.[176]

For Mormons these Missouri days were a low point. John
Pulsipher wrote of this period in his diary: "It seamed that the devil
was in almost every man in Missouri. They would declare, from the
governor in his chair, down to the meanest man there, who would
stand up and *swear*, with a bottle of whiskey in one hand and a knife
in the other that the Mormons should not stay there."[177] Anxiety
turned to fury as the wagons of the exiles from DeWitt rolled into
Far West. The prophet protested to John Corrill on 14 October that a
plea for assistance had been made to the governor and none had
been rendered. Corrill recalled that then and there Joseph and
Hyrum Smith determined "to withstand the mob" and drive them
out of the country.[178] That Sunday Smith learned from General
Doniphan that a large body of troops was hurrying to Adam-ondi-
Ahman to begin a new siege, and it was this, according to Corrill,
which got the prophet "much excited."[179] It was recorded in Smith's
history afterward that the general told the prophet at this point to
form his own militia and protect the northern settlement.[180] But several Mormons informed the editor of the *Missouri Republican* that
when Smith called the elders to arms on Monday, 15 October, it was
to retaliate for driving the Saints from DeWitt.[181]

In the morning two to three hundred Mormons collected at the
public square to hear Smith exclaim the time had come to take up
arms. According to non-Mormon and dissenter sources, Joseph Smith
angrily said the law was "unequally administered—all against us, and
none for us."[182] The Saints must, he continued,

TAKE OUR AFFAIRS INTO OUR OWN HANDS AND MAN-
AGE FOR OURSELVES. We have applied to the Governor and
he will do nothing for us; the militia of the county we have tried
and they will do nothing. All are mob; the Governor's mob, the
militia mob, and the whole State is mob. . . . I am determined
that we will not give another foot, and I care not how many come
against us. . . . God will send angels to our deliverance and we
can conquer 10,000 as easily as ten.[183]

Smith told the elders that they might have to live off plundered supplies, but it was justified because they were at war.[184] He illustrated
his point with a story of a Dutchman who would not sell his potatoes
to a military captain, only to find in the morning that the potatoes
had been taken despite the captain's pledge to the contrary.[185]

Sidney Rigdon now addressed the throng and demanded that
all able-bodied men join the task force. Perhaps as many as a third
of the elders opposed the expedition,[186] but when Smith threatened
to place dissenters at the head of the column, most quickly
joined.[187] George Hinkle was placed in command of two hundred
men who marched to Adam-ondi-Ahman.[188]

Once a base was established in the northern town, the elders
were organized into scouting parties and sent to comb the region
for supplies.[189] On 17 October General Parks arrived, and Mormon
accounts state that he ordered them to "go and put the mob
down."[190] Ephraim Owens recalled that Parks told George Hinkle
that the Saints "must help themselves" but would not give them a
written order to call out Mormon troops. Owens observed that Mormons were thus "compelled to defend themselves by
themselves."[191] Parley Pratt said that it was a Mormon judge, Elias
Higbee, who called out the militia under Colonel Hinkle.[192] During
the week that followed, according to Phineas Richards, the elders
"went at it and drove the mob by the hundreds, hunted them from
every valley, from every secret place. They fled like wind . . . leaving
their cannon and many other valuable things behind which were
taken as spoil."[193]

During the campaign Mormon troops drove into Gallatin, the
county seat, Millport, and Grindstone Fork and confiscated the property of old citizens.[194] Some of the elders evidently affirmed during
the raid that the time had come when the riches of the Gentiles should
be consecrated to the Saints.[195] Most of the property was placed in
the bishop's storehouse.[196] At Gallatin the brethren took all the goods
in one store and burned the building to the ground.[197] At Millport

they raided and burned houses,[198] including the home of William
Penniston,[199] and at Grindstone Fork citizens who had stashed away
enemy arms were driven out and their houses burned.[200]

The elders who took to their arms had not done so without provocation. Non-Mormons had driven off Mormon livestock[201] and seized
and burned houses.[203] Two Mormons had been compelled to ride
for three days astride a cannon which the Missourians had brought
from Carroll County.[204] Some of the brethren were tied to trees and
beaten.[205] Nonetheless, many of the Mormon troops had gone to war
rejoicing that the "Saints shall take the kingdom and possess it
forever," fulfilling the prophecy of Daniel.[206] It had been whispered
among the Danites since July that they would live to fight the battle
of Gog and Magog,[207] and one of them affirmed in William
Swartzell's hearing that they expected to fight "until the blood shall
come up to the horse-bridles."[208] Albert Rockwood, who was in Far
West when the elders returned from their northern campaign, was
convinced that millennial events were unfolding and that the Lord's
will had been done:

> Far West is head-quarters for the Mormon war. The Armies of
> Israel that were established by Revelation from God are seen
> from my door every day. . . . The mob have been dispersed by
> the Brethren they ask no favors of the Militia—the Missouri mob
> have all left Davis Co. The f[e]ar of God rests down upon them
> and they flee when no man persueth. The brethren are fast
> returning from the northern campaign with hearts full of grat-
> itude, not a drop of blood has been spilt, the Mob disperse by
> hundreds on the approach of the Danites. . . . The word of the
> Lord is for the Saints to gather to Zion in haste . . . for the per-
> plexities of the nations have commenced.

In an appeal to his family to hurry to Far West, Rockwood said, "Now
Father, come to Zion and fight for the religion of Jesus, many a hoary
head is seen with their armour about them bold to defend their Mas-
ters cause." Rockwood concluded with wonder: "The Prophet now
goes before his people as in times of old. Bro. Joseph has unsheathed
his sword & in the name of Jesus declares that it will not be sheathed
again until he can go into any country or state in safety and
peace."[209]

Smith had indeed unsheathed his sword, but it was a move that
he and his people would regret. In the heat of the Daviess County
campaign, he proclaimed revolutionary intentions. He said he would

"hoist a flag, or standard, on the square in Far West, on which he intended to write, 'Religion aside, and free toleration to all religions, and to all people that would flock to it,' and that he believed thousands in the surrounding country would flock to it, and give him force sufficient to accomplish his designs in maintaining his flag and in carrying the war."[210] Apostle Thomas Marsh, disaffected by these events, confirmed these radical plans "to take this state, and . . . [Joseph Smith] professes to his people to intend taking the United States, and ultimately, the whole world. This is the belief of the church, and my own opinion of the prophet's plans and intentions."[211] Even consistently loyal Mormons expressed dismay at the actions of Mormon forces against innocent Missourians.

Already by 1838 dreams of a theocratic empire were solidifying. In September Nathan Marsh had written to the governor that "the fears of the people are greatly excited . . . [the Mormon] teachers have recently been very urgent in soliciting the people to fly to their towns for protection, as the time has arrived when the 'Flying Angel' should pass through the land, accompanied by the Indians."[212] A resident of Randolph County reported with concern in the *Missouri Republican* that their "object is a Kingly government . . . they seem confident that all the wicked in Missouri will be cut off and the Mormons will take peaceable possession."[213]

When the elders struck towns in Daviess County in October, terror naturally seized the nearby communities. Rumors flew wildly of the intentions of Mormons to devastate the whole state,[214] and in Ray County word was received that they planned to burn the village of Buncombe.[215] Frightened citizens sent a communication to Governor Boggs asking for military assistance,[216] and Boggs responded by calling out two thousand militia to repel invaders.[217] Citizens of Ray County did not wait for the state militia but mobilized their own troops under Captain Samuel Bogart.[218] These troops crossed the line into Caldwell County and drove some Mormons from their homes.[219] Hearing of mob activity in the southern part of their county, Mormon leaders sent Apostle David Patten with seventy Danites to drive Bogart's army out,[220] but in the ensuing fight on 24 October, Patten and two other Mormons were killed.[221]

Word spread throughout western Missouri that the Mormons had annihilated Bogart's men,[222] and the governor immediately issued a proclamation that the Mormons be exterminated.[223] Thousands of Missourians happily seized their muskets to end once and for all the Mormon menace in their midst.[224] On 30 October at

Haun's Mill, a small Mormon village, a company of state militia acting on Boggs's extermination order fell upon the community and
slaughtered eighteen elders as well as a boy of eight years.[225] Talk of
extermination first by Rigdon and then by Boggs had its effect. The
men in the Haun's Mill village were not part of the Mormon army,
and the slaughter of these innocents burned into the minds of the
Saints a hatred of Missourians that a full generation would not wipe
away.[226]

"Many respectable men" responded to Bogg's order and began
collecting at Richmond in Ray County to expel the Mormons.[227] General John Clark had been placed in command of the state's forces by
the governor but was stationed in Charlton County, and he and his
troops were slow in arriving.[228] Meanwhile, troops at Richmond
under Generals Samuel Lucas and David Atchison moved toward Far
West.[229] Albert Rockwood anxiously watched the masses of militia
approach the city and noted that the army was "many miles in
length." The Saints had a mere five hundred men to face a force
which Rockwood estimated to be 1,700. Assured that the Lord would
tip the scales in the Mormon favor, he wrote, "the work of death seems
to be before us."[230]

The prophet perceived the situation for what it was and determined to seek whatever terms he could, perhaps at last recognizing
that for the moment most citizens of western Missouri had turned
against his people.[231] He sent Reed Peck and John Corrill to General Doniphan to sue for peace.[232] Before anything had come of this
General Samuel Lucas, who had hurried into the field without
orders,[233] intervened to present the Saints with a "treaty" which
required that their leaders—Joseph Smith, Sidney Rigdon, Parley P.
Pratt, Lyman Wight, and George W. Robinson—surrender themselves
as hostages until a final settlement could be reached. The treaty
demanded that all the Saints leave the state,[234] a demand that would
satisfy the second alternative in Governor Boggs's extermination
order.

When Joseph Smith promptly accepted these terms he was taken
into custody and "treated with the utmost contempt."[235] General
Lucas and some of the other militia officers held a court martial on 1
November and sentenced the Mormon leaders to be shot at dawn.[236]
Despite the seeming doom that faced the Mormons, all did not yet
despair. Albert Rockwood wrote in his extended letter: "We are now
in the hands of our enemies, that are our judges, jurors, and execu-
tioners. God only can deliver us . . . [we] have only to wait and see

the salvation of God."[237] Rockwood's faith was partially rewarded when General Alexander Doniphan, who was commanded to carry out the executions, refused on the grounds that the proceeding was unlawful.[238] His staunch opposition saved the Mormon leaders from a quick death.

The Saints in Far West did not fare so well. Once they surrendered the militia poured into the town and reaped vengeance upon those who had participated in the Daviess County raid.[239] Hyrum Smith told Dimick B. Huntington to take the Mormon militia men "out of the state for they will be shot down like dogs."[240] But those in the militia were not the only ones who would be menaced. Nancy Tracy wrote:

> They abused women and children destroyed crops killed beaves and made a general havoc. Once Bogarts company was camped near my house and they searched . . . for my husband and weapons but they got neither. They placed a double guard at the door and windows so there was no going or coming without their leave. [A]ll this time I was sick in bed a child 3 weeks old and shaking with ague by day burning with a fever at night with no one to care for me but my little boy 5 years old.[241]

Meanwhile, sixty[242] of the leading elders were marched to Richmond where on 12 November they were charged with treason in a court of inquiry presided over by Judge Austin King, who had already condemned the prisoners in the newspapers.[243] The hearing, although legally valid, was fiercely partisan as King refused to allow Mormons to testify for the defense and allowed no cross examinations.[244] The few Mormons who did testify for the state were intimidated by threats of violence.[245]

Following the hearing Smith and Rigdon were held over for trial. On 25 January they petitioned to have their case heard in Clay County, where citizens were not as hostile as those in Ray County, but Judge Joel Turnham at Liberty found just cause to hold Smith and four others. On 10 April at a session presided over by Thomas C. Burch, judge of Missouri's eleventh judicial circuit, a Daviess County grand jury brought indictments against the Mormons for riot, arson, burglary, and treason.[246] The prisoners gained a change of venue to Boone County after this[247] and while in transit to Columbia apparently bribed a guard and escaped.[248] They fled to Illinois where the Saints had begun to gather along the banks of the Mississippi River.

The Mormon experience in Kirtland and Missouri accentuated the anti-plural tendencies within the movement, vastly increasing the authority of the Mormon prophet and limiting the possibility of loyal dissent. The Danite injunction that the prophet must be obeyed right or wrong became an irresistible demand that all were forced to comply with or leave the community. Those who opposed going to war in Missouri were silenced, forced to flee or put at the head of the Armies of Israel as they marched into battle. Even Brigham Young, who in somewhat similar circumstances later in Nauvoo, Illinois, opposed Rigdon's call to arms,[249] made no protest in Far West.[250]

Only two apostles spoke against the war after the Danite raids had begun: Thomas Marsh, one of the prophet's staunchest supporters and president of the twelve apostles, and Apostle Orson Hyde. They fled Far West before daring to express their opposition. In Ray County they testified before a local judge on 24 October[251] and then wrote to "Bro & Sister Abbott" on the following day to explain their reasons. Marsh said, "I have left the Mormons & Joseph Smith jr. for conscience sake and that alone." Marsh declared "the disposition in J. Smith and S. Rigdon to pillage, rob, plunder, assassinate and murder, was never equalled, in my estimation, unless by some desperado Bandit. O my what principles to be called the religion of Jesus Christ." Hyde concurred, "I can say with him that I have left the church . . . for conscience sake, fully believing that God is not with them."[252] When Hyde wrote to Brigham Young several months afterward to plead for readmission into the church, he said, "I felt like taking no part in the Danite movements. The convictions of my mind were, that it was not a good and virtuous institution."[253]

Wilford Woodruff, expressing the more common views of most of the Saints, said that the dissenting apostles were guilty of "high handed wickedness." Woodruff wrote that the apostles had "jeopardized the church by bearing false witness against the presidency & the church before authorities of the state of Missouri which was the leading cause of the Governor calling out thirty thousand of the Militia against the Church."[254] Actually, there is no evidence that the testimony of the two apostles before Justice Henry Jacobs on the 24th[255] had any influence on Boggs. Boggs's letter to General Clark on the 26th demonstrates that it was the Danite raids on Gallatin and Millport that caused him to call out the militia.[256] It is also evident that the exterminating order on the following day came in the wake of reports that the elders had attacked Bogart.[257] Military retaliation by the Mormons, not apostolic testimony, had once and for all turned Missouri state officials against the Saints.

Had warnings of those opposed to retaliation been heeded, misery, loss of property, and life might have been avoided.[258] Still, it does not seem possible that Mormons could have remained in Missouri for long. Given the anti-pluralistic tendencies developing among the Mormons in Missouri, no opposing voices could have been heard and no alternative course considered. Hyde's and Marsh's apprehensions might have been considered humane and supportive of lawful procedures in another time and place.

Yet Wilford Woodruff might have been right to some extent in saying that the two apostles had borne "false witness," in that they quoted exaggerated Danite promises which probably did not indicate serious Danite intent.[259] They told of the formation of a Danite "destruction company" to burn Buncombe, Liberty, and Richmond if the residents made any military move against the Saints. They described plans to poison corn and fruit and to say that it was the work of the Lord. They reported Joseph Smith saying "he should yet tread down his enemies, and walk over their dead bodies," and it would soon be "Joseph Smith or the sword."[260] Smith was inclined when under great stress to talk in exaggerated terms and would do so again in Illinois.[261] But the actual response to belligerence when it occurred was much more restrained.[262] Although the elders did confiscate property and burn houses, their attacks were generally aimed at specific enemies.[263] Mormons had neither the inclination nor means to wage a general war of extermination against all mobbers, despite menacing talk. The only fatalities occurred in the skirmish with Bogart, where the elders got the worst of the fight. Had the prophet been intent on waging total war, it is unlikely he would have allowed Rigdon to issue his 4th of July warning, which only put the Missourians on guard.

If Marsh and Hyde in fact exaggerated the vicious side of Danite intentions, it may have been because they were misinformed. Hyde confessed to Brigham Young that "tales of some who had been initiated into the mysteries" had prompted him to flee Far West,[264] although he insisted that his basic views had been formed before this.

Neither Hyde nor Marsh spoke out against driving dissenters from Far West earlier in the year. It was the war preparations that caused them to flee. Afterward Smith himself came to believe that

Danite plundering was wrong, or at least a tactical error,[265] which may have influenced him to welcome Hyde back to the twelve in 1839.[266] Hyde told Brigham Young at the time of his return that "as to the terms upon which I can be received back into my place I shall not be particular; for to live this way [apart from the Saints] I cannot."[267] Hyde never denied the specifics of his testimony before Jacobs,[268] although later in Nauvoo he was more inclined to blame Rigdon rather than Smith for Danite excesses.[269] Marsh did not deny his testimony either, although he wrote to Apostle Heber C. Kimball years later that he had "betrayed a trust."[270]

The prophet and his people paid a heavy price for their resort to arms in 1838. A majority of state legislators believed that the Saints were at fault and offered no reparations, despite a protest from some in and out of the legislature that the Mormons had been needlessly provoked.[271] The legislature's decision to table investigation of the causes of the Mormon war precluded any chance, however remote, that the federal government would intervene to demand reparations.[272] The consequences psychologically on the Mormon people were enormous as they faced the future fearful that no one in the state or nation cared about their rights or safety.

CHAPTER 6

"Everything God Does is to Aggrandize His Kingdom"[1]

The five thousand Saints who staggered out of Missouri in the winter of 1838-39 did not flee further west but turned east to Illinois and a new refuge.[2] Most collected around Quincy, the largest town on the upper Mississippi, and looked for housing and employment.[3] Elders sent to scout the countryside for a new gathering place found the village of Commerce, fifty-three miles north of Quincy and opposite Montrose in Iowa.[4] On the Iowa side of the Mississippi River they found the barracks of old Fort Des Moines, which could serve as a temporary shelter.[5] But in February 1839, when the brethren at Quincy discussed the location, they were reluctant to proceed, wondering if it would be wise to congregate again and thus risk further persecution.[6] For the moment the gathering seemed stalled by the waning enthusiasm of such prominent churchmen as Sidney Rigdon, now released from incarceration, Bishop Edward Partridge, and William Marks.[7]

Meanwhile, Brigham Young and a few apostles still in Missouri were determined that the poor should not be forsaken. Young persuaded the Saints who had found accommodations to assist the destitute,[8] and a committee was formed, working with characteristic cooperation into the spring to bring the exiles to Quincy.[9] There, on 17 March, Young told the Saints to organize branches of the church and maintain order.[10] By encouraging a new gathering at Quincy Young gained stature in the kingdom for himself and the Quorum of Twelve Apostles he represented.

When Joseph Smith finally joined the Saints in April, the evacuation from Missouri was largely accomplished,[11] and they resolved to make a fresh start in the new state. Wilford Woodruff wrote in his journal that church members were "determined to build a city wherever their lot is cast."[12] Prospects seemed excellent, for the people of Quincy looked upon the Mormons with sympathy. These Illinoisans went out of their way to find shelter and work for the refugees—happy to serve as well as to have settlers who might strengthen the western part of the state politically.[13] But Quincy could not provide a permanent location for all the immigrants, and Smith turned his attention elsewhere. He negotiated with several landowners around Commerce, purchasing large amounts of land there and in Iowa.[14] He said that the Saints must hasten to build a city, because "the time is soon coming, when no man will have any peace but in Zion and her stakes."[15]

But where was Zion to be, especially if its establishment in Jackson County was to be delayed? Some, such as Alanson Ripley, were still militant and seethed at the violence levied against the Saints and the incarceration of church leaders. Ripley wrote to Smith in early April,

> when I reflect upon the cause of your afflictions it is like fire in my bones, and burns against your enemies to the bare hild [hilt], and I never can be satisfied while there is one of them to piss against a wall or draw a sword or spring a trigger, for my sword never has been sheathed in peace; for the blood of D. W. Patten and those who were butchered at Haun's Mill crieth for vengeance from the ground therefore hear it, Oh-ye heavens . . . that I from this day declare myself the Avenger of the blood of those innocent men, and the innocent cause of Zion.[16]

Those more pacific, such as David Foote, explained the expulsion from the promised land by finding that the Old Testament prophet Micah had predicted that Zion would be driven into the wilderness.[17]

Still another response was to take refuge in apocalypticism. Eliza R. Snow wrote that the inhabitants of the earth are, . . . beginning to be in haste to fill up their measure, before the Lord shall come. . . . The nations of the world can never fill the cup of their iniquity without shedding innocent blood, and the blood of the 'Latter Day Saints' will be required. . . . The Lord has commenc'd a work that is destin'd to try the sincerity and the strength, yes, and the legality too, of every creed and profession, both political and religious.[18]

More typical perhaps was the position of Parley Pratt, who affirmed that Zion must tarry but a short time "until the indignation of a just God has disencumbered the land and made room for the rights of man and the laws of the Lord to be restored." Pratt vented his anger against the American government in a letter to his wife, Mary Ann, in April 1839, saying that the Saints had been "banished" from Missouri only "because they belong to the church." With deep bitterness he protested the injustice. "This is called in this country," he wrote, "a just, impartial, and equitable administration of the laws, of a free and independent Republic—This is liberty!!!!!! American liberty!!!!" With intense resentment he exclaimed, "This is the government established in these modern times as a kind of Sample, a model or pattern for the nations of the earth . . . O' tell it not in England, nor let the sound be heard in Europe; Lest Britannia Laugh us to scorn,—Lest the daughter of Monarchy Tryumph."[19]

Other Saints looked to the government for redress. Sidney Rigdon went to the governor of Illinois with a proposal for a joint condemnation of the Missourians by all the state legislatures in the Union.[20] He also called for an investigation by Congress of the recent war in Missouri.[21] Joseph Smith planned a personal mission to Washington, D.C., to set forth the facts of the expulsion and to ask the federal government for compensation for their property losses.[22] In the spring of 1840, Smith, Rigdon, and Elias Higbee went to the nation's capital, armed with affidavits intended to prove that the Saints had been victims of religious persecution.[23] But the petitions and pleadings fell on deaf ears, as neither the president nor Congress would intervene to help the Mormons. Smith called personally on President Martin Van Buren, who exclaimed, "What can I do? I can do nothing for you! If I do anything, I shall come in contact with the whole state of Missouri."[24] Smith later wrote bitterly of Van Buren that he is "so much a fop or a fool, for he judged our cause before he knew it, we could find no place to put truth into him." Smith remarked that "we do not intend that he shall have our vote."[25] The prophet hunted up congressmen and senators, hoping that they might do something for his people.[26] But efforts failed in the Senate when representatives of Missouri maintained that the Saints had defied the law and waged war on the state. Missourians exhibited evidence presented at the preliminary hearing before Judge King[27] and convinced the judiciary committee of Mormon wrong-doing.[28] The Mormon emissaries were told that the affair was a matter for the state to settle and that they should appeal to the local courts.[29] Despite this the Saints hoped for a change of attitude. As late as May 1840, Elias Smith, representing the high council at Montrose, Iowa, wrote to Elias Higbee in Washington that the Saints still expected redress at the hands of the federal government. "You are not to give in an inch," he said, "on any position that has been taken, especially in relation to our damages. . . . Our rights we want and must have of the Government of the United States; and nothing short of that can be received." Elias Smith, like the prophet, blamed the "Golden Humbug firm of Van Buren & Co whose aim has been to aggrandize themselves at the expense of the laboring class."[30]

It was unrealistic for the Saints to expect the federal government to intervene in the 1840s on behalf of an unpopular minority when the Democratic party advocated states' rights.[31] Martin Van Buren was understandably reluctant to risk further civil war in Missouri in an unpopular cause. Even Andrew Jackson, Van Buren's predecessor whom Joseph Smith viewed as a champion of minorities, preferred to compromise with South Carolina on the tariff question even though he believed resistance to federal law by armed force was treason.[32] And when the abolitionists, a small minority like the Mormons, were mobbed between 1834 and 1836, Jackson had encouraged the attacks, saying that citizens in every state should frown on any proceedings within "her borders likely to disturb the tranquility of their political brethren in other portions of the union." He stated flatly: "each state has the unquestionable right to regulate its own internal concerns according to its own pleasure."[33] Such a man would not have intervened in Missouri in 1840 any more than Van Buren, especially since Missouri state officials were judged to be the upholders of law and order and the Saints in rebellion.

When Mormon leaders were told that they should seek redress in Missouri courts, they found the suggestion outrageous, since their old enemies in Daviess County were still in control.[34] George Adams summarized their feelings when he wrote that this was "the worst

insult we have ever received."[35] The Mormons' inability to gain con-
cessions deepened their alienation from American society and government. They were convinced that the leaders of the federal government who had refused to respond to their pleadings were
culpable. Smith even advocated that those who would not intervene
to protect the rights of citizens should be declared eligible for capital punishment.[36] He declared that the nation was on the verge of
destruction: "my heart faints within me when I see, by the visions of
the Almighty, the end of this nation, if she continues to disregard
the cries and petitions of her virtuous citizens, as she has done and
is now doing."[37] Ironically, however, Smith was speaking of an inter-
ventionist United States government that did not exist until the Civil
War and Reconstruction.

Reconsidering his chiliastic expectations, the prophet in July
1840 gave a panoramic view of what seemed in store for the Saints
and the nation. He said the elders would have to redeem the nation,
because it had failed in its divinely ordained mission. Smith told the
congregation that Zion, the place of refuge, might be in South as
well as North America, or anywhere the Saints might gather. The
redemption of Zion, then, "is the redemption of all N[orth] & S[outh]
America." The Saints must build up twelve stakes, scattered abroad,
and they will have peace while doing so, although the "Nations of
the earth will be at war." He said that "we may plead at the feet of
Magistrates and at the feet of Judges, at the feet of Governors and at
the feet of senators & at the feet of Pre[s]idents for 8 years it will be
of no avail. We shall find no favor in any of the courts of this
government." Smith told his people they would build a temple with
a great watchtower on top to know if the enemy was advancing "as a
thief in the night." God's servants would then be scattered abroad
to "wake up the Nations of the earth." Then "this Nation will be on
the very verge of crumbling to pieces and tumbling to the ground
and when the constitution is upon the brink of ruin this people will
be the Staff up[on] which the Nation shall lean and they shall bear
the constitution away from the very verge of destruction." Then the
Lord will call "all my servants who are the strength of the Lord's
house . . . [to] come to the Land of my vinyard and fight for the
Lord."[38]

In Martha Jane Coray's account of this discourse, there is no
indication against whom the servants of the Lord's house would fight.
Parley P. Pratt interpreted Smith to mean that when the government
of the United States had "come so near dessolation as to stand as it

were by a single hair," God's servants would gather for "the strength of the Lord's house 'a mighty army.' . . . And this is the redemption of Zion—when the Saints shall have redeemed that government and reinstated it in all its purity & glory." Pratt saw this military action as a way of gaining control of the government for its purification, whereas Coray's version of the speech does not convey that idea clearly since the resort to arms comes after redemption in her sequence.[40] In his account Pratt relished the idea that the Saints would be on the side of the Constitution and their enemies against it. He failed to perceive that a seizure of power by the Mormon elders through military means, however benign their intentions, might not ever be pleasing to the American people, whatever the circumstances.

Nauvoo had become a boom town by the time Joseph Smith returned from Washington, D.C., in the spring of 1840, but he was not especially satisfied with the progress. He had made heavy investments in land, and to keep the church solvent the lots had to be sold quickly to large numbers of Saints. Accordingly, Smith stressed upon his return that everyone should hurry to the gathering and build a temple where converts might worship during the final dispensation.[41] In June 1840, a new newspaper, the *Times and Seasons*, caught the booster spirit, proclaiming that "for immigration and growth, this place must assuredly take the lead of all other places that ever came under our observation." The editor affirmed with enthusiasm,

> We behold, amidst all these sceneries, the saints comfortably situated, with already about 250 houses put up by their own hands. . . . There has been . . . several commodious framed houses built; and several more now in lively operation. Also several large stone buildings now in contemplation to be erected this season, one of which is designed as a place of worship; also a large and splendid brick building, the foundation of which is already laid, intended for a public house. A saw mill has been erected here. . . . A grist and saw mill is now erecting upon an improved plan, to be carried by water power. . . . This place is bound, according to the common source of things, to become a great depot of commercial and mechanical operations.[42]

In January 1841, the editor observed that there were 3,000 inhabitants in the city, with more being added daily.[43] Many newcomers were immigrants from England, generally from the poorer classes.[44] By November even non-Mormons were impressed at how fast the city was growing. One visitor described how "several hundred new houses erected within the last few months attest to the passing traveller the energy, industry, and self-denial with which the community is imbued."[45] Another warned, however, that although the city contin- ued to grow in 1842, it was composed mostly of log huts and cabins, and insufficient land was under cultivation to feed the masses flock- ing to the area.[46]

As in Missouri, the rapid gathering saw Mormons squeezed into every corner of Hancock County[47] and into Lee County, Iowa. Grow- ing dissatisfaction among some non-Mormons followed. At Houston, as early as March 1840, a notice was tacked to the schoolhouse door warning "all those who claim the name Mormon" to "depart from this neighborhood." The Saints were told that their "false doctrines" were not wanted in the community and that hundreds were ready "to assist in ridding this part of the county of such vile trash."[48]

But such expressions of outright antagonism were rare and ineffectual.[49] What was more potent in spreading antipathy was the threat of the economic power of the kingdom. When Smith and sev- eral Elders journeyed fifteen miles south to the outskirts of Warsaw to survey a site for the town of Warren, there was increasing opposi- tion from businessmen and land speculators in the town. Those opposed were led by Thomas Sharp, editor of the *Warsaw Signal*, who maintained that the arrival of so many Mormons had prevented other capitalists from investing in the area.[50] According to an unnamed correspondent writing in 1844, Sharp "made himself the organ of a gang of town lot speculators . . . who are afraid that Nauvoo is about to kill off their town!"[51] Feelings were bitter when the citizens of Warsaw began charging high rents and inflated prices for commod- ities of the Mormons who had come to settle.[52] Smith had to cancel immigration to Warsaw for a time but remarked that "the first thing toward building up Warsaw was to break it down, to break down them that are there."[53] These intentions were not lost on the leading men of the city, including Calvin Warren to whom Smith made his remark. Soon Warren and the others were some of the most relentless ene- mies of the prophet and Saints.[54]

In Iowa in 1841 there was acute hostility to Mormon expansion. One of the Gentile leaders was David Kilbourne, town father, store owner, and land speculator at Montrose,[55] who protested in an Iowa newspaper that in March Alanson Ripley visited the town "with com- pass and chain and strided through gates and over fences to the very doors of the 'Gentiles' and drove stakes for lots of a city."[56] The antip- athy toward the Mormons became so intense that by the end of the year the Iowans were threatening to expel them by force.[57]

To add to these difficulties the Saints, as a result of their enduring hatred toward Missourians,[58] began organizing raids into Missouri. According to loyal Mormon Joel Hills Johnson, a "secret
combination" was formed to proclaim "that it was no harm to steal
from Missourians." Johnson said that a bishop, a councilor, four high
councilmen, and ten or twelve elders were involved.[59] Despite Joseph
Smith's denunciation of this group,[60] his brother Hyrum believed
they were still functioning as late as 1843.[61]

In early July 1840, some Missourians, led by a local sheriff,
Chauncey Durkee, retaliated by seizing four of the elders on the Illinois side of the river and forcibly taking them to Tully, a town in
Missouri twenty-eight miles south of Nauvoo. There the elders were
beaten, humiliated, and temporarily incarcerated. No legal extradition was sought from Illinois authorities.[62] Durkee maintained, nonetheless, that he was acting in an official capacity since the Mormons
were guilty of stealing.[63] Mormon leaders countercharged that the
Elders had been kidnapped and appealed to Governor Carlin of Illinois to take steps to bring the perpetrators to justice.[64]

In September Governor Lilburn Boggs of Missouri revived the
old charges of treason against Joseph Smith and demanded of Governor Carlin that Smith be returned to Missouri for trial.[65] The editor of the *Quincy Whig* said that Boggs's demand came as a direct
response to his being asked to turn the abductors of the elders in
the Tully affair over to Carlin.[66] Whether or not this was so, Smith
was determined not to be taken back to Missouri and sought ways to
legally prevent this. He sent John C. Bennett, Quartermaster General of Illinois and a new convert,[67] to the state capitol to secure an
act of incorporation for Nauvoo that would offer protection from
legal and military assaults by Missourians.[68]

Bennett and the Mormons were extraordinarily successful in
receiving a charter with unique powers.[69] Joseph Smith took an
expansive view of the power given him. "I concocted it for the salvation of the church," he said, "and on principles so broad, that every
honest man might dwell secure under its protective influence."[70]
Smith believed that the Nauvoo charter would provide a legal refuge for Mormons, with veto power to act independently of state and
national laws in certain situations. When he took steps to implement
his sweeping conception of Mormon rights, many Illinoisans were
outraged.

From the time of the Mormon arrival in Illinois, Whigs and Democrats both tried to win the Mormon vote,[71] and before many months

had passed the Saints, with their anti-plural tendencies, had committed themselves collectively to a single party and were once more
embroiled in political conflict.

As soon as Sidney Rigdon and the other elders had first begun
drifting into town, the editor of the *Quincy Whig* courted their favor,
affirming that "the whole proceedings towards this people by the
authorities of Missouri, must stand as a lasting stigma to the state."[72]
The editor reminded Mormons that the Missouri officials who had
caused them grief were Democrats and drew the logical moral:
"We . . . hope from the speciman that they have received of the lib-
erality and justice of *loco-focoism*, when carried out, as it has been by
the dominant party in Missouri—that they have come among us with
more enlightened opinions in regard to those *levelling and destroying*
doctrines so characteristic in Missouri." The Whig spokesman made
a strong appeal for support by reminding the Saints that the Whig
newspapers in Missouri had protested the violation of their rights.[73]

Not to be outdone, Quincy Democrats held a meeting in which
they offered material aid to the needy Saints.[74] The *Quincy Whig*
denounced this as a "queer" sort of meeting, led by a "little knot of
politicians," including the editor of the *Quincy Argus*, and fumed that
as part of the arrangement the Saints were expected to support the
Democratic party in the August election. The Whig editor said, "we
do hope that they [the Mormons] will stand aloof . . . treat all overtures from either part as an intrusion upon their rights."[75] The Whig
editor would recommend that the Saints remain neutral rather than
side with the Democrats.

The bantering between these party partisans continued in this
vein when the *Argus* charged that Governor Boggs was actually a
Whig.[76] The editor of the *Quincy Whig* countered by asserting that it
was the radical Democrats of Missouri who blocked any investigation by the state of the causes of the Mormon War.[77] Now the *Quincy
Argus* made a grandiose move for Mormon sympathy by urging that
Missouri be stricken from the union, but the *Whig* editor would not
be outdone and denounced the Democratic newspaper for its blatant efforts to gather Mormon votes.[78] At this point belligerent Lyman
Wight entered into the fray by declaring in the columns of the *Whig*
that the Democratic party led by Lilburn W. Boggs was responsible
for all the Mormons' troubles in Missouri.[79] A committee of five of
the elders chastised Wight for "presenting his political views to the
press in a manner derogatory to the church." Wight was told that he
was "closing up what public feeling there was manifested in our

favor."[80] But Wight was adamant and wrote to the *Quincy Whig* to lament that the Saints would not support him.[81] Joseph Smith tried to counter Wight's influence by writing to the Whig newspaper that politics was not an issue in Missouri: "it is not doing our cause justice to make a political question of it in any manner whatever. . . . We have not at any time thought that there was a political party as such, chargable with the Missouri barbarities."[82] Wight would still not heed council and wrote on 30 May that "the first Mob ever commenced upon us in the State of Missouri, was commenced by a gang of Ruffians with Moses G. Wilson at their head, and it is well known he is a Loco-Foco, and was supported in it by L. W. Boggs." Wight said it was the Democrat Boggs who issued the exterminating order.[83] No doubt Smith and the elders were right in trying to silence Wight, for up to this time both parties were inclined to be sympathetic. To make a party issue of what happened in Missouri would turn the Democrats against the Saints.

But Smith left for Washington, D.C., in 1840 where his experience in seeking redress for property losses in Missouri altered his thinking, and he returned embittered like Wight against the Democratic party. Smith told a congregation of Saints in Nauvoo in March 1840 that the Democrats would not have his support in the November elections. He observed afterward that his anti-Democratic convictions were shared by his people and that the "effect has been to turn the entire mass of people, even to an individual . . . on the other side of the political question."[84] A few days later Udney H. Jacob wrote to President Van Buren, the Democratic leader in Washington, that the Mormon prophet was determined to "throw his weight with all his followers against you."[85]

In commenting on the Mormon swing to the Whig party, Smith said that it did not hurt the Saints, "we have lost nothing by our change, but have gained friends and influence." He insisted that he was compelled to change in "consequence of seeing a disposition manifest to turn a deaf ear to the cries of suffering innocense."[86] According to Thomas Gregg, in March the prophet participated in a Whig political meeting at Carthage, demanding that Martin Hopkins be removed from the ticket and that John F. Charles be put in his place as a candidate for the state legislature. Charles was later influential in helping get the Nauvoo charter through the state assembly.[87]

But Smith sensed that his direct involvement in politics created resentment and told the Saints at April conference that "he did not wish to have any political influence." Despite this he also informed them that he "wished the Saints to use their political franchise to the best of their knowledge," thus making it clear that he did not actually want them to disregard his strong anti-Democratic feelings.[88] Prior to the county elections in August, the Saints held a political meeting of their own and agreed that they would "make their weight felt." It was affirmed in the caucus that "any man who would vote for Van Buren was a knave, a thief, a murderer and a robber."[89] When the August election returns came in for the county, it was evident that the Saints had reversed their party allegiances and voted strictly Whig.[90] The editor of the Democratic *Illinois State Register* commented on the vigorous part Smith had played in the election.[91]

In November Nauvoo gave William Henry Harrison and the Whigs a 410-vote majority.[92] With the Whigs conducting an effective log-cabin-and-hard-cider campaign and benefitting from the reaction to the panic of 1839, Harrison defeated Van Buren in the presidential election, although he did not take Illinois.[93] Ebenezer Robinson said of Van Buren's defeat that he "received a rebuke which will long be remembered by him and his supporters." Robinson said, "nothing short of the power of the great Jehovah could have produced such a change in the minds of the people."[94]

So long as Mormons remained in the Whig camp politically they were generally treated with consideration by the party press in the state.[95] Criticism of the church by the *Illinois State Register* was denounced by the Whig-controlled *Sangamo Journal* in Springfield as motivated by religious prejudice.[96] At times, in Iowa, where the Saints lacked a large block of voters, they were criticized by Whig newspapers.[97] But in Illinois the Saints lost what tolerance they had garnered from the Whigs when, following Van Buren's defeat, they began to gravitate once more toward the Democrats, a party with which they may have had a greater political affinity on a broad spectrum of issues.[98]

Joseph Smith initially acknowledged a possible rapprochement with the Democrats when he noted in December that party leaders had been helpful in securing the charter for Nauvoo, which granted "every power we asked."[99] When in June 1841 Judge Stephen A. Douglas, champion of western Democrats, declared in the circuit court of Warren County that the writ issued by Governor Carlin for Smith's arrest was defective,[100] even the Whigs began wondering if political winds were changing in Nauvoo.[101] In December their fears were confirmed. Smith told the Saints in the *Times and Seasons* that past loyalties had been to Harrison, not to the Whig party. Harrison, who passed away in April, is dead, Smith said, and "all his friends are not ours." Smith candidly confessed that "we care not a fig for the Whig or Democrat; they are both alike to us, but we shall go for our friends . . . and the cause of human liberty." He warned, "we are aware that 'divide and conquor' is the watchword with many, but with us it cannot be done." He made his intentions absolutely clear by saying, "Douglas is a master spirit," and "his friends are our friends—we are willing to cast our banners in the air, and fight by his side in the cause of humanity and equal rights." Smith said that Adam Snyder, the Democratic candidate for governor, and his running mate, Moore, were Douglas's friends "and they are ours. These men are free from prejudices and superstitions of the age, and such men we love, and such men will ever receive our support."[102]

Such political opportunism by Smith was not likely to win enduring friends among either party and threatened to leave the Saints politically isolated. As might be expected, Whig spokesmen who had been willing to give Mormons the benefit of a doubt on controversial issues now became bitter enemies. The editor of the *Quincy Whig* said of the prophet's public commitment to Stephen Douglas and friends: "this clannish principle of voting in a mass, at the dictation of one man who has acquired an influence over the minds of the people through a peculiar religious creed . . . is so repugnant to the principles of our Republican form of government, that its consequences and future effects will be disagreeable."[103] By switching parties for the second time in Illinois, Smith guaranteed that a block of influential critics would persistently denounce him and his people as politically menacing.[104] Only at election time would Whigs soften their attack,[105] hoping that the Saints might again switch their allegiances.

Most Democrats were pleased to have Mormons in the fold again, but not everyone was reassured. The editor of the *Quincy Herald* said he was uncertain as to what Smith's actual motives were, but if Smith intended his proclamation in the Mormon newspaper to be a "royal edict" binding upon all the Saints, then despite possible advantage to his party, he would agree with the *Quincy Whig* "that it is presumption in the extreme."[106] In Iowa the editor of the *Lee County Democrat* called Smith a "pretty cute fellow" for influencing his people's political allegiances so cavalierly.[107] The prophet had

made some important Democrats distrustful and incurred the enduring wrath of the Whigs, a party beginning to lose some support in
the state[108] and therefore all the more hostile.

While Mormons were moving toward political isolation in Illinois, they were also heading toward a quasi-independent status militarily. As part of the city charter the state legislature had granted
the right to organize a self-governing military body termed the
Nauvoo Legion, whose only tie to the rest of the state militia was that
both owed ultimate allegiance to the governor.[109] Stephen Douglas
informed Smith that in his opinion the elders owed service to no
other segment of the state militia.[110] The officers at Nauvoo, com-
prising a court martial, were empowered to enact any laws not repugnant to the constitutions of Illinois or the United States, with nothing explicitly stated as to their compliance to the laws made by the
legislatures of the state or nation.[111]

In February 1841, the legion was fully organized with its officers
choosing Smith as Lieutenant-General,[112] a choice that seemed natural enough at the time but made the prophet the focus of intense
fear and hatred among non-Mormons in Hancock County. Receiving his military commission in March, Smith assumed a role he had
been careful to avoid in Missouri. The result was that where Missourians did not always focus their hate on Joseph Smith personally,
Illinoisans did. A contributing factor was the unprecedented size of
the Mormon military force. Within six months enrollment in the
legion reached 1,450.[113]

In the Mormon mind the legion was to assist the Saints in fulfilling their prophetic destiny. Eliza R. Snow, a Mormon poetess and
eventual plural wife of Joseph Smith, stressed the peculiar mission
the legion would serve in the Mormon millennialist perspective. She
referred to the legion as "a phoenix," which "Missouri's oppressor's
laid low in the dust." Snow envisioned a "day of vexation" when these
"warriors" would stand as a "bulwark of Freedom." And, should they
falter, "there is still a reserve, a strong Cohort above; 'Lo! the chariots
of Israel and horsemen thereof.'"[114]

As historian Robert Flanders has shown, the legion played a
prominent role in social and ceremonial life in Nauvoo, taking part
in the major holidays and religious functions of the city.[115] Something of the pomp and enthusiasm with which the elders pursued
their military exercises is described by an eyewitness in the *Banner of
Peace*:

Joe Smith in splendid regimentals, in the character of lieuten-
ant general, as the head of a thousand troops. He was attended
by six of his principle officers on horseback, constituting the
front rank, as they moved. Directly in the rear were six ladies on
horseback, with black caps and feathers, constituting the second
rank and in the rear of these were two ranks of six each of body-
guards in white frocks with black belts. Joe carried a large tin
speaking trumpet, and uttered his prophecies through that
instead of giving his orders to his aids.[116]

Despite its showy, amateurish qualities, the legion seemed menacing to non-Mormons. In May, John Nevius, who lived at Bluff, Illinois, noted the fears of the community in a letter to a relative in
Pennsylvania. The Saints, he said,

are looked upon with a jealous eye, and that for the reason they
believe . . . they must and will take the world. And if they cannot
do it by preaching they will by the force of arms. They therefore
incorporate militerry tacticks with their religeion it is said they
train every saturday and are well disciplined . . . it is said they
take the liberty to tell the people that they now come with the
Bible in their hands but ere long they will come with a sword
also by their side.[117]

When Smith and John C. Bennett came to Iowa in September
and were treated with military honors by the marshalled elders, David
Kilbourne protested to the assembled men: "Citizens of Iowa: The
laws of Iowa do not require you to muster under, or be reviewed by
Joe Smith or General Bennett, and should they have the impudence
to attempt it, it is hoped that every person having respect for himself, will at once leave the ranks." Smith noted with satisfaction that
Kilbourne's protest had no effect.[118] But a prophet who combined
the rolls of land speculator, political boss, and commanding general of an independent militia invited the hostility of men like
Kilbourne, who were economic rivals and who feared the concentration of power in their opponent's hands. Within a few months the
press in Illinois and Iowa began to express apprehensions regarding Smith's activities. Thomas Sharp voiced a general feeling when
he warned that so long as Smith remained "near the sanctuary and
prophe[s]ies of religion he is guiltless of offense; but . . . when he
uses the religious influence he possesses, under the military garb he
has acquired, he becomes a dangerous man, and must look to the

consequences."[119] By assuming multiple routes to power, the Mormon prophet had taken a course that most Americans would resent and fear: the consolidation of power into the hands of a single man. Mormons were certain that their leader was inspired and that his power would bring good ends, but the American people, sired in the traditions of Jefferson and Madison, believed that men are more or less corrupt and not to be trusted with too much power. This distrust in time would swing the majority in the state against the Mormons and their leader and bring him and his brother, Hyrum, to the jail at Carthage.

In the face of their near disaster in Missouri, the Saints closed ranks when they reached Nauvoo and moved toward complete intellectual isolation and morality based exclusively on in-group values.[120] The trend was apparent when dissenters were blamed for all the Missouri mishaps[121] and the twelve apostles were told bluntly that no sin compared to "proving a traitor to the brethren."[122] Orson Spencer wrote that "compliance with the divine will is the only true standard of character,"[123] and John D. Lee was instructed that "no man could commit sin so long as he acted in the way that he was directed by his church superiors."[124] Among Mormons loyalty to priesthood was emerging as the paramount virtue. This loyalty was to be demonstrated by strict obedience to the ordinances which priesthood officers administered[125] and by a willingness to heed their council and to make any sacrifice they requested to build the kingdom of God.[126]

New powers granted to the priesthood were instruments of group cohesion. Smith announced in the summer of 1840 that the leading elders had been given authority to baptize vicariously for the dead, so that the Saints' ancestors might comply with gospel standards[127] and the elect be fused into a "whole and complete, and perfect union."[128] Later, in 1842, Smith declared that the keys had been restored whereby priesthood leaders could "seal" family members on earth and the ordinance would be confirmed in heaven.[129] Through the sealing power the elders would have the opportunity of "adoption," as well. Smith said in 1844 that "the doctrine of sealing of Elijah is as follows: The first thing you do, go and seal on earth your sons and daughters to yourself, and yourself unto your fathers in eternal glory, and go-ahead, and not go back, but use a little craftyness, and seal all you can and when you get to heaven, tell your Father that what you seal on earth should be sealed in heaven, according to his promise."[130] It was thought that the larger one's family—through bearing children, taking additional wives, or adoption—the greater one's kingdom and glory in the hereafter.[131]

J. W. Gunnison, who came to Utah in the 1850s and observed Mormon institutions closely, said that adoption also "consists in taking whole families and adopting them as part and parcel of the family chief."[132] But Heber Kimball indicated that many Saints were hesitant to embrace the new doctrine. "When any seemed disposed to enlarge their kingdom and godhead the old women and young women run with their old kettles & pans & cow Bells to drown the sound of their leaders and throw the saints into confusion and keep them shut up in their old traditions."[133] In July 1845, Orson Hyde attempted to overcome this reluctance by urging some Saints in Iowa to "give him a pledge to come into his kingdom when the ordinances could be attended to, but wished all to select a man whom they chose."[134] William Smith said that Brigham Young had all the seventies sealed to him before they left Nauvoo.[135] Parley Pratt said in the *Millennial Star* that in the celestial kingdom there would be a "gradation" which will "descend in regular degrees from the throne of the Ancient of Days with his innumerable subjects, down to the least and last Saint . . . who may be worthy of a throne and septre, although his kingdom may, perhaps, consist of a wife and a single child."[136]

The goal of the Saints was to become gods. Joseph Smith told his flock in 1844, "You have to learn to be gods yourselves, and to be kings and priests to gods, the same as all gods before you, namely by going from one small degree to another."[137] The prophet admitted William Clayton and others into an inner prayer circle where washings and anointings were administered, ordinances later performed in the temple.[138] Some were even given second anointings whereby their "calling and election" was confirmed and they were pronounced kings, priests, and gods.[139] The highest orders of salvation were thus institutionalized and governed by priesthood authority, setting the Mormons apart from evangelical Protestants, who valued first one's personal relationship to God.

The most controversial means of adding to one's kingdom was plural marriage. By 1841 Smith had begun adding additional wives to his household and introducing the concept to some of his most trusted followers.[140] Orson Pratt later justified this innovation by saying that "a man's posterity, in the eternal worlds, are to constitute his glory, his kingdom and dominion." The more wives, the more posterity. Pratt told the Saints that the Lord "intends to make them a kingdom of Kings and Priests, a Kingdom unto himself, or in other words, a Kingdom of Gods, if they will hearken unto his law" of "celestial marriage."[141] Smith promised Sarah Ann Whitney, one of his plural wives, that if she remained within the "new and everlasting covenant" of marriage until the end, she and her father's house "shall be saved in the same eternal glory," and even if they should wander from the fold they could still repent and "be crowned with a fulness of glory."[142] Smith told William Clayton that "nothing but the unpardonable sin [of shedding innocent blood] could prevent him . . . from inheriting eternal glory for he is sealed up by the power of the priesthood unto eternal life having taken the step that is necessary for that purpose." Clayton had just entered into a plural marriage relationship.[143]

Initially only a few of the Saints were introduced to the new order.[144] Many were strongly opposed, even though a small faction had been secretly encouraging the practice.[145] Mrs. Joseph Horne remembered that "the brethren and sisters were so averse to polygamy that it could hardly be mentioned."[146] When Benjamin Johnson heard that Smith wanted his sister he told the prophet "as the Lord lives" Johnson would kill him if his sister was degraded.[147] When Brigham Young learned of polygamy "it was the first time in my life that I desired the grave, and could hardly get over it for a long time."[148] Hyrum Smith told the elders in 1843 that "if an angel from heaven should come and preach such doctrine some would be sure to see his cloven foot & a cloud of blackness over his head."[149] John Taylor said that when Smith made plural marriage known to him, Orson Hyde, Heber Kimball, and others, they "were in no great hurry to enter into it."[150] Helen Mar Whitney, Kimball's daughter, added that when Smith commanded her father to take a second wife "if it had been his death sentence he could not have felt worse."[151] Don Carlos Smith, the younger brother of Joseph Smith, also opposed polygamy, saying that any man "who will teach and practice the doctrine . . . will go to hell, I don't care if it is my brother Joseph."[152]

For many women plural marriage was a severe trial. Phoebe Woodruff wrote, "I opposed it to the best of my ability until I became sick and wretched."[153] Mrs. Eliza Maria Partridge Lyman, sealed to Smith in 1843, said that it "was truly a trial for me."[154] Orson Hyde's third wife said, "I resisted it with every argument I could command, for with my tradition, it was most repulsive."[155] When Lucy Kimball was informed that Smith wanted her, she recalled, "I was tempted and tortured beyond endurance until life was not desirable."[156]

Catherine Lewis heard one of Smith's wives say that she supposed plurality was necessary, but she would "rather that *her kingdom* were small."[157] Joseph Fielding, a devout elder, said that he was anxious to do "the will of the God and obtain all the glory I can" but admitted later that "it appears in general to have given great offence to the [first] wife, in some instances their Anger and Resentment have risen to a very high pitch saying it is an abomination." Fielding observed "this is a strong Charge against Joseph especially."[158]

When the John C. Bennett scandal erupted in the summer of 1842, plural marriage was brought into the open for Mormons and non-Mormons alike, although it was still officially denied by church leaders. Bennett was mayor of Nauvoo, a general in the legion, and a self-advertised physician.[159] Oliver Olney recorded that Bennett had been "for months . . . in clover up to his ears in women that think they have ben abused by their husbands."[160] Smith became alarmed when he learned that his name was being used by Bennett to solicit sexual favors. He wrote to the women of the Nauvoo Female Relief Society in mid-April to beware of a "man who may be aspiring after power and authority, and yet without principle." The sisters were not to be imposed upon "by believing such men, because they say they have authority from Joseph, or the First Presidency." Smith said, "We do not want any one to believe anything as coming from us, contrary to the old established morals and virtues," even though "such principles be taught by lord-mayors, generals, . . . elders priests or the devil, [they] are alike culpable and shall be damned."[161]

In May a crisis arose when Smith learned that increasing numbers were being misled and indulging in sexual experimentation outside of plural marriage. According to Smith's history Bennett was confronted and forced to resign as mayor on 19 May, "because his whoredoms and abominations were fast coming to light."[162] More reliable sources show that Smith was not yet ready for a showdown on this date and that he gave Bennett permission to leave the church without recrimination on the 17th. On the 19th the city council gave Bennett a vote of thanks "for having good & wholesome laws adopted." Bennett was told that he had performed the "faithful discharge of his duty."[163] Fearing retaliation, Smith hoped to avoid an open break with Bennett.

On the 23rd, however, Chauncey Higbee was cut off from the church for unchaste conduct and for teaching that it was right if kept secret.[164] Two days later Mrs. Catherine Warren was charged by the Nauvoo high council with having sexual relations with Bennett, and she testified at her hearing that several Saints had taught her that plural relations were right and that the heads of the church sanctioned them.[165] At this point, with rumors flying, any hope of keeping the issue under wraps had become remote. In a last desperate effort to quiet Bennett, Smith met with him and about one hundred elders on the 26th to hear his confession and earnest pleadings not to be publicized. Smith asked the group to show Bennett mercy.[166] But recurring exposures of sexual misconduct and rising feelings against him in the Mormon community forced the ex-mayor to flee the city.[167]

Within two weeks polygamy among the Mormons had become a national scandal, as Bennett published charges that Smith had been involved with Nancy Rigdon, Sidney Rigdon's daughter, and also with Sarah Pratt, the wife of Apostle Orson Pratt.[168] Smith published counter-charges against Bennett, who evidently had a wife in Ohio at the time of his amorous affairs in Nauvoo, as well as against Sarah Pratt and Nancy Rigdon.[169] Embarrassed by all of this, even the loyal Joseph Fielding now concluded that the "Lord had pushed things forward rather prematurely."[170]

The Mormon churches in Philadelphia were torn apart by plurality, with bitter conflict occurring between missionary Benjamin Winchester and others, including William Smith. Winchester, who would be scolded by the prophet, soon left the church over the issue.[171]

One of the major casualties over the plurality doctrine was Orson Pratt. The *Alton Telegraph* noted on 23 July that Pratt had fled Nauvoo, leaving behind a note which revealed that the apostle was devastated by reports that Smith had made advances toward his wife. Pratt wrote: "I am a ruined man. My future prospects are blasted. The testimony seems to be equal. . . . my sorrows are greater than I can bear." Pratt lamented that if Smith's testimony was correct, then his family life was ruined, but if Sarah's version was correct, then fourteen years of work in the church had been wasted.[172]

Oliver Olney added a dimension to Pratt's torment not touched on in the note. Olney observed that it was openly discussed in Nauvoo how Bennett was at the Pratt home at night while Orson was away. But Sarah charged that Smith had "used the name of the Lord to seduce her several times. In company she declares it to be a fact." Olney said that some in Nauvoo still held that Sarah was a "respectable lady," but "others say not."[173] Brigham Young recorded in his history that he spent several days laboring with Pratt "whose mind became so darkened by the influence and statements of his wife, that he came out in rebellion against Joseph, refusing to believe his testimony or obey his council. Joseph told him if he did believe his wife and followed her suggestions he would go to hell." Pratt refused at church meetings to acknowledge that Smith was "good, moral, virtuous and patriotic."[174]

Pratt was suspended from the Quorum of the Twelve Apostles on 20 August, but several months later, in January, returned and "repented in dust and ashes." At the council of the twelve meeting where Pratt was restored to his apostleship, Brigham Young said that Orson's only fault was that "he loved his wife better than David." Smith told Pratt that Sarah "lied about me—I never made the offer she said I did." He suggested that Pratt might consider getting a new wife, "marry a virtuous woman—and sire a new family that if you do not do it she'll ever throw it in your teeth." Sarah was also rebaptized but remained bitter with regard to this matter for the rest of her life.[175]

Smith's own wife, Emma, was another casualty of the new order. The story of her troubles over plural marriage is well known,[176] but it is worth noting again that at one point she came close to leaving Joseph,[177] fluctuating between grudging acceptance and bitter and at times hysterical opposition.[178] Determined to preserve his plural marriages, Smith at one point told Emma that he would give them up entirely only to confess to William Clayton that he had no such intention.[179]

Emma's continued opposition forced Smith to justify plurality to her and to certain elders. He presented Emma with a revelation which affirmed that "all covenants, contracts, bonds, obligations, oaths, vows . . . connections, associations . . . that are not made and entered into and sealed by the Holy Spirit of promise, of him who is anointed . . . are of no efficacy, virtue, or force in or after the resurrection from the dead; for all contracts that are not made unto this end have an end when men are dead." He warned that "those who have this law revealed to them must obey the same" or "be damned."[180] Whoever refused would be "ministering angels to minister to those who are worthy of a far more, and an exceeding weight of glory." The prophet promised, "If a man marry a wife according to my word, and they are sealed by the Holy Spirit of promise . . . and he or she shall commit any sin or transgression of the new and ever-lasting covenant, and all manner of blasphemies, and if they commit no murder wherein they shed innocent blood, yet they shall

come forth in the first resurrection, and enter into their exaltation."
By assuring Emma that her salvation would be virtually certain and
all but the unpardonable sin would be merely visited "with judgment in the flesh," Smith placed enormous pressure on his reluctant wife to accept plural marriage. But according to William Clayton,
for the moment she "said she did not believe a word of it and
appeared very rebellious."[181]

The Bennett affair raised new questions in the minds of some
Illinoisans as to the moral situation at Nauvoo. The scandal had developed on the eve of the 1842 election, and the *Sangamo Journal* made
the most of it by publishing Bennett's allegations.[182] At Quincy in
July the editor of the *Whig* first accepted Smith's charges that Bennett
had seduced married women in Smith's name, but within a week he
was beginning to suspect that where there was smoke there was also
fire. When Bennett published his accusation in book-form, the editor said despite Bennett's dubious character he had presented substantial evidence.[183] The same month Abraham Lincoln wrote from
Springfield that Bennett's "disclosures are making some stir here
but not very great."[184] The editor of the *Hawk-Eye and Iowa Patriot* in
September cited the *New York Journal of Commerce*'s evaluation of
Bennett's lectures on the topic, saying that Bennett "tells his stories
with a leer and a laugh, occasionally, which showed the lecturer's
mind was in a vulgar and debased condition and totally destitute of
that stern disapprobation of crime that should characterize a
reformer." The editor said, "We do not think the Gen. carried any
very strong conviction to the minds of his audience, that what he
said was conclusive evidence of the real state of things at
Nauvoo."[185]

The editor of the *Missouri Republican* commented in October
that the book was "not chaste" and that "much of it the young should
not read." He said that he did not accept it at face value, yet he could
not discount all of it either.[186] At Peoria an editor wrote in January
that the court house was packed to hear Bennett, and that "the general belief is that he [Bennett] told the truth."[187]

Despite this mixed reaction by the public, Mormon missionaries and church officials reported that the church was hurt. Robert D.
Foster wrote to Smith from New York on 16 July 1842 that "many have
been the interrogations prepounded to me respecting yourself family Church &c. &c." Foster reassured Smith that while Bennett had
found many voteries, "they are mostly birdes of the same feather viz.

(blackbirds)." He said, "The effects upon the respectable community is equal to the effects of water upon the gooses back."[188] But
John E. Page reported at Pittsburgh on 8 August that "the disclosures of Bennett has done much to injure the cause here the people
are enxiously looking for the fully and effectual downfall of
Mormonism." Page urged Smith to respond to put down Bennett's
influence. On the 15th Page told Smith that the "elders abroad are
the sufferers" and pleaded for evidence to counter accusations.[189]
Smith published affidavits impugning Bennett's character which cast
some doubt on his veracity in Illinois and elsewhere.[190] At Carthage, however, Thomas C. Sharp took Bennett's allegations at full value
and began a periodic harangue against Smith in his *Warsaw Signal.*[191]

For a time, in response to the criticism in local and national
press due to Bennett's allegations, Smith entertained the idea of finding refuge further west. Oliver Olney learned of this and wrote him
a letter dated 20 July 1842 from Quincy. He inquired, "They say with
your numerous wifes and maidens you are about to start west as far
as the Rocky Mountains where you will raise up a Righteous Branch
without being molested by the Laws of the Land." Olney later noted
that the Saints "are fast a fixing to go West where they can live in
peace without being molested By the laws of the land. They say soon
to start If what I hear is correct as far West as Origen Territory and
establish a stake of Zion." But Willard Richards indicated in a letter
to James Arlington Bennett of New York, written in November, that
the Saints desired to go no further west unless compelled, so that by
the latter date they felt reasonably certain that they had weathered
the storm stirred by Bennett.[192]

Nonetheless, the conflicts within and without the church over
plural marriage were not over, and the issue placed many within
the inner circle in a terrible moral dilemma. Divine revelation
informed them that to achieve the highest glory in the next life they
had to accept and live the principle, yet they could not openly advocate it or even admit to it, except to a few within their own group. To
the non-Mormon world they continued to publish strong denials.[193]
Only by this means could the rising protest be abated and the kingdom preserved. Mormons were left in a morally ambivalent situation, with many believing the published denials, and others, better
informed, aware that the denials were a subterfuge. For some this
created a trauma they could not endure, and they left the church.
One church member who deplored the apparent duplicity was Sarah

Scott. She wrote to her parents in Massachusetts in 1844 that the doctrines of plurality of gods and wives and of unconditional sealing to salvation had been taught secretly in the church for two years despite emphatic denials. She could only remark, "Cursed is he that putteth his trust in men." For some the full culmination came in the summer of 1843, when Hyrum Smith read the revelation on plural marriage to a select group of high councilmen. Many were fiercely opposed. Soon these men and others began to hold secret meetings and to preach that Smith was a fallen prophet.[194]

In addition to these difficulties, the Saints had drifted into a precarious situation politically in 1842. With an election coming and Mormons having switched their allegiance to the Democrats, the Whigs and their gubernatorial candidate, Joseph Duncan, hammered at them, drawing attention to the unusual power concentrated in the hands of the prophet and to the scandal associated with John Bennett.[195] Duncan especially denounced Smith for his public commitment to Douglas and the Democrats:

> Joe Smith, as LIEUTENANT GENERAL of the Nauvoo Legion, *commanding* his followers to vote for this or that candidate, is too bold a stride toward despotism ever to be long countenanced by a free and intelligent people . . . it ill becomes Joseph Smith professing obedience to our laws, and asking our protection, not only towards himself but his people . . . to issue [a proclamation] both in his *spiritual* and military capacity, commanding his followers to vote as he shall direct.[196]

The editor of the *Telegraph* noted that the Saints had nominated a full ticket of county officers of their denomination and warned that "they intend either to rule or ruin."[197] Duncan now demanded that the Nauvoo charter be repealed and made this the main object of his campaign oratory.[198] The Democrats handled the Mormon question more gingerly, accusing the Whigs of stirring religious prejudice.[199] But in July, during the heat of the election struggle, Thomas Ford, newly named Democratic candidate replacing the deceased Adam Snyder, moved to undercut Duncan's advantage by also demanding that the charter for the Mormon city be repealed.[200] This was a shrewd maneuver[201] and gave Ford enough of a margin that the Mormon vote was of no statewide significance when he won the election.[202] Ford was now free to act on his campaign pledge if he chose. Thus the Mormon tactic of voting en bloc to gain a statewide balance of power had been thwarted.[203] The disgruntled editor of

the *Alton Telegraph*, whose party had lost the election, took the opportunity to hit at the Mormons again:

> It will open the eyes of all parties to the dangerous and
> antirepublican tendency of a political, religious and military
> band of men, organized in our midst, and trained to obey the
> will and dictation of one man—to vote according to his resent-
> ments and prejudices—to sacrifice their own honest convictions
> of right and duty at the beck and nod of a petty dictator.[204]

In time others in addition to the Whigs would agree with the editor
of the *Telegraph*. The gubernatorial election of 1842 foreshadowed
things to come.

On 8 August, immediately after the election, Smith was arrested
on a charge of being an accessory to the recent attempted murder of
former Governor Boggs of Missouri.[205] But the deputy sheriff was
unable to apprehend Smith, as he was quickly presented with a writ
from the municipal court of Nauvoo demanding that Smith be
brought before its chambers for a ruling on the impending
arrest.[206] The next day the city council passed an ill-advised law which
affirmed that it had full right to review the merits of every arrest
within its jurisdiction and to release under a writ of habeas corpus
any prisoner held on charges originating out of "private pique, mali-
cious intent, or religious or other persecution."[207] In November city
fathers passed another ordinance threatening indefinite confine-
ment without bail to any public official who refused to heed the
court's writ.[208]

In the meantime Smith went into hiding, refusing to be taken
again to Missouri where he feared for his life.[209] But this attempt to
thwart legal process was deeply resented in Illinois. Tom Sharp wrote
indignantly in the *Warsaw Signal*, "What think you of this barefaced
defiance of our laws by the city council of Nauvoo, and if persisted
in what must be the final result?" Sharp predicted that soon every
criminal in the area would seek asylum in the Mormon city.[210]

The editor of the *Sangamo Journal*, in Springfield, raised a similar question when he published a letter by John Bennett alleging
that Smith "designs to abolish all human law and establish a Theocracy in which the word of God . . . shall be the only law; and he now
orders that his followers shall only obey such laws as they are compelled to do."[211] Even Governor Carlin was concerned about the question of Mormon exemption from legal process. He wrote to Emma
Smith a month later that he did not believe the state legislature

intended to grant Nauvoo a right to release prisoners held under writs issued by state courts. The actions of the Nauvoo city council, he fumed, are a "gross usurpation of power that cannot be tolerated."[212] In his inaugural address in December he asked the state legislature to repeal the Mormon city and agricultural charters, observing that the people are "aroused" and "anxiously desire that these charters should be modified so as to give the inhabitants of Nauvoo no greater privilege than those enjoyed by others of our fellow citizens."[213]

The question of the repeal of the Nauvoo charters now became embroiled in an ongoing conflict with Quincy and other rural towns in western Illinois. A demand was made in the legislature that the charters of several such towns be abrogated,[214] thus shifting the focus for the moment away from the Mormons. Two charges leveled against Mormons were the menace of their legion and the misuse of habeas corpus.[215] In the legislature William Smith took the position that repeal was a threat to property rights.[216] The issue was decided when several Whigs voted against repeal, preferring to amend Mormon powers rather than abolish them.[217] The vote in the senate was 22 against repeal and 13 in favor.[218] It was a narrow escape for the Mormons, with five votes making the difference. But the matter of special exemption from legal process had occasioned the first general opposition to Mormons in the state and played into the hands of a small but outspoken group of anti-Mormons in Hancock County who were determined to curb Mormon power one way or another.

This group was led by Thomas Sharp, who had come to Hancock County in September 1840 from New York where he had been a Whig, active in the anti-Masonic movement. At twenty-three he was young and ambitious and had switched to the Democrats in Illinois in time to become a leader in the anti-Mormon movement in the county.[219] By mid-1841 Sharp had purchased the *Western World*, published at Warsaw, and begun directing his editorials against the Saints. On 9 June he explained his reasons, warning that there was every indication that the Mormons intended becoming a "political church." If this is not so, he asked,

> why is it that General Bennett told us that they designed always to make their power felt at the ballot box? Why is it that when a highly respectable citizen remarked that the Mormons would soon have a majority in this county, D[on] C[arlos] Smith ... replied that "the country would be *safe* in their hands?" Why is

it that a proclamation is made by the Prophet just at this time calling in all the "saints abroad" to settle in that county? Why is it that the Mormons have, in all former contests, uniformly voted as one man in favor of the candidate of Joseph Smith's choice?

Whatever is thought of their present strength, it is certain that if not checked in another year, they will have the decided majority in this county. . . . Now we ask the citizens of Hancock County, are you prepared for this? Are you prepared to see one man control your affairs? Are you prepared to see the important offices of sheriff and county commissioner selected by an unparalleled knave, and thus have power to select your jurymen, who are to sit and try our rights to life, liberty, and property? . . . Ask yourselves what means this array of military force which is paraded under the direction of this church. Is an army necessary to propagate religion? Is it necessary to protect their civil rights?[220]

Responding to this rhetoric, which gave voice to their own, innate fears, the old citizens met on 19 June at Warsaw to elect delegates to an anti-Mormon convention, and on 28 June they chose a slate of candidates for county office. They pledged at this time that they would "lay aside former party feelings and oppose, as independent freedmen, political and military Mormonism."[221] Their effort proved initially successful for Sharp announced in the *Warsaw Signal* on 25 August that its candidates had won the elections for county and school commissioners, although the vote was close.[222]

So long as Sharp remained editor of the *Signal*, he continued to attack various dimensions of the Mormon kingdom, warning of the Saints' intentions to occupy Warren,[223] cautioning Smith that excessive political ambition could be dangerous,[224] and detailing the vagaries of "spiritual wifery."[225] He was especially angry at the alleged Mormon manipulation of the processes of the law.[226] But despite these efforts to maintain a solid front against the Saints in preparation for the election of 1842, he was outmaneuvered by Smith, who appealed to the uncommitted in the county[227] and with a "mongrel ticket" of Mormons and non-Mormons carried all the county offices.[228] After this Sharp was unable to pay his publishing costs and was forced to sell the *Signal* to Thomas Gregg at the end of the year.[229] Smith had won the first round, but preserving the loyalty of the uncommitted and those who joined with him out of political ambition was difficult, and in time risky. One of the politicos who went along with the prophet at this time was Mark Aldrich, who later came to doubt the political advantage of siding with the Mormons and became a bitter anti-Mormon who would be indicted for Smith's murder.[230]

Meanwhile, Mormons moved to have tested in a federal court the validity of Governor Carlin's writ. Their efforts were rewarded when Pope, a Whig judge, declared the writ void since Smith had not fled Missouri to escape punishment for the abortive effort on Boggs's life.[231] Mormons were pleased at the results, but some of the citizens at Carthage, and elsewhere, viewed with alarm Smith's apparent immunity from legal prosecution. William Weston wrote to his brother at Rockville that although Smith had a reward of $400 on his head, "we cannot bring him or any of his crew to justice for any of these iniquit[ie]s without fighting."[232] The fear would continue to grow inside the county that Mormons were not subject to the same law as the rest of the population. Such unique privilege seemed particularly undemocratic to many, and one editor warned the prophet this early that a day of reckoning would come.[233]

Furthermore, with both political parties still unusually anxious as to whither Mormon political support was tending, the Pope decision naturally caused a stir. The *Quincy Herald*, a Democratic journal, promptly labeled the affair a Whig effort to gather Mormon votes, while the *Warsaw Message*, a Whig supporter, saw the decision as judicious.[234] Governor Ford may have feared these developments, urging Smith personally to "refrain from all political electioneering." Smith replied, diplomatically, that he had "always acted upon that principle."[235] The Mormon leader may indeed have intended to retire from the political arena, for he informed the church in January that "it would be well for politicians to regulate their own affairs. I wish to be let alone, that I may attend strictly to the spiritual welfare of the church."[236] However, the prophet's sense of destiny was still as much concerned with the acquisition of political power as, in fact, with the fulfillment of prophecy, and he would not refrain from using this means to advance the kingdom. Seeking to gain social control over the divisive and secular elements in American society, he believed that this could only be achieved through political power. He plainly affirmed his intentions a month after his pledge to Ford, telling the Saints, "Tis right, politically, for a man who has influence to use it, as well as for a man who has no influence to use his. From henceforth I will maintain all the influence I can get. In relation to politics I will speak as a man; but in relation to religion I will speak in authority."[237] Yet the kingdom was organized to blur all distinctions between secular and religious, politics and the parish, and the

Saints assumed that what the prophet said was God's will, whatever
the subject matter. By announcing that he would build the kingdom
through political power, Smith stirred an automatic reaction by non-
Mormons who believed in pluralism. Non-Mormons would work with
as much conviction as the Saints, but to thwart the prophet's quest.
These Gentiles had a much larger constituency upon which they
could ultimately depend for support.

CHAPTER 7

Appeal to a "Higher Power"

The middle years of the Mormon sojourn in Illinois were ones of rapid growth and expansion as converts from the eastern states and England swarmed into the bustling city of Nauvoo.[1] But with this growth came familiar economic problems.[2] As early as March 1840, Joseph Smith had determined to abandon the impractical Law of Consecration,[3] and increasingly afterward he and the other leaders hoped and planned for a more diversified and self sufficient economy.[4] But providing the city with a stable business life was a formidable task, one that the Saints would not fully master before their exodus in 1846.[5]

From the first, land speculation and housing construction were, as in Kirtland, important enterprises because of the incoming converts.[6] Many of the immigrants were impoverished upon arrival and had no cash to buy land or housing. The per capita wealth was depressed by their coming.[7] Currency was chronically lacking, making trade by barter and payment in kind common.[8] Hanna Ford commented in February 1844 that despite the scarcity of hard money, supplies in the city were generally plentiful.[9]

Drawn into the gospel net was a host of skilled craftsmen—textile workers, bootmakers, and cabinet and carriage makers—who clamored for industrialization.[10] Church leaders responded by gaining a charter from the legislature to incorporate the "Nauvoo Agricultural and Mechanical Association," an institution for pooling Mormon resources to manufacture flour and produce lumber and other needed commodities.[11] At a trade meeting in November 1844, Brigham Young and others spoke of the need for independence by manufacturing everything they would require.[12] But the Saints were reluctant to invest in these new enterprises,[13] so that through 1844 leaders were still searching for ways to promote them.[14] Successful industries were those of the small craft and home variety—a steam mill, grist mill, match factory and leather works, bakery, meat-packing plant, brick yards, and others.[15] There is no evidence in the non-Mormon newspapers that these businesses competed successfully outside Nauvoo.[16]

Due to the dearth of coin and the inability to produce profitable exports, prices were generally high in Nauvoo. David Jenkins reported in September 1841 that staples cost more than in eastern cities, with coffee, sugar, muslin, and calicoes nearly double in price. Woodwork, including bedsteads, tables, chairs, and other household goods were also high.[17] People were still complaining of high prices in 1843, and John Taylor admitted that prices were 25-50 percent higher than elsewhere.[18] A few determined to relieve the money shortage by providing an imitation variety,[19] but when this found its way into non-Mormon hands, the general distrust of the community was increased.[20]

By the summer of 1844 the Nauvoo economy was hurting. The editor of the *Missouri Republican*, who visited in July, said that there were but a few workshops or "manufactories" and that provisions were scarce.[21] Sidney Rigdon indicated that there were more houses available than buyers and that building trades were therefore languishing.[22] Many had to leave the city to find employment elsewhere.[23] Despite this, leaders tried to maintain an optimistic front in their correspondence.[24] But even boosters such as Orson Spencer had to admit that many were impoverished among them.[25] As Rigdon observed, from an economic standpoint the Saints were in need of the good will of non-Mormons,[26] but their activities associated with the kingdom tended repeatedly to alienate them from their neighbors.

A turning point in Mormon-non-Mormon relations in Illinois came in June 1843 after events at Dixon and the legal and political maneuverings that followed. When Joseph and Emma Smith visited Emma's sister near Dixon, Illinois, nearly two hundred miles east of Nauvoo, Joseph was taken into custody by two deputies, Reynolds from Missouri and Wilson from Carthage, under an extradition order issued by Governor Thomas Ford.[27] The state of Missouri, with encouragement from renegade Mormon leader John C. Bennett, sought Smith for alleged involvement with Orrin Porter Rockwell in the attempted murder of Lilburn W. Boggs.[28] After suffering abuse and insults from the deputies and being denied legal council for a time,[29] Smith succeeded in contacting Cyrus Walker, a leading lawyer and candidate for congress on the Whig ticket. To secure Walker's legal assistance, Smith pledged that he would vote for him.[30] According to his official history, Smith only committed his personal vote, but Walker understood otherwise since the Saints had followed the lead of their leader unanimously in other elections.[31]

Walker secured writs against the deputies for threatening Smith's life and placed them in the custody of the sheriff of Lee County.[32] But in the meantime word had reached Nauvoo of the arrest of the Mormon leader, and 170 members of the Nauvoo Legion hurried to Monmouth, where they expected to prevent the deputies from taking him into Missouri.[33] Smith had instructed Major General Wilson Law as early as August 1842 that "if I by any means should be taken [into custody by Missourians] these [orders] are to command you forthwith, without delay, regardless of life or death, to rescue me out of their hands."[34] Smith was convinced that a return to Missouri would place his life in jeopardy.

The deputies charged upon reaching Nauvoo that they had been taken there by force,[35] although they were well treated and dined at the prophet's table.[36] The incident caused alarm in the press,[37] so that Governor Ford sent Mason Brayman as a special representative to Nauvoo to learn the truth about the charges. He concluded that the legioneers had exerted no overt force themselves but that the sheriff of Lee County had done so.[38]

In a court presided over by friends at Nauvoo Smith was released from custody.[39] But the editor of the *Quincy Herald* wrote that if it was true that two hundred armed Mormons had effected the release of Smith "it is high time that the laws were most rigidly enforced, without respect to persons."[40]

Jubilant that their prophet had been rescued, the whole town of Nauvoo turned out to welcome his return.[41] Shaken by his encounter with the Missouri deputy, Smith promised a crowd that in the future he might appeal to a higher law: "If our enemies are determined to oppress us & deprive us of our rights & privileges as they have done & if the Authorities that be on the earth will not assist us in our rights nor give us that protection which the Laws & Constitution of the United States & of this State garrentees unto us: then we will claim them from higher power from heaven & from God Almighty." Smith said with respect to the deputies who had taken him into custody: "I SWEAR I will not deal so mildly with them again for the time has come when forbearance is no longer a virtue. And if you are again taken unlawfully you are at liberty to give loose to Blood and Thunder. But act with Almighty Power."

Much in the spirit of Sidney Rigdon's 4th of July address in Missouri Smith warned his enemies still further:

> the time has come when their shall be such a flocking to the standard of Liberty as never has been Nor never shall be hereafter. . . . Shall the Prophecys be established by the Sword? Shall we always bear? NO. Will not the State of Missouri stay her hand and in her unhallowed persecutions against the Saints? If not, I restrain you not any longer. I say in the name of Jesus Christ I this day turn the key that opens the heavens to restrain you no longer from this time forth. I will lead you to battle & if you are not afraid to die & feel disposed to spill your Blood in your own defence you will not offend me. Be not the aggressor. Bear untill they strike on the one cheeck. Offer the other & they will be sure to strike that. Then defend yourselves & God shall bear you off. Will any part of Illinois say we shall not have our rights? Treat them as strangers & not friends & let them go to Hell.

Smith believed that the Nauvoo charters were part of his guaranteed rights:

> If I [am] under the necessity of giving up our chart[er]ed rights, privileges and freedom . . . I will do it at the point of the Bayonet & Sword. . . . Lawyiers say that the powers of the Nauvoo Charter are dangerous. But I ask is the constitution of the United States or of this State dangerous. No. Neither are the charters granted unto Nauvoo by the legislator[s] of Illinois dangerous, & those that say they are fools. . . . If mobs come upon you any more here, dung your gardings with them.

The prophet concluded on a revolutionary note, saying "We will rise up Washington like & break of[f] the wait [weight] that bears us down & we will not be mob[b]ed."[42]

The threat of an appeal to arms by the prophet was matched in August by a similar declaration from Missouri. J. Hall wrote from Independence, "If Illinois by her own authority cannot capture the prophet, it will be but a small matter to raise volunteers enough here to raze the city of Nauvoo to the ground." Hall asserted that he had it from high authority in his state that "Missouri will hold the whole state [of Illinois] responsible for the treatment of our messenger and the delivery of the prophet."[43]

Smith feared additional attempts to take him into Missouri, and the city council passed a law on 29 June requiring newcomers to the city to give their names, former residence, and purpose. Any refusal or rendering of false information would be considered a violation of vagrancy laws. Nauvoo officers were empowered to enter hotels, houses, and places of amusement to inquire as to the intentions of all inhabitants.[44] At the end of July some of the citizens of Adams and McDonough counties responded by resolving that henceforth no Mormons could reside among them.[45] The spirit of suspicion, fear, and retaliation thus picked up momentum.

Only the impending election curbed further hostile exchanges as the two national political parties sought the Mormon vote in Illinois. Even the editor of the *Warsaw Message* spoke of the unfortunate treatment of the prophet, saying that Missouri's harassment involved a "relentless persecution."[46] Congressional candidates of both parties, Cyrus Walker of the Whigs and Joseph P. Hoge of the Democrats, visited the Mormon city and paid their compliments to the Saints.[47]

According to Thomas Ford, J. B. Backenstos was sent by the Saints to Springfield to learn what they might gain if they remained in the Democratic fold. A prominent party leader, in Ford's absence from the city, reportedly promised that special favors would ensue and that the state militia would not be called out to enforce the extradition order from Missouri.[48]

On July 29 Mason Brayman confirmed the promise, writing to Smith to say that although he could not speak for Governor Ford, he was certain that he represented his views. Brayman said that when he came to Nauvoo as a special investigator for the governor he sought to learn whether unlawful means had been used to arrest the prophet and that Ford had not issued his writ for Smith's arrest out of hostility. He said that he was now convinced that Smith was not a fugitive from Missouri in the usual sense and that Governor Ford "will not in my opinion find least difficulty in refusing to issue another warrant, should an hundred be demanded." Brayman reassured the prophet, "Vote, preach, pray, and worship God as you please, so that you violate no law, you have nothing to fear from the Executive or his advisers."[49]

Oliver Olney noted the day after Walker and Hoge had addressed the Saints at length in Nauvoo that the Mormon leaders met in the temple and decided to form a "Political union in favor of the Democratic Party. . . . In the name of the Lord They in union move together to lay a foundation to put in office Such men as they pleas." Olney quoted the leaders to say that they would "first rule the county By going with one of the regular partys By thus doing they have much strength Besides their own." Olney said Mormon political ambitions went beyond the county. He quoted the leaders saying that "the time is not far distant when they will sway the [s]cepter Over the American soil."[50]

Thus before Smith had received Brayman's letter he had decided to go Democratic, despite his pledge to Walker. But no doubt the letter from Brayman reinforced this decision. On election day Smith told the Saints he would vote for Walker but "would not electioneer, would not controul or influence" the voting.[51] He then informed them that Hyrum Smith had received a "testimony that it will be better for this people to vote for hoge & I never knew Hyrum [to] say he ever had a revelation & it failed."[52] The result was a certainty. When election returns came in the Democrats carried Hancock County by over 1,300 votes. They also carried the state 7,796 to 7,222.[53] Ford held to his promise and wrote to the governor of Missouri that there was no legal justification to call out the state militia to arrest Smith.[54] But Ford wrote of this that "from this time forth the Whigs generally, and a part of the Democrats, determined upon driving the Mormons from the state."[55] The editor of the *Davenport Gazette*, speaking for the Whig party, denounced Hyrum Smith's revelation as a "ruse" and a "blasphemy."[56]

Perhaps the prophet sensed that he had no genuine political allies in the state, even among Democrats, because he said on 13 August that "all our wrongs have arisen under the power and authority of democracy [the Democratic party] and I have sworn that these arms shall fall from my shoulders and this tongue cleave to the roof of my mouth before I will vote for them, unless they make satisfaction."[57] In selling the Mormon vote for favors and attempted security to two different parties, Smith caused both parties to distrust him. The consequence was a still greater feeling of alienation between Mormons and their neighbors.

Anti-Mormon feelings were particularly intense in Hancock County at Warsaw and Carthage. Thomas Gregg, editor of the *Warsaw Message*, announced the election results on 6 September, writing, "Revelation now has the balance of power."[58] At Carthage two victorious candidates whom the Mormons had supported for school commissioner and clerk of the county court were met by armed men and warned that they would never be sworn into office.[59] Notices were posted that the Mormons must leave the state.[60] In an effort to determine ways to force the Saints to leave, a call was made for an assembly at Carthage on August 19.[61] People met briefly on the designated day, then decided to reconvene on 6 September when they would be better organized.[62] Most of those who came were Whigs, but there were a few Democrats,[63] the leaders being older citizens who had come to the county before the Mormons[64] or people who resided in the eastern half of the county and felt disfranchised by Mormon power at Nauvoo.[65] They all agreed that the Saints must no longer be allowed to hold the balance of political power in the county.[66]

From the subsequent meeting came a declaration of independence from the Mormon kingdom. The old citizens affirmed that the prophet had "set aside . . . all those moral and religious institutions which have been established by the Bible." They felt that Joseph Smith had shown "a most shameless disregard for all the forms and restraints of law," by having his "city council pass laws contrary to the laws of the State" and by causing "the writ of *habeas corpus* to be issued by the municipal court of the city . . . in a case not provided for in the charter . . . thereby procuring his own rescue from the custody of the law." Further, they said, "citizens from the adjoining counties have been denied the right to regain property stolen and taken to Nauvoo." Of the election, they felt that men "of the most vicious and abominable habits" have been "imposed upon us to fill our most important county offices." To "crown it all," the disgruntled citizens added, Smith "claims to merge all religion, all law, and both moral and political justice, in the knavish pretension that he receives fresh from heaven divine instructions in all matters pertaining to these things." After deprecating Smith's recent escape from the Missouri officials, the citizens resolved that henceforth they would "resist all wrongs which may hereafter be attempted by the Mormons, to the utmost of our ability," and would "stand by and support each other in every emergency up to the death."

At the conclusion was a call for armed assistance from Hancock and other counties and for the authorities in the state of Missouri to make another request for the prophet's extradition. This time they would cooperate in his apprehension. Addressing the heart of their frustration, they fumed that "it has been too common for several years past for politicians of both parties, not only in this county but also in the state to go to Nauvoo and truckle to the heads of the Mormon clan." In justifying their call to arms, they affirmed that when a government ceases to protect the people," the "citizens of course fall back upon their original inherent right to self-defense."[67]

The Saints requested that Governor Ford give them public arms and protection from invasion.[68] But in their press they blustered, warning the Carthaginians that should they attack Nauvoo their lot might be that of Hannibal of old.[69] John Greenhow, writing for the *Nauvoo Neighbor*, threatened "Little Tommy" Sharp with the fate of Humpty Dumpty should his ambition become too exalted.[70] Such bellicosity did not help the cause of a non-Mormon like Thomas Gregg, who, although a fierce Whig partisan, deplored violence and insisted that the anti-Mormons must find a remedy "that will not interfere with the majesty and SUPREMACY OF THE LAW."[71]

There were those even at Carthage who lamented the growing belligerence and sought means other than violence to resolve the differences between the two hostile groups. Andrew Moore, an old citizen, said, "The Mormons are still making considerable stir here but not making many converts. They have ruled the elections in this county this last election and their is considerable stir here about it and some strong talk about driving them from the County." He said that "Them and the democrats have played a deep game here I mean some of the leaders of the democrats they have Screened Joe from justice to secure their vote . . . " But Moore, probably a Whig, said not everyone had joined the anti-Mormon mob spirit. There was still an alternative: "Our neighbors are some trading out to the mormons and leaving their is but few left in the settlement that was here when I Came to it and I think their will be few here if the mormons continue to come as they have been doing I will all trade out to them and let them have the county."[72]

Those determined to use violence were more resolute than those ready to cooperate with the Mormons, and soon violence would become the order of the day. Joseph Smith learned on 8 December that two citizens of Nauvoo had been taken hostage by armed men from Missouri and Hancock County and was told that rumors were circulating that these men intended taking others. To protect himself and others against this possibility Smith, as mayor, ordered a portion of the Nauvoo Legion to be ready to enforce city ordinances and keep the peace. He also asked the city council to grant additional legal protection,[73] and the council responded with an ordinance stating that if any person came to Nauvoo with a legal demand based on old Missouri charges, he would be subject to arrest and, if convicted, to imprisonment for life. Pardon from the governor would only be possible with the consent of the mayor.[74]

On 18 December a Nauvoo city constable arrested non-Mormon John Elliott for kidnapping. A writ was also issued for the arrest of Levi Williams, who was similarly charged with kidnapping. At Elliott's hearing, testimony was given that there was a conspiracy against Smith and others and that "some of them would be shot."[75] That same day two visitors to the city informed Smith that a group was collecting at Warsaw to protect Williams. Willard Richards in a sworn affidavit said that the group intended to attack Nauvoo.[76] The city council reacted by passing another ordinance which stipulated that all warrants issued outside Nauvoo must be examined by the mayor, with fines to be levied against violators.[77] This ordinance further embittered anti-Mormons, who vowed they would respond in kind.

With the flight of the non-combatants and mounting militancy among those who remained, any middle ground between Saints and the old citizens was barely possible by this time. Thomas Gregg, who had earlier stood for a temperate, lawful response, now published in the *Warsaw Message* his fears of "an irresponsible and growing power at Nauvoo." This threat must be "met rightly," he proclaimed in an *Extra*, noting that a crisis was irreversibly approaching in the county and adjoining counties.[78]

In early 1844 anti-Mormons at Carthage found an opportunity to retaliate against the Nauvoo ordinance restricting outside legal process. When an officer of the county attempted to arrest Milton Cook of Hancock in January, he was prevented, and a cluster of armed men gathered around Cook and insisted that he not be taken to Nauvoo for a hearing.[79] Intra-county comity had thus broken down, and the drums of war sounded. In Green Plains men had been drilling since mid-September 1843,[80] and on 10 January 1844 militant Carthaginians announced their readiness to march on Nauvoo.[81]

Meanwhile, frightened by these developments and disregarding the instructions of the governor,[82] Smith called out the Nauvoo Legion to enforce city ordinances and chase down insurgents.[83] The editor of the *Missouri Republican* accurately observed: "It is quite evident that law has lost all its obligations in the county in which the Mormons are principally located, and an embittered and hostile feeling is taking possession of the minds of both parties."[84]

Joseph Smith had been aware since July that there were dissenters within the fold who were opposed to his policies. The editors of his history quote him as saying, "I have secret enemies in the city intermingling with the Saints."[85] After the Dixon affair he was so distraught by his near capture that he wrongly accused Sidney Rigdon of informing his enemies that he would be in that vicinity.[86] In December he told his police force, "I am exposed to far greater danger from traitors among ourselves than from enemies without."[87]

Feeling threatened on all sides, Smith and his followers took refuge in apocalyptic hopes. Orson Pratt in April 1843 cited prophecies of Daniel, who had predicted a time when the kingdom of God would "sway a universal Sceptre over all the earth." Then more power would be conferred on the Saints and the "condemnation and judgment of Some corrupt powers of the earth" would take place.[88] That fall Apostle Brigham Young told a congregation in New York that the "time is come for God to set up his kingdom" and that kings would come to "inquire after the wisdom of Zion."[89] Apostle Parley P. Pratt admonished the same audience that consensus was mandatory among them so that "a great nation may be saved from all nations." He said he longed for the coming of a messianic leader who could save the nation and the world: "If I were an infidel, I would like to have the Lord raise up a Joseph or a Daniel, or a Mordecai, or an Esther, to obtain political, temporal and spiritual power, and cause a change for the good of the world."[90] The Mormons had little confidence in democratic government at this time.

Convinced that legal appeals were in vain, Smith resorted to unpromising, desperate schemes to protect Nauvoo. He called on the citizens of several states to come to the rescue of his people.[91] In a letter to the "Green Mountain Boys" of Vermont written in late November, Smith called for retaliation: "Whenever a nation, kingdom, state, family, or individual has received an insult or an injury from a superior force, it has been the custom to call the aid of friends to assist in obtaining redress." Smith said it was his intention to "humble and chastise or abase" Missouri for "the disgrace she has wrought upon constitutional liberty until she atones for her sins." He pleaded with the men of Vermont, "by all honorable means to help bring Missouri to the bar of justice." He said his only desire was to "frustrate the designs of evil men . . . show presidents, governors, and rulers prudence . . . teach judges justice." He said he would "execute justice and judgment upon the earth in righteousness, and prepare to meet the judge of the quick and the dead, for the hour of his coming is nigh."[92]

To secure legal sanction for his call to arms, Smith petitioned Congress to form Nauvoo into a federal district[93] and grant him authority to command federal troops in defense of the city.[94] He warned his closest friends that "if Congress will not hear our petition and grant us protection, they will be broken up as a government, and God shall damn them, and there shall be nothing left of them—not even a grease spot."[95]

Actually, Smith already despaired for the nation, telling U.S. senator John C. Calhoun that "if the Latter-day Saints are not restored to all their rights and paid for all their losses . . . God will come out of his hiding place, and vex this nation with a sore vexation—yea, the consuming wrath of an offended God shall smoke through the nation."[96] He told Henry Clay, also a U.S. senator, that the "glory of America is departed."[97]

The prophet announced his candidacy for president of the United States in January, saying that unless he was elected the nation would be doomed. George Laub recorded his prophecy that "if they elect him ruler of the nation he would save them & set them at liberty, but if they refuse they shall be swept off."[98] Benjamin Andrews wrote to the Saints in the east: "The Lord, the mighty God, has ordained him a deliverer and Saviour to this generation, if they will hear his council. . . . Gen. Smith is in every way calculated to preside over a great and mighty people."[99] Smith promised, "If ever I get into the presidential chair, I will protect the people in their rights and liberties."[100] He wanted a refuge for his people, but he also wanted vengeance against his enemies. He said that he would give the president power to send an army to suppress mobs, independent of a governor's request.[101] He said there were wicked men in the church and elsewhere that the president should deal with: "We should lift up our voice against wickedness of all kinds. But will the rulers of our land do it? No, they will not; they will be cowards until there is no man left to fight, and then they will be brave. When government will not do it, some man should take the helm of government who will do it."[102] Orson Hyde would say in June that Smith was "God's messenger to execute justice and judgment in the earth."[103] Smith himself would promise at the funeral of King Follett in April that if dissenters felt justified in taking his life because he was a fallen prophet, "upon the same principle am I authorized to take away the life of every false teacher."[104]

Smith sought the presidency also as a means of eliminating divisive pluralism. As early as 1842 an editorial in the *Times and Seasons* had argued that the absence of priesthood authority in America had led to

> conflicting opinions, the clash of doctrines, the diversity of sentiment, and the woefully benighted state that the religious world presents itself in at the present time. Let the Melchisedec priesthood be introduced, and men be subject to their teaching, and their sectarian, narrow contracted notions would flee away . . . the anarchy and confusion that prevails among men would disappear, and the world would be organized upon principles of intelligence, purity, justice, truth and righteousness.[105]

If Smith reached the presidency he would have the power to achieve these ends. His brother Hyrum told the Saints in April 1844: "We want a President of the U.S., not a party president, but a President of the whole people; for a party President disfranchises the opposite party. Have a President who will maintain every man in his rights. . . . We will try and convert the nations into one solid union. I despise the principle that divides the nation into party and faction."[106]

Putting the prophet in the White House was calculated to dissolve all distinctions between sacred and secular and make them one. Brigham Young said in April: "The government belongs to God. No man can draw the dividing line between the government of God and the government of the children of men. You can't touch the gospel without infringing upon the common avocations of men."[107] A "friend to the Mormons" wrote in even stronger terms to the *Times and Seasons* that "the church must not triumph over the state, but actually swallow it up like Moses' rod swallowed up the rods of the Egyptians."[108]

Despite the tremendous odds against them,[109] Smith and his people evidently hoped that by gaining a balance of power nationally (as they assumed they had in Illinois) they could actually win the election of 1844. The Council of Fifty, which would be the executive, legislative, and judicial arm of the Kingdom of God, was first outlined by Smith in 1842 but fully organized in March 1844.[110] The council's first major task was to plan Smith's presidential campaign.[111] Elders were sent to several cities and states, and rallies and conventions were planned.[112] Apostle Willard Richards wrote to James Arlington Bennett in New York that "General Smith is the greatest statesman of the 19th century" and urged Bennett to run with him as the vice-presidential candidate. He told Bennett to "get up an electoral ticket" in New York, New Jersey, Pennsylvania, and any other state within your reach." He informed Bennett they expected to win since "we will go it with the rush of a whirlwind, so peaceful, so gentle, that it will not be felt by the nation till the battle is won."[113]

Apostle John Taylor exhorted the Saints at Nauvoo in March that "we must do what we can to elect Joseph President and not be cowards."[114] Elder Richards wrote to Elder Orson Hyde in Washington in May that "our faith must be manifest by our works, and every honorable exertion made to elect Gen Smith."[115] Writing to Hugh Clark, an alderman in Philadelphia, in behalf of the "Central Committee of Correspondence for the election of Gen. Joseph Smith," Richards said that Mormons and Roman Catholics were "most obnoxious to the Sectarian world" yet had not persecuted each other. He urged the alderman to join them in establishing "Jeffersonian Democracy, Free trade and Sailors rights and protection of persons and property." Help us to elect Joseph Smith, he pleaded, "and we shall help you to secure those privileges which belong to *you* and to break every yoke."[116]

At a party convention in Jackson, Michigan, on 6 July, before news of Smith's death had reached them, the Saints voted not to "cease until a full & entire revolution should be effected in the administration of the government."[117] Two days later Brigham Young wrote to Richards from Salem, Massachusetts, to say, "We shall do all we can and leave the event with God."[118]

As early as mid-April, James Arlington Bennett had written from New York to say that he thought the prophet had no chance to win, that the best that could be hoped for was the gaining of some political influence.[119] Richards's reply, "we mean to elect him,"[120] revealed

the serious intentions of the Council of Fifty. But Mormons—despite
a few hastily organized rallies—had no party organization, no patron-
age jobs to reward non-Mormons who would support the campaign,
and a candidate who was not popular in the national press.[121] Thus
D. S. Hollister wrote from Wilmington, Delaware, on 26 June that he
was greatly disappointed that he could rally little support in Balti-
more, and on the 28th he said no delegates had been selected for the
party convention from Philadelphia. He intended to attend the convention on 13 July but was doubtful that much had been done to prepare for it in other states.[122]

James Arlington Bennett believed that the Saints would have
better success at finding peace if they pursued another course. He
had for some time urged them to establish a government of their
own in the west. In April 1844 he urged Willard Richards: "The Mormons should settle out of the States and have an empire of their own.
Not only thousands but millions would flock to an independent people. In this case a Patriarchal government with Joseph at the head
would be just the thing. In unity there is power. Nothing could resist
such a people."[123]

In establishing the Council of Fifty, Smith set up a political
agency for just such a "patriarchal" government. Whether it would
be established in the United States, with Nauvoo as the capitol, or in
the far west, the Saints would still rule. Plans were made in early
1844 to establish a settlement in Oregon or California.[124]

As relations with Illinoisans grew worse in 1844, Smith authorized Lyman Wight to seek an alliance with Texans, to settle the "table
lands" of Texas, and to establish a theocracy there. He told the Council of Fifty in March to "Send 25 men . . . and if [Houston] will
embrace the gospel [. . .] [We] can amend the constitution and make
it the voice of Jehovah and shame the U[nited] S[tates]."[125]

Thus Smith would either gain the White House or establish an
independent government. George Miller, a bishop, described the two
alternatives as they appeared at the time. He said they must "do everything in our power to have Joseph Smith elected President, and if we
succeeded in making a majority of the voters converts to our faith
and elected Joseph Smith President, in such an event the dominion
of the kingdom would be forever established in the United States.
And if not successful, we could still fall back on Texas and be a kingdom notwithstanding."[126]

Smith did not relish force as a means to power and told the
Saints in May: "it will not be by the Sword or Gun that this kingdom

will roll on—the power of truth is such that—all nations will be under the necessity of obeying the gospel." Yet he added, "The prediction is that army will be against army—it may be that the Saints will have to beat their ploughes into Swords. It will not do for men to set down and see their women & children destroyed patiently."[127]

If possible, Smith preferred to gain power through the electoral process. The editor of the *Times and Seasons* said that Smith's election would curb the increasing secularism in the nation:

> There are peculiar notions extant in relation to the propriety of mixing religion and politics, many of which we consider wild and visionary. . . . We cannot but think that the course taken by many of our politicians is altogether culpable, that the division [between church and state] is extending too far, and that in our jealousy lest a union of this kind should take place, we have thrust God from all of our political movements.

The editor said that he feared the nation would soon become "directed by human wisdom alone."[128]

In case he did not win the election and the Saints had to seek their refuge in the west, Smith memorialized Congress in March to allow Mormons to raise an army of 100,000 volunteers to protect American emigrants going to the far west.[129]

The prophet's ambition for the White House, according to Thomas Ford, brought him into "conflict with the zealots and bigots of all parties."[130] Ford's contention seems plausible given the aspirations of the down-state Whigs, who entertained the idea of a reconciliation with the Saints. A. G. Henry said "the Mormons are worth coaxing a little. They are violent against Van & intend to go for Clay."[131] But later a Whig booster said "our Mormon neighbors cannot be relied on. Joe is a candidate for President he will not vote for Mr. Clay."[132]

Mormon political isolation was now complete, as neither party could hope for their support. In 1844 the Mormon prophet placed himself at the head of his own political party, dedicated to carrying out his will in national politics.

Meanwhile, the conviction hardened in Hancock County that the Mormon question had drifted long enough. The determined attitude was evidenced in the return of Thomas Sharp as editor of the Warsaw newspaper in January and the marked increase in its circulation the next month.[133] Many were now ready to listen when Sharp insisted that non-Mormons must unite to curb the "encroachments of the fanatical band located in our midst."[134] Although some were primed to expel the Saints immediately by force, others were hesitant and awaited the next move of the Mormons.[135]

Sharp was in the vanguard of those dubious of delay. He lashed out at Mormon marriage practices[136] and depicted as futile any tendency to temporize.[137] He was unmoved when, in a belated attempt at conciliation, Smith repealed the law against "foreign" legal processes.[138] If the Mormons want peace, he said,

> they must cease from screening each other from the operation of the law—cease from sham trials, intended to let off offenders by a mere nominal penalty—cease from releasing persons in custody of state officers, by their city Habeas Corpus—cease from insulting the laws, and desecrating public morals by substituting for the laws of the state a set of abominable ordinances, which give to all who believe in their validity a free scope of licentiousness—cease from threatening the liberties of our citizens by their city authorities & cease from dictating who shall be our county officers. These are the only terms on which they can have peace.[139]

For an agitator like Sharp the emerging schism at Nauvoo over plural marriage was made to order. As soon as Mormon dissenters began to differ openly with Smith, Sharp was ready to champion their cause. Noting at the end of April that two had been charged with conspiracy by the *Nauvoo Neighbor*, Sharp warned, "Let Jo dare to harm one of them and he will awaken a spirit to which resistance will be useless."[140]

The leader of the Mormon rebels was William Law, a former member of the First Presidency[141] who had first quarreled with Smith during the August election. Law publicly opposed Hyrum Smith's political revelation, contending that Hyrum was angling for a seat in Congress if he could deliver the Mormon vote for Hoge.[142] Also prominent in the opposition to Smith were Wilson Law, William's brother, formerly a commander of the Nauvoo Legion[143]; Robert D. Foster, a physician, land owner, and brigadier general in the legion[144]; and Francis and Chauncey Higbee, two sons of former high councilor Elias Higbee, recently deceased.[145] Nearly all had quarreled with Smith over polygamy, some claiming that he had "tried to get their wives away from them and had many times committed adultery."[146] Foster expressed the disillusionment with Smith that the dissenters felt, writing to him in June: "You have trampled upon everything we hold dear and sacred. You have set all law at defiance, and profaned the name of the Most High to carry out your damnable purposes."[147]

On 6 and 7 April at General Conference, doctrines were publicly advocated which the Laws believed were blasphemous—that there exists a plurality of gods, that God was once a man, that Joseph Smith was a god to this generation, and that the kingdom of God on earth required a human king.[148] Wilford Woodruff recorded in his diary as early as 24 March that church leaders had been told that the Laws, the Higbees, and Foster were part of a conspiracy to kill the entire Smith family. Hyrum said at conference that he did not believe this, that "they would not do any thing to injure me or any man's life."[149]

Despite Hyrum's dissent, charges were leveled against the Laws and Foster, and they were excommunicated on 18 April.[150] The cryptic minutes of the Council of the Twelve Apostles indicate that Foster called Joseph Smith a "murderer, Bogus maker counterfiter, [and] adulterer." John Scott testified that William Law had "spoke[n] against Joseph," claiming that Joseph had gone to his wife "to attempt to seduce her—Joseph wanted her to come into the order." Scott also said that Law was angry that Joseph would not seal Law to his wife, Jane, which confirmed to him that Smith wanted her for himself.[151] Law believed that the hearing was unlawful, since he was not informed of the identity of his accusers and since Sidney Rigdon, one of Smith's councilors in the First Presidency, was not present.[152]

The dissenters responded to their excommunication by organizing their own church in May, with William Law as prophet.[153] They began holding weekly meetings on Sunday,[154] attracting approximately three hundred people.[155] The discontented group made plans to publish a newspaper at Nauvoo to defend their stand against Smith, and Francis Higbee described to Thomas Gregg the purpose of the forthcoming publication:

> The paper I think we will call the Nauvoo Expositor; for it will be fraught with Joe's peculiar and particular mode of Legislation; and a discitation [dissertation] upon his *delectable* plan of Government; and above all, it shall be the organ through which we will herald his mormon ribaldry. It shall also contain a full and complete expose of his mormon seraglio, or Nauvoo House, and his unparalleled and unheard of attempts of seduction.[156]

According to William Law, Smith sent Rigdon to him on 13 May "to negotiate terms of peace." Rigdon informed him that if they would "let all difficulties drop," church officials would restore William, his wife, and Foster to their "standing in the church and to all [their] offices." Rigdon acknowledged that the excommunication proceedings had been improper and said this would be published in the newspaper. Law demanded that Smith admit publicly that he had taught and practiced polygamy. He warned that otherwise he would "publish all to the world." Rigdon replied that he was not authorized to yield this much.[157]

At the end of May several of the dissenters moved to bring Smith to trial at Carthage, leveling charges that included adultery and falsely accusing a visitor to Nauvoo of murder. These allegations led to two indictments against Smith.[158] Smith tried to avoid falling into the hands of his enemies at Carthage by making a secret trip to the town and demanding an immediate trial. His case was held over until the following month. The atmosphere in Carthage was extremely hostile. Sharp warned in his newspaper:

> We have seen and heard enough to convince us that Joe Smith is not safe out of Nauvoo, and we would not be surprised to hear of his death by violent means in a short time. He has deadly enemies—men whose wrongs have maddened them—whose lives have been sought by Joe, and who are prepared at all times to avenge themselves. . . . The feeling in this country is now lashed to its utmost pitch, will break forth in fury upon the slightest provocation.[159]

Thus it was that the Mormon prophet was backed into an inevitable corner. To journey to Carthage for trial would give his bitterest enemies an opportunity to take his life. But not to submit to the jurisdiction of those in authority in Carthage could bring retaliation against Nauvoo. When Smith sought to resolve this dilemma by once again utilizing his writ issuing powers at Nauvoo, the non-Mormon community was outraged. As far away as Rock Island the editor of the *Upper Mississippian* warned ominously, "If the laws and authority of the state can thus be set at defiance by a single individual, it is high time that the people should know it."[160]

Once more Smith tried to reconcile his differences with church dissenters as a way out of his menacing situation. On the day the *Nauvoo Expositor* was due for publication Smith sent Dimick Huntington to Robert Foster to propose a conference. He coldly rejected the offer. Foster replied: "I have consulted my friends in relation to your proposal of settlement, and as they as well as myself are of the opinion that your conduct and that of your unworthy unprincipled clan are so base that it would be morally wrong & detract the dignity of gentlemen to hold any conference with you."[161]

When the *Expositor* appeared on the streets of the city the prophet was alarmed. The newspaper denounced the attempt to "Christianize a world by political schemes and intrigue" and urged church members to repudiate recent innovations in doctrine.[162] Smith saw the publication as a threat to church unity and Mormon security. In a meeting of the city council he declared, "The conduct of such men and such papers are calculated to destroy the peace of the city, and it is not safe that such things exist, on account of the mob spirit which they tend to produce."[163]

Smith moved that the newspaper and printing press be destroyed. The councilmen generally agreed, but a non-Mormon named Warren suggested that it might be better to impose a fine on the publishers rather than destroy their property. Smith disagreed, saying that no Mormon could otherwise safely journey to Carthage. He said he was "sorry to have one dissenting voice in declaring the newspaper a nuisance."[164] The council voted to destroy the paper and the press at once.[165] A large group of legionnaires and citizens promptly marched to the *Expositor* office, smashed the press, and scattered its type in the street.[166]

Smith had made the mistake his enemies were waiting for. The public reaction was immediate and overwhelming. The editor of the *Quincy Whig* denounced the action as "HIGH HANDED OUTRAGE" and declared that it "really seems to us that their intention is to put the law at defiance." The editor exclaimed, "These people are unworthy to be trusted with power."[167] The *Alton Telegraph* decried the blatant act as "Mormon violence,"[168] while the editor of the *Lee County Democrat* in Iowa said that the destruction of the opposition press "has aroused the people of Illinois and . . . hundreds of them properly armed and equiped, hold themselves in readyness at a moment's notice to go to Nauvoo to aid . . . the authorities."[169] The editor of the *Quincy Herald*, a Democratic newspaper, published excerpts from the *Warsaw Signal*, which declared war and remarked that "the evidence speaks for itself."[170] H. H. Bliss of LaHarpe reflected the prevailing public disposition when he said that the issue is "whether the *Law* should have its corse on Smith or not."[171] At Warsaw Tom

Sharp frenetically declared that "War and Extermination is inevitable. Citizens ARISE ONE AND ALL!"[172]

William Law now headed to Carthage to charge Smith with instigating a riot. He insisted in his diary that he told the people of Carthage that legal process would be sufficient to correct Mormon wrongdoing.[173] Sheriff David Bettisworth of Carthage acted on Law's charges and went to Nauvoo to apprehend Smith. Bettisworth arrived in Nauvoo on 12 June, only to find that Smith refused to be taken to Carthage. He offered to stand trial before any judge, but the proceeding would have to be held in Nauvoo.[174] When Bettisworth insisted that Smith return with him, the prophet secured a writ of custody from a Nauvoo court. He was tried on 17 June in Nauvoo and was acquitted.[175]

In assuming that by taking this step he had met the law's requirements, Smith misjudged the temper of the citizens of Illinois. One older citizen said that they would "not be caught with this trap. Joe had tried the game too often."[176] When Bettisworth returned without his prisoner, emotions reached a peak.[177] Samuel O. Williams, who was among the throng who received the sheriff, said, "Such an excitement I have never witnessed in my life."[178] Messages were sent to all the older citizens for three hundred miles around to gather to Carthage with arms for a march on Nauvoo.[179] Two emissaries were sent to Governor Ford to ask for support from the state militia.[180] If Ford did not respond favorably, the citizens were determined to form a "posse comitatus" and head for Nauvoo. Mormons were given the choice of surrendering their prophet or going to war.[181]

Within a week citizens began to collect from many directions. The *Warsaw Signal* reported how at "Carthage and Green Plains, the citizens are all in arms . . . throughout the county every man is ready for conflict. In Clark Co., Mo. many hold themselves in readyness. . . . From Rushville . . . 3,000 men have enlisted for the struggle, McDonough County is alive and ready. . . . From Keokuk and the river towns . . . all are coming."[182]

Meanwhile, Smith wrote to Ford to justify the action he had taken against the *Expositor* and offered to submit to an investigation before "any legal tribunal at the capitol."[183] On 17 June Smith placed Nauvoo under martial law and addressed the legion in a manner reminiscent of Missouri. He said, "I call God and angels to witness that I have unsheathed my sword with a firm and unalterable determination that this people shall have their rights." He added militantly, "I call upon all friends of truth and liberty to come to our assistance and may the thunders of the Almighty and the forked light-nings of heaven and pestilence, and war and bloodshed come down on those ungodly men who seek to destroy my life and the lives of innocent people."[184] To further implement this call to arms, Wil-lard Richards wrote to James Arlington Bennett to come "with as many volunteers as you can bring." He said, "If the mob cannot be dispersed, and the Government will not espouse our righteous cause, you may soon, very soon, behold the second birth of our nation's freedom."[185] In accord with this revolutionary thinking, Smith ordered on 22 June that a "standard be prepared for the nations."[186]

Hoping to learn the facts and avert civil war, Governor Ford came to Carthage on 21 June. After a brief investigation of the charges and the Mormon defense,[187] Ford made the only choice open to him if he wished to avoid civil war. He decided that the Mormons had broken the law on several counts and violated the American consti-tution. He wrote to Smith on 22 June to argue these points, saying that the cause of the "existing disturbance" in Hancock County was the destruction of the *Nauvoo Expositor* and the "subsequent refusal of the individuals accused to be accountable therefore . . . only before your own municipal courts."

Ford said, "You have violated the Constitution in at least four particulars. You have violated that part of it which declares that the printing press shall be free . . . It may have been libelous, but this did not authorize you to destroy it," a point on which scholars would later agree.[188] The dissenters should have been brought to trial for libel and given an opportunity to present evidence in support of the truth of their allegations, according to Ford. The second violation of the Constitution, in Ford's mind, was that the city council had not recognized the right of people to be protected "against unreason-able searches and seizures of their property except by judgment of [their] peers." The third point, he said, was that "your Council, which has no judicial powers, and can only pass ordinances of a general nature, have undertaken to pass judgment as a court and convict with-out a jury . . . The Constitution," Ford explained, "abhors and will not tolerate the union of legislative and judicial power, in the same body of magistracy, because, as in this case, they will first make a tyrannical law, and then execute it in a tyrannical manner."

Ford next took up the matter of Nauvoo's chartered rights and insisted that Smith had exceeded its privileges by initiating writs to free from legal process himself and others accused of crimes. Ford admitted that certain lawyers in the state had encouraged Smith in his interpretation, in hopes of political favor. But, he insisted, "You have ... assumed to yourselves more power than you are entitled to." He maintained that it was "never supposed by the legislature, nor can the language of your charter be tortured to mean that a jurisdiction was intended to be conferred which would apply to all cases of imprisonment under the general laws of the state or of the United States."[189]

The Illinois governor thus struck at some of the anti-pluralistic aspects of the kingdom at Nauvoo: the concentration of the power of mayor and judge in the hands of one man who seemed to claim accountability only to himself; the intolerance to criticism; and the apparent indifference to rights of property.

In demanding that Smith come to Carthage, Ford seemed indifferent to threats made against his life. Ford may have later regretted this decision, but at the moment he wanted to avert civil war and establish the sovereignty of state law. In siding with anti-Mormons on this issue, he left himself open to charges made by the Mormons that he had been part of the conspiracy to take Smith's life.

Ford was most anxious that Mormons do nothing to further antagonize the old citizens and advised Smith: "All of you who are or shall be accused or sued [are] to submit in all cases implicitly to the process of the court, and to interpose no obstacles to an arrest, either by writ of *habeas corpus*, or otherwise." He said that Smith and others were required to submit to the authorities at Carthage: "I tell you plainly that if no such submission is made as I have indicated, I will be obliged to call out the militia; and if a few thousand will not be sufficient, many thousands will be."[190]

Isolated, with no friends other than his own people, who were divided, Smith had either to submit to authorities at Carthage, where those who had proclaimed their intention to kill him waited menacingly,[191] or flee to a refuge in the east or west,[192] with the risk that the city would be attacked in retaliation.[193] Fearing for his life, Smith initially crossed the Mississippi River to go into hiding.[194] But pleadings from his wife and close friends, and a charge of cowardice, persuaded him to return and submit to trial.[195] His attorney, James Woods, arranged for Smith's surrender to state authorities, and he and fifteen others started toward Carthage on the 24th, only to find that Captain Dunn, acting on the governor's orders, wanted him to return to Nauvoo to encourage the Saints to surrender the arms given them by the state.[196]

In Nauvoo, Smith said that he was going to Carthage "like a lamb to the slaughter."[197] He was aware of great risks, but his actions and statements afterward made it clear that he expected to remain among the living. His brother, who had argued that they should surrender to authorities, said, "Let us go back and put our trust in God, and we shall not be harmed," a belief Joseph shared.[198] Stopping at a plural wife's house en route out of Nauvoo, Smith spoke with some uncertainty but not despair. He said, "If I never see you again, or if I never come back remember I love you."[199] He saw his death as a possibility, not an inevitability.

The party reached Carthage at midnight, and Smith was placed under guard at the Hamilton Hotel. On the following morning Governor Ford marched the Mormon prisoner in front of the Carthage Greys, who showed their mounting hostility by threatening him with their rifles.[200]

At the preliminary hearing on the perjury charge, Smith met the legal requirements and might have been released, but his enemies acted quickly and charged him with treason, thus requiring that he be held over in Carthage.[201] Tensions continued to mount when Smith was placed in the jail at Carthage and clusters of armed men whispered their hatred of the Mormon leader.[202] Smith sensed his danger and told his lawyer, James Woods, on the 27th that he would "never live to see another sun."[203]

Yet he still hoped to survive. He wrote to his wife shortly after eight o'clock in the morning:

> There is no danger of any "exterminating order." Should there be a mutiny among the troops, (which we do not anticipate, excitement is abating,) a part will remain loyal, and stand for the defence. . . . There is one principle which is Eternal, it is the duty of all men to protect their lives . . . whenever . . . occasion requires, and no power has a right to forbid it. . . . Should the last extreme arrive, but I *anticipate no such extreme*, - but caution is the parent of safety.[204]

When he learned two hours later that he would not accompany the governor to Nauvoo to urge the Mormons to keep the peace, as planned,[205] he was not dismayed. He wrote to Emma: "I just saw that the governor is about to disband his troops,—all but a guard to protect us and the peace.—and come himself to Nauvoo and deliver a speech to the people. This is right as I suppose."[206] When two more hours had passed he addressed a letter to lawyer Browning: "Myself and brother Hyrum are in jail on [a] charge of treason, to come for examination on Saturday morning 29th inst. and we request your professional services at that time."[207] Smith had underestimated the intensity of personal hatred toward himself and his people. Thomas Sharp would later write that a "Committee of Safety" in Carthage had already determined upon "summary execution" of Joseph and Hyrum.[208] They had to await their opportunity. After Governor Ford dismissed the troops at noon on the 27th, and militiamen from Green Plains and Warsaw, disappointed that they had not been led in an attack on Nauvoo,[209] stopped at a crossroads to consider their alternatives, Sharp argued that now was the time to join together and rid themselves of the brothers Smith. At this some turned back, unwilling to kill men who were incarcerated and helpless. Others marched toward the jail, faces blackened, intent on murder. They were assured by a note from the captain of the Carthage Greys on guard that they would not meet serious opposition. Arriving at the jail, they brushed aside the few men stationed there and rushed up the stairs to the room where Joseph and Hyrum Smith with two apostles were held.[210]

The accused, trapped inside, tried to hold the door shut, but some of their assailants managed to shoot into the room, killing Hyrum with a shot through the head. Joseph ran to the window, hoping for an escape, but armed men below fired at him as others did so from the door. The prophet was struck with four musket balls and fell out of the window to the ground below.[211] Then one of the assassins stabbed him with a bayonet, making sure of the work.[212]

The men who committed the cold-blooded murder of the Smith brothers were militia men who despised Joseph for his military pretense and politicos who feared the continuation of Mormon political power. They justified the killings as self defense, appealing to the American revolutionary tradition, saying that the prophet had placed himself above the law.[213] This was the same charge Mormons leveled against their tormentors. The murderers hoped that by killing the Smiths it would cause the Saints to dissolve their gathering and their political maneuvering.[214] But they misjudged the resiliency of the Mormon people.

Of the dissenters who had stirred the wrath against Smith to a fever pitch, the evidence is contradictory as to whether any were at the jail at five o'clock. The Laws and Foster were in town that morning, but Law said that they left and were in Fort Madison by the afternoon.[215] Others claimed to have seen them at the jail.[216] There or not, William Law approved of the murder. He said that at the end the Smiths "knew no mercy . . . [and] they found none." He said that the man he had once sustained as a prophet of God had one aim— "to demoralize the world, to give it to Satan, his master." Ignoring his own part in swearing the writs which brought Smith to Carthage, he said, "God stopped him in his mad career & gave him to his destroyers." Law concluded, "He claimed to be a god, whereas he was only a servant of the Devil, and as such he met his fate."[217] Whether or not he came to the jail, Law, by transforming Joseph Smith from a god to a devil, eased his guilt for the part he played in the murderous affair.

CHAPTER 8

"To the Wilderness for Safety and Refuge"

The grief the Mormon people felt at the death of their prophet and his brother was more intense and enduring than anything they had yet experienced. Job Smith said that on the morning of 28 June when a horseman rode through Nauvoo shouting that the leaders had been assassinated "the weeping was general."[1] Eight thousand Saints turned out to mourn when the bodies were brought back to the city in rough pine caskets. Emma and Mary Fielding, Joseph's and Hyrum's widows, were devastated and wept bitterly at the public viewing.[2] In utter despair, Lucy Mack Smith could only acknowledge the condolences of Sarah M. Kimball by holding her hand for a long time without speaking. Finally she managed, "How could they kill my boys O how could they kill them when they were so *Precious*! I am shure they would not harm any boddy in the world . . . there was poor Hyrum what could they kill him for he was always *mild*."[3]

A "momentary panic ensued immediately after the tragical event," according to the editor of the *Times and Seasons*, and "gloom overspread the minds of the Saints; they felt that every principle of humanity was violated, and that they were among a horde of savage barbarians."[4] George Morris said that some "could neither shed tears nor speak," while others prayed "for vengeance on their murderers." Still others wanted to retaliate by "laying Carthage in ashes."[5]

Most reacted like Henry W. Bigler who said, "At first I felt mad and could have fought a tiger, but soon I felt like weeping and a feeling of loneliness came over me."[6] As time passed many Saints felt as did Jacob Gibson in Philadelphia. He lamented that there was "no profit to lead no Sear to discern the calamities."[7] The question of who would succeed as church president and prophet deeply troubled the Mormon people in the months that followed 27 June 1844.

To Apostle Willard Richards at Nauvoo it seemed paramount following the funeral that the twelve be recalled from the east.[8] These authorities were scattered from New York to Boston, preaching and campaigning for the fallen prophet. They did not hear of the murders until 9 July. Wilford Woodruff said he first read about them in the *Boston Times* that day.[9] Heber C. Kimball, en route to New York to meet with the prophet's brother, William, reported that the morning papers in Salem were filled with the news. His reaction was typical of the rest: "I was not willen to believe it, fore it was to[o] much to bare. . . . It struck me at the heart."[10]

The next day, a Sunday, Brigham Young informed the Boston Saints of the deaths, explaining that the prophet had finished his work and left the keys to men on earth. Significantly, he did not say to whom.[11] Young may have been referring to the secret conferral the previous March of special authority on the twelve to perform sacred temple rites.[12] But at the time of this conferral, Young and others would not have imagined an inherent right of succession since prior to 27 June they did not expect Joseph's death. To be sure, Smith had told the twelve that spring, "I may soon be taken from you,"[13] but the twelve did not take this literally or they never would have left Nauvoo. Young said afterward that had Smith heeded "the Spirit of revelation in him he would never have gone to Carthage. . . . This he did through the persuasion of others."[14] Brigham did not see the martyrdom as foreordained but rather as the consequence of human error. As late as 24 July, the twelve were still hoping that the reported deaths were a mistake. Kimball said on the day they learned by letter that Smith had surrendered to state authorities, "[it] satisfide us that the Brethren ware dead." Only then did they fully realize what had happened, and Kimball wrote, "O what feelings we had."[15]

Years later Young admitted to his family his complete surprise. He said that when he first heard the news, he wondered whether the keys of authority were still with the church. Even when he decided that the authority to preside over the church was still on earth, he did not know exactly where. He remembered, "I had no more idea of it falling upon me than of the most unlikely thing in the world. . . . I did not think it was with me."[16]

Once Young and those of the twelve who were in the east had collected themselves, they instructed Orson Hyde to write to Smith's first counselor, Sidney Rigdon, at Pittsburgh to have him and Apostle John Page meet them at Nauvoo. Hyde said they wanted to meet with Rigdon before any "action was taken before the public."[17] They made the long journey to Illinois still planning to include Rigdon in the difficult decisions which had to be made regarding succession and church leadership. Church stalwarts still in Nauvoo—W. W. Phelps, Willard Richards, and John Taylor—were thinking along similar lines for they informed the Saints in the city that "as soon as the 'Twelve' and the other *authorities* assemble, or a majority of them, the onward course . . . will be pointed out."[18] As yet, it had not been determined on whom Joseph's mantle would eventually rest.

By the time the distant apostles reached Nauvoo on 6 August 1844, a crisis in leadership had developed. William Clayton perceived the essential problem as early as 6 July, noting in his journal: "The greatest danger that now threatens us is dissensions and strifes amongst the Church. There are already 4 or 5 men pointed out as successors to the Trustees and President & there is danger of feelings being manifest All the brethren who stand at the head seem to feel the delicacy of the business."

Emma Smith feared the uncertainties of her claim on her husband's property, some of which belonged to the church, and wished that Nauvoo stake president William Marks would be named immediately as Trustee in Trust and church president. Emma and Marks both bitterly opposed plural marriage, and Emma wanted him to lead the fight against it. But Clayton had won a degree of her confidence and did not trust Marks. Clayton feared that if Marks headed the church "the most important matters" would be endangered. To pacify Emma, Clayton was named acting trustee.[19]

Meanwhile, George Miller and Alexander Badlam began to advocate that the Council of Fifty was to head the church, a view with which Apostle Lyman Wight came to agree when he moved to Texas in October.[20] To complicate the situation, Sidney Rigdon had hurried to Nauvoo ahead of the apostles and claimed a special revelation that he was to be the guardian of the church. Rigdon's move caused him to shun the twelve when they arrived.[21] Since Rigdon and Marks opposed plural marriage,[22] and the "most important matters" were at stake,[23] the twelve were forced to advance their own claim to church succession. It did not help Rigdon with the twelve that he had been relatively inactive in church councils for five years and was blamed for the Missouri expulsion. Some of the brethren may even have considered him insane.[24]

No one at this point gave consideration to William Smith, the prophet's youngest brother and member of the Quorum of the Twelve Apostles, who had remained in New York with a sick wife. Samuel, another brother, may have been a contender, but he died on 30 July under circumstances some considered suspicious.[25] Neither Lucy, Emma, nor William Smith made a proposal at this time that Joseph Smith III succeed his father.[26] A boy of eleven years, he seemed too young for consideration. Lucy appeared willing to see what the twelve would do, giving them her early support.[27] Oliver Cowdery and David Whitmer, two who might have had a claim earlier,[28] were now out of the church.[29]

James J. Strang, a relative newcomer to the church, affirmed in August that he had received a letter from Joseph Smith written on 19 June naming him stake president at Voree, Wisconsin, and "leader of the flock" should Smith fall.[30] Claiming to be a prophet and seer, Strang would in time prove to be a threat to the twelve, securing the allegiance for a time of William Smith, and perhaps others in the Smith family, William Marks, George Miller, and Apostle John E. Page.[31] But he was of no concern to the twelve at Nauvoo when decisive actions were being taken.

Thus the struggle for the prophetic mantle turned out to be a tug-of-war between Rigdon and the Quorum of the Twelve Apostles. It was a struggle that Rigdon had no chance to win, due to his personal limitations and the inherent theoretical weakness of his position. When the twelve arrived on 6 August, they listened to Rigdon present his claims to a large audience of Saints.[32] Rigdon proposed that a meeting be held on the 8th to choose a guardian, but the twelve succeeded in converting this into a general church conference over which they would preside. They arranged to hear a report of Rigdon's vision on 7 August at 4 o'clock at the Seventies Hall. The high council and high priests were invited.

Wilford Woodruff considered what he heard from Rigdon to be a "kind of second class vision." Rigdon maintained that he had been appointed "to lead the church,"[33] that there were otherwise no authorities to govern and that a guardian must be chosen to pre-side over a restructuring of the organization.[34] At the church con-ference on the 8th, Brigham Young began his remarks by inquiring if the Saints wanted to choose a guardian or "a Prophet evangelist or sumthing els as your head to lead you. All that are in favor of it manifest by raising the right hand."[35] According to Wilford Woodruff, no hands were raised.[36] Young then insisted that Rigdon could not continue to act as spokesman for or counselor to Joseph Smith in his absence without going beyond the veil where the prophet had gone. Rather the twelve held the keys of the kingdom to be "the Presidency of the Church." He said that the Saints could not appoint anyone to stand ahead of the twelve unless the twelve ordained him themselves. Joseph Smith had "laid the foundation," Young announced, "& we shall build upon it."[37] The church organization was already established and no innovations were needed.

Amasa Lyman spoke next, "I believe their is no power or offices or means wanted to carry on the work but what is in the Twelve." W. W. Phelps rose and proclaimed, "The twelve are chosen to rise up and bear the Church off triumphant."[38] Young then asked the con-gregation if they wanted the twelve apostles "to Stand at the head, the first presidency of the Church and at the head of this kingdom in all the world." Woodruff reported that the vote was unanimous in the affirmative, although there were those in the audience who favored Rigdon.[39]

The vote of the Saints was to retain the existing church order, which meant that its presiding officers were still in their places.[40] No prophet was named to replace Joseph Smith. Brigham Young admitted as much in his "Epistle of the Twelve," published in the *Times and Seasons* in August: "You are now without a prophet present with you in the flesh to guide you; But you are not without apostles, who hold the keys of power to seal on earth that which shall be sealed in heaven and to preside over all the affairs of the church in all the world." Young, who had great veneration for Joseph Smith, stressed that no one would take his place in the institution: "Let no man pre-sume for a moment that his place will be filled by another; for, *remember he stands in his own place*, and always will; and the Twelve Apostles of this dispensation stand in their own places and always will, both in time and in eternity, who minister, preside and regu-late the affairs of the whole church."[41]

Thus Young revealed no plans to reestablish the First Presi-dency in 1844; the twelve were to remain as they were. Young did not

believe that his calling was of the same nature as the prophet's. Concerning Joseph Smith, he said that God, not the people, had called
him to be a prophet and that he was accountable to God and the
angel who had delivered to him his gospel dispensation.[42] Of his
own authority to lead the church, Young said that it derived from
the people of the church who were the "sole controllers of it."[43]

Young made the same point in the Salt Lake Tabernacle in April
1852. He asked, "Who ordained me to be First President of this
Church on earth? I answer, it is the choice of the people, and that is
sufficient."[44] Young was a reluctant successor to Joseph Smith but
assumed the reigns of authority because he feared the effects of division and plurality. He noted in his journal on 8 August 1844: "I
perseved [perceived] a Spirit to hurry business, to get a Trustee in
Trust and a Presede[n]cy over the Church Priesthood or no Priesthood right or wrong this grieved my h[e]art, now Joseph is gon[e] it
seems as though manny wanted to draw off a party and be leaders,
but this cannot be, the Church must be one or they are not the Lords."

Rigdon, meanwhile, made himself increasingly unpopular at
Nauvoo. On the Sunday following the special conference, he told a
congregation that he had received the keys of David, the keys of con-
quest, and that the elders would soon sweep through the nation and
conquer their enemies. He promised to go with them to England to
take Queen Victoria "by the nose" and demand her dominions. He
claimed to have seen everything to the time of Gog and Magog.[45]
The Saints, however, had heard enough of such talk, and the church
counsellor lost even more credibility.

Rigdon met with the twelve on 3 September and told them that
he had more power and authority than they.[46] William Clayton noted
that he "had come out full" against the twelve and "said he would
not be controlled by them." Clayton noted there was "considerable
feeling prevailing" and that at least five elders sided with Rigdon,
some of whom he ordained to be prophets, priests, and kings.[47]
Finally, when it was rumored that Rigdon was conspiring with apostates to bring mobs to the city, Young went to Rigdon's house and
demanded his preaching license.[48] On 8 September Rigdon was
excommunicated.[49]

Rigdon returned to Pittsburgh and in October began publishing a new periodical. In his first issues, Rigdon recalled that he and
Frederick G. Williams were "equal with . . . [Joseph Smith] in holding the keys of this last kingdom," according to an early revelation[50]; explained that he would carry out only those measures of

Smith's "which are according to holiness"; alleged that Smith was a fallen prophet due to plural marriage and that "the Lord smote him for it"[51]; and reported that Brigham Young had scoffed at Rigdon's prophecy that great battles were soon to be fought. Rigdon insisted that "all nations are in one general scene of confusion, consternation and dismay" and that "this nation will, at a period now future, divide into parties and . . . go to war . . . until the government shall lose its power."[52]

Rigdon soon won over some former Mormon leaders who had defected at Kirtland and Far West. William E. McLellin and George Hinkle had originally combined efforts in 1840 to form "The Church of Jesus Christ the Bride the Lamb's Wife." They had initiated a gathering at Buffalo, Iowa, and recently begun publishing their own journal. They had said they would practice all the ordinances which were mandatory in the New Testament[53] and stay out of politics.[54]

By October 1844 the McLellin/Hinkle group had begun to quarrel over leadership.[55] As a result Hinkle traveled east to investigate Rigdon's church at Pittsburgh. In response, Rigdon conceived a new hierarchy for the kingdom, with himself as prophet and seventy-three kings and priests in command.[56] Rigdon was finally claiming the mantle of Joseph Smith. John A. Forgeus, one of Rigdon's converts, was excited about prospects under the new prophet, saying, "Zion will be redeemed by power, and a man will lead them like Moses."[57]

In his periodical Rigdon began attacking plural marriage practiced by the twelve[58] and won to his side such former Saints as Harvey Whitlock, E. B. Wingate, Thomas A. Lyne, Joseph M. Cole, and George Morey, as well as McLellin and Hinkle.[59] One of the Mormon church's most effective former missionaries was also converted for a time. Benjamin Winchester, living in Philadelphia, had been at odds with Joseph Smith and then the twelve over plural marriage[60] and launched his own crusade even before he joined up with Rigdon. Apostle William Smith reported that Winchester had rented a lecture hall and "done the 12 all the harm he can." Winchester spoke of Joseph, Hyrum, and the twelve and reportedly "sunk them as low as he had the power to do." He charged Joseph with having an affair with Heber Kimball's daughter and "implicated all the heads of the church."[61] Winchester was excommunicated at Nauvoo in September. By Christmas he was named by Rigdon as one of Rigdon's new apostles. But Winchester was too restless to remain in one denomination very long and soon left.[62]

Meanwhile, William Smith became a leading defender of the twelve in the east. Concerned that he might be denied a loftier position in church hierarchy, he wrote to Brigham Young in August 1844 that no one could take the place of his fallen brother, but that Young as head of the twelve was entitled to revelations from the martyred prophet. William reasoned that when Jesus Christ died, Peter, the chief apostle, became the head of the church. But he told Young that the church patriarch was next in authority to the chief apostle and stood "as father to the whole church." William contended that the patriarch could also be a prophet and revelator but was not to govern the church.[63] Because the office had belonged to his father and to his brother Hyrum it was intended to remain in the Smith family.[64]

In November William attacked Benjamin Winchester in a published pamphlet, saying that he was a disciple of William Law, a "wanton falsifier and base calumniator," and was a companion of "bad women." In response, Winchester brought suit against Smith, who was unable to find sufficient proof for his allegations and retracted.[65] Toward the end of the year, Apostle Parley P. Pratt was named the principle church authority in the east,[66] which did not set well with Smith. Smith complained that he had stood up against Rigdon, saving the eastern churches, and demanded equal rights with the apostle who was coming to supersede him. "I hold my office & power in spite of Earth or hell," he warned.[67]

But Smith's status in Zion was on the wane. As early as October Apostle Wilford Woodruff had written to Brigham Young from Boston that William himself had been preaching "spiritual wifery" and claiming the right to perform plural marriages. Woodruff complained that wherever William went the churches were disrupted and the "worst off."[68] In December Woodruff wrote Young that William had been working primarily for his own interests and gratifying his "propensities." Woodruff accused him of using funds meant for building the temple and said that it was actually Jedediah Grant who had "saved the church in Philadelphia."[69]

While Smith thus battled Woodruff, Pratt, and Young, William McLellin had a falling out with Rigdon and Hinkle. In December 1846, he wrote to David Whitmer at Richmond, Missouri, relating that he had heard from Leonard Rich and Benjamin Winchester that Whitmer had been ordained in 1834 to succeed Joseph Smith should he fall.[70] McLellin believed that Whitmer was a prophet and seer and that regardless of his personal reluctance he must assume the responsibilities of his calling. McLellin longed for the days of early Kirtland when, he believed, the church had been less worldly.[71]

With McLellin's encouragement Whitmer wrote to Oliver Cowdery in September 1847 and convinced the former assistant president to resume his place in church councils next to David Whitmer.[72] Jacob Whitmer and Hiram Page were designated High Priests, while McLellin became a counselor, standing next to David Whitmer as Oliver Cowdery had stood to Joseph Smith, that is "to assist in presiding over the whole church."[73]

Thus in the three years that had passed after the death of Joseph Smith, several independent churches had been organized from Mormon stock, each claiming to be the true successor with a prophet at the head. As Thomas Sharp had hoped, the Mormons became divided, some breaking off and settling elsewhere.[74] But the majority, much to Sharp's chagrin, remained in Nauvoo and accepted Brigham Young as their leader. The twelve were sustained at a general church conference in April 1845 as "the first presidency and leaders of the church," the vote being apparently unanimous. Yet nothing was said about any of the apostles becoming a prophet.[75]

Within a month of this the twelve faced their most serious challenge. William Smith returned to Nauvoo on 4 May, saying that his wife had recovered sufficiently to make the long journey.[76] Smith had been acknowledged in an earlier church conference as the patriarch "to the whole church," to "preside over all other Patriarchs."[77] Despite the fact that Joseph Smith had once affirmed that "the Patriarchal office is the highest office in the church,"[78] no such status was conferred on William when he was ordained on 24 May 1845.[79]

Yet there was some confusion in the matter. When W. W. Phelps described the office in the *Times and Seasons* prior to William's ordination, he had said that William would inherit his father's office as patriarch "over the whole church."[80] Apostle John Taylor published an immediate clarification in the next issue, insisting that William was patriarch to the church but not over it. He noted that neither Father Smith nor Hyrum had ever led the church.[81] But the damage was done, and the mishandling simply emphasized the ambiguity regarding where the office stood in the hierarchy.

Just prior to William Smith's ordination as patriarch, William Clayton had recorded in his journal that Smith had already turned against the twelve:

> Wm Smith is coming out in opposition to the Twelve and in favor
> of [George] Adams. The latter has organized a church at Augusta,
> Iowa Territory with young Joseph for President, Wm. Smith for
> Patriarch, Jared Carter for President of the stake and himself as
> spokesman to Joseph. William says he has sealed some women
> to men and he considers he is not accountable to Brigham nor
> the Twelve nor any one else. There is more danger from Wil-
> liam than from any other source, and I fear his course will bring
> us much trouble.[82]

In light of this entry it appears that the ordination of William to the
patriarchal office, twenty days after his return to Nauvoo, was a desperate effort by Brigham Young to appease William and to avoid an
open break with the Smith family. Young may have advanced William as far as he dared in the organization without surrendering ultimate authority in the church.

At stake for William was more than a high church position.
James Monroe recorded that William wished to gain some leeway in
publishing church books, which might provide him with some additional revenue.[83] Stewardship over church publications had belonged
exclusively to Joseph Smith prior to his death but since then had
been controlled by the twelve.

The relationship between William Smith and the twelve reached
a critical point on 28 May, when William Clayton reported that Lucy
Mack Smith had received and was circulating a revelation which
seemed to designate William as the rightful successor to Joseph.
Clayton said the revelation had been changed in critical places by
William, but the situation was serious nonetheless.[84] Brigham Young
and the other apostles met at the home of Willard Richards on 29
May and "prayed that the Lord would overrule the movements of
Wm Smith who is endeavoring to ride the Twelve down."[85]

Young and the twelve allowed nearly a month to pass after this,
perhaps hoping that the situation might improve. But when William
had an altercation with the city police with respect to a prisoner he
wished released, the brethren arranged to meet with him at the
Masonic Hall on 25 June. William contended that the police had not
shown him sufficient deference, and Young countered that William
had intruded where he had no authority and had physically accosted
a police officer. William wrote to Young prior to the meeting that he
feared for his life since there were those in the city who wanted to
"put me out of the way."[86] After hearing William's explanation Young
said that his excuse was "pathetic." William reminded the elders that

they were dependent upon the Smith family for their priesthood, but Young shot back that they owed their priesthood to God. William then allegedly pronounced "fearful anathemas" on those who would not support him.[87] Mary B. Smith, Samuel Smith's daughter, wrote years later that William was told to leave the city at once, but this may be an exaggeration since he remained in Nauvoo for weeks afterward.[88] Church historians recorded that things were patched up for the time being.[89]

The police at the meeting with William had been heavily armed, and this alarmed his mother. Lucy Mack Smith received a revelation on the 27th that things were wrong in the church. She recorded that a voice informed her that a snare was laid for her only remaining son, William. The spirit told her that Joseph Sr. and Joseph Jr., as well as Hyrum, were the "first founders, *Fathers* and *Heads*" of the church and that she should now "arise and take thy place." Her vision showed her a room full of armed men who menaced William, intending to crush him. Lucy was promised, nonetheless, that William "shall have power over the churches, he is Father in Israel, over the Patriarchs, and the whole church . . . he is President over all the church." In a second vision Lucy received a visit from her son Joseph who informed her that "the day is coming when I shall have the sceptre of power over my enemies. Be patient."[90]

Young wrote to Apostle Woodruff on the same day Lucy received her revelations, commenting that since his return to Nauvoo William had not acted "as we could have wished." William "seems to think he ought to be president of the church," that the calling to the office of patriarch had made him even more determined. Young observed caustically: "we think to the contrary knowing better."[91]

On 28 June Uncle John Smith and his cousin, George Albert Smith, called on William to discuss Lucy's visions but found that "he evinced a bitter spirit, declared himself President of the Church, and said he would have his rights."[92] Lucy was less belligerent. She said that she was satisfied with the leadership of the twelve,[93] apparently deciding to be patient as her vision had advised. On 2 August Young and the twelve deeded a piece of land to Mother Smith in hopes that she would continue to be loyal to them.[94] But William stated that he would acknowledge Young as church president only if the latter would grant him full freedom to perform all church ordinances as he pleased.[95] Specifically, William wanted power to seal plural wives. Young did not want this rite performed indiscriminately or in a way that would advertise it beyond a small circle at Nauvoo.

In August William presented Young with a bill for $74.24 for his expenses, but the president of the twelve refused to honor it, saying that William had already received more assistance than the rest of the twelve combined. He said that should William receive a house as had his mother, it would belong to the church. He questioned William about why he wanted sealing authority, which was the greater concern to Young.[96]

On the 17th William and John Taylor exchanged bitter remarks when William protested that he could not be seen with a woman in his carriage without gossipers spreading it all over town. Taylor responded that just because Jacob had many wives, we should not infer that every man is so entitled, an allusion to William's demand for sealing authority. William was furious and vowed that he would disrupt the rest of the meeting.[97] On the 20th William wrote privately to a friend that "some people would fain make us believe that the Twelve are the perpetual heads of this church to the exclusion of the Smith family." William believed that "the Twelve are however the Presidents for the time being" and predicted that soon a mob would come and destroy the city.[98]

By the end of the month William had decided to leave Nauvoo, despite Willard Richards's letter urging him to stay.[99] He fled to Augusta, Iowa, where on 25 September he wrote to Young that a mob was searching for him and that he could not get back to the city.[100] A few weeks later he described his true feelings in a letter: "Brigham is a tirant and usurper & he shall not prosper in his fals claims. . . . And no man need tell me that B. Young does not clame to be the prophet, Seer and perpetual head of this church." William said that his calling "lawfully and legely belongs to Lidle Joseph But I shall say no further only I am not a Brighamite." Smith promised: "I shall not resign the Smith family rights to be a slave to usurpers."[101]

William began drifting from one small gathering of Saints to another, looking for those who would support family claims and provide him a more lofty place in the church organization. He joined James J. Strang for a time and promised, with John C. Bennett's urging, to bring the rest of the family with him to Voree.[102] Later, in 1849, he joined Isaac Sheen in a new reorganization and was named prophet with the keys of Elijah, Elias, and John.[103]

Although Brigham Young would never have acknowledged William Smith as church president, he was not opposed to the idea that one day a descendent of Joseph would be. Speaking at the Bowery in Salt Lake City in 1863 Young said that Smith had told him, "I shall have a son born to me, and his name shall be called David; and on him, in some future time, will rest the responsibility that now rests on me." Young continued that "if [the] one that the prophet predicted should step forth to become the leader of this church, he will come to us like a little child, saying, 'God says so-and-so through me.' " Young declared that in that event "I will be as ready to receive him as any man that lives."[104]

Meanwhile Young was ardently defending his own calling, saying in October 1844, "if you want to know whose right it is to give revelations, I will tell you, it is I." Young explained that according to the New Testament, the Lord set apostles ahead of prophets in the church "because the keys and power of the Apostleship are greater than that of the Prophets."[105] Thus Young believed that he was the proper successor to Joseph Smith and had the right to receive revelations for the church but was reluctant to claim such at this time, preferring instead to rest his authority again on his apostolic calling and the approval of the Saints.

Once he had left Nauvoo and the objection that would be raised there to anyone claiming to be Joseph's successor, Young became bolder and reorganized a first presidency with himself as head. In late 1846 he urged fellow apostles to support him in calling two counselors to fill positions next to him. Young argued that the proper function of the twelve was to direct missionary efforts only, that Joseph had never been formally ordained to his office as prophet, seer, and revelator but that his authority had come from his own apostleship. Thus Young argued that he could make the reorganization without additional power being bestowed. His strongest opponent in this move was Apostle Orson Pratt, who contended that the twelve could not ordain one of their members to an office higher than their own. Young overcame Pratt's objections by reassuring him that he had received revelations "as plain as ever Joseph had."[106]

Despite this, Young still would not call himself a prophet. He told the Saints in April 1852: "A person was mentioned today who did not believe that Brigham Young was a Prophet, Seer and Revelator. I wish to ask every member of this whole community, if they ever heard him profess to be a Prophet, Seer, and Revelator, as Joseph Smith was? He professed to be an Apostle of Jesus Christ, called and sent of God to save Israel."[107] After several more years as church president Young was somewhat more affirmative: "I have never particularly desired any man to testify that I am a prophet; nevertheless, if any man feels joy in doing this, he shall be blest for it. I have never said that I am not a Prophet; but, if I am not, one thing is certain, I have been very profitable to this people."[108]

Whatever Young's opinion, to the people at Nauvoo who in 1846 went west, Young had become a prophet indeed. Hosea Stout spoke for them when he paid Young's taxes for the police—"as a token of respect due him from us as a prophet and leader to this people."[109] Nevertheless, the Saints longed for a prophet who would speak definitively and say "thus saith the Lord." George Miller argued this point repeatedly to Brigham Young in Nauvoo in 1846, insisting "no prophet, no church."[110] It was a conviction that had given birth to Mormonism in the beginning and was the one belief upon which all the groups that had looked to Joseph Smith for leadership ultimately agreed.[111] To "discern the calamities," to offset pluralism and secularism, to counsel and command them, the Latter-day Saints demanded a prophet like Joseph.[112]

The Mormon people had other worries after the death of Joseph Smith. They had to survive continuing anti-Mormon attacks and for this looked in part to Governor Thomas Ford, despite their belief that he had betrayed their trust in not protecting their leaders at Carthage. On 29 June Ford issued a proclamation to the people of Illinois, saying that if his pledge of safety for the Smiths was broken, it was the responsibility of the militia at the jail.[113] Ford said he was determined to keep the peace. He sent emissaries to Nauvoo and Warsaw to determine whether further hostilities were planned.[114] On the 30th he wrote to Brigadier General Deming at Carthage that he believed the Mormons "will not commit any further outbreak" but that some in the county "are in favor of violent measures." He said that they had circulated thousands of rumors to rally a larger military force. Ford continued, "I am afraid the people of Hancock are fast depriving themselves of the sympathy of their fellow citizens, and of the world. I strictly order and enjoin you that you permit no attack on Nauvoo."[115]

Ford perceived that most of the people of the state considered the murders at Carthage an atrocity. The editor of the *Quincy Whig* said they were "dreadful,"[116] while the editor of the *Illinois State Register* condemned them as "cold blooded and cowardly."[117] Even George Davis, editor of the *Alton Telegraph*, strongly pro-Whig in his politics, wrote that the old citizens had been wrong in taking the law into their own hands, however right their cause.[118]

Despite this negative reaction in the press, the old citizens were still bitterly hostile toward Mormons. On 2 July, Jonathan Dunham, commander of the Nauvoo Legion, informed Governor Ford that citizen militia were still milling around Warsaw and Golden's Point, waiting for an opportunity to attack Nauvoo.[119] Upon learning this, Ford called out the militia from Marquette, Pike, Brown, and Schuyler counties for a twelve-day campaign.[120] According to the editor of the *Missouri Republican*, many of the mob had come across the border from his state, being "very bitter" against the Saints and wanting to protect the anti-Mormon headquarters at Warsaw.[121] The editor of the pro-Democratic *Quincy Herald* praised Ford's efforts to maintain civil order and said he believed that the murders were the work of a "few desperate characters,"[122] thus minimizing the general civil disorder which actually prevailed in the county.

In a letter to Ford on 3 July, members of the Warsaw Committee of Safety, which had planned the murders, wrote that they were determined to drive the Mormons from the county. They said that they had employed every means to remedy the evils of Mormon political solidarity but were disfranchised by their more numerous enemies. They reaffirmed that the Saints disregarded legal process and contended that the two groups could therefore not coexist in the same region.[123] Ford responded by saying that the public found their "base deed" abhorrent, adding, "I know of no law authorizing their expulsion."[124]

Thomas Sharp, who had participated in the assassination, was temporarily placed on the defensive by public reaction. He admitted that the killings brought on "us the severest censure of nearly the whole newspaper press." Sharp maintained that the lives of the anti-Mormons had been endangered and that they owed allegiance to the law only insofar as it protected them. He said they regretted taking the law into their own hands, but "sooner or later it would have to be done." The Warsaw editor admitted that troops from his town and Green Plains had participated in the murders, feeling that the governor had "trifled" with them in disbanding the militia. He said they had feared that the Nauvoo Legion would attempt to rescue the Smiths that night. The old citizens had to act "or surrender all their dearest rights and leave the county."[125] Levi Williams, one of the more militant anti-Mormons, confessed that the real motive was that the Saints "ruled the county, elected who they pleased, and the old citizens had no chance; that it was the only way they could get rid of them."[126]

The editor of the *Quincy Whig* regarded the issues between the Saints and the older citizens as unresolved and irreconcilable. He said that nothing had been settled by the murders. The old citizens acquired rights of priority by settling the county first, and the Mormons had come in and attempted to reorganize everything to their liking. They combined religious, civil, and military authority in the hands of one or a few men. Such a society could not be tolerated by those abiding existing laws. He warned that "what has been will be again."[127]

Governor Ford had similar fears. In a letter to Willard Richards and W. W. Phelps on 22 July, he said that he had learned that Mormons believed there had been a universal reaction in the state in their favor but warned that this was not so:

> The naked truth is, that most well-informed persons condemn in the most unqualified manner the mode in which the Smiths were put to death, but nine out of every ten of such accompany the expression of their disapprobation by a manifestation of their pleasure that . . . [they] are dead. . . . The unfortunate victims of this assassination were generally and thoroughly hated throughout the country, and it is not reasonable to suppose that their death had produced any reaction in the public mind resulting in active sympathy; if you think so you are mistaken.

Ford told the Mormons that he could not raise a sufficient military force to protect their people from attack.[128]

Three days later Ford wrote to correct misunderstandings in the minds of the old citizens. He told them that they had placed themselves in the wrong with the public and that current threats of expulsion or extermination of the Mormons did not help their situation. The governor said that the Mormons had submitted to the law and kept the peace and that the public would not tolerate expulsion. He warned that if necessary he would use the force of the state to prevent it. He cautioned against mob activity at Lima or Macedonia, where a small number of Mormons lived.[129]

Ford's letter was published in the *Warsaw Signal* with a reply by Sharp on 10 July. Sharp wrote that it was too late for the old citizens to reconsider their course of action, that they had resolved in June to exterminate the Mormon leaders and that the "essential part" had been carried out. "As to the balance," he explained, "we are content to await the result of certain circumstances." The circumstances to which he alluded hinged on the reaction of Illinoisans to the propaganda and civil disorder planned by Mormon antagonists. Miner Deming, a general in the state militia and sympathetic non-Mormon, accurately assessed the disposition of anti-Mormons in a letter to his parents written in August:

> We have had war, murder, politics and animosity bitter and desperate in Hancock, without stint for the last three months. . . . The excite[men]t has been far greater than the a[nti]-masonic that once raged furiously in N[ew] York. The exterminators are of the two, more fanatical than the Mormons and less regardful of the law. They threaten death to all who have enough daring or humanity to oppose them. . . . The Mormon question since the murder of the Smiths has become political and the venum of party spirit breathes in detraction. . . . there were some 2[oo] or 300 engaged in the murder and they with their friends and the alliance of the Whig party in the county, who mean to sustain and protect the murderers makes a strong party that by threats, violence & desperation aim at supremacy above the law and justice.[130]

The most immediate concern of the old citizens was the county elections scheduled for 6 August 1844. Sharp and his friends feared the prosecution of the murderers[131] should the election of a pro-Mormon sheriff encourage Ford to proceed. The governor had delayed legal action thus far because he suspected the state militia might not cooperate and because he hoped that federal troops would be sent for support. He learned on 10 August that no federal troops would be made available.[132]

But a clean sweep by the Mormon candidates in the elections,[133] as well as the victory of Miner Deming as county sheriff, bolstered Ford's determination to prosecute. Deming had written to Ford on 3 July that "it is necessary for the honor of the State and the vindication of your character . . . that the truth in the matter should be fully known."[134] Franklin Worrell, on guard at the jail and subsequently accused of firing blanks at the mob,[135] immediately perceived the danger. He wrote defiantly to Thomas Gregg, a Whig sympathizer, on the 8th: "We are badly beaten in this county . . . I hope Deming will attempt to arrest some of the mob if he does—we will have some more sport—& no mistake."[136]

Ford suggested to W. W. Phelps in September that the Saints should initiate legal complaints against the supposed murderers before a non-Mormon justice of the peace. If there was any resistance by the accused, he promised to intervene. Ford said he would "make the trial to sustain the laws and ascertain how far I will be seconded

by the militia." He indicated that he would bring only the main insti-
gators to trial.[137]

The anti-Mormons now sought to intimidate Ford, Deming, and
the county commissioners who were to choose the grand jury. They
called for a military encampment at Warsaw from 27 September to 2
October to "keep a proper military spirit among the several
companies." Four out of ten leaders who called for this "wolf hunt"
were later indicted for the murders.[138] Ford responded by asking
for 2,500 volunteers to prevent the military assembly in Hancock
County.[139]

Thomas Sharp turned to ridicule, insisting that the assembly
was not anti-Mormon in purpose. Whig editors took up the theme,
hoping to make Ford's call for militia seem foolish. Ford found that
he could muster only 450 of the men he asked for, but before they
reached the county the "wolf hunt" was called off.[140]

John Taylor, who had been wounded at the jail, swore before a
justice of the peace that Levi Williams and Thomas Sharp were
responsible for the murders. On this basis, with a military force now
at his back, Ford was able to demand the surrender of the two anti-
Mormon leaders. But he was unable to apprehend them when they
fled to Alexandria, Missouri. Ford offered a $200 reward for their
capture.

Ford then opened lengthy negotiations to bring the men back
for trial. He promised that they could appear before a non-Mormon
judge for their preliminary hearing and that they would be guaranteed bail. As a result Sharp and Williams surrendered and were
brought before a grand jury in October. At these proceedings they
were indicted for the murder of Joseph Smith, as were John Wills,
William Voras, William Grover, Jacob C. Davis (a state senator), Mark
Aldrich, and two men named Allen and Gallaher, who were never
apprehended nor brought to trial.[141]

Mormon apostles John Taylor and Willard Richards, both eye
witnesses, never testified in court, fearing that "they would have
murdererd us." Taylor told Deming in March that "it was no use any
one coming with a writ for me for I will not go." Taylor said the trial
would be rigged and the murderers set free.[142] He went into hiding
to avoid attempts to subpoena him.

The trial opened on 19 May 1845, and many witnesses were
heard, mostly from Warsaw and Carthage. Only three witnesses sympathetic to the Mormons were brought to court, and their testimony

was so clouded by inconsistencies and exaggerations that it was easily discredited by opposing attorneys and then dismissed by Josiah Lamborn, the prosecutor. Since the jury was selected solely from bystanders who were from Carthage, and since Mormons would not testify, the verdict of not guilty on 30 May was inevitable.[143]

The not guilty verdict further disillusioned Mormons with the legal process. According to the editor of the *Nauvoo Neighbor,* had the accused been found guilty, "it would have been a novel case. . . . The murderers can rest assured that their case, independent of earthly tribunals, will be tried by the Supreme Judge of the universe, who has said vengeance is mine and I will repay."[144] A full year after Joseph Smith's death, in June 1845, Brigham Young recalled the trial verdict with anger: "this matter was decided as we supposed it would be, for we consider that it belongs to God & his people to avenge the blood [of his] servants. We did not expect that the laws of the land would do it."[145]

Because Thomas Sharp had been granted bail, he had been free during the trial to continue his anti-Mormon crusade. On the eve of the trial, 14 May, he had headlined an article in his paper, "HORRIBLE MURDER. TWO MORMONS ARRESTED," recounting how an old man named Miller and his son had been killed in Lee County, Iowa, by men traced to Nauvoo. Sharp prophesied that new waves of violence were imminent. He had held his peace of late but now must speak out. The people of Hancock "never can be at rest, until Nauvoo is made desolate, or filled up with a population of a character entirely different from those who now occupy it." Sharp declared a continuing war on the Mormons.[146]

On 4 June Sharp complained of new outrages at Nauvoo against non-Mormons, saying that Porter Rockwell had warned at least one outsider to stay away from Nauvoo.[147] A week later he published a letter from a follower of Rigdon alluding to the polygamist relations of Nancy Hyde, Orson's wife.[148] In the following issue he said that "some features in the doctrines of Mormonism . . . have a tendency to corrupt the morals and to degrade the character of its adherents." He said that one such doctrine was that the land of the Gentiles would one day belong to the Saints, and complained that "there are many who think it but a small sin to shorten the Lord's time."[149]

On 24 June violence erupted when Sheriff Deming was accosted at the county clerk's office by an older citizen named Sam Marshall, who said he was opposed to Mormon thieving. Deming had sold some of Marshall's land for back taxes, but Marshall showed him a receipt and demanded payment. Deming found that the description of the land on Marshall's receipt did not match the land he had sold. Marshall grabbed Deming by the collar, choking and pushing him. Surrounded, Deming drew his pistol and shot Marshall in the stomach.[150] Deming was convinced the attack had been calculated to provoke him, "to get him in a quarrel by insult and abuse, hoping to get him out of the way."[151]

The *Quincy Whig* accused Deming of being "vain, conceited, pompous, and an instrument of God and his right hand friends the Mormons." The editor wrote, "We can expect such violence until the Mormons are removed from the state."[152] Thomas Sharp also identified the incident as Mormon related.[153] The Warsaw and Whig newspapers would allow nothing to pass that might serve as a means to agitate the Mormon question.

Shortly afterwards, when thieves broke into the home of George Davenport in Rock Island on 4 July and robbed and murdered him, rumors spread that the Mormons had done it. In Camden, William Dickson wrote to his son, a minister, that the murderers were generally believed to be Mormons: "it is hard to tell what will become of these Mormons. They have got to be subdued, either by the sword or the Gospel, & I have no idea that it will be the later."[154] When the editor of the *Quincy Whig* learned from the *Chicago Democrat* that a group of non-Mormons had been arrested for the crime, he reported it,[155] but the damage had been done. Non-Mormons in outlying areas of the state were becoming agitated.[156]

Sharp reported violence in Warsaw on election day, when thirty to forty Mormon elders came to Warsaw to vote against two candidates whom the anti-Mormons had put up for election at the last minute. The citizens of Warsaw had held secret meetings to choose their candidates, but the Mormon candidates easily carried the county despite these efforts.[157]

Sharp did not like the newly elected sheriff, J. B. Backenstos, any better than Deming. He complained that Backenstos had defamed the older citizens by declaring that they had stolen from each other and accused the Mormons. Sharp said the sheriff was a "despicable puppy."[158] Privately, Brigham Young acknowledged that there were bands of "consecrating thieves" at Nauvoo, sometimes with church leaders in command, who "pretend to say they have a right to consecrate, from the Gentiles." Young said he did not want them publicly exposed so as to jeopardize the lives of thousands of innocent Saints but that those who continued to steal would be excommunicated.[159] Young wanted to avoid open conflict with the Gentiles until the temple was finished and they had conducted the ceremonies that would bind the people together. He told Wilford Woodruff that they would not leave Nauvoo before the temple endowments were performed, which would begin in two months.[160] On 28 August he sent word to make preparations for a company of 3,000 to journey to Upper California next spring.[161]

Young's resolve to avoid trouble with the anti-Mormons was tested in September. On the 9th, while the older citizens were holding a meeting in the school house at Green Plains, shots were fired. Sharp admitted later that no one knew who was responsible, but leaders at Green Plains, with Levi Williams in command, decided to retaliate against the Mormons and burned several houses at Morley's settlement. Sharp said that only two or three houses were burned,[162] but the *Nauvoo Neighbor* reported first that eight and then forty-four houses and an out house were destroyed.[163]

The day the burnings began, a church council resolved to send 1,500 emigrants to the Great Salt Lake Valley as soon as possible and appointed a committee of five to gather vital information.[164] Special efforts were made to see that several of the Council of Fifty would be in this group.[165]

Sheriff Backenstos issued a proclamation requesting all citizens to assist him in dispersing the mob operating in the southwestern part of the county.[166] On 11 September a church council encouraged Backenstos now to "quell" the mob but said nothing about using Mormon troops. William Clayton noted in his diary that the council was praying to "manage affairs with the mob so as to keep them off till we can get ready to leave." Letters were sent to outlying Mormon settlements advising them to sell out and gather to Nauvoo.[167] Young told Solomon Hancock to move to Nauvoo but to be ready for a much longer move in the spring.[168]

Mormon leaders learned on 11 September that Miner Deming had died of a sudden illness. This "causes us sorrow," said Young.[169] Deming's wife informed her sister that when the news reached Warsaw, they "threw up their hands and shouted as if they had gained a political triumph."[170] The next day Young told Solomon Hancock to move the women and children from "Yelrome," a code name for the Morley settlement. The brethren were to stay to save the grain. Young told Hancock to let the sheriff worry about the mob or to "see whether he and the 'Jack Mormons' so called, the friends of law and

order, will calmly sit down and watch the funeral procession of Illinois liberty."[171]

Sheriff Backenstos asked Young on the 14th for Mormon militia
to fight the mob, but Young answered that he preferred to let them
burn houses, "until the surrounding counties should become convinced that the Saints were not the aggressors."[172] On the 15th
Backenstos wrote to Young that Levi Williams had called out the
Warsaw militia, and said, "We must whip them." But Young told the
impetuous sheriff to wait a few days to see what might happen.[173]

The anti-Mormons now sought to place greater pressure on Mormon leaders to force them from the state. They brought charges
against several of the leaders for treason, for conspiring with Joseph
Smith, for having an arsenal, and for meeting with the Indians. Constable Michael Barnes of Carthage came to Nauvoo with writs for
the arrest of Brigham Young, Heber Kimball, Willard Richards, and
others.[174] Clayton remarked that "there seems to be a desperate effort
to break us up."[175]

On the 16th an event occurred for which the anti-Mormons had
been waiting. After being harassed and ridiculed at Carthage, Sheriff Backenstos decided to move to Nauvoo. En route he was followed
by armed men and took refuge with a friend at Warsaw overnight.
The next morning, starting out in his buggy, he was chased by ten or
twelve men on horseback, with Franklin Worrell of the Carthage
Greys in the lead. At this point Backenstos encountered Mormon
militia who were escorting burned out Saints back to Nauvoo. He
appealed to them for assistance. Backed by these men, he demanded
that his pursuers halt. When they continued approaching, he ordered
the Mormons to fire. Porter Rockwell responded by shooting Worrell
from the saddle. Thomas Bullock believed that Worrell was the one
"who first went to the stairs" at the Carthage jail "& had the knife in
his hand to cut off Joseph's head."[176]

Sharp immediately denounced the "MURDER OF ONE OF
OUR BEST MEN" and called again, "TO ARMS! TO ARMS!"[177] He
said the citizens must have revenge. When Backenstos burst into a
church council at Nauvoo to report what had happened, the brethren were stunned. Kimball wrote in his diary, "My Father in Heaven
wilt Thou help Thy people and deliver us from our enimies."[178] The
Saints feared instant retaliation.

The editor of the *Missouri Republican* hurried to the scene and
witnessed a "state of excitement of which it is very hard to give a just
description." He found that the anti-Mormons had justified in their

minds the use of any amount of violence to drive the Mormons out. He said he stood on a small knoll as Backenstos and the troops of Levi Williams confronted each other ready for a fight and was disappointed when one did not develop. The Mormons were holding back, trying to avoid another provocation. The editor said he loathed men who would stand by and watch mobbers burn their homes without retaliating. "There is no such thing in the Mormon dictionary as the word courage," he lamented. But he said that it was Levi Williams and his men who finally fled across the river, making excuses as they did so.[179]

Brigham Young wanted to avoid past mistakes by shunning warfare that the Mormons could not win. On the 16th he sent a committee of five with a letter to Levi Williams offering exodus in the spring in return for a cessation of house burnings and other violence.[180] He told Backenstos that he should keep a small force at Carthage to prevent easy access to Nauvoo but that he should bring his main force back home. Young wrote, "The time will come that . . . [the mob] may be dealt with according to the law of God and not endanger the lives of the Saints." On the 19th the citizens of Carthage voted for peace.[181]

There was some bitterness among the brethren as a result of the course they had to take. William Clayton recorded that at a meeting at Bishop George Miller's, they prayed "the Lord would preserve his servants and deliver those who had been active in the mob that killed Joseph and Hyrum into our hands that they might receive their just deserts."[182]

By the 21st Governor Ford had learned of Backenstos's drive to purge Carthage of insurgents and had dispatched a military force to the county under John J. Hardin to take Backenstos into custody. Ford said that anti-Mormons intended to kill him and that citizens from Adams, Brown, Marquette, McDonough, and Henderson counties had met and demanded his arrest. Ford warned the sheriff that the alternative to surrender was an immediate attack on Nauvoo.[183]

When citizens from Macomb came to Nauvoo on the 22nd, they inquired whether Young and his people really intended to leave the state. Young replied that they were not bound to do so because Levi Williams had not accepted their terms, but that they would in fact leave if the law suits against church leaders were dropped and the Saints received a fair price for their property. Young said they would be happy to be paid in groceries, oxen, wagons, and mules. Above all, he said, they wanted peace until their departure.[184]

The citizens of Quincy held a meeting on the 22nd to evaluate the Mormon situation. A majority voted that they were against the Mormons and that the latter must leave. Calvin A. Warren and O. H. Browning, lawyers who had defended the accused murderers of Joseph and Hyrum Smith, were leaders at the Quincy meeting.[185] That same day Constable Michael Barnes came from Carthage and took several church leaders into custody for destroying the *Nauvoo Expositor*. After a preliminary hearing the prisoners were released. The prosecution confessed that they had no direct evidence that the accused were involved in the press's destruction.[186]

By the end of September it was becoming clear throughout the state that tolerance of Mormons had run low. The editor of the *Sangamo Journal* headlined on 1 October: "PUBLIC SENTIMENT IS DECIDEDLY AGAINST THE MORMONS—THEY MUST GO!" The editor of the *Quincy Whig* urged non-Mormons of every party, also on 1 October, to "all be united—put by everything like party or sect— and our state will be relieved of a great grievance now and hereafter." In a conversation with Brigham Young two weeks later, Stephen A. Douglas, a Democrat, and John J. Hardin, a Whig, told the church leader that the prejudice against his people was so great that they could not protect them, and that it was "advisable for us to remove as the only conditions of peace." Young told a committee from Quincy that his people would leave when "grass grows and water runs."[187]

Meanwhile at Carthage on 1 October, citizens from several counties met to consider whether they would wait for a voluntary exodus by the Saints in the spring or drive them out at once. After considerable discussion they decided to accept Young's offer to leave if no legal processes would be served on Mormon leaders and if the older citizens would help in the sale of Mormon property. The non-Mormons demanded that the Mormons not press legal action against the house burners and that Mormon "lawlessness" must cease or vigilantes would march on Nauvoo. County officers elected by Mormon vote in August would have to resign, including the county sheriff, commissioners, and coroner.[188] The anti-Mormons wanted complete political control of Hancock County, even without an election.

The Saints accepted the inevitable in their General Conference on 6 October, voting to "move west in masse."[189] Young told them that "the ranklings of violence and intolerance and religious and political strife that have long been walking in the bosom of the nation, together with the occasional scintillations of settled vengeance, and

blood-guiltiness [will no] long[er] be suppressed. . . . The direful erup-
tion must take place."[190] The Saints were preparing to leave Illinois
and the United States, convinced that the nation was falling into ruin.
Parley Pratt spoke candidly at the conference regarding his view of
Mormon destiny: "We know that the great work of God must all the
while be on the increase and grow greater. The people must enlarge
in numbers and extend their borders; they cannot always live in one
city, nor in [one] county; they cannot always wear the yoke; Israel
must be the head and not the tail."[191]

On the 10th rumors circulated that John Hardin's men, now stationed in Nauvoo, had sworn to take Porter Rockwell into custody
for shooting Worrell or "unroof every house in Nauvoo." It was said
that three hundred volunteers were ready to come to Nauvoo. Clayton
wrote that "there seems to be no disposition abroad but to massacre
the whole body of this people, and nothing but the power of God
can save us."[192]

Many in Illinois doubted that the Mormons intended to leave.
The editor of the *Illinois State Register* said that there remained a great
deal of excitement among non-Mormons.[193] To calm the Mormons
John Hardin rode out of Nauvoo in search of house burners. But
Young wrote to Woodruff that Hardin's men accomplished nothing
against the mobbers "and never will." Young wrote that 150 Mormon
homes had been destroyed, but he still hoped to remain in Nauvoo
until 1 May.[194] Meanwhile, Governor Ford wrote to Hardin to praise
his work in keeping the peace and persuading the Saints to leave the
state "voluntarily."[195]

In the weeks that followed an uneasy peace settled on Hancock
County, preserved only by the small force of men under Major William B. Warren, whom Hardin left in charge. There were occasional
burnings of Mormon houses[196] and tension between church leaders
and troops stationed in the town. Mormons called these troops a
"legalized mob"[197] and urged Governor Ford to remove them from
the city.[198] The governor replied that they kept theft under control.[199]

Testimony of Mormon counterfeiting in Iowa brought an indictment against the twelve apostles by a Hancock County grand jury in
late October, and only Governor Ford's fear that legal proceedings
against them would delay the exodus prevented action by county
officials.[200] When citizens of Carthage learned of this, they said they
were ready to march. The presence of Warren's men prevented
this.[201] Ford wrote to Backenstos that he feared a possible federal

indictment against the twelve and that U.S. president James K. Polk might use the army to prevent the Saints from going west. Ford said the government had doubts about Mormon loyalty should a war break out with England over Oregon, as national leaders feared.[202]

In fact, federal officers accompanied by the Quincy Rifles arrived at Nauvoo on 5 November with writs for counterfeiting against Mormon leaders.[203] Young was furious. He told authorities there must be no more writs or they would not leave.

On 15 November a Mormon named Edmund Durfee was shot and killed as he struggled to put out a fire near his barn. The assailant, a man Ford termed a "swarthy, grim and sanguinary tyrant,"[204] boasted that he could hit a Mormon on the first shot. The suspect was arrested after a state authority threatened to unleash Backenstos.[205] The editor of the *Quincy Whig* said he believed Durfee was killed by a drunk, not an anti-Mormon.[206] The Whigs were anxious to avoid conflict and allow the Mormons to leave the state, and nothing more was said in protest of the arrest.

In mid-November the editor of the *Times and Seasons* assured neighboring communities that 3,285 families were ready to leave Nauvoo, with 1,508 wagons built and 1,982 more in process.[207] On 1 December the editor published Orson Pratt's farewell address to Saints in the east, expressing openly his deep resentment at the forced exodus. He said that the choice his people faced was either "DEATH OR BANISHMENT" beyond the Rockies and that the latter seemed preferable:

> It is with the greatest joy that I foresake this Republic; and all the Saints have abundant reasons to rejoice that they are counted worthy to be cast out as exiles from this wicked nation. . . . If our heavenly father will preserve us, and deliver us out of the hands of the bloodthirsty Christians of these United States, and not suffer any more of us to [be] martyred to gratify holy piety, I for one shall be very thankful.[208]

For Pratt, religious bigotry, not fear of political domination, was the root of anti-Mormon opposition. That Joseph Smith and the twelve concentrated political power in their own hands did not seem menacing to the Saints, who saw their leaders as pure and incapable of tyranny.

Brigham Young believed that what was happening to the Saints proved people could not govern themselves. He told Wilford Woodruff on 19 November: "we have verily seen the fraility of all government and long to see the Kingdom of God spread its domain over the whole earth & reign predominant."[209]

The Saints were anxious to leave. Jeremiah Willey told his brother at the end of the month that they would soon journey "beyond this government." He said, "this land is no longer my home."[210] Willard Richards told Benjamin Wiley that "the commandment to every man and every woman is to come out of Babylon, that you may not be partakers of her plagues."[211]

On 23 December a grand jury of the U.S. Circuit Court at Springfield returned an indictment against the twelve apostles for counterfeiting. At two o'clock that afternoon state militia came to Nauvoo with writs against them. Quickly sizing up the situation when the troops arrived, G. D. Grant turned to William Miller outside the temple and addressed him as Brigham Young, asking if he would like a ride in his carriage. An officer immediately placed Miller under arrest and reached Carthage with his prisoner before realizing his mistake.[212]

Young remained in hiding in Nauvoo and addressed the Saints at length in the temple on 2 January 1846, promising that things would be different: "We will go to a land where there are at last no old settlers to quarrel with us—where we can say that we have killed the snakes & made the roads, and we will leave this wicked nation, to themselves, for they have rejected the gospel, and I hope and pray that the wicked will kill one another & save us the trouble of doing it." Continuing in this vein he said:

> The U.S. Government says if we let the Mormons go out from this Nation they will give us trouble—well perhaps their fears will come upon them—Where is there a city of refuge, on the face of the earth but this? . . . they have got writs out for me, but they have not got me yet, and when they do get me they will get some thing else, I assure you. From [President James K.] Polk, down to the nastiest Bogusmaker, or whiskey seller—it was resolved to break up the Mormons this fall.

Young promised that where they were going, pluralism and secularism would not exist. "One thing I will do," he said, "I will not have divisions & contentions. I mean that there shall not be a fiddle in this Church but what has holiness to the Lord upon it."[213]

Joseph L. Heywood pleaded with Young afterward to leave for the west as soon as possible. He said, "However agreeable it might be to your brethren here to have your society . . . your safety will be greatly endangered."[214]

Sam Brannan, writing from Washington, D.C., informed church leaders at the end of January that Amos Kendall had told him the federal government meant to station troops west of Nauvoo and demand their arms.[215] Hearing this, the elders huddled and decided to leave as soon as possible, believing that "if we are here many days our enemies have resolved to intercept us whenever we start."[216] Young told the Saints at the temple on 3 February that he was going to gather his family and head west.[217]

The next day, on a cold winter's morning, the first wagons left Nauvoo, crossing the river for the Iowa side. By the end of the day, it was reported, 1,700 wagons had made the journey.[218] Hosea Stout, one of the policemen in Nauvoo, crossed and recrossed the river several times in the days that followed, preparing himself and others for the exodus. On the 16th he posted a white flag in front of his tent in Iowa, saying that it was a "token of peace." But he wrote in his journal that it "refused to waive in the air notwithstanding there was a light breeze." Stout saw the flag as symbolic: it "seemed to say that it would not proclaim peace in the United States when there was naught but oppression and tyranny towards the people of God by the ruler of the government and the saints fleeing from her borders to the wilderness for safety and refuge from her iron yoke."[219]

Thomas Ford indicated that over the next three months as many as 16,000 Saints may have left Nauvoo, with about 1,000 remaining who were too poor to make the move.[220] To the old citizens this was not enough, and on 6 June they met to declare that the Mormons were stalling and vowed to take up arms.[221] Sharp wrote in July that "THERE IS NO PEACE FOR HANCOCK WHILE A MORMON REMAINS."[222] Ford said that the anti-Mormons took "measures to get up a new quarrel with the remaining Mormons." They seized a few Mormon men and whipped them. When writs were issued out of Nauvoo to apprehend the perpetrators, counter writs were dispensed at Carthage, and a posse of several hundred rounded up to attack the Mormon city.[223] A special committee was sent ahead to Nauvoo to require a pledge that the Saints would not vote in the coming August elections as a condition of peace. But on election day the elders changed their minds and voted Democratic.[224] Although furious, the anti-Mormons soon learned that they had carried the county anyway. Sharp told readers that at last the old citizens had gained the advantage so long held by the Mormons. They would not have to resort to extra-legal means to have their way.[225]

"It is with much satisfaction that I am enabled to state," Ford told the legislature on 7 December 1846, that the "people called Mormons have removed from the State." Ford continued to maintain that the removal had been voluntary, although he confessed that a small remnant were later expelled by force "in a manner which reflects but little credit on the State or its institutions." Ford said that if the Mormons had remained in Illinois, their presence would have been a continued source of war, "encouraging anarchy and disregard for law, subversive of republican government."[226]

In truth, the Mormon experience in Illinois had been disruptive to Saints and citizens alike. In gathering by the thousands and voting en bloc, the Saints had sought power, but the more political power they gained the more they were hated. Illinoisans preferred power diffused and constantly reallocated. They despised the newcomers for balancing one party against the other for political advantage. They instinctively feared a society where church leaders commanded voting behavior and military force. Other irritants were Joseph Smith's claim of sovereignty for Nauvoo under the Nauvoo Charter and of exemption from legal process, as well as Mormon thieving and counterfeiting in retaliation for property losses. These things gave Thomas Sharp issues to win the noncommitted in Illinois. Plural marriage was a factor, but it was not decisive any more than it had been in Kirtland or Missouri. Anti-pluralism was the main cause of persecution.

But the Mormon experience also pointed to basic limitations within the American democratic political order before the Civil War. As Alexis De Toqueville perceived, there was no appeal of a minority against the will of American democratic majority.

> When an individual or a party is wronged in the United States, to whom can he apply for redress? If to public opinion, public opinion constitutes the majority; if to the legislature, it represents the majority and implicitly obeys it; if to the executive power, it is appointed by the majority and serves as a passive tool in its hands. The public force consists of the majority under arms; the jury is the majority invested with the right of hearing judicial cases; and in certain states even the judges are elected by the majority.[227]

When Stephen A. Douglas and John J. Hardin told Brigham Young that the state could not protect them and that they had no choice but to take their leave, the two Illinois leaders spoke truthfully. Once Thomas Sharp had won his propaganda campaign, the issue was effectively decided. Brigham Young thus made the only decision open to his people if they intended to remain a gathered and largely theocratic society: to remove to an unsettled area where they could become the old citizens, establish their peculiar institutions, and demand the rights of priority for themselves.

Before they could secure a more tranquil place for their society within the confines of the American Republic, however, they would have to give up their unique political party, their plural marriages, their army, and their loyalties to a theocratic political kingdom. By 1907 or so this would be effected and the Mormons would become a somewhat grudgingly accepted denomination among many, thus enabling them to make their own distinctive contribution to the pluralism that nurtures American freedom.

Notes

ABBREVIATIONS

BC   [Joseph Smith, Jr.,] A Book of Commandments for the Gov-
            ernment of the Church of Christ (Zion, MO: by W. W.
            Phelps & Co., 1833).

BM   [Joseph Smith, Jr.,] The Book of Mormon (Palmyra, NY: E.
            B. Grandin, For the Author, 1830).

Brodie   Fawn M. Brodie, *No Man Knows My History: The Life of Joseph
            Smith* (New York: Alfred A. Knopf, 1945).

Bushman   Richard L. Bushman, *Joseph Smith and the Beginnings of Mor-
            monism* (Urbana: University of Illinois Press, 1984).

DC   [Joseph Smith, Jr., et al.,] Doctrine and Covenants of the
            Church of Jesus Christ of Latter-day Saints (Salt Lake City:
            The Church of Jesus Christ of Latter-day Saints, 1921), fol-
            lowed by section and verse numbers.

Faulring   Scott H. Faulring, ed., *An American Prophet's Record: The
            Diaries and Journals of Joseph Smith* (Salt Lake City: Signature
            Books in association with Smith Research Associates, 1987).

HC   Joseph Smith, Jr., et al., *History of the Church of Jesus Christ of
            Latter-day Saints*, 6 vols., ed. Brigham H. Roberts (Salt Lake
            City: Deseret Book Co., 1951).

JD   *Journal of Discourses*, 26 vols. (Liverpool and London: F. D.
            Richards and S. W. Richards, 1853–86).

JH   Journal History of the Church of Jesus Christ of Latter-day
            Saints, LDSCA.

Kenney   Scott G. Kenney, ed., *Wilford Woodruff's Journal*, 9 vols. (Salt
            Lake City: Signature Books, 1983–85).

LDSCA   Archives, Historical Department, Church of Jesus Christ
            of Latter-day Saints, Salt Lake City, Utah.

LDSMS	*Latter-day Saints' Millennial Star*, followed by volume and page numbers.
LMSms	Lucy Mack Smith, preliminary manuscript to her history of Joseph Smith, LDSCA.
PGP	[Joseph Smith, Jr.,] The Pearl of Great Price (Salt Lake City: The Church of Jesus Christ of Latter-day Saints, 1928).
PW	Dean C. Jessee, ed., *The Personal Writings of Joseph Smith* (Salt Lake City: Deseret Book, 1984).
RLDSCA	Archives, Reorganized Church of Jesus Christ of Latter Day Saints, The Auditorium, Independence, Missouri.

INTRODUCTION

1. *Times and Seasons* 3 (15 March 1842): 727; Daniel Rupp, comp., *An Original History of Religious Denominations Existing in the United States* (Philadelphia: J. Y. Humphreys, 1844), 404; 1 (Dec. 1834): 39.

2. See "Is the End Near?" in *Messenger and Advocate* 1 (July 1835): 149; compare Michael Feldberg, *The Turbulent Era: Riot and Disorder in Jacksonian America* (New York: Oxford University PRess, 1980), 5–6, who finds "a higher frequency and variety of urban collective violence and disorder among private groups than in any equivalent period int he nation's past int he 1830s and 1840s." Gordon Wood, "Evangelical America and Early Mormonism," *New York History* 61 (Oct. 1980): 365–66.

3. Alexis de Tocqueville, *Democracy in America* (New York: Vintage Books, 1955), 2:115–16, esp. pp. 105–28.

4. An entire reading of the Book ofMormon makes this point clear, but see 1 Ne. 18:9–11; 2 Ne. 19–24; Jac. 1:15; Enos 20; Mos. 11:1–22, 26:1–12; Al. 1:23, 30:1–59, 45:23–24, 46:13–15, 48.

5. 2 Ne. 2:11 (1920 ed.). Mos. 1:15–16 (1920 ed.). The mouths of the false Christs were "shut" and false teachers and prophets were "punished according to their crimes." Apparently their crimes consisted of stirring up controversy. Al. 30 (1920 ed.). Alma approved of this dissenter's fate, saying, "thus we see the end of him who perverteth the ways of the Lord."

6. Martin E. Marty, *Righteous Empire: Protestant Experience in America* (New York: Dial Press, 1970), 44–77. The Constitution was a compromise document, but most scholars concede that Madison had a major role in its shaping by drawing up the Virginia Plan and writing some of the most important *Federalist Papers*.

7. See Federalist 10 in Michael Kammen, ed., *The Origins of the American Constitution* (New York: Penguin Books, 1986), 145–52.

8. In Article 6 the Constitution provides that "no religious test shall ever be required as a qualification to any office or public trust under the United States."

9. On Thomas Jefferson's religious views, see Dumas Malone, *Jefferson the Virginian*, vol. 1 of *Jefferson and His Time* (Boston: Little, Brown and Company, 1948), 274–79. For an understanding of Jefferson's epistemology, see Daniel Boorstin, *The Lost World of Thomas Jefferson* (Boston: Beacon Press, 1948), 119–23. The Virginia legislature modified Jefferson's Bill for Religious Freedom but retained its basic ideas.

10. For the conflicting views of the founding fathers on establishment, see Winthrop Hudson, *Religion in America* (New York: Charles Scribner's Sons, 1981), 104–105; see also Edwin S. Gaustad, *A Religious History of America* (New York: Harper & Row, 1974), 124.

11. As one historian has said, "The culture allows no City of God to rule, much less chiefly to inspire, all its many cities of man." For a perceptive analysis of the role of religion in America as a consequence of pluralism and the "wall between church and state," see William A. Clebsch, *From Sacred to Profane: The Role of Religion in American History* (Ann Arbor: Scholars Press, 1968). The quotation is on page 218.

12. Compare B. H. Roberts's vigorous affirmation of Mormon loyalty to the United States in *Mormonism, Its Origin and History* (Independence, MO: Press of Zion's Printing and Publishing Co., 1923), 24–28. Roberts claimed that the Saints were "misrepresented in the East" by the charge that Brigham Young headed a government "superior to the United States, in civil as in religious affairs." But compare an earlier work by Roberts wherein he writes that "the kingdom of God . . . is to be a political institution that shall hold sway over all the earth; to which all other governments will be subordinate and by which they will be dominated" (*The Rise and Fall of Nauvoo* [Salt Lake City: Deseret News, 1900], 180).

13. No non-Mormon looked with favor upon the Mormon kingdom in the late nineteenth century, as it was viewed as undemocratic and dangerous. More will be said on early nineteenth-century views, but see Bruce Kinney, *Mormonism the Islam of America* (New York: Fleming H. Revell, 1912), 6–9, who wrote, "The hierarchy has extended its influence into so many lines of our national concern, that Mormonism has ceased to be of merely theological or religious significance. It must be studied in relationship to government and commerce. . . . They are promising their followers nothing less than that they will in time control things politically in the United States."

Hyrum L. Andrus's *Joseph Smith and World Government* (Salt Lake City: Deseret Book, 1958) acknowledges that Smith organized a political government in preparation for the Millennium but insists, strangely, that it embodied the principle of separation of church and state, since the political government would constitute a separate body, with some non-Mormons in it. He maintains that the kingdom would be basically democratic, because although fundamental decisions would be made by the priesthood, the citizenry would have the right to approve. He contends that under such a system there would be no need for divisive politicking and that parties would be unnecessary. He attempts to compare this ideal form of government with that intended by the founding fathers, since they had not planned for parties under the Constitution.

14. Thomas F. O'Dea, "Mormonism and the Avoidance of Sectarian Stagnation: A Study of Church, Sect, and Incipient Nationality," *The American Journal of Sociology* 60 (Nov. 1954): 285–93.

15. E. E. Ericksen does not deal with the kingdom to any extent but does discuss perceptively the growth of what might be called Mormon isolationism. He sees their exclusiveness as mostly due to persecution. Most Mormon ethical values, he insists, came from this experience. This insight is, nonetheless, in some respects erroneous, as I hope to demonstrate in what follows. See his *The Psychological and Ethical Aspects of Mormon Group Life* (Chicago: University of Chicago Press, 1922), vii, 4, 8–9.

16. See Arthur E. Bestor's article on the communitarian movement which flourished in western New York and the Old Northwest in this period, "Patent-Office Models of the Good Society: Some Relationships Between Social Reform and Westward Expansion," *Mississippi Valley Historical Review* 58 (April 1953): 505–26. The name of this periodical has since been changed to *Journal of American History*.

17. Thomas Ford, *History of Illinois* (Chicago: S. C. Greggs, 1954), 268.

18. Quincy's visit to Nauvoo in 1844 formed the basis for his comments. They were published in his *Figures of the Past* (Boston, 1883) but are more accessible in William Mulder and A. Russell Mortensen, eds., *Among the Mormons: Historic Accounts by Contemporary Observers* (New York: Alfred A. Knopf, 1958), 142.

19. W. P. Strickland, ed., *Autobiography of Peter Cartwright* (New York: Carlton & Porter, 1857), 345. Some support for the accuracy of Cartwright's recollection comes from the statements of apostles Orson Hyde and Thomas B. Marsh, who in 1838 were temporarily estranged from the Saints in Missouri and testified at the trial of Joseph Smith for treason. They affirmed that the prophet intended "taking the United States, and ultimately the world." See *Document Containing the Correspondence, Orders, &c., in Relation to the Disturbances with the Mormons and the Evidence Given Before the Hon. Austin A. King, Judge of the Fifth Judicial Circuit of the State of Missouri, at the Court-House in Richmond, in a Criminal Court of Inquiry, Begun November 12, 1838, on the Trial of Joseph Smith Jr., and Others for High Treason and Other Crimes Against the State* (Fayette, MO: Published by order of the General Assembly at the office of *Boon's Lick Democrat*, 1841), 57–59. This will be referred to as *Correspondence and Orders*.

20. *Proclamation of the Twelve Apostles of the Church of Jesus Christ of Latter-day Saints. To All the Kings of the World, to the President of the United States of America; to the Governors of the Several States, and to the Rulers and People of All Nations* (Liverpool: F. D. Richards, 1845), 1, 6. A copy of this proclamation is in the

Yale University Library and is also quoted in part in G. Homer Durham, "A Political Interpretation of Mormon History," *Pacific Historical Review* 13 (June 1944): 141.

21. 2 (Aug. 1834): 353. Compare also *Messenger and Advocate* 1 (Dec. 1834): 40.

22. The kingdom in Utah has been studied from an economic standpoint by Leonard J. Arrington, Feramorz Fox, and Dean L. May, *Building the City of God: Community and Cooperation Among the Mormons* (Salt Lake City: Deseret Book, 1976). Robert Bruce Flanders's *Nauvoo: Kingdom on the Mississippi* (Urbana: University of Illinois Press, 1965) surveyed both political and economic aspects but neglected some of the doctrinal developments. Warren Abner Jennings in a dissertation at the University of Florida in 1962 studied Mormon-Gentile social relationships in Jackson County, Missouri. His work is entitled "Zion is Fled: The Expulsion of the Mormons from Jackson County, Missouri."

23. The above work by Arrington, Fox, and May is an exception but deals with economics, not politics.

24. Klaus J. Hansen, *Quest for Empire* (East Lansing: Michigan State University Press, 1967).

25. Fawn Brodie mentions charges of Mormon apostates that the Saints had established an independent government but fails to give it credence (pp. 244, 314–15). Compare Hansen, 4–5, 11, 65–66. Leonard J. Arrington and Davis Bitton largely ignore it (*The Mormon Experience* [New York: Alfred A. Knopf, 1979], 52, 206).

26. See James R. Clark, "The Kingdom of God, the Council of Fifty, and the State of Deseret," *Utah Historical Quarterly* 26 (April 1958): 131–48. For a short time the council contained a small number of non-Mormons.

27. Hansen, 7–9.

28. D. Michael Quinn, "The Council of Fifty and its Members, 1844 to 1945," *Brigham Young University Studies* 20 (Winter 1980): 163–93. That the council was not convened by the twelve apostles until February 1845 may only mean that they were struggling to establish their own authority in the confusion following Joseph Smith's 1844 assassination and that they were fearful to convene a rival. This says nothing about what the council meant to Joseph Smith, who thought the end of the U.S. government was at hand and that the kingdom would replace it. See the "Journal of William Clayton" (LDSCA) where, on 13 April 1844, Smith "prophesied the entire overthrow of the nation in a few years."

29. Thus Hansen argues (pp. 20–21) that the Saints by 1844 had tied themselves to the idea of progress and had become determined that they would build the kingdom themselves, with a minimum amount of help from the Lord. There is some truth in this, but it captures only part of their thought.

30. *Times and Seasons* 3 (15 July 1842): 855–56. There is some evidence to suggest that some of the prophet's theocratic ideas may have come from his paternal grandfather, Asael Smith, who wrote, "For my part I am willing to trust the government of the world in the hand of the Supreme Ruler of the Universe . . . He has conducted us through a glorious Revolution and brought us into the promised land of peace and liberty; and I believe that He is about to bring all the world in the same latitude in His own time and way . . . And I believe that the stone is now cut out of the mountain, without hands, spoken of by Daniel, and has smitten the image upon his feet . . . (viz. all the monarchical and ecclesiastical tyranny) shall be broken to pieces and become as chaff" (*The Historical Collections of the Topsfield Historical Society* 10:74–76).

31. HC 2:4–24 (the quotation is on p. 21).

32. *Messenger and Advocate* 1 (Dec. 1834): 40.

33. Mulder and Mortensen, 115. Compare also the *Gospel Reflector* 1 (15 May 1841): 261, where Benjamin Winchester argues a similar idea.

34. The *Gospel Reflector* 1 (15 Jan. 1841): 38.

35. Ibid., 39, and 1 (15 April 1841): 202–203.

36. *The Prophet* 4 (8 June 1844): 2. Some support for Rigdon's contention that the early Saints believed in the triumph of the kingdom is seen in Nancy Towles comment in 1831 that the Mormons expected to "increase and tread down all their enemies and bruise them beneath their feet" (Mulder and Mortensen, 60). E. D. Howe, *Mormonism Unvailed* (Painesville, OH: for the author, 1834) noted that the Saints planned an empire that would begin in Kirtland and reach all the way to the Pacific Ocean. He wrote (pp. 110, 145) that they intended to control "all the secular power in the country." And W. W. Phelps exclaimed in the *Messenger and Advocate* in 1834, "Away with crowns, and Kingdoms, away with fame and fashions—all are vanity . . . when the Lord comes, the riches of eternity will be given the Saints . . . the whole world will become the garden of God and his people. The land of the north, the land of the east, the land of the south, and the land of the 'west' will be the land of Israel . . . and the seat of the beloved city." Theocratic ideas in the Book of Mormon also suggest the early commitments to the theocratic kingdom.

37. Howe, 14.

38. Parley P. Pratt, *A Voice of Warning* (London: F. D. Richards, 1854).

39. Pratt, *Autobiography*, 160.

40. Pratt, *A Voice of Warning*, 26–30.

41. Ibid., 30.

42. Ibid., 96.

43. Ibid., 31.

44. Ibid., 71–77, 92.

45. Ibid., 185–86. Compare *The Evening and the Morning Star* 1 (Oct. 1832): 79 and 1 (Dec. 1832): 107.

46. Ibid., 176. Compare Parley P. Pratt's *Millennium and Other Poems* (New York: W. Molineux, 1840), 1–2, and *Mormonism Unvailed* (New York, 1838), 5. Pratt comments in the latter that "if God has provided the great west for a refuge, from . . . wrath, it is no more than he has done for his saints in former ages."

47. Pratt, *Mormonism Unvailed*, 15. Compare BM, 500–501, 512, 520. Parley's brother Orson wrote in *An Interesting Account of Several Remarkable Visions* (New York: Joseph W. Harrison, 1841), 32–33, "We believe that the nations are fast ripening in wickedness, and that judgments, fearful and terrible, speedily await them. . . . In the midst of all these commotions, just as every government seems to be on the very eve of crumbling to pieces, . . . a way of safety for the meek of the earth is clearly pointed out. The kingdom of God is reorganized on earth, which alone will stand secure and triumphant in the midst of the dissolution of all earthly governments."

48. Amos Hayden, *Early History of the Disciples in the Western Reserve, Ohio* (Cincinnati: Chase & Hall, 1876), 183.

49. Pratt, *A Voice of Warning*, 177. Pratt insists if the city is not built by the Saints the Lord will not come.

50. DC 1:1–14, 35.

51. Pratt, *A Voice of Warning*, 13.

52. Missouri in 1838 may have been an exception.

53. HC 2:182.

54. Faulring, 349.

55. See Clebsch, 212, for the gradual adjustment most denominations made in the nineteenth century to pluralism. But compare Sidney E. Mead, *The Old Religion in the Brave New World* (Berkeley: University of California Press, 1977), 88–90, for some of the difficulties American religious leaders have had. A very good recent discussion of Mormon anti-pluralism is Richard T. Hughes and C. Leonard Allen, *Illusions of Innocence: Protestant Primitivism in America, 1630–1875* (Chicago: University of Chicago Press, 1988), 133–52.

CHAPTER 1
WANTED: A REFUGE FOR THE UNCONVERTED,
RELIGIOUSLY DISORIENTED, AND POOR

1. This is noted in LMSms, which Lucy Mack Smith dictated in her old age and which has been published in two somewhat different versions. The edition which is most accessible, and which I have cited unless otherwise noted, was edited by Preston Nibley under the title *History of Joseph Smith by His Mother, Lucy Mack Smith* (Salt Lake City: Bookcraft, 1954); see pages 31–32, 46. Orson Pratt edited and published the first edition in England in 1853, titled *Biographical Sketches of Joseph Smith, the Prophet and His Progenitors for Many Generations* (Liverpool: by S. W. Richards, 1853), which is cited below

on one occasion. Where necessary I have compared these with LMSms, citing the latter where the original wording is important.

    2. Ibid., 31–32, 37, 46, but compare the remarks of Asael Smith, Joseph's
father, who wrote on 4 January 1796 that his son was farming his "old farm"
at "halves" and that he himself intended to move to a new location. Since
Lucy dictated her history so many years afterward she may have erred. She
also seems to have been very sensitive on the subject of their poverty. See
The Historical Collections of the Topsfield Historical Society (Topsfield, MA: by
the Society, 1905), 10:74.

    3. Bushman, 30.

    4. Ibid., 40.

    5. Joseph himself acknowledged a period of drunkenness at a time
when his son Hyrum was young. In a patriarchal blessing he gave to Hyrum
in 1834 he said that "though he [i.e., Hyrum's father] has been out of the way
through wine, thou hast never forsaken him nor laughed him to scorn"
(Hyrum Smith papers, LDSCA). It is unlikely that Hyrum, born in 1800,
would have laughed at his father after reaching maturity, so this probably
refers to a time before 1820. That father Smith drank to excess in New York
after moving there in 1816 is also attested by Lorenzo Saunders in 1884, as
interviewed by a sympathetic member of the Reorganized Church of Jesus
Christ of Latter Day Saints, E. L. Kelley. Saunders, a long-time neighbor of
the Smiths, said that the "old man [i.e., Smith] would go to turkey shoots
and get tight." His brother Orlando added that he once went into Joseph's
cooper shop and found him dressed in the "raggedest and dirtiest shirt
and all full of holes," suggesting not only his poverty but apparent lack of
self-esteem at the time. "Interview with Lorenzo Saunders," E. L. Kelley
papers, RLDSCA.

    6. There is no account in LDSCA that Joseph Sr. drank to excess after
he joined the church in 1830. His conversion, together with that of Martin
Harris, caused his son the prophet to break down in wrenching sobs, evidence of his deep concern and relief. Joseph Knight remembered "that
evening that old Brother Smith and Martin Harris was Baptised Joseph was
fild with the Spirrit to a grate Degre to see his Father and Mr. Harris . . . he
Bast out with greaf and Joy and seamed as tho the world Could not hold
him. He went out into the Lot and appeared to want to get out of site of
every Body and would sob and Crie and seamed to Be so full that he could
not live" (Dean C. Jessee, "Joseph's Knight's Recollection of Early Mormon
History," *Brigham Young University Studies* 17 [Autumn 1976]: 37).

    7. Bushman, 40.

    8. Ibid., 48.

    9. Whitney Cross, *The Burned-Over District* (New York: Cornell Univer-
sity Press, 1950), 139–40; Brodie, 10.

    10. Cross, 139.

11. "William Smith to E. C. Briggs and J. W. Peterson," *Deseret Evening News*, 20 Jan. 1894, 11.

12. Kelley, "Interview with Lorenzo Saunders."

13. Lucy Mack Smith, 93.

14. Bushman (p. 48) indicates that the family paid between seven and eight hundred dollars over several years, making one-hundred-dollar payments each year. Yet, as Brodie argues (p. 10), this estimate may be too high.

15. James H. Hotchkin, a Presbyterian minister in western New York, comments on the poverty of many who migrated to the area. See *A History of the Purchase and Settlement of Western New York* (New York: M. W. Dodd, 1848), 24–25.

16. These statements were published by E. D. Howe in *Mormonism Unvailed* (Painesville, OH: 1834), 232–68.

17. "William Smith to E. C. Briggs," 11.

18. *Palmyra Reflector*, 19 April 1830, 130; 12 June 1830, 36–37; 30 June 1830, 53; and 6 Jan. 1831, 76.

19. The records of the Presbyterian church in Palmyra show that Lucy, Hyrum, and Samuel Smith were active until the fall of 1828. They were suspended from church sacraments in March 1830 for not having attended meetings during the preceding eighteen months. There is no other charge against them. Milton V. Backman reproduces these sources in *Joseph Smith's First Vision* (Salt Lake City: Bookcraft, 1971), 182–83.

20. *Palmyra Reflector*, 1 Jan. through 28 Jan. 1831, carries a series of editorials on the money-digging origins of Mormonism.

21. I have taken my quotations here and below from LMSms. The pages are unnumbered but are roughly in chronological order.

22. BC, 19. The revelation is dated April 1829.

23. "Journal of Priddy Meeks," *Utah Historical Quarterly* 10 (1942): 180. There is a great deal of evidence, much of it from Mormon sources, which shows that Joseph and other members of the Smith family were deeply involved in treasure hunting. See my "Money-Digging Folklore and the Beginnings of Mormonism: An Interpretive Suggestion," *Brigham Young University Studies* 24 (Fall 1984): 473–88. Also in the same issue, see Ronald W. Walker, "The Persisting Idea of American Treasure Hunting," 429–60, and his "Joseph Smith: The Palmyra Seer," 461–88. The most detailed discussion to date of Joseph Smith and magic is D. Michael Quinn, *Early Mormonism and the Magic World View* (Salt Lake City: Signature Books, 1987).

24. Brodie, 16–33.

25. Keith Thomas, *Religion and the Decline of Magic* (London: Weidenfield and Nicolson, 1971), 22–50, 70–93, 117–28, 200–13, 224–45, 643–66. Jon Butler argues that Thomas errs in distinguishing between religion and magic, which serve a common function (see his "Magic, Astrology, and the Early American Religious Heritage, 1600–1760," *American Historical Review* 84 [April 1979]:

317–46). I have sided with Butler in arguing that magic had religious meaning for early Mormons in "Money Digging Folklore," 474–75, 482–86. See
also Jan Shipps, "The Prophet Puzzle: Suggestions Leading Toward a More
Comprehensive Interpretation of Joseph Smith," *Journal of Mormon History* 1
(1974): 3–20; Alan Taylor, "Rediscovering the Context of Joseph Smith's Treasure Seeking," *Dialogue: A Journal of Mormon Thought* 19 (Winter 1986): 18–28;
and Quinn, *Magic World View*.

26. Sidney Ahlstrom, *A Religious History of the American People* (New
Haven: Yale University Press, 1972), 436–39, 481–83.

27. William Warren Sweet, *Religion in the Development of American Culture, 1765–1840* (New York: Charles Scribner's Sons, 1952), 190–233; Sidney E.
Mead, *Nathaniel William Taylor, 1786–1858: A Connecticut Liberal* (Chicago: University of Chicago Press, 1942).

28. For an analysis of the strands of Seekerism, see Dan Vogel, *Religious Seekers and the Advent of Mormonism* (Salt Lake City: Signature Books,
1988).

29. LMSms.

30. Bushman, 28.

31. William Smith, "Notes Written on Chamber's Life of Joseph Smith,"
LDSCA.

32. LMSms.

33. Ibid.

34. Joshua Bradley, *Accounts of the Religious Revivals in Many Parts of the
United States from 1815 to 1818* (Albany: G. J. Loomis, 1819), 223, and Hotchkin,
126.

35. *Memoirs of Rev. Charles G. Finney* (New York, 1876), 78.

36. Cross, 3–28.

37. Sec. K-M, 1827, American Home Missionary Files, Chicago Theological Seminary. The letter is dated 9 Feb. 1827.

38. Amos Hayden, *Early History of the Disciples in the Western Reserve,
Ohio* (Cincinnati: Chase & Hall, 1876), 20–21.

39. *Wayne Sentinel*, 31 Oct. 1828, 2; 26 March 1830, 2; 21 May 1830, 2; 23 July
1830, 2. Obadiah Dogberry also noticed a minister's mixing of politics and
religion in the *Palmyra Reflector*, 2 Jan. 1830, 12; 1 Feb. 1831, 95.

40. James Hotchkin lamented that French ideas thrived in America at
this time, bringing infidelity and atheism. He wrote (p. 26), "Some who were
deeply imbued with these principles were among the first settlers of western New York and were zealous in propagating their sentiments."

41. 16 Feb. 1825, 2.

42. A religious leader who partook of this mood was John Humphrey
Noyes. See Robert David Thomas, *The Man Who Would Be Perfect* (Philadelphia: University of Pennsylvania Press, 1977), 1–41.

43. Richards voiced his opposition to Finney's new measures in a letter to Asahel Nettleton, a bitter enemy of Finney. See Richards Family Correspondence, 1821–43, LDSCA.

44. Cross, 151–69.

45. "History of Willard Richards," LDSMS 27 (Feb. 1865): 118–19.

46. Joseph F. Kett, *Rites of Passage: Adolescence in America, 1790 to the Present* (New York, 1977), 62–85. Kett indicates that many young people berated themselves when they did not have the coveted experience.

47. *Wayne Sentinel*, 2 Mar. 1825, 2.

48. Ibid., 23 Oct. 1823, 4.

49. The several different versions of the first vision are reproduced in Backman, 155–69. An account by William Smith in the *New York Observer*, July 1841, recounts how an angel was the first heavenly messenger to visit his older brother "About the year 1823."

50. Neal E. Lambert and Richard Cracroft, "Literary Form and Historical Understanding: Joseph Smith's First Vision," *Journal of Mormon History* 7 (1980): 31–42.

51. HC 1:3–6.

52. Brodie, 21–25.

53. Wesley P. Walters, "Joseph Smith's First Vision Story Revisited," *Journal of Pastoral Practice* 4 (1980).

54. "The First Vision Controversy: A Critique and Reconciliation," *Dialogue: A Journal of Mormon Thought* 15 (Summer 1982): 31–47. I set down here my reasons for believing that none of the small revivals around Palmyra and environs before 1823 and described by Backman satisfy all the conditions in Joseph's descriptions.

55. LMSms and my piece cited above.

56. Alexander Neibaur Journal, n.d. (LDSCA), but reproduced in Backman.

57. Bushman portrays relationships within the family as always harmonious but misses Lucy's confession of hurt feelings (pp. 31–40).

58. "William Smith to E. C. Briggs."

59. "William Smith on Mormonism," reprinted in Francis W. Kirkham, *A New Witness for Christ in America* (Independence, MO: Zion's Printing and Publishing Co., 1951), 414; and HC 1:3.

60. Lucy Mack Smith, *Biographical Sketches*, 36–37. This quotation does not appear in Preston Nibley's edition.

61. William Garrett West, *Barton W. Stone: Early American Advocate of Christian Unity* (Nashville: The Disciples of Christ Historical Society, 1954), 6.

62. See the recollections of W. D. Purple, who took notes at the trial, in the *Chenango Union*, 3 May 1877. It is significant that Joseph Smith never mentioned this trial in any of his writings.

63. Linda King Newell and Valeen Tippetts Avery, *Mormon Enigma: Emma Hale Smith* (New York: Doubleday, 1984), 18, 24–25.

64. Ibid. This account comes from Emma Smith's two cousins who witnessed the event and wrote to the *Amboy Journal* in 1879.

65. HC 1:3.

66. "Biographical Sketch of George Albert Smith," LDSMS 27 (July 1865): 407.

67. "History of Willard Richards"; and Claire Noall, *Intimate Disciple: A Portrait of Willard Richards* (Salt Lake City: University of Utah Press, 1957).

68. From a source shared with me by Steven Pratt, a descendant who has some of Pratt's papers. Compare *Autobiography of Parley P. Pratt*, 5th Ed. (Salt Lake City: Deseret Book, 1961), 25–26.

69. Eugene England, ed., "George Laub's Nauvoo Journal," *Brigham Young University Studies* 18 (Winter 1978): 155.

70. "Life of George Whitaker A Utah Pioneer as Written by Himself," 1. A copy of these memoirs is in the Southern Illinois University Library at Edwardsville.

71. Ben E. Rich, *Scrapbook of Mormon Literature* (Chicago: Henry C. Etten, n.d.), 1:543–45.

72. "Autobiography of Warren Foote," 4, Harold B. Lee Library, Brigham Young University, Provo, Utah.

73. Paul Hokanson, "Lewis Warren Shurtliff: A Great Man in Israel," M.A. thesis, Brigham Young University, 1979, 8–11.

74. In I. Woodbridge Riley, *The Founder of Mormonism: A Psychological Study of Joseph Smith, Jr.* (New York: Dodd, Mead, 1902), 47.

75. Charles G. Finney, *Lectures on Revivals of Religion* (New York: Leavitt, Lord, 1835), 385.

76. Peter L. Berger, *The Sacred Canopy* (New York: Doubleday Anchor, 1969), 111–12.

77. "Diary of Hosea Stout," 1:61, 68, Harold B. Lee Library, Brigham Young University.

78. Andrew Jenson, comp., *Latter-day Saint Biographical Encyclopedia*, 4 vols. (Salt Lake City: Andrew Jenson History Co., 1902), 1:227.

79. "Testimony of Martin Harris," 4 Sept. 1870, in the hand of Edward Stevenson, located in his papers at LDSCA.

80. "Reminiscences of Sarah Leavitt," Huntington Library, San Marino, California.

81. "Journal of John Murdock," LDSCA.

82. "Life of Laban Morrill, Written by His Grandson, with Quotations from his Autobiography," 90–91, Special Collections, Harold B. Lee Library, Brigham Young University, Provo, Utah.

83. "Journal of Lewis Barney," 16, Special Collections, Harold B. Lee Library, Brigham Young University.

84. *The Evening and the Morning Star* 1 (April 1834): 290.

85. "Isaac Haight Journal," 1, Huntington Library.

86. From notes given to me by Leonard J. Arrington.

87. "Journal of Wandle Mace," 1, Special Collections, Harold B. Lee Library, Brigham Young University.

88. *The Evening and the Morning Star* 1 (Sept. 1832): 64.

89. BM (1830), 13.

90. Ibid., 108.

91. M. R. Werner, *Brigham Young* (London: Jonathan Cape, 1925), 7; Matthias F. Cowley, ed., *Wilford Woodruff* (Salt Lake City: Deseret News Co., 1909), 4; Brigham H. Roberts, *The Life of John Taylor* (Salt Lake City: Bookcraft, 1963), 23; Eliza R. Snow Smith, *Biography and Family Record of Lorenzo Snow* (Salt Lake City: Deseret News Co., 1884), 2; *Autobiography of Parley Parker Pratt*, 30–31; and "History of Lyman Wright," LDSMS 27 (22 July 1865): 455. These findings compare favorably with Orson Spencer's statement in 1842 that "our people are mostly the working class" (see *Letters Exhibiting the Most Prominent Doctrines of the Church of Jesus Christ of Latter-day Saints* [Salt Lake City: Deseret News Co., 1889], 38).

92. Spencer, 38.

93. Mark P. Leone, *Roots of Modern Mormonism* (Cambridge: Harvard University Press, 1979), 16. Most Mormon converts appear pre-industrial in their farming and crafts.

94. Ronald W. Walker traces the contours of this early form of religion in the two articles cited in note 23. Barnes Frisbie recalls some of the religious beliefs of money diggers in 1800 in *History of Middletown, Vermont* (Middletown: Middletown Historical Society, 1867), 49–60.

CHAPTER 2

"A PRINCIPLE MEANS IN THE HANDS OF GOD"

1. Joseph Knight wrote that "when he Began to translate he was poor and was put to it for provisions . . . : He and his wife Came up to see me the first of the winter 1828 and told me his Case. But I was not in easy Circumstances and did not know what it mite amount to my wife and family all against me about helping him. But I let him have some little provisions and some few things out of the Store apair of shoes and three Dollars" (Dean C. Jessee, ed., "Joseph Knight's Recollections of Early Mormon History," *Brigham Young University Studies* 17 [Autumn 1976]: 35//36). Knight speaks of Smith's poverty throughout the translation time.

2. Bushman, 66–68.

3. LMSms.

4. Eber D. Howe, *Mormonism Unvailed* (Painesville, OH: the Author, 1834), 260.

5. See Faulring, 5–7, for Joseph Smith's 1832 dictated history. Oliver Cowdery repeated much of the same attitude on Joseph's part in a letter to

W. W. Phelps in 1834 (*Latter-day Saints Messenger and Advocate* 2 [Oct. 1835]: 197).

6. Jesse Smith to Hyrum Smith, 17 June 1829, in Joseph Smith's Kirtland Letter Book, LDSCA.

7. Letter dated 22 Oct. 1829 from Harmony, Pennsylvania, in Kirtland Letter Book.

8. Lucy Smith recalled this during a conference in Nauvoo, Illinois, 7 Oct. 1845 (see the minutes in LDSCA).

9. Hiram Page's letter, dated 2 Feb. 1848, to brother "William" (probably William E. McLellin), is in RLDSCA. David Whitmer, a witness to the Book of Mormon plates, also recalled the attempt to sell the copyright in his *An Address to All Believers in Christ, by A Witness to the Divine Authenticity of The Book of Mormon* (Richmond, 1887), 30.

10. The agreement to allow Martin Harris to sell copies of the Book of Mormon until he was repaid his $3,000 loan is dated Manchester, 16 Jan. 1830, and is in LDSCA.

11. Jessee, "Joseph Knight's Recollections," 37.

12. *Evangelical Magazine and Gospel Advocate* 2 (9 April 1931).

13. Whitmer, 31–32.

14. Brodie (p. 33) argued that Smith outgrew money digging to assume his prophetic role. Bushman (p. 76) contends that Joseph gave up money digging as early as 1826.

15. The 1832 account of the first vision makes it clear that this was a personal vision reassuring Smith of his acceptance with God and included no call to the ministry at this time.

16. Smith's later polygamous proposals to other men's wives (especially those he did not want) could be a type of this role testing. James Monroe recounted (in an account located in the library of the Utah State Historical Society, Salt Lake City) that Smith once came into his Nauvoo store, where the diminutive Monroe was clerking, put his large leg on Monroe's shoulder, and commented, "You are stouter than I thought." He then wrestled with Monroe and broke Monroe's leg. Smith often tested how much his loyal followers would take.

17. Keith Thomas, *Religion and the Decline of Magic* (London: Weidenfield and Nicolson, 1971), 117–30, 151–73, 200–13, 224–45, 643–66; compare Jon Butler, "Magic, Astrology, and the Early American Religious Heritage, 1600–1760," *American Historical Review* 84 (April 1979): 317–46.

18. BM, title page and 497.

19. Ibid., 108, 113.

20. Ibid., 466, 478.

21. Ibid., 32, 67, 104–105.

22. Ibid., 32, 67. Martin Harris, one of the three witnesses to the Book of Mormon plates, told John A. Clark that the scripture would "settle all religious controversies and speedily bring on the millennium. (See Clark,

Gleanings by the Way [Philadelphia: Simon Brothers, 1842], 223–24). Compare Pomeroy Tucker, *Origin, Rise and Progress of Mormonism* (New York: D. Appleton & Co., 1857), 78, who heard Sidney Rigdon emphasize in a sermon in Palmyra the common purposes of the Bible and Book of Mormon.

23. George A. Arbaugh, "Evolution of Mormon Doctrine," *Church History* 9 (June 1940): 169.

24. BM, 25, 80, 160, 186, 453, but compare passages in the Book of Ether where Jesus on the eve of mortality appears to the brother of Jared (p. 544). Notice also that after Jesus ministers to the Nephites he then mentions his ascension to "my father" (pp. 22, 476–510, especially 485).

25. See ibid., 23 and 586 where Jesus, the Father, and the Holy Ghost seem to be different persons. It is significant that Joseph Smith later revised several of these passages to conform to his developing tri-theism.

26. Ibid., 439–40.

27. Ibid., 85.

28. Ibid., 306.

29. Ibid., 315. Alma says, "But behold, if ye will awake and arouse your facilities, even to an experiment upon my words, and exercise a particle of faith; yea, even if ye can no more than desire to believe."

30. Ibid., 38.

31. Ibid., 108.

32. Ibid., 32, 159, 162.

33. Thomas F. O'Dea, *The Mormons* (Chicago: University of Chicago Press, 1957).

34. BM, 221–22. The apostate Nehor preaches that all humanity will be saved.

35. Ibid., 311. The apostate Zoramites preach that God "hast elected us to be thy holy children" but are discredited for this.

36. Ibid., 501. That the Book of Mormon was not merely a history of the Nephites and Lamanites but a warning to contemporary Americans is plain in many passages (see ibid., 60//61, 75, 107–110, 527–28, 535–38).

37. Parley P. Pratt, *Autobiography of Parley Parker Pratt* (Salt Lake City: Deseret Book, 1961), 37.

38. "Lecture written by John M. Rigdon on the Early History of the Mormon Church," Special Collections, Harold B. Lee Library, Brigham Young University.

39. W. W. Phelps to William Smith, 25 Dec. 1844, in *Times and Seasons* 5 (1 Jan. 1845): 757.

40. JD 4:77.

41. Obadiah Dogberry (Abner Cole) took this view, publishing a caricature of the Mormon scripture called the "Book of Pukei," in the *Palmyra Reflector*, 12 June 1830, 36–37, and 7 July 1830, 60.

42. This appeared under the title "Delusions" in the *Painesville Telegraph*, 8 March 1831, 1–2, and "Internal Evidences," 15 March 1831, 1–2.

Campbell also published this attack in his *Millennial Harbinger*, Feb. 1831, and as a brochure in 1832. See Brodie, 471.

43. Amos Hayden, *Early History of the Disciples in the Western Reserve* (Cincinnati: Chase and Hall, 1876), 215–250, and James Harrison Kennedy, *Early Days of Mormonism* (New York: Charles Scribner's Sons, 1881), 980–91. Campbell gave as his reason for writing "Delusions" that "several hundred persons of different denominations believed" the Book of Mormon (see *Painesville Telegraph*, 8 March 1831, 2).

44. *Painesville Telegraph*, 15 March 1831, 1.

45. The compilers of JH estimate that there were approximately 1,500 Mormons in Ohio as of 31 December 1831.

46. Kennedy, 90–91. Kennedy reports that the Campbellites took the lead in opposing the spread of Mormonism but that other denominations joined in. He indicates that it was Sidney Rigdon's "former high standing" in the Campbellite church which caused Alexander Campbell to come to Ohio for twenty-two days and oppose "the new creed." Possibly, too, the similarity in doctrine made the two denominations natural rivals.

47. Benjamin Winchester, a Mormon missionary in Pennsylvania when Hurlbut first traveled through, claimed that Hurlbut learned about Spaulding in Pennsylvania in a place called Jackson Settlement (see Winchester's *The Origin of the Spaulding Story Concerning the Manuscript Found* [Philadelphia: Brown, Bicking & Guilbert, 1840], 8–11). However, Charles Shook (*The True Origin of the Book of Mormon* [Cincinnati: Standard Publishing Co., 1914], 64), maintained that the residents of Conneaut (New Salem), Ohio, recognized the similarities between the two works as early as 1832 when Mormon missionaries first visited the region. This is countered by Orson Hyde, a missionary who traveled through Conneaut in 1832, converting some of Spaulding's neighbors. Hyde insisted that none "intimated to me that there was any similarity between the Book of Mormon and Mr. Spaulding's Romance." Hyde acknowledged that these neighbors had frequently heard the manuscript read aloud. Hyde's observations appear in Benjamin Winchester's *Plain Facts Showing the Origin of the Spaulding Story. Concerning the Manuscript Found, and its Being Transformed in the Book of Mormon* (Bedford, England: George J. Adams, 1841), 25. Joseph E. Johnson, a Mormon in Kirtland at the time, declared that the charge that the Spaulding manuscript had been the source of the Book of Mormon was made before Hurlbut went east to collect testimony (see Thomas Gregg, *The Prophet of Palmyra* [New York: John B. Allen, 1890], 428).

48. George A. Smith, Joseph Smith's cousin, said that Hurlbut had threatened that he would "wash his hands" in the prophet's blood and that the court proceedings which resulted from his threats discredited him in Ohio and caused Howe to assume authorship of the book (see "Historical Discourse," in JD 11:8).

49. See *Chardon Spectator and Geauga Gazette*, 18 Jan. 1834, 2, which reports that Hurlbut searched in New York "on behalf of his fellow townsmen" (the article originally appeared in the *Wayne Sentinel*). Compare the *Cleveland Herald*, 22 March 1834, 2, where it is affirmed that Hurlbut was sent from Kirtland by a committee appointed during a "public meeting." Howe himself writes that he undertook the book after being solicited by "a great number of friends" (see the "advertisement" in front of the book).

50. This is suggested by Shook who alleges that the parallels between the two were discovered "in a meeting in Conneaut in 1832 or 1833 where a woman preacher read some of it" (p. 64).

51. Ibid., ix. On the all-but-universal acceptance of the theory until the turn of the century or a little after, see Lester E. Bush, Jr., "The Spaulding Theory Then and Now," *Dialogue: A Journal of Mormon Thought* 10 ((Autumn 1977): 40–69.

52. William Alexander Linn, *The Story of the Mormons* (New York: Russell and Russell, 1963), 50.

53. See Daryl Chase, "Sidney Rigdon—Early Mormon," M.A. thesis, University of Chicago Divinity School, 1931, 36–37; compare "Faith of the Church of Christ in These Last Days," *The Evening and the Morning Star* 1 (April 1834): 290.

54. Ibid., 27, and compare Hayden, 299.

55. Campbell had changed his mind as to the authorship of the Book of Mormon. See *Millennial Harbinger*, 3rd Series, 1 (Jan. 1844): 38, and 4th Series, 6 (Dec. 1856): also *Painesville Telegraph*, 15 Mar. 1831, 1.

56. Linn, 62.

57. The Manuscript Found was later located in Hawaii but bore little resemblance to the Book of Mormon. Some witnesses claimed that Spaulding had written another work closer to the Book of Mormon, but this manuscript, it if exists, has never been found. For a thorough critique of the argument, see Bush, 53–61.

58. Compare *Millennial Harbinger*, 3rd Series, 1:38; and Linn, 63.

59. Isaac Woodbridge Riley, *The Founder of Mormonism* (New York: Dodd, Mead & Co., 1902), 369–95; Chase, 39–70; Brodie, 419–433; and Bush.

60. Brodie, 46–48.

61. See my "Secular or Sectarian History?: A Critique of *No Man Knows My History*," *Church History* 43 (March 1974): 78–96.

62. Among those newspapers editorializing on the Book of Mormon are the *Rochester Daily Advertizer*, 2 April 1830; *The Gem* (Rochester), 15 May 1830; *The Chenango Republican* (Oxford), 19 May 1830; the *Ohio Star* (Ravenna), 9 Dec. 1830. The *Painesville Telegraph*, which was to become a focal point of anti-Mormonism in Ohio, carried a piece on the book as early as 16 November 1830.

63. No contemporary caught the excitement in some circles better than Lucius Fenn, who wrote of the forthcoming book in February 1830 from

Covert, New York, some fifty miles from Palmyra. Fenn observed, "There is something that has taken place lately that is mysterious to us . . . there has been a bible found. . . . It speaks of the millennium day and night and tells when it is going to take place" (in William Mulder and A. Russell Mortensen, eds., *Among the Mormons* [New York: Alfred A. Knopf, 1958], 38).

64. Until June the revelations, later published in DC, had dealt entirely with the translation of the Book of Mormon.

65. Whitmer, 32.

66. BC, 34–39. The revelation was given to Oliver Cowdery and David Whitmer in June and is now DC 18. In the Book of Commandments the twelve were designated "disciples" as they had been in the Book of Mormon. Later editions, however, termed the twelve "apostles." See BM, 477–85, especially 485, and compare BC, 34, and DC (1835 edition), 172.

67. R. Kent Fielding, "The Growth of the Mormon Church in Kirtland, Ohio," Ph.D. diss., University of Indiana, 1957, 111–13. More recently, Mormon historian Richard Bushman (p. 240–55) acknowledged that the restoration of higher priesthood probably did not occur until two months after the church was organized.

68. Whitmer, 36, 64. Whitmer was wrong about the Book of Mormon not mentioning high priests. He was also inconsistent, ordaining high priests himself in the reorganization he planned with William E. McLellin in 1847 (see his letter to Oliver Cowdery, 8 Sept. 1847, in *The Ensign of Liberty of the Church of Christ* 1 [May 1848]: 83). Cowdery's views may be contained in *Defence in a Rehearsal of My Grounds for Separating Myself from the Latter Day Saints* (Norton, OH: Pressley's Job Office, 1839), 4 (although Richard L. Anderson, a professor of religion at Brigham Young University, questions the authenticity of this source, contending that there was no press in Norton in 1839). "The Book of John Whitmer," 8–9, copy in LDSCA. For McLellin's position, see LDSMS 40 (Dec. 1878): 770. John Corrill, *A Brief History of the Church of Jesus Christ of Latter-day Saints, Including Their Doctrine and Discipline* (St. Louis: by the author, 1839), 18. Brewster's views are found in *The Olive Branch* 2 (Dec. 1849): 89–91. See also *William Smith on Mormonism* (Lamoni, IA: Herald Steam Book & Job Office, 1883), 20, and JD 9:89 for Brigham Young's address of 7 May 1861.

69. HC 1:175–76. Church historian John Whitmer wrote that at that time Joseph Smith "laid his hands upon Lyman Wight and ordained him to the high priesthood after the holy order of God" ("Book of John Whitmer," 8–9).

70. P. Pratt, 42, 68.

71. Whitmer, 64.

72. *William Smith on Mormonism*, 20.

73. JD 9:89.

74. HC 1:176n (the note was written by B. H. Roberts). Also see Bushman, 241.

75. Dan Vogel, *Religious Seekers and the Advent of Mormonism* (Salt Lake City: Signature Books, 1988).

76. 1 (Oct. 1834): 15.

77. BM, 575. Compare Moroni 3 in current LDS editions.

78. Ibid., 258–60. Compare Alma 13 in current LDS editions.

79. Whitmer, 66.

80. *Painesville Telegraph*, 7 Dec. 1830, 3.

81. I have elaborated on the primitive gospel movement in America and its impact on early Mormonism in "Christian Primitivism in the Origin and Development of the Mormon Kingdom," Ph.D. diss., University of Chicago, 1968.

82. Wesley P. Lloyd, a Mormon, wrote with some insight about the strengths and weaknesses of lay leadership in the Mormon church in "The Rise and Development of Lay Leadership in the Latter-day Saint Movement," Ph.D. diss., University of Chicago Divinity School, 1937. Significantly, Lloyd begins his chapter on "General Historical Background" with a description of "Lay Leadership in the Early Christian Church" (see pp. 6–8).

83. There is a difference of opinion on this. Compare David Whitmer's estimate of between sixty and seventy members (pp. 32//33) with the assessment of thirty made by Joseph Smith and supported by B. H. Roberts (HC 1:76–77, 84). Whitmer insists that the church was fully organized by the fall of 1829.

84. Whitmer, 33, writes that there was a branch at Fayette, one in Manchester, and one at Colesville. Later there may also have been one at Waterloo (see LMSms). Apparently, the Mormons had little success in Palmyra (see Brodie, 87, but compare LMSms, and Tucker, 79).

85. Smith said the church organization was formed "according to the order of the Church as recorded in the New Testament" (HC 1:79).

86. See BC, 48. This compares with DC 20:2.

87. BC, 45. Here Oliver Cowdery was told to ordain Smith a "prophet and seer" and that the church was to "give heed unto all his words and commandments."

88. Ibid., 48. Compare DC 20. The wording has been altered in the more recent version to make it clear that Smith was the first elder and Cowdery the second. But this comes through well enough in the original. See also Cowdery, 1.

89. BC, 51. Compare DC 20:39–44.

90. BC, 51–52, and HC 1:67–68.

91. HC 1:68. Compare BC, 54.

92. HC 1:69. Compare BC, 53. The convert had to be of the "age of accountability" and capable of repentance.

93. As indicated by Pearson H. Corbett in *Hyrum Smith, Patriarch* (Salt Lake City: Deseret Book Co., 1963), 75–78, thirty-two new members joined the Fayette branch from June to October 1830; a total of approximately 250 joined the church during the last nine months of 1830.

94. LMSms.

95. BC, 73, 75, 81, 82.

96. Ibid., 45. David Whitmer, Oliver Cowdery, and Hiram Page, one of the eight witnesses of the Book of Mormon, disapproved of this move (see Whitmer, 32–34, 45–48; Cowdery, 1; and *The Olive Branch* 2 [Aug. 1849]: 28).

97. They held that it contradicted the Book of Mormon. The revelation treated the sequence involved in repentance, baptism, and the forgiveness of sins. Cowdery believed that the church was claiming too much of the latter power, labeling this "priestcraft." See HC 1:104–105, and compare BM, 119, and BC, 51. Compare also Arbaugh, 60.

98. Newell Knight described these events in "Journal of Newell Knight," *Scraps of Biography, Tenth Book of the Faith Promoting Series* (Salt Lake City, 1883), 64–65. Compare the recollections of Ezra Booth in the *Painesville Telegraph*, 20 Dec. 1831, who reports that Page's revelations were widely believed until Joseph's revelation condemned him. In 1953, official Mormon historian Joseph Fielding Smith wrote that "among other things [Page] claimed to have received a revelation making known the place where the City of Zion would be built" (*Church History and Modern Revelation* [Salt Lake City: Council of the Twelve Apostles of the Church of Jesus Christ of Latter-day Saints, 1953], 1:134–35).

99. According to David Whitmer, Smith gave up the seer stone after the Book of Mormon was translated. Whitmer believed that Joseph led the Saints astray afterward (p. 32).

100. Compare *RLDS Saints' Herald* 34 (5 Feb. 1887), where Whitmer denied that secret meetings were held "in any house."

101. Oliver may indeed have received some revelations of his own at this time. In BC, 67, he was told "thou shalt not write by way of commandment but by wisdom." Ezra Booth indicated that Cowdery received some of the revelations. Booth's eighth letter, dated 20 Nov. 1831, appeared in the *Painesville Telegraph*, 20 Dec. 1831, 2–3. A revelation in Cowdery's hand, dating from 1829, some of which Booth quotes, is located in LDSCA.

102. God told Cowdery "no one shall receive revelations in this church excepting my servant Joseph" (BC, 67).

103. Ibid., 61. The gathering in New York into small communities may have come as a defensive measure as a result of persecution. See LMSms and notice that Hiram Page complained later that the gathering, "is sowing the seeds of discord." He does not say whether he opposed the gathering this early. Page's letter to J. C. Brewster, written in June 1849, appears in *The Olive Branch* 2 (Aug. 1849):28.

104. In his *Autobiography* (p. 55) Parley Pratt wrote that he told the Indians they would be restored to all their "rights and privileges" if they accepted the Book of Mormon. This no doubt referred to a restoration of their lands which Andrew Jackson had taken from them.

105. BC, 82.

106. Ibid., 80, 83. These revelations on going to Ohio were given after Rigdon joined the church and came east in December to visit Smith. Rigdon was told in a revelation that the Lord had chosen "the weak things of the world, those who are unlearned and despised, to thrash the nations by the power of my spirit. . . . and their enemies shall be under their feet and I will let the sword fall in their behalf" (ibid., 77).

107. Ibid., 83. The Saints were promised "ye shall have no king nor ruler, for I will be your king. . . . and ye shall have no laws, when I come, for I am your lawgiver" (ibid., 82).

108. Ibid., 83–84. Compare page 82 where the Saints were told that every man must "esteem his brother as himself," for "what man among you, having twelve sons . . . and he saith unto one be thou clothed in rags." The Law of Consecration which established communitarianism among the Mormons was not given until a month after this.

109. Ibid., 83.

110. See Whitney R. Cross, *The Burned-over District: The Social and Intellectual History of Enthusiastic Religion in Western New York, 1800–1850* (New York: Cornell University Press, 1950), 146–50, who views early Mormonism as an eastern, not western, movement.

The Mormon elders had been cautioned by God to tarry until the Book of Mormon was translated before taking the gospel to distant cities (BC, 29–30; this is section 20 in more recent editions). John Corrill, who joined the church in January 1831, tells of the dramatic announcement of a new revelation by the first missionaries (see Corrill, 10, and compare Orson Pratt, "Divine Authority, or the Question Was Joseph Smith Sent of God?" *Series of Pamphlets*, 4–6). Also see P. Pratt, 84–89.

A typical, if unusually talented, convert was Sidney Rigdon. Hayden, 186, recalled Rigdon's enthusiasm for the Millennium while still a Campbellite. Alexander Campbell said that Rigdon told him that "were Joseph to be proved a liar, or say himself that he never found the Book of Mormon as he reported, still he would believe it, and believe that all who did not believe shall be damned" (*Millennial Harbinger* 2 [4 July 1831]: 331).

111. Orson Pratt, "Divine Authenticity of the Book of Mormon," LDSMS 12 (Dec. 1850): 318–82. This series of articles by Pratt appears at the back of vol. 12 as a separate brochure. I have continued the paging of the *Star*, however, so that the exact pages can be found quickly.

112. Winthrop H. Hudson discussed with insight the basic assumptions American pluralism imposed. He sees the notion that God's truth could only be adequately manifest through many different church doctrines and

organizations as basic to American thinking and maintains that the concept was hammered out during the Puritan revolution in England and trans-
ported to the United States. The "theory," if it were that formal, was hardly
articulated so clearly by most Americans but came more in the nature of a
tacit understanding or compromise. Nonetheless, support for the existing
variety of denominations was overwhelming, and the Mormons could win
no favor for themselves by staunchly insisting that theirs was the only road
to Jesus Christ's kingdom. See *American Protestantism* (Chicago: University
of Chicago Press, 1961), 37–48, but compare Perry Miller, "The Contribution of the Protestant Church to Religious Liberty in America," *Church History* 4 (March 1935), 57–66, and Sidney E. Mead, in *Church History* 25:317, 334–35.

113. See HC 1:9, 18–19, 43–44, 59, 84, 86–96, 108. Compare LMSms. Some
of these situations occurred in Pennsylvania but during the years indicated.
Compare "Journal of Newell Knight," 53, for confirmation of one incident
in which opposition to Mormon baptisms led to the tearing down of a dam
that had been constructed for that purpose. HC 1: 88 records the charges
against Smith. Compare "Journal of Newell Knight," 55.

114. *Evangelical Magazine and Gospel Advocate* 2 (April 1831).

115. HC 6:393. Reid told this story in 1844.

116. *Palmyra Reflector*, 1 Feb. 1831, 95.

117. Ibid., 19 April 1830, 130.

118. Ibid., 30 June 1830, 53. Compare also "Book of John Whitmer," 2,
where Whitmer reports a prophecy by Smith made at this time that God
would soon destroy this generation. See also JH, 21 Aug. 1830, where Newell
Knight heard Smith prophesy that the wrath of God would overtake their
persecutors.

119. Smith acknowledged that "the first *public* discourse delivered by
any Mormon came on April 11, 1830 and was given by Oliver Cowdery" (HC
1:81). "A. W. B." charged that Smith met secretly in South Bainbridge with
his followers *(Evangelical Magazine and Gospel Advocate* 2 [9 April 1831]). These
meetings may have been held before 1830. John Whitmer confirms the secret
meetings. He indicates that while in the church's "infancy" the "disciples
used to exclude unbelievers, which caused some to marvel, and converse
about this matter because of the things that were written in the Book of
Mormon" (see "Book of John Whitmer," 6).

120. *The Prophet*, 8 June 1844, 2.

CHAPTER 3
"I SAY UNTO YOU, BE ONE"—SOCIAL UNITY AND ECONOMIC EQUALITY

1. Religious experimentalism was not unique to the Mormons. See
Jerald C. Brauer, *Protestantism in America* (Philadelphia: Westminster Press,

1953) 7, and compare Alice Felt Tyler, *Freedom's Ferment* (New York: Harper Torchbooks, 1962), 46, 109–39, 166–95.

2. *Palmyra Reflector*, 9 March 1831, 116. Compare Leonard J. Arrington, "Early Mormon Communitarianism: The Law of Consecration and Stewardship," *Western Humanities Review* 7 (Autumn 1953): 349n26.

3. DC 38:27. Compare BC, 82–83.

4. *Painesville Telegraph*, 16 Nov. 1830, 3. Howe said the missionaries had been there two weeks.

5. Daryl Chase, "Sidney Rigdon—Early Mormon," M.A. thesis, University of Chicago, 1931, 71–72. Parley Pratt, an ex-Campbellite and associate of Rigdon, had encouraged them to take a roundabout route west to present the Book of Mormon to his friend. Kent Fielding describes how much more convenient it would have been to go to Missouri via the National Road (see "The Growth of the Mormon Church in Kirtland, Ohio," Ph.D. diss., University of Indiana, 1957, 29–30).

6. *Painesville Telegraph*, 16 Nov. 1830, 3.

7. Lucy Mack Smith wrote to Solomon Mack on 6 Jan. 1831 that 300 had been added to the church in Ohio (see Ben E. Rich, *Scrapbook of Mormon Literature* [Chicago: Henry C. Etten, 1910?], 543–45).

8. Parley P. Pratt, *Autobiography of Parley Parker Pratt* 5th ed. (Salt Lake City: Deseret Book, 1961), 48.

9. Rigdon's conversion added prestige to the movement in Ohio. John Corrill said he was himself partly persuaded by Rigdon's congregation joining the Mormons since he knew they were well versed in the Bible. See *A Brief History of the Church of Christ of Latter-day Saints, Including their Doctrine and Discipline* (St. Louis: For the author, 1839), 7–8, and compare Chase, 73–74.

10. See Willis Thornton, "Gentile and Saint in Kirtland," *Ohio State Archaeological and Historical Quarterly* 63 (1954): 8.

11. Ibid., 9, and Amos Sutton Hayden, *Early History of the Disciples in Hiram, Portage County, Ohio* (Cleveland: Robison, Savage, 1876), 20.

12. Thornton, 9. Hayden said the Mormons made "little headway among the Disciples" except at Kirtland where "the way was paved by the common stock principle" (see p. 216).

13. Fielding makes the basis of the Mormon appeal too narrow when he says that spiritual gifts were the decisive factor (see p. 34). It was the whole primitive Christian appeal.

14. Quoted by Corrill, 8.

15. Ibid., 10

16. Ibid., 14.

17. *Naked Truths About Mormonism* 1 (Jan. 1888). The statement was made by S. F. Whitney, brother of Newell K. Whitney.

18. See "Ezra Booth's Letters," *Painesville Telegraph*, 1 Nov. 1831, 3.

19. This version of the emotional excesses at Kirtland was told by Mathew Clapp, a Campbellite (see ibid., 15 Feb. 1831, 1). Clapp's observations

are confirmed by Mormon sources. See Corrill, 16; John Whitmer, "The Book of John Whitmer," 3–4, copy in LDSCA; as well as P. Pratt, *Autobiography*, 61. Pratt says that the frenzied ecstasies of some members continued into the spring in many branches outside Kirtland.

20. *Naked Truths About Mormonism* 1 (Jan. 1888).

21. Richards described a much milder form of spiritual manifestation than that which came in Kirtland and told of his feelings after the Saints had emigrated to Utah. See "Narrative of Franklin Dewey Richards" (San Francisco, 1880), p. 15, part of a large collection of personal reminiscences collected by Hubert Howe Bancroft in the Bancroft Library at Berkeley, California.

22. Corrill, 17.

23. "Recollections of the Prophet Joseph Smith," *Juvenile Instructor* 27 (1892): 22.

24. Joseph Smith to Hyrum Smith, 31 March 1831, in PW, 230.

25. According to David Whitmer, "many had the gift of prophecy in those days" (*Saints' Herald* 34 [Feb. 1887]: 90).

26. "Book of John Whitmer," 4–5.

27. DC 43:3–4. This revelation came in February in response to Hubble's manifestations. Compare HC 1:154 and BC, 96.

28. DC 50:23. Compare BC, 121.

29. DC 50:31. Compare BC, 121–22.

30. JD 11:4.

31. See "The Equality and Oneness of the Saints," *The Seer* 2 (July 1854): 289.

32. The Lord had told them before they fled New York, "go ye out from among the wicked" (BC, 84; compare DC 38: 42).

33. E. D. Howe commented on separatist tendencies in Kirtland in *Mormonism Unvailed* (Painesville, OH: By the author), 128.

34. This point is made by Kent Fielding, "Historical Perspectives for a Liberal Mormonism," *Western Humanities Review* 14 (Winter 1960): 74. In fact, Mormons were not just fleeing New York but inheriting Ohio. E. D. Howe quoted a letter by Rigdon to Ohio Saints saying that Kirtland would be part of the eternal inheritance of the Saints (see pp. 110–11). Compare *Painesville Telegraph*, 18 Jan. 1831, 3, where Howe made the same observation three years before his book was published. Here he noted that converts in Ohio had been told to sell no more land but to purchase as much as they could. Compare also John Whitmer's statement that some of the Saints believed Kirtland would be the place for building the New Jerusalem ("Book of John Whitmer," 6). Joseph Smith himself wrote to Martin Harris in February 1831 to tell those Saints still in New York to hurry to Ohio. He said of the New York elders that the Lord "has a great work for them all in this our inheritance" (see

JH, 22 Feb. 1831). W. W. Phelps in 1832 designated the area from the Mississippi River to the Pacific Ocean as Zion (see *The Evening and the Morning Star*
1 [Sept. 1832]: 71).

35. Oliver Cowdery's letter to his brother, Warren, dated 30 Oct. 1833,
reflects this mood. This is in a collection of Oliver Cowdery's letters at
Huntington Library, San Marino, California. It will be referred to below as
Oliver Cowdery's Letters.

36. DC (1835 edition), 119.

37. Smith told Martin Harris in February, "We have received the laws
of the kingdom since we came here" (JH, 22 Feb. 1831).

38. It is significant that nothing was said in the 1833 BC about the Saints
being subject to the laws of the land. Should the sins of the Saints include
murder or stealing, they were to be held accountable to church law alone.
Later, as the church began to have trouble over legal matters, the revelation
was changed, and in the 1835 DC, members were made accountable to the
law of the land touching these two crimes. Compare BC, 91–92, with DC
(1835 edition), vv. 79–86, which were added to the original. The additions
appear on p. 125 of the 1835 edition.

39. BC, 91–92, 95. Compare DC 42: 18–28, 65. The wording of this latter
verse was altered in the later edition.

40. This caption is often employed by the Mormons today and is used
by Leonard J. Arrington in his excellent article describing how the law operated economically in Ohio and Missouri (see "Early Mormon
Communitarianism," 7, 341–69).

41. BC, 92. This law was changed in some respects later and the DC
was adjusted accordingly (compare DC 42: 30–35).

42. Accordinq to Lyman Wight, those Disciples of "Morley's Family"
who joined the Mormons had been basing their communal experiment on
an interpretation of Acts 2. (Wight's journal is quoted by Eva L. Pancoast,
"The Mormons at Kirtland," M.A. thesis, Western Reserve University, 1929,
p. 65.)

43. *The Seer* 2 (July 1854): 290–91. Compare W. W. Phelps's similar views
in *The Evening and the Morning Star* 1 (Dec. 1832): 6. This is from the original
edition.

44. Ibid., 2:293.

45. Ibid.

46. Arrinqton describes these as two social purposes of the law ("Early
Mormon Communitarianism," 347).

47. *St. Louis Times*, 9 July 1831, 2, carried a piece from a Ravenna, Ohio,
newspaper noting the settling of the Saints at Thompson in May.

48. Arrington implies that when Lemon Copley withdrew his consecration the farm was abandoned. But according to Ezra Booth, Partridge
was commanded to buy the farm at a very low price and to borrow money to

do it. That this was done is indicated by Lucy Smith, who, with her husband, continued to live on the farm under the consecration law until 1835. See "Early Mormon Communitarianism," 349, and "Ezra Booth's Letters," *Painesville Telegraph*, 6 Dec. 1831, 1. Compare Lucy Mack Smith, *History of Joseph Smith by his Mother*, Preston Nibley, ed. (Salt Lake City: Bookcraft, 1954), 209–37.

49. Arrington does not say so, but according to George Albert Smith, the Campbellites composing the "family," who had been living under a communistic arrangement, were baptized into the Mormon church while still living in this manner. They struggled over the sharing of each other's property, and this may have been one reason why in Smith's revelation the Saints were told they must buy what they needed from their neighbor. See "Early Mormon Communitarianism," 347n18; G. A. Smith's sermon in JD 11:3–4; and BC, 94. Compare also Howe, 103, and *Palmyra Reflector*, 14 Feb. 1831, 102, which confirms that the early Mormons in Ohio had a community of goods.

50. Arrinqton, "Early Mormon Communitarianism," 349, and Lucy Mack Smith, 237. The departure of the Colesville Saints came in June or July 1831 (see JH, 25 July 1831).

51. Arrington, "Early Mormon Communitarianism," 342–43.

52. Arrington does not discuss this purpose of the law, but its importance is shown by the fact that when Smith in 1838 sought from the high council a fixed salary for his service, it was vigorously opposed by the body of the church. A revised Law of Consecration and tithing had to be substituted. See HC 3:32, and compare Ebenezer Robinson, ed., *The Return* 1 (Sept. 1889): 136–38. Robinson indicates that although the high council voted to give the salary, they later had to rescind the resolution. For further ramifications of this controversy, see below.

53. Arrington, along with Feramorz Y. Fox and Dean L. May, have treated Mormonism's communitarian experience on a grand scale in their *Building the City of God: Community and Cooperation Among the Mormons* (Salt Lake City: Deseret Book Co., 1976). Their treatment of early communitarianism in Kirtland follows closely Arrington's article but with some additional details (see pp. 15–33). Compare "Early Mormon Communitarianism," 344.

54. "Book of John Whitmer," 4. Howe's account of this phase of the experiment substantiates Whitmer. Howe is quoted by John A. Clark, *Gleanings by the Way* (Philadelphia: Simon Brothers, 1842), 323. Warren A. Jennings ("Zion is Fled: The Expulsion of the Mormons from Jackson County, Missouri," Ph.D. diss., University of Florida, 1962, 99) inaccurately uses these passages to apply to Missouri. Before and after page 4 Whitmer is describing events in Kirtland and gives no indication of any change of subject. Howe specifically says the poor in Kirtland wished for a sharing of goods.

55. HC 1:215.

56. Hayden, 250–51.

57. Ryder was converted by a Mormon girl's prophecy of destruction in China, in addition to Smith's healing powers (ibid., 250–51). Ezra Booth was also converted at this time.

58. As quoted from the "Life and Character of Symonds Ryder," in Burke Aaron Hinsdale, *A History of the Disciples in Hiram, Portage County, Ohio* (Cleveland: Robison, Savage & Co., 1876), 19. With consecration failing to provide adequate funds for land purchase, the Lord in September authorized the Saints to borrow money from the Gentiles, saying, "Behold it is said in my laws or forbidden to get in debt to thine enemies; But behold it is not said at any time, that the Lord should not take when he please, and pay as seemeth him good: Wherefore as ye are agents, and ye are on the Lord's errand; and whatever ye do according to the will of the Lord, it is the Lord's business, and it is the Lord's business to provide for his saints in these last days, that they may obtain an inheritance in the land of Zion" (BC, 160). That Bishop Partridge objected to this injunction is indicated by Ezra Booth, who predicted Partridge would soon be removed from his managerial position. Booth said the borrowed money was used to buy land at Thompson. This loan of "several hundred dollars" may have been an important factor in keeping the remaining Mormons in Ohio. Compare "Ezra Booth's Letters," *Painesville Telegraph*, 6 Dec. 1831, 1, and Fielding, "The Growth of the Mormon Church," 46–47, where he gives evidence that the Mormons were thinking of migrating en masse to Missouri.

59. Brodie, 116.

60. HC 1:236.

61. BC, 95. These lesser officers were to be given a stewardship from the consecrated property or be cared for from the storehouse (compare DC [1835 ed.], 124).

62. Arrinqton, "Early Mormon Communitarianism," 356.

63. DC (1835 edition), 220. Compare DC 82:11–24.

64. Arrington, "Early Mormon Communitarianism," 356n52.

65. Fielding, "The Growth of the Mormon Church," 86–88.

66. DC 78:5–6.

67. Ibid., 14.

68. Arrington, "Early Mormon Communitarianism," 356n53.

69. Fielding argues in "The Growth of the Mormon Church," 87–88, that one of the reasons for breaking up the United Firm was to allow the prophet to secure a stewardship since he had none before and that he probably borrowed $2,000 on the farm. It is possible, however, that the money was used for Zion's Camp, since Smith was having difficulty raising funds for the expedition. A revelation given April 23, two weeks before the camp's departure, authorized the borrowing of money "to deliver yourselves from bondage" (DC 104:83–84). On Zion's Camp, see below, pp. 41–46.

70. Arrington, "Early Mormon Communitarianism," 358n64. But notice in Wilford Woodruff's diary that on 31 December 1834 Woodruff consecrated

$240 worth of property to the church in Missouri—his total assets (Kenney, 1:16). I cannot agree with Arrington's initial view that the Law of Consecration was not revived in 1838. But Arrington modifies his position in his recent book, saying the law was never reinstated but a lesser law was introduced, which was "not greatly different from the so-called celestial law of 1831" (Arrington, Fox, and May, 33–34; see also 202–204).

71. JD 1:215. Probably the period referred to dates after 1835, since Fielding indicates Smith operated a variety store after the United Firm was broken up ("The Growth of the Mormon Church," 87).

72. The missionaries had neglected to secure a permit for their work and also unintentionally disrupted the efforts underway by ministers of other denominations (Jennings, 7–8). Jennings in another publication quotes the wife of one of the Baptist missionaries in Independence that an "agent has driven them off this side of the line and forbits their crossing it" (see his "Isaac McCoy and the Mormons," *Missouri Historical Review* 61 [Oct. 1966]: 65).

73. Ibid., 8, 30, and P. Pratt, *Autobiography*, 61. Pratt does not indicate what reports he made to Smith. But his information plus that learned from correspondence with the missionaries in Missouri must have been favorable enough or the expedition west would not have been launched. Fielding shows that many Saints sold their land in Ohio before departure, so they intended to make Missouri a permanent home (see "The Growth of the Mormon Church," 46–47, and compare HC 1:181–82). Smith indicates here how anxious the Ohio Saints were for information about Missouri.

74. HC 1:177. The Lord by revelation had already designated Missouri as a land of inheritance for the Saints (compare Jennings, 30, 36). The Saints planned a settlement upon the public domain.

75. HC 1:188, 191.

76. Jennings, 37.

77. 9Ibid., 36. Compare DC 57:1–4, and HC 1:189.

78. HC 1:199. Compare Jennings, 38–39.

79. Howe, 130, and Fielding, "The Growth of the Mormon Church," 50.

80. Both Josiah Gregg and Thomas Pitcher reported that relations between Mormons and Gentiles were good at the start (see their statements in Jennings, 120n3).

81. Emily Austin, *Mormonism: or Life Among the Mormons* (Madison, WI: M. J. Cantwell Book and Job Printer, 1882), 68. Emily was a sister-in-law to Newel Knight (see p. 30).

82. Mosiah Gregg, *Commerce of the Prairies*, in Reuben Gold Thwaites, *Early Western Travels*, Pt. II (Cleveland: Arthur H. Clark, 1905), 20:95. Isaac McCoy, a Baptist missionary to the Indians whom the Mormons said was a primary leader among their enemies, maintained that Mormons did not get

into politics initially, but he feared their potential power (see his letter of 28 Nov. 1833 in *Missouri Intelligencer*, 21 Dec. 1833).

83. Jenninqs, 120. Compare Corrill, 19. By December 1832, the Saints had 538 members in Missouri ("Book of John Whitmer," p. 39).

84. Corrill, 19.

85. Compare B. Pixley's comments in a letter written 7 Nov. 1833, from Independence, in William Mulder and A. Russell Mortensen, eds., *Among the Mormons* [New York: Alfred A. Knopf, 1958], 82, with Howe, 145, and Joseph Thorp, *Early Days in the West Along the Missouri One Hundred Years Ago* (Liberty, MO: Irving Gilmer, reprinted 1924), 74.

86. Jennings, 60–62, quotes Alexander Majors to this effect.

87. Alexander Majors, as a young observer of these events, emphasized the degree to which Mormon claims to special authority were offensive to the other denominations (see Prentiss Ingraham, ed., *Seventy Years on the Frontier: Alexander Majors' Memoirs of a Lifetime on the Border* [Chicago: Rand, McNally & Co., 1893], 43–45, 47, 52–53). Also, many ministers were irked by enthusiastic Mormon missionary efforts and were particularly disturbed by the Mormon argument that the Bible was intended mostly for ancient Christians (Jennings, 62, 74–75). Rigdon was preaching these views in Missouri in 1832. Compare also the "Secret Constitution" of the Missourians drawn up against the Mormons in 1833. The pertinent part is quoted by Jennings, 308. Compare Jennings's comments and appropriate quotations on sectarian opposition to the Saints (pp. 128–29, 309–12).

88. Jennings, 54–55, 298, and compare *An Appeal to the American People*, 2nd ed. (Cincinnati: Shepard & Stearns, 1840), 7. According to William Alexander Linn (*The Story of the Mormons* [reprint; New York: Russell & Russell, 1963], 21), this pamphlet was written by Rigdon. Daniel Boorstin's shrewd commentary on how the first comers to a community tended to reap the maximum benefits in American society is relevant here. It was customary for the squatters to band together to safeguard their rights regardless of the law. Meanwhile the Mormons expected that this traditional mode of handling land rights should be set aside in their favor. It was their contention throughout their sojourn in Missouri that they had paid for their land and were entitled to it. But squatters' rights and the rights of priority could not be offset by formal legal claims. See Boorstin, *The Americans: The National Experience* (New York: Random House, 1965), 78–81.

89. Jennings, 296–98.

90. Ibid., 299.

91. "O" stressed this point in defending the anti-Mormon activities of Samuel Owens (see *Missouri Argus*, 29 July 1836).

92. Jennings, 124.

93. Ibid., 125.

94. Ibid., 127

95. Ibid., 129–30. Among other things, Phelps revealed that free people of color must have a certificate of citizenship from another state. He
insisted afterward that he was trying to discourage free Negroes who were
converts from immigrating by making known how difficult satisfying Missouri laws could be.

96. Ibid., 22.

97. Ibid., 131–35. Jennings describes how fearful the Missourians were
of free Negroes living among them. B. H. Roberts quotes the *Western Moni-
tor*, a non-Mormon newspaper published in Fayette, 2 Aug. 1833, that "a considerable number of this degraded caste were only waiting this information before they should set out on their journey" (*The Missouri Persecutions*
[Salt Lake City: George Q. Cannon and Sons, 1900], 80).

98. After Phelps's blunder, the leading civil authorities in Jackson
County were ready to oust the Mormons. A jailer, an Indian agent, a constable and his deputy, a county clerk, a postmaster, the judge of the county
court, and justices of the peace signed the Secret Constitution. This document enumerates the several aspects of the Mormon kingdom which the
Missourians opposed. But it is worth noticing that not all Missourians were
against the Mormons, as they themselves sometimes held. See editorials which
especially deplored violence in *Missouri Intelligencer and Boon's Lick
Advertizer*, 10 Aug. 1833, 3; 16 Nov. 1833, 2; 23 Nov. 1833, 2; and 30 Nov. 1833, 1.
This is referred to below as *Missouri Intelligencer*.

99. Jennings, 137–38.

100. Ibid., 137–47.

101. Ibid., 154–56

102. Ibid., 134, 162–64, 168–69, 171–72, and *History of Jackson County Missouri* (Kansas City, MO: Union Historical Co., 1881), 256.

103. Jennings, 158–59.

104. Ibid., 160–64.

105. Ibid., 166–80.

106. These facts are told by Jennings, 211–26. His information came
largely from "The History of Joseph Smith," published in the *Times and Seasons*. For convenience, compare HC 1:424–25.

107. *Missouri Intelligencer*, 8 March 1834, 1–2, recounts these happenings.
Compare W. W. Phelps's account of the morning's events in HC 1:481–82.
Phelps indicates Jackson Countians flooded into Independence and assumed
"a boisterous and mobocratic appearance."

108. Jennings, 216, 221–25. The western Missouri newspapers contain
much information about these events. See not only the *Missouri Intelligencer*
but also the *Missouri Republican* from March to July 1834. I was generously
supplied these newspapers on microfilm by the State Historical Society of
Missouri at Columbia.

109. See HC 1:491–92, which contains a letter written in April from
church leaders to the governor informing him of their intention to arm

themselves and their expectation that in the summer reinforcements would arrive to help them defend their homes. They thanked the governor for enforcing the laws "so far as he can consistently 'with the means furnished by the legislature.' "

110. Oliver Cowdery's Letters, 30 March 1834. This was written to W. W. Phelps in Missouri.

111. Thus Oliver Cowdery explained the purpose of the Camp in a circular letter to the Saints written on 10 May 1834 (see the Oliver Cowdery Letters, Huntington Library, San Marino, California). Peter Crawley and Richard L. Anderson argue this point in "Political and Social Realities of Zion's Camp," *Brigham Young University Studies* 14 (Summer 1974): 406–20.

112. *Painesville Telegraph*, 9 May 1834, 3. Brigham Young said he took with him "a good gun, the bayonet, plenty of ammunition, a dirk, an ax, a saw, a chisel, spade, hoe, and other necessary tools" ("History of Brigham Young," LDSMS 25 [July 1863]: 455).

113. BC, 237–38. This is DC 101:55–58. Compare Joseph Smith's prophetic promise made on 30 March: "God will strike through kings in the day of his wrath . . . and what do you suppose he should do with a few mobbers in Jackson County, where ere long he will set his feet, when earth and heaven shall tremble!" (Oliver Cowdery's Letters, 30 March 1834). See also the account by an Ohioan that some of the elders maintained they were "going to fight the battle of the Lord" (*Missouri Intelligencer*, 7 June 1834, 3).

114. BC, 239. Compare DC 101:86–89.

115. See the letter of a citizen from "Chagrin," Ohio, dated 29 April 1834, *Missouri Intelligencer*, 7 June 1834, 3.

116. George Albert Smith recounts a promise made by the prophet that "if they were faithful and did not murmur against the Lord and his servants they should all return safely and not one shall fall upon the mission" (LDSMS 27 [July 1865]: 439).

117. See "Extract from the Journal of Elder Heber C. Kimball," *Times and Seasons* 6 (15 Jan. 1845): 772–73, 787. Kimball tells how careful the members of the camp were not to reveal their identity.

118. *Missouri Intelligencer*, 7 June 1834, 3. See also *St. Louis Observer*, 19 June 1834, 123; *Jeffersonian Republican*, 21 June, 1834, 4; and *Missouri Republican*, 23 June 1834, 2.

119. *Missouri Intelligencer*, 7 June and 3, 14 June 1834.

120. Joseph Smith to Orson Hyde, 7 April 1834, in Joseph Smith Letterbook, LDSCA.

121. PW, 323.

122. Howe, 172–75.

123. See Zacharin Linville's letter warning of such military action addressed to Joseph Smith on 23 June 1834, Smith papers, LDSCA.

124. P. Pratt, *Autobiography*, 115.

125. See Charles C. Rich's "Day Book," 14 June 1834, in LDSCA.

126. Winchester's "Primitive Mormonism," appears in Charles L. Woodward's "First Half Century of Mormonism," 195, in the New York Public Library.

127. "Diary of Hosea Stout," 1:79, Special Collections, Harold B. Lee Library, Brigham Young University, Provo, Utah.

128. "Nathan Tanner Biographical History," 13, Special Collections, Harold B. Lee Library, Brigham Young University.

129. "A Short Sketch of the Life of Harrison Burgess," 3, LDSCA.

130. Oliver Cowdery Letterbook, May 1834.

131. PW, 323.

132. Kimball, *Times and Seasons* 6 (Feb. 1845): 790.

133. Ibid. L. O. Littlefield gives a figure of forty feet. However, when the Saints actually measured the river some time afterward, it was down to a few feet (see Alan H. Gerber, "Church Manuscripts," 2:17, Harold B. Lee Library, Brigham Young University).

134. Ibid.

135. Ibid. Kimball's narrative indicates this.

136. Ibid., and see "Proposition of the Mormons," *Painesville Telegraph*, 8 Aug. 1834, 1. Compare HC 2:121–22. Cornelius Gilliam, who confronted the Mormons in Clay County along with Colonel Searcy, repeats the Mormon version of their intentions, which had been signed by the leader of the camp. This account agrees substantially with Kimball, stressing the peaceful purposes of the Mormon task force by this time.

137. See the details of this meeting in the *Missouri Intelligencer*, 28 June 1834, 3. This was Monday, 23 June.

138. HC 2:107, 115, 119.

139. According to Reed Peck in *Peepstone Joe and the Peck Manuscript*, L. B. Cake, ed., (New York: By the editor, 1899), 82. Compare DC 105:15, where the Lord said, "The destroyer I have sent forth to destroy and lay waste mine enemies and not many years hence they shall not be left to pollute mine heritage." This revelation was given in Missouri at a time when cholera had struck the state.

140. DC 105:16–17.

141. Ibid., v. 4.

142. Ibid., vv. 24–25.

143. Ibid., v. 26.

144. Ibid., v. 30.

145. Ibid., vv. 31–32.

146. HC 2:122–24. Afterward there would develop much disagreement as to what position Whitmer had actually been called. Whitmer himself and some of the other dissenters held he had been made a successor to the prophet should he falter. See William E. McLellin's argument to this effect, *The Ensign of Liberty* 1:5, and compare David Whitmer, *Address to All Believers in Christ* (Richmond, MO: By the author, 1887), 55; Woodward, 195; and "Book

of John Whitmer," 42, which all indicate that David was ordained a "Prophet, Seer, and Revelator."

147. HC 2:145. This letter was written on 16 Aug. 1834.

148. Ibid.

149. *Ensign of Liberty* 1:4.

150. John Zahnd mss, New York Public Library.

151. Howe, 162.

152. "Book of John Whitmer," 32, and HC 2:160.

153. HC 2:180–200 records the selection of the Twelve but omits the promises (but see LDSMS 25 [March 1853]: 206–207).

154. Fielding, "The Growth of the Mormon Church," 134.

155. Grant Underwood has persuasively argued how slowly Mormon thought deviated from Protestant norms, even on the question of heaven and hell ("Saved or Damned: Tracing a Persistent Protestantism in Early Mormon Thought," *Brigham Young University Studies* 25 [Summer 1985]: 85–103).

156. HC 5:499. For a shrewd and frequently neglected evaluation of this and other aspects of Mormon thought see Jules Remy's perceptive perusal of Mormon institutions in Utah. Remy was a Roman Catholic who saw Mormonism in a Protestant context. See *A Journey to Great Salt Lake City* (London: W. Jeffs, 1861), 1:cxv-cxvi.

157. DC 19:10–12. This was declared in a revelation to Martin Harris in March 1830. Compare *The Historical Collections of the Topsfield Historical Society*, 8:93, for the views of Asael Smith.

158. DC 76 develops Mormon eschatology for this period.

159. Ibid.. vv. 50–70.

160. Underwood, 94, 99. See Fielding, "The Growth of the Mormon Church," 136.

161. DC 76:71–80.

162. Ibid., vv. 81–88.

163. See the fifth "Lecture on Faith" published with the 1835 DC, 52–53. Compare the *LDS Messenger and Advocate* 1 (15 May 1835): 115, 122–23.

164. See DC 93:21–30. Compare DC (1835 edition), 211–12. The Book of Abraham, which Smith claimed to have translated from Egyptian papyrus rolls at this time but did not publish until 1842, explained the principle in more detail, holding that some of God's elect had attended a great council before the world was created to decide the course of action which would save human souls (see Book of Abraham, 3:22–28, in PGP).

165. Compare Book of Abraham, 3:23, and DC 131:7, which reproduces a revelation given in 1834.

166. DC 93:29–30.

167. For a discussion of these ideas, their proponents, and possible influence on Smith, see Robert E. Paul, "Joseph Smith and the Plurality of Worlds Idea," *Dialogue: A Journal of Mormon Thought* 19 (Summer 1986): 12–38.

168. See Brodie, 171–72, where the views of Dick are discussed in relationship to the Book of Abraham. Brodie rightly notes that Dick's *Philosophy of a Future State* was being read in Kirtland in the fall of 1836. It was not Sidney Rigdon, however, who commented on Dick, as Brodie maintains, but Oliver Cowdery, the editor of the *LDS Messenger and Advocate*. Brodie stresses too much the parallels between the ideas in Dick and those in the Book of Abraham and not enough the book's possible effect on the broader range of Mormon eschatological thought. There is no evidence extant that Dick was being generally discussed among the Mormons before 1836, but the parallels to earlier Mormon thought are apparent. See *LDS Messenger and Advocate* 3 (Nov. 1836): 423, for Cowdery's discussion of Dick's work.

169. See Thomas Dick, *The Philosophy of a Future State*, 2d ed. (Brookfield, MA: E. & G. Merriam, 1830), 48, 101, 176.

170. Compare HC 2:8; DC 93:33, and 88:34–38, 61; and *The Evening and the Morning Star* 1 (Aug. 1832): 45, for evidence that Smith had formulated his basic ideas between 1832 and 1834.

171. Moses 7:30, 35–36, in PGP.

172. DC 131:7. This scripture indicates that all spirit is matter of a purer type.

173. Ibid. 93:33. Compare Dick, 88.

174. Jefferson's views are given in a letter to John Adams, dated 1820, in *Painesville Telegraph*, 20 April 1830.

175. See Pratt's "Absurdities of Immaterialism," LDSMS 11 (Dec. 1849): 11. The brochure by Pratt, along with several others, actually appears at the end of vol. 10. The page number given here is that of the pamphlet. By the time Pratt wrote, the Saints had long held that God, like Christ, had a body of flesh.

176. Oliver Cowdery's Letters, 22 Dec. 1835.

177. In 1903 Benjamin F. Johnson, who had lived in Kirtland, recalled some of the rumors which he heard in his letter to George S. Gibbs (see the typewritten copy of "An Interesting Letter from Patriarch Benjamin F. Johnson to Elder George S. Gibbs," 9–10, Special Collections, Harold B. Lee Library, Brigham Young University; referred to below as Johnson to Gibbs). For other rumors linking Smith to several women in Kirtland, see Richard S. Van Wagoner, *Mormon Polygamy: A History* (Salt Lake City: Signature Books, 1986), 4–6.

178. DC (1835 edition), 251.

179. Based on Acts 3:19–21. Compare John E. Benson's comment that even the patriarchal order must be restored. See his letter of 17 Feb. 1844 in Richards Family Correspondence, Kimball Collection, LDSCA. See also *The Evening and the Morning Star* 2 (Feb. 1834): 265, where the author of "Millennium" cites this passage.

180. A sister who practiced polygamy in Utah thus termed the institution (see "Autobiographic Sketch of Phebe W. Woodruff" [Salt Lake City, 1880], 3, in Bancroft Manuscripts).

181. Phelps's letter of 17 July 1831, is in the Brigham Young Collection, LDSCA. Compare Van Wagoner's contention (p. 223), however, that Phelps made no mention of this to his wife in a letter of 16 Sept. 1835.

182. Johnson to Gibbs, 9.

183. "Last Testimony of Sister Emma," *Saints' Advocate* 2 (Oct. 1879): 50. Emma denied that Joseph had ever been a polygamist.

184. Thus the *LDS Messenger and Advocate* (2 [May 1837]: 511) reported that the seventies leaders voted to disfellowship quorum members indulging in the practice.

185. Kirtland Council Minute Book, 7 Sept. 1836, LDSCA.

186. John Whitmer maintained that polygamy divided the church in 1836. Mary E. Lightner, who claimed to be one of the first of Smith's plural wives, wrote in 1905 that an angel came to Smith three times between 1834 and 1842 demanding that he obey the principle (see Gerber, 2:61–65).

187. HC 2:161, 167.

188. Kimball, *Times and Seasons* 6 (15 March 1845): 804–805. William E. McLellin indicated that this endowment was to be a gift of tongues so that the elders might take the gospel to the nations (see *Ensign of Liberty* 1:5).

189. HC 2:169–70, 176.

190. *Times and Seasons* 6 (15 April 1845): 867.

191. Ibid., 867–68.

192. Fielding, "The Growth of the Mormon Church," 91, 164–65.

193. Ibid., 92–94.

194. Ibid., 94, 164, 167. Marvin S. Hill, Keith Rooker, and Larry T. Wimmer estimate the total population a bit more closely than Fielding in "The Kirtland Economy Revisited," *Brigham Young University Studies* 17 (Summer 1977): 408.

195. One of their investments was in a farm where they hoped the clay soil would prove suitable for brick making. They were never able to get the kiln to work (ibid., 80).

196. Compare two letters by Phelps in JH, 26 May and 18 Dec. 1835, for evidence of money shortage and inflation. See also Oliver Olney's eye-witness account, *The Absurdities of Mormonism Portrayed* (Hancock County, IL: n.p., 1843), 4. On the general inflation at this time, see Max Parkin, *Conflict at Kirtland* (Provo, UT: LDS Department of Seminaries and Institutes, 1966), 160.

197. Ibid., 26 May 1835.

198. For a generally favorable view of the Kirtland economy and some reasons for optimism for the future, see Hill, Rooker, and Wimmer, 394–405.

199. HC 2:281–82.

200. Ibid., 287, 291. Oliver Cowdery discouraged Samson Avard in December 1835 from coming to Kirtland because most of the church would go west in the spring (Oliver Cowdery's Letters, 15 Dec. 1835).

201. Ibid., 407.

202. Ibid., 432.

203. "Book of John Whitmer," 37–38.

204. This appeared in *The Far West* some time in the spring of 1836 and was reproduced in the *Daily Cleveland Herald*, 21 July 1836, 2; also in *St. Louis Observer*, 19 May 1836.

205. *The Far West*, 11 Aug. 1836, 1. According to "O.P.Q.," Smith was furious when he learned his plans were known in Missouri.

206. As quoted in the *Daily Cleveland Herald*, 21 July 1836, 2.

207. HC 2:449.

208. Ibid.

209. Ibid., 455.

210. Ibid., 467.

211. *The Far West*, 25 Aug. 1836.

212. This was a point of some controversy afterward, but see Doniphan's recollections of his arrangement in the *Kansas City Journal*, 12 June 1881. Newell Knight, in his unpublished diary, LDSCA, recalled that it was agreed that the Saints were to have "set . . . up a county by themselves," which lends some credence to Doniphan's contention.

213. Cornelius Gilliam expressed this commonly held view in a letter published in the *Missouri Republican*, 15 Feb. 1839. Gilliam said it was agreed that the Saints in Caldwell "would never settle north of the line but soon as they established themselves they sent in immigrants." Compare *Missouri Argus*, 5 Nov. 1838, for a "Letter to the Editors" supporting this.

214. See the protest of the editor of the *St. Louis Commercial Bulletin*, 27 Sept. 1838.

215. JH, 2 June 1837.

216. HC 2:467.

C H A P T E R   4
ESTABLISHING A THEOCRATIC GOVERNMENT

1. Winchester's "Primitive Mormonism" appears in Charles L. Woodward's "First Half Century of Mormonism," 195, in the New York Public Library. Winchester said this revelation came in the fall of 1837. This date, however, is obviously too late, since the revelation preceded the establishment of a bank.

2. Richards Family Correspondence, 27 Oct. 1836, LDSCA.

3. In JH, 25 Nov. 1836.

4. *LDS Messenger and Advocate* 3 (Dec. 1836): 443, and R. Kent Fielding, "The Growth of the Mormon Church in Kirtland, Ohio," Ph.D. diss., University of Indiana, 1957, 209–39.

5. Fielding, 209–39, and Brodie, 189–94.

6. Marvin S. Hill, Keith Rooker, and Larry T. Wimmer, "The Kirtland Economy Revisited," *Brigham Young University Studies* 17 (Summer 1977): 419–30.

7. Dale W. Adams, "Chartering the Kirtland Bank," *Brigham Young University Studies* 23 (Fall 1983): 467–82, esp. pp. 474–75.

8. Ibid.

9. Ibid. See also the *Cleveland Herald and Gazette*, 6 Oct. 1837, which comments on the anti-monopoly stand of the Mormon leaders at Kirtland.

10. 23 Jan. 1837.

11. Adams; Kenney, 1:120; and Hill, Rooker, and Wimmer, 437–41.

12. Hill, Rooker, and Wimmer, 445.

13. *Cleveland Daily Gazette*, 24 Jan. 1837, and *Painesville Telegraph*, 27 Jan. 1837.

14. See ibid., 20, 25 Jan. and 3 Feb. 1837 for attacks on the soundness of the Safety Society. Also *Scioto Gazette*, 15 Feb. 1837; *Ohio Repository*, 29 Dec. 1836; and *Daily Herald and Gazette*, 1 May 1837.

15. 17 Jan. 1837, 2.

16. Hill, Rooker, and Wimmer, 448, where the total amount of notes issued is estimated at $85,000.

17. Ibid., 456. Smith continued to invest in the bank as late as March 1837.

18. Kenney, 1:131–39.

19. Ibid., 137–39.

20. *Daily Herald and Gazette*, 8 July 1837. The newspaper indicated that Warren Parrish, a growing critic of the prophet, had reissued the notes. The *Cleveland Daily Advertizer*, 13 July 1837, reported that old bills were being used with new signatures. See also Benjamin F. Johnson, *My Life's Review* (Independence, MO: Zion's Printing and Publishing Co., 1947), 29, who says Parrish and Frederick G. Williams were pushing the resigned notes.

21. *LDS Messenger and Advocate* 3 (Aug. 1837): 560.

22. Hill, Rooker, and Wimmer, 438. See pp. 437–41 for a discussion of the legal issues at stake in the trial.

23. Ibid., 434.

24. For a list of Zion's Camp members, see HC 2:183–85. Parrish's hostile evaluation of the prophet appears in the *Painesville Telegraph*, 15 Feb. 1838. Others who were dissatisfied with Smith's leadership are listed in Ebenezer Robinson's *The Return* 1 (Aug. 1889): 116. See also Fielding, 278, and Alan H. Gerber, "Church Manuscripts," 1:94, Harold B. Lee Library, Brigham Young University, Provo, Utah.

25. William E. McLellin to Orson Pratt, 29 April 1854, McLellin papers, LDSCA.

26. *Ensign of Liberty* 1 (March 1847): 7.

27. Ibid., (Dec. 1847): 46.

28. Ibid., (March 1847): 7.

29. The Kirtland Safety Society Stock Ledger Book in the Chicago Historical Society lists subscribers and the amounts they invested.

30. *Painesville Republican*, 15 Feb. 1838.

31. Kenney, 1:131–36.

32. Reproduced in Richard Livesey, *An Exposure of Mormonism* (Preston, England: J. Livesey, 1838), 9.

33. The original complaint is in the Newell K. Whitney Collection, Special Collections, Harold B. Lee Library, Brigham Young University.

34. This letter is in the possession of Steven Pratt.

35. "History of Brigham Young," LDSMS 25 (1 Aug. 1863): 487.

36. HC 2:489–95.

37. Boynton and the Johnsons were disfellowshipped on 22 October for "mingling with the world and dancing," but obviously more was at stake (see Kirtland Council Minutes, 251, LDSCA).

38. HC 2:126.

39. See discussion below.

40. Journal of Newell Knight, 23 Nov. 1835, LDSCA. Smith taught the couple the "ancient order of God concerning marriage," possibly confirming his introduction of plural marriage at this time.

41. Woodward, 195.

42. David Whitmer, *Address to All Believers in Christ* (Richmond, MO: By the author, 1887), 26, 33–35, 42, 47, 49–51, 56–62, 71–72.

43. John Whitmer, "Book of John Whitmer," 40, copy in LDSCA.

44. Lucy Mack Smith, *History of Joseph Smith by his Mother, Lucy Mack Smith*, Preston Nibley, ed. (Salt Lake City: Bookcraft, 1954), 241–42.

45. Oliver Cowdery to Lyman Cowdery, 13 Jan. 1834, in Oliver Cowdery Letters, Huntington Library, San Marino, California.

46. *LDS Messenger and Advocate* 3 (July 1837): 538.

47The letter, cited in fn35, was addressed to Mary Thompson.

48. The letter, dated Aug., is addressed to Elias Smith and is in Special Collections, University of Utah Library, Salt Lake City. Internal evidence makes it clear the year is 1837.

49. HC 2:518–21, 524–25, and "Conference Minutes and Record Book of Christ's Church of Latter-day Saints," or Far West Record, 73, LDSCA.

50. *Elders' Journal* 1 (Nov. 1837): 28.

51. HC 2:521.

52. Oliver Cowdery Letters, 10, 21 Jan. and 24 Feb. 1838. See also Richard S. Van Wagoner, *Mormon Polygamy: A History* (Salt Lake City: Signature Books, 1986), 10–11.

53. Oliver Cowdery Letters, 21 Jan. 1838.

54. HC 2:521–24.

55. Johnson, *My Life's Review*, 29.

56. Ibid., and "Historical Discourse Delivered by Elder George A. Smith," Tabernacle at Ogden, 15 Nov. 1864, in JD 11:11. Smith included among the disaffected leading elders, members of the Seventy, the high council, "and many others."

57. Oliver Cowdery Letters, 30 Jan. 1838.

58. James H. Kennedy, *Early Days of Mormonism* (New York: Charles Scribner's Sons, 1888), 166–69.

59. Both revelations, under this date, are in George W. Robinson's "Scriptory Book," which he kept for Joseph Smith (Faulring, 192–93).

60. E. D. Howe indicates that several lawsuits were initiated by non-Mormons "to counteract the progress of so dangerous an enemy" (*Autobiography and Recollections of a Pioneer Printer* [Painesville: Telegraph Steam Printing House, 1878], 45). Compare the "Private Journal of Anson Call" (LDSCA) in mid-1836 for a list of lawsuits up to that time.

61. JH, 19 Feb. 1839. George W. Robinson wrote in the "Scriptory Book" that Kirtland "was broken up by those who have professed the name of Latter-Day Saints" (Faulring, 198).

62. See HC 1: 261–65; 2:2; 3:1; and George A. Smith's recollection, LDSMS 27 (July 1865): 439. According to Smith, non-Mormons feared that an influx of poor Saints into Kirtland would burden the town. They demanded Mormon removal.

63. See Willis Thornton, "Gentile and Saint at Kirtland," *Ohio State Archaeological and Historical Quarterly* 63 (1954): 10–17.

64. *Painesville Telegraph*, 30 Nov. 1830, 3.

65. Ibid., 14 Dec. 1830, 2.

66. Ibid., 15 Feb. 1831, 1.

67. Ibid.

68. I counted four articles published by Howe in 1830, twenty-five in 1831, three in 1832, two in 1833, and seven in 1834 when Missouri events received attention.

69. Howe himself noted that the "Gold Bible fever seems to be abating in this vicinity" (29 March 1831, 2).

70. Thornton, 18–19.

71. 2*Painesville Telegraph*, 22 March 1831, 2.

72. PW, 287. The letter to W. W. Phelps and others is dated 18 Aug; see Max Parkin, *Conflict at Kirtland* (Provo, UT: LDS Department of Seminaries and Institutes, 1966), 184.

73. 4HC 1:450–51.

74. *Anti-Masonic Telegraph*, 16 Oct. 1833, 2.

75. *Chardon Spectator and Geauga Gazette*, 18 Oct. 1834, and *Painesville Telegraph*, 10 Oct. 1834, 2–3.

76. Ibid., 20 Feb. 1835, 2. Two issues of the *Northern Times*, dated 2 and 9 Oct., are preserved in LDSCA. Compare Parkin, 188.

77. *Northern Times*, 2 Oct. 1835.

78. Interview by Arthur Deming of E. D. Howe, April 1885, in the Mormon Collection, Chicago Historical Society. Howe recalled of Rigdon's remarks that "many of our citizens feared his prediction would prove true."

79. *Painesville Telegraph*, 17 April 1835.

80. The final notice of Mormon political efforts came in 8 August 1837 when the editor of the *Cleveland Daily Herald and Gazette* said that the Mormons had become advocates of the "no-party" cause.

81. *Cleveland Daily Gazette*, 20 Jan. 1837, 2.

82. Ibid., 15 Sept. 1837, 1.

83. Thus L. L. Rice termed the banking notes from Kirtland "Mormon money" and they were so designated by most non-Mormon newspapers. Nor was any distinction made between the banking activities of Joseph Smith and those of Warren Parrish and Frederick G. Williams. Compare *Cleveland Daily Gazette*, 17, 20 Jan. 1837; *Daily Herald and Gazette*, 1 May, 8, 17 July 1837; and *Scioto Gazette*, 15 Feb. 1837, 3.

84. Compare Prentiss Ingraham, ed., *Seventy Years on the Frontier: Alexander Majors' Memoirs of a Lifetime on the Border* (Chicago: Rand, McNally & Co., 1893), 55.

85. "O.P.Q." said as of this date the Mormons only held 2,000 acres in the township (*The Far West*, 11 Aug. 1836, 1).

86. Noah Packard believed a by-product of Gentile strife and wickedness was the refusal of Ohioans to support the Kirtland Safety Society, an institution which would have given life's blood to an emaciated American nation (see *Political and Religious Detector in Which Millerism Is Exposed* [Medina, OH: Michael Hayes, 1843], 3, 5–6, 10, 14–16).

87. George S. Richards to his parents, 1 March 1838, in Richards Family Correspondence.

C H A P T E R   5
"IN A MILITARY SPIRIT"

1. Benjamin F. Johnson, "An Interesting Letter from Patriarch Benjamin F. Johnson to Elder George S. Gibbs," Special Collections, Harold B. Lee Library, Brigham Young University, Provo, Utah.

2. Richard L. Anderson points out Mormon dependence upon the natural rights philosophy, without considering whether it was appropriate for a Christian people. See his "Atchison Letters and the Causes of Mormon Expulsion from Missouri," *Brigham Young University Studies* 26 (Summer 1986): 3–47. One of the dominating types in the Mormon scripture is the warrior-saint like Mormon and Moroni who defends faith and country. For the ambivalence in Mormon militancy, see D. Michael Quinn, "The Mormon Church

and the Spanish American War: An End to Selective Pacifism," *Pacific Historical Review* 43 (Aug. 1974).

3. This is demonstrated by events in 1836 described above, but compare the Albert P. Rockwood Letters, 29 Oct. 1838, at the Beinecke Library, Yale University.

4. See Thomas B. Marsh's letter to Joseph Smith, written between 5 and 13 March 1838, in the *Elders' Journal* 1 (July 1838): 45. Marsh indicated that his chief concern in Far West was church unity.

5. See Leland H. Gentry, "A History of the Latter-day Saints in Northern Missouri from 1836 to 1839," Ph.D. diss., Brigham Young University, 1965, 133n75, where W. W. Phelps and David and John Whitmer question whether the Word of Wisdom required abstinence from tea and coffee. The Whitmers did not consider these "hot drinks" according to the definition in the Doctrine and Covenants. See section 89 in the recent edition.

6. Oliver Cowdery to Warren Cowdery, 4 Feb. 1838, Huntington Library, San Marino, California; hereafter Cowdery Letters.

7. Heber C. Kimball Journal, 21 Dec. 1845, LDSCA. Kimball reports George A. Smith recalling this in a Sunday meeting.

8. See A. Ripley's letter to the "Elders Abroad" in May, in *Elders' Journal* 1 (July 1838): 39.

9. Cowdery Letters, 4 Feb. 1838.

10. See David Whitmer's explanation as to why his brother sold his land in Missouri in *Saints' Herald* 34 (5 Feb. 1887): 90. That Phelps was also heavily in debt and therefore sold his land is revealed in his letter to John Whitmer from Bellbrook, Ohio, 4 March 1840. A typewritten copy of this letter is in Special Collections, Harold B. Lee Library, Brigham Young University.

11. HC 3:3–4.

12. Ibid., 6.

13. See "Minutes of High Council," *Elders' Journal* 1 (July 1838): 46.

14. Ibid.

15. "Far West Record," 101, LDSCA.

16. *Elders' Journal* 1 (July 1838): 38.

17. HC 3:11.

18. Faulring, 160. This would be 16 or 17 March 1838.

19. HC 3:11.

20. Gentry, 146–47, 151–53.

21. Ibid., 140, 149, 151. Whitmer was accused of trying to damage the reputation of Joseph Smith, not of bringing lawsuits to court.

22. Ibid., 140, 146.

23. Ibid., 140.

24. Ibid., 152. Compare "Far West Record," 119.

25. "Far West Record," 123.

26. W. W. Phelps quoted Joseph Smith to this effect in *Circuit Court, Davis County, State of Missouri vs. Joseph Smith, 1839*. These records are in the Missouri Historical Society, Columbia. Orson Hyde, in *The Prophet*, 2 Nov. 1844, cited Rigdon that "it was the imperative duty of the Church to obey the word of Joseph Smith . . . without question or inquiry."

27. Gentry, 149

28. Ibid., 149–51. Whitmer insisted that he should not be tried by the high council but by a bishop's court, but Joseph Smith who was present at the trial disagreed.

29. HC 3:18.

30. Edward Partridge to James Partridge, 30 Oct. 1837, Missouri Historical Society, Columbia.

31. *Elders' Journal* 1 (July 1838): 33. Smith wrote his editorial in May.

32. Ibid., 39.

33. DC 115:6–7.

34. Ibid., vv. 8, 13–14.

35. HC 3:27.

36. Reed Peck, "Manuscript," in L. B. Cake, *Peepstone Joe and the Peck Manuscript* (New York: By the author, 1899), 85.

37. HC 3:32.

38. *The Return* 1 (Sept. 1889): 136–37.

39. Ibid.

40. DC 119:2.

41. HC 3:34–35.

42. Rollin J. Britton, *Early Days on the Grand River and the Mormon War* (Columbia, MO: The State Historical Society, 1920), 7–8.

43. Gentry, 241–43.

44. Reed Peck, 87.

45. Joseph Thorp, *Early Days in the West Along the Missouri One Hundred Years Ago* (Liberty, MO: Irving Gilmer, 1924), 84.

46. Gentry, 241–43.

47. *Document Containing the Correspondence, Orders, &c., in Relation to the Disturbances with the Mormons and the Evidence Given Before the Hon. Austin A. King, Judge of the Fifth Judicial Circuit of the State of Missouri, at the Court-House in Richmond, in a Criminal Court of Inquiry, Begun November 12, 1838, on the Trial of Joseph Smith Jr., and Others for High Treason and Other Crimes Against the State* (Fayette, MO: Published by order of the General Assembly at the office of *Boon's Lick Democrat*, 1841), 103–106; hereafter *Correspondence and Orders*.

48. Reed Peck, 83–84.

49. See "Extract of a Letter to the Editors," *Missouri Argus*, 8 Nov. 1838.

50. *Correspondence and Orders*, 138–39. It should be recalled that George W. Robinson in the "Scriptory Book" (Faulring, 160), quoted Smith warning against those who "seek out unrighteous and vexatious lawsuits under the pretext or color of law."

51. Ibid. Rigdon protested that since Whitmer and Cowdery had come to Far West they had instituted a system of vexatious lawsuits similar to those in Kirtland (p. 8).

52. John Corrill, *A Brief History of the Church of Christ of Latter-day Saints, Including Their Doctrine and Discipline* (St. Louis: For the author, 1839), 59.

53. Ibid., 30.

54. See John Corrill's statement, "I think the original object of the Danite band was to operate on dissenters" (*Correspondence and Orders*, 112); and William E. McLellin's similar belief in *Ensign of Liberty* 1 (March 1847): 8.

55. "Book of John Whitmer," 24, LDSCA.

56. HC 3:180; *Correspondence and Orders*, 101–102; and Reed Peck, 93.

57. HC 3:180. Anson Call also indicates that initially the Danites were composed of the captains in the armies of Israel. See his recollections of 10 Dec. 1885 in the Utah State Historical Society, Salt Lake City.

58. Ibid.

59. Albert P. Rockwood Letters, 29 Oct. 1838; and Anson Call, 10 Dec. 1885.

60. "Diary of Oliver Boardman Huntington," 1:36. A typewritten copy of this diary is in the Special Collections, Harold B. Lee Library, Brigham Young University.

61. *Correspondence and Orders*, 101–102

62. Corrill, 31.

63. Ibid.

64. *Correspondence and Orders*, 114.

65. Albert P. Rockwood Letters, 29 Oct. 1838. The recent argument by Dean C. Jessee and David J. Whittaker, partly in response to Stephen C. LaSueur, *The Mormon War in Missouri* (Columbia: University of Missouri Press, 1987), that the Rockwood letters provide a basis for a new, positive interpretation of the Danites and their intentions does not hold up well. Most of the negative view of the Danites comes not from Avard but from Joseph Smith, Orson Hyde, Thomas B. Marsh, Robinson, and Rockwood, to name the most reliable. Nor can John Corrill be ignored, for despite the fact that he left the church he did his best for the Mormons afterward and wrote what historians generally regard as one of the most temperate accounts of the period. Jessee and Whittaker also ignore Joseph Smith's very explicit warnings that if persecution continued he would retaliate. He acted on this, exactly as he and Rigdon said they would. The Saints were on the defensive at DeWitt, but after this they went on the offensive and raided Missouri towns. If the Danites were but a small, divergent group Joseph Smith would have stamped them out before March 1839. See Jessee's and Whittaker's "The Last Months of Mormonism in Missouri: The Albert Perry Rockwood Journal," in *Brigham Young University Studies* 28 (Winter 1988): 5–41.

66. Corrill, 31. Corrill said the Presidency were "the wire pullers." Gentry argues that Smith was unaware of Danite activities (see pp. 341–53). Lyman Wight said that Avard frequently did things of which Smith did not approve. See Britton, 86.

67. "Diary of John Smith," 4, 18 Aug. and 1 Sept. 1838, LDSCA. For evidence of Hyde's and Marsh's awareness, see below, p. 96.

68. Faulring, 198.

69. Reed Peck, 87–89.

70. Peck believed the threats of mortal harm were largely intended to frighten the dissenters. See p. 89.

71. The entire decree is found in *Correspondence and Orders*, 103.

72. Reed Peck, 91. That Smith approved of driving out the dissenters is made clear in the "Scriptory Book" written for him by Robinson. He spoke with approval regarding Rigdon's later 4th of July sermon and said "these men took warning and soon were seen bounding over the prairie."

73. *The Return* 1 (Oct. 1889): 147.

74. *Saints' Herald* 34 (5 Feb. 1887): 91.

75. *Elders' Journal* 1 (July 1838): 42. Compare Smith's explanation of the important pre-millennial role of Adam in HC 3:386–87, 390–91; and William Swartzell's notation in his day-by-day account of events at Far West that at the end of July "strange rumors [circulated] respecting the appearance of Adam, the Ancient of Days, . . . who is to put the Church to rights for the glorious reception of Christ." *Mormonism Exposed* (Pekin, OH: by the author, 1840), 26.

76. *Oration Delivered by Mr. S. Rigdon on the 4th of July, 1838* (Far West, MO: The Journal Office, 1838), 6–12. The pamphlet is located in the Chicago Historical Society.

77. Emily Austin, *Mormonism: or, Life Among the Mormons* (Madison, WI: M. J. Cantwell, Book and Job Printer, 1882), 88.

78. *Correspondence and Orders*, 122; *The Return* 1 (Nov. 1889): 170.

79. *Elders' Journal* 1 (Aug. 1838): 54.

80. *Missouri Argus*, 27 Sept. 1838.

81. Jedediah M. Grant acknowledged in 1844 that Rigdon's oration "was the main auxiliary that fanned into flame the burning wrath of the mobocratic spirit of the Missourians." He neglected to say that Rigdon spoke for Joseph Smith. See *A Collection of Facts Relative to the Course Taken by Elder Sidney Rigdon in the States of Ohio, Missouri, Illinois and Pennsylvania* (Philadelphia: Brown, Bicking & Cuilbert, 1844), 11.

82. *Elders' Journal* 1 (July 1838): 33. Smith wrote in May that "the Saints are at perfect peace with all surrounding inhabitants." There is no indication that when the *Elders' Journal* went to press in July the situation had changed. See the evidence presented by LaSueur, 51. Richard Anderson's counter, arguing that the Saints were innocent of wrong doing and always acted on the defensive, begins the story much too late to perceive the entire

picture. Anderson leaves out the war preparations that began in 1834 and minimizes Rigdon's threat to block legal process in Caldwell County, saying that the veto would effect vexatious lawsuits only. But who was to decide whether the lawsuits were vexatious? Lawsuits by those considered anti-Mormon or dissenters would be excluded, thus nullifying the mediating purpose of the law in a pluralistic, democratic society. Anderson plays down Rigdon's threat to take the war to Gentile homes and families. His contention that "if the law would not protect their minority from expulsion, they served notice that they would protect themselves" is an appeal to higher law, of the same sort that got the Mormons into difficulty in the first place. It ignores the fact that when Rigdon made his speech, although Mormons were not welcome everywhere, no expulsion was threatened. See R. Anderson's "Atchison Letters," 3–47, especially 14–16.

83. *Missouri Argus*, 27 Sept. 1838.

84. *Correspondence and Orders*, 114.

85. Ibid., 122.

86. *Jeffersonian Republican*, 18 Jan. 1838.

87. Kenney, 2:378.

88. HC 4:504.

89. "Inner Facts of the Social Life in Utah" (San Francisco, 1880), 87. This is an interview by Hubert H. Bancroft, in the Bancroft Manuscripts, a filmed copy of which is in the Harold B. Lee Library, Brigham Young University.

90. *Correspondence and Orders*, 114. The suit in question involved a claim of trespass against Smith.

91. Ibid., 139.

92. Ibid., 122.

93. R. Anderson, "Atchison Letters," 15, agrees that Rigdon's address represented Smith's "defensive views."

94. Corrill, 32.

95. John D. Lee, *Mormonism Unveiled* (St. Louis: Bryan, Brand & Co., 1877), 61.

96. Ibid.

97. R. Peck, p. 92.

98. Corrill, 46; and J. D. Lee, 62.

99. J. D. Lee, 62, 65.

100. Luman Andros Shurtliff Journal, typewritten copy, Special Collections, Harold B. Lee Library, Brigham Young University.

101. "Journal of John Smith," 15 Oct. 1838.

102. Albert P. Rockwood Letters, 6 Oct. 1838. Compare also Swartzell, 23–24, for a description of the layout of the fields at Adam-ondi-Ahman.

103. Ibid.

104. Ibid.

105. According to the testimony of Ephraim Owens, a Mormon, in U.S., *House of Representatives, Memorial of Ephraim Owens, Jr., Late of Green County, Indiana, now of Davis County, Missouri, Asking of Congress to Afford Protection to the People Called Mormons, in the Enjoyment of Their Civil Rights As Citizens of the United States and Complaining of Loss of Property*, U.S. Document No. 42, 25th Cong., 3d Sess. (Washington, D.C.: U.S. Government Printing Office, 1839), 1. This will be referred to as *Memorial of Ephraim Owens*. Compare "Extract of a Letter to the Editors," *Missouri Argus*, 8 Nov. 1838, where a Missourian maintained that some resentment was there initially.

106. Peter H. Burnett, *Recollections of An Old Pioneer* (New York: D. Appleton & Co., 1880), 34.

107. "Extract of a Letter to the Editors," *Missouri Argus*, 8 Nov. 1838. Compare also the *Saint Louis Commercial Bulletin*, 27 Sept. 1838, which reproduces a piece from the *Columbia Patriot*, and HC 3:59.

108. HC 3:27, 30.

109. *An Appeal to the American People*, 15.

110. Ibid., 16, and *Memorial of Ephraim Owens*, 2.

111. HC 3:30–31; also see "James O. Broadhead Papers," Missouri Historical Society, St. Louis, where a clipping from the *St. Louis Globe Democrat* explains the party allegiance at Far West. See also a letter dated 11 Sept. 1838 by George Churchill noting the Democratic leanings of the Mormons and the fact that most Missourians in the "old counties" were Whig. This is in the "Railroad Papers" of the society. Compare also a letter of Phineas Richards to Wealthy Richards, 7 Jan. 1839, in Richards Family Correspondence, where the Missourians of Daviess County, contrasted with the Mormons, are designated as Whigs.

112. J. D. Lee, 53, and William Earl Parrish, "The Life of David Rice Atchison: A study in the Politics of a Border State," Ph. D. diss., University of Missouri, 1955, 17.

113. Gentry, 248, indicates that long before the election Adam Black and Penniston went from house to house warning the Saints to leave the county.

114. J. D. Lee, 56.

115. "Autobiography of John Lowe Butler, 1808–1861," Special Collections, Harold B. Lee Library, Brigham Young University. Butler, a Danite, was one of those who went to Gallatin.

116. HC 3:56–57.

117. John Butler's description of the Gallatin Fight is in JH, 6 Aug. 1838.

118. *Nauvoo Neighbor*, 25 July 1843.

119. JH, 6 Aug. 1838.

120. *Nauvoo Neighbor*, 25 July 1843.

121. Vincent Knight to William Cooper, 3 Feb. 1839, LDSCA.

122. *Peoria Register and Northwestern Gazeteer*, 17 April 1840, has the Caldwell County election returns for 1838.

123. *An Appeal to the American People*, 19.
124. Faulring, 213.
125. Vinson Knight to William Cooper, 3 Feb. 1839.
126. Faulring, 213.
127. Ibid.
128. *Nauvoo Neighbor*, 25 July 1843.
129. Faulring, 213.
130. Missouri State Dept., Commission Dept., Mormon War, 1838–41, File Box 139. This includes Adam Black's deposition of 9 Aug. 1838, in which he says he was forced to sign a pledge "that he would not molest the people called Mormons." John Taylor in 1839 published a copy of what he claimed was the original agreement signed by Black which affirmed that "so long as they will not molest me I will not molest them." See Taylor's *Short History of the Murders, Robberies, Burnings* [in Missouri] (1839), 2.
131. Faulring, 213.
132. Missouri State Dept., File Box 139, for Black's deposition.
133. HC 3:61. This includes Penniston's affidavit.
134. *Missouri Republican*, 25 Aug., 3 Sept. 1838; *St. Louis Commercial Bulletin*, 22 Sept. 1838; *Missouri Argus*, 6 Sept. 1838; *Southern Advocate*, 8 Sept. 1838.
135. Ibid., 3 Sept. 1838.
136. *Missouri Argus*, 6 Sept. 1838.
137. Gentry, 289.
138. *Missouri Republican*, 18 Aug. 1838. John Taylor in his *Short History of the Murders*, 9, stated that the anti-Mormons at DeWitt were led by two ministers, a Presbyterian and a Methodist. Compare Hanna Ford to her brother, Stephen, 16 June 1839, in the Kimball Collection. An old citizen wrote after the Mormons had departed that politics was a more decisive factor. "I have no hesitation in saying that in three years from this time every office in Carroll would have been filled by a Mormon! Therefore . . . the citizens of Carroll considered themselves fighting for liberty." *Saint Louis Commercial Bulletin*, 1 Nov. 1838, 2.
139. Ibid.
140. Ibid.
141. HC 3:69.
142. *Correspondence and Orders*, 20–21.
143. Faulring, 211.
144. HC 3:69.
145. Gentry, 272–74.
146. "Philo Dibble's Narrative," *Early Scenes in Church History* (Salt Lake: Juvenile Instructor Office, 1882), 88–89.
147. This piece from the *Western Star* was republished in the *Missouri Republican*, 22 Sept. 1838. The editor of the *Missouri Argus* also exonerated the Mormons. See the issue of 27 Sept. 1838.
148. Ibid., 19 Sept. 1838.

149. HC 3:79–81, which includes two letters by Atchison. See also Gentry, 279–83.

150. *Daily Commercial Bulletin*, 22 Sept. 1838, citing the *Western Star*.

151. Gentry, 283, 285–86.

152. *Correspondence and Orders*, 33.

153. HC 3:84–85. According to Elders Higbee and Thompson, the old citizens agreed to sell out for $25,000. See *Petition of the Latter-day Saints*, 7.

154. In R. L. Anderson, "Atchison Letters," 20. The editor of the *Missouri Argus* urged on 27 September that Mormons should not be judged too hastily or "opposed for religious reasons."

155. Albert P. Rockwood Letters, 6 Oct. 1838.

156. Gentry, 294.

157. Ibid., 294–95.

158. Thorp, 84.

159. "Journal of John Murdock," 61, LDSCA.

160. Gentry, 297. George Hinkle was in charge of the Mormon defense.

161. HC 3:150. The entire letter is found in *Correspondence and Orders*, 34–35. Lucas was an old enemy of the Mormons from their Jackson County days. See Warren A. Jennings, "Zion is Fled: The Expulsion of the Mormons from Jackson County, Missouri," Ph.D. diss., University of Florida, 1962, 144, 184.

162. In *Jeffersonian Republican*, 6 Oct. 1838, 3.

163. *Missouri Republican*, 8 Oct. 1838.

164. Ibid., 11 Oct. 1838.

165. Ibid.

166. Thorp, 85. Phineas Richards noted that one hundred men were sent to DeWitt. Letter of Phineas Richards to Wealthy Richards, 21 Jan. 1839.

167. Gentry, 302–303; and *Correspondence and Orders*, 40, for a letter of 7 October 1838 sent by the citizens of DeWitt to those of Howard County.

168. Ibid., 305. Albert Rockwood maintained that the militia were unwilling to turn out against their fellow Missourians. See his letter of 6 October. Compare the testimony of Henry Root, in HC 4:63; and R. L. Anderson, "Atchison Letters," 22–23.

169. See Gentry, 308; and *Missouri Republican*, 5 Nov. 1838. Boggs later told the members of the state legislature that sufficient forces were already at the scene. Boggs's letter to the House, 5 December 1838, is reproduced in *Correspondence and Orders*, 13.

170. Ibid., 307; *Quincy Whig*, 17 Nov. 1838, 2; *Sangamo Journal*, 17 Nov. 1838, 2. This message had severe consequences for the Saints.

171. Ibid., 311; and *Missouri Republican*, 18 Oct. 1838.

172. The Saints accepted these terms but never received any compensation.

173. *Missouri Republican*, 18 Oct. 1838.

174. *An Appeal to the American People*, 30–31.

175. Samual Bogard to Governor Lilburn Boggs, 15 Oct. 1838. A hand-written copy of this letter is in Missouri State Dept., File Box 139, Mormon War 1838–41, Missouri Historical Society, St. Louis.

176. *Correspondence and Orders*, 39; and R. L. Anderson, "Atchison Letters," 24.

177. "Diary of John Pulsipher," 1, 6, Special Collections, Harold B. Lee Library, Brigham Young University.

178. *Correspondence and Orders*, 112.

179. Corrill, 36.

180. HC 3:161–62. Compare Smith's petition to Congress, November 1838, in HC 4:32.

181. *Missouri Republican*, 9 Nov. 1838.

182. *Correspondence and Orders*, 117.

183. *Missouri Republican*, 3 Nov. 1838, for King's letter of 24 October.

184. J. D. Lee, 71.

185. *Correspondence and Orders*, 117. Compare Reed Peck's testimony with that of John Cleminson, 114, and W. W. Phelps, 122.

186. As reported by the *Missouri Republican*, 9 Nov. 1838, 2.

187. *Correspondence and Orders*, 123, for the testimony of W. W. Phelps.

188. Corrill, 37, gives the number as 200; Reed Peck, 111, says it was 300.

189. Ibid., 38; R. Peck, 111; and Johnson, *My Life's Review*, 37.

190. HC 3:165; and Phineas Richards to Wealthy Richards, 21 Jan. 1839, in Richards Family Correspondence.

191. *Memorial of Ephraim Owens*, 3.

192. "Testimony of Parley P. Pratt Before the Municipal Court of Nauvoo," 1 July 1843, LDSCA.

193. Phineas Richards to Wealthy Richards, 21 Jan. 1839.

194. Gentry, 378–83.

195. *Correspondence and Orders*, 112–16, for the testimonies of John Corrill and John Cleminson; "The Book of John Whitmer," 22. See also *Elders' Journal* 1 (Oct. 1837): 32, where Thomas Marsh in a poem looks forward to the day when "the substance of the Gentile nations round; shall come to thee [Zion], and in thy streets abound." Compare Isa. 61:6.

196. See the testimonies of Apostles Thomas Marsh and Orson Hyde in *Correspondence and Orders*, 57–59. That the goods confiscated at Gallatin were given to the bishop is attested by Oliver B. Huntington, 1:31–32. Compare Gentry, 383.

197. *Correspondence and Orders*, 113–14, 131, 145 reproduces the testimonies of Ezra Williams, a member of the Mormon troops that attacked the town, and John Raglin and Patrick Lynch, also eye witnesses. See also the testimony of Philip Covington, 43, who with friends and family was driven from the county by the Mormons. Compare the recollections of Ebenezer Robinson in *The Return* 2 (Jan. 1890): 203; and that of Thomas Marsh in *Correspondence and Orders*, 57–59. John Corrill said that Joseph and Hyrum Smith

led the raid on Gallatin. His testimony appears in *Circuit Court, Davis County . . . vs. Joseph Smith.*

198. Gentry, 378–83, 385, maintains that the Missourians burned Millport, but the Missouri witnesses he cites merely say that Joseph Smith and others were there on the following day, after the town was burned, which does not prove that they were not there the day before also. Compare the testimonies of Charles Bleckley, James B. Turner, and W. W. Phelps in *Correspondence and Orders*, 125–29, 136–40. Phelps indicates that he went on the expedition "in which Gallatin and Millport were burnt." John Corrill said Mormons burned between eighty and one hundred and fifty cabins. See Corrill, 38.

199. Penniston testified to this in *Correspondence and Orders*, 43. Compare the statement of James Morehead, William Thornton and Jacob Gadgel in the *Missouri Republican*, 2 Nov. 1838, 2, who verify this but indicate that Senator Morin's house was not burned.

200. Gentry, 381–82; and Johnson, *My Life's Review*, 38–39, 42.

201. John P. Green, *Facts Relative to the Expulsion of the Mormons or Latter-day Saints, from the State of Missouri* (Cincinnati: R. P. Brooks, 1839), 12.

202. Shurtliff, 34.

203. "Journal of John Smith," 20 Oct. 1838.

204. Gentry, 371; Greene, 12; and R. Peck, 108, who indicates that the cannon came from Carroll County.

205. Gentry, 371–72.

206. Albert P. Rockwood Letters, 29 Oct. 1838.

207. Swartzel, 23; and compare Eze. 37–38, and Rev. 20:8.

208. Ibid.

209. Albert P. Rockwood Letters, 29 Oct. 1838.

210. *Correspondence and Orders*, 128, for the testimony of George Hinkle. Compare J. Lee, 63, who quotes Sidney Rigdon similarly.

211. Ibid., 59.

212. Ibid., 16. Compare a piece in the *Messenger and Advocate* 2 (Oct. 1835): 193 on the vital role of the Indians in the "day of the Lord's power."

213. *Missouri Republican*, 29 Sept. 1838, 2.

214. *Missouri Argus*, 1 Nov. 1838, for the piece by "Accidentalist," and *Missouri Republican*, 3 Nov. 1838, 2.

215. See *Jeffersonian Republican*, 3 Nov. 1838, 2, for the statement by Morehead, Thornton, and Gudgel.

216. Ibid. for the editorial by Gunn; also Gentry, 410.

217. Lilburn W. Boggs to Col. Joseph Hawkins, 26 Oct. 1838. This letter is in the Forest Smith papers, Missouri Historical Society, Columbia.

218. *Correspondence and Orders*, 48, reproduces Bogart's letter to Atchison explaining his decision to order out a company to "range the line between Caldwell and Ray."

219. *An Appeal to the American People*, 35; Burnett, 58; and Gentry, 399.

220. HC 3:169–71. Mormon troops were mustered by Caldwell County judge, Elias Higbee, or so Smith maintained in his journal. If so, it only pointed up the dilemma in which the Mormons placed themselves by organizing their own militia. Later the elders were tried at Richmond for the murder of one of Bogart's men. See HC 3:212.

221. Gentry indicates that three Mormons and one non-Mormon were killed.

222. See the letter of E. M. Ryland published in the *Jeffersonian Republican*, 3 Nov. 1838, which claimed that the Mormons had "cut off" Bogart's whole company. Compare *Missouri Argus*, 8 Nov. 1838, 1, where an account by William Claude Jones is equally exaggerated.

223. The extermination order of 27 October is reproduced in HC 3:175.

224. *Missouri Republican*, 5 Nov. 1838, 2. The editor stated that Ray County had collected 2,500 men, Howard and Chariton counties 1,500 to 2,000.

225. Britton, 36–43, has a detailed account of the massacre from a non-Mormon viewpoint. Compare HC 3:183–86 for Joseph Young's eye witness account. Compare the *Missouri Republican*, 12 Nov. 1838, 2, which indicates that a member of the state legislature was in the detachment of Missourians.

226. See Juanita Brooks, *The Mountain Meadows Massacre* (Norman: University of Oklahoma Press, 1962), 46–47, 52–57, for an account of the influence of Haun's Mill on Mormon thinking prior to the massacre in 1857 of one hundred members of a wagon train, including some Missourians.

227. *Missouri Republican*, 1 Nov. 1838, 2.

228. Gentry, 467.

229. *Correspondence and Orders*, 72.

230. Albert P. Rockwood Letters, 29 Oct. 1838. Rockwood added to this letter as events unfolded so that he was still writing it on 1 November.

231. Thus the editor of the *Missouri Republican* wrote on 1 November that there was "little division among the citizens in opposition to the Mormons." The editor of the *Missouri Commercial Bulletin*, 5 Nov., said, "They can never live among us," and the editor of the *Missouri Argus*, 8 Nov., stated flatly, "The Mormons must leave the state, or we will, one and all."

232. R. Peck, 120–22, and Corrill, 41.

233. See Corrill, 42, and compare Gentry, 473, and *Missouri Republican*, 14 Nov. 1838, 2.

234. Corrill, 42, recounts the terms of the so-called treaty offered by General Lucas. Mormons were required to surrender all their property to pay for damages from the Daviess County raid. Compare R. Peck, 128. See also Britton, 47, who observed that the treaty "put the Mormons in the light of being a foreign nation."

235. HC 3:189. Compare Pratt's account in a footnote.

236. Ibid., 190. Compare Britton, 45. The officers voted three to one for execution of the Mormon leaders. See *History of Clay and Platt Counties, Missouri* (St. Louis: National Historical Co., 1885), 134.

237. Albert P. Rockwood Letters, 29 Oct. 1838. Compare similar views by Shurtliff, 35.

238. HC 3:190–91. Peter H. Burnett, 63, claimed that most of the Clay Countians opposed the court martial. Compare Britton, 46, and "Diary of a Mormon in California, by H. W. Bigler," 2–3, in Bancroft Manuscripts.

239. See Austin A. King's letter of 23 December to Governor Boggs, confessing some brutalities at this time and the reasons given by the Missourians. King's letter is reproduced in *Correspondence and Orders*, 95. See also Britton, 45, and compare the *Saint Louis Bulletin*, 12 Nov. 1838, which confirms the abuse given Mormons and recounts two killings of Mormons after the surrender.

240. Dimick B. Huntington Letters, 1 Nov. 1838, LDSCA.

241. "A Brief Narrative of the Life of Nancy Tracy," 15, Bancroft Manuscripts.

242. This figure is given by David Pettigrew, one of the prisoners. See HC 4:73.

243. See King's letter of 24 October, criticizing the Mormons for seizing the sword in Daviess County, in the *Missouri Argus*, 8 Nov. 1838, 1. On King's general unfitness for hearing the case, see the views of representative Scott of the Missouri legislature in *Missouri Republican*, 9 Jan. 1839, 2.

244. Whereas forty-two witnesses were called for the state, only seven appeared for the defendants. The testimony of the witnesses is reproduced in *Correspondence and Orders*.

245. On the intimidation of the witnesses compare HC 3:210–11, and Gentry, 556. See also the statement by W. W. Phelps who testified for the state in 1838 but after returning to the church recounted how he had acted under duress. See the *Nauvoo Neighbor*, 12 June 1844, 255.

246. Dean Jessee, "Walls, Grates and Screeking Iron Doors: The Prison Experience of Mormon Leaders in Missouri, 1838–39," 29, 33, for an account of the charges and several hearings in which true bills were brought against Joseph Smith. Jessee's article appears in Davis Bitton and Maureen Ursenbach Beecher, eds., *New Views of Mormon History* (Salt Lake City: University of Utah Press, 1987).

247. Ibid., 33.

248. Smith said that the guards were intoxicated, but Parley P. Pratt remarked "some say that the guards got beastly drunk and let them escape; others that they were bought for the paltry sum of $250." Joseph H. McGee indicated that one of the guards who allowed the escape was ridden through Gallatin on a bar of steel and died after the brutal experience. See HC 3:320; Parley P. Pratt, *History of the Late Persecution Inflicted by the State of Missouri*

Upon the Mormons (Mexico, NY: Office of the Oswego County Democrat, 1840), 29; and Britton, 109.

249. See below, and Dallin H. Oaks and Marvin S. Hill, *Carthage Conspiracy* (Urbana: University of Illinois Press, 1975), 195–96. Twice, in 1844 and 1845 Young opposed waging war, when proposed by Rigdon and then sheriff Jacob Backenstos.

250. HC 3:152–54.

251. *Correspondence and Orders*, 57–59.

252. The Marsh and Hyde letter of 25 October is copied into Joseph Smith's Kirtland Letter Book, LDSCA.

253. Hyde's letter to Young, dated 30 March 1839, is copied into Young's "Journal, 1837–45," LDSCA.

254. Kenney, 1:340.

255. *Correspondence and Orders*, 57–59.

256. HC 3:173–74. See also Boggs to Joseph Hawkins, 26 Oct. 1838.

257. HC includes a letter of E. M. Ryland to Rees and Williams, dated 25 Oct., recounting the attack on Bogard, Boggs cites information from this letter in his exterminating order of the 27th. See HC 3:172–73, 175, and compare.

258. Richard Anderson argues that by going to war in defense of the Saints, Smith saved lives in Missouri. But no lives had been lost up to the time of the Crooked River battle. It was reported that the Mormons "had burnt to ashes the towns of Gallatin and Millport" that caused loss of lives and property. It is hard to see how the Danite war benefitted the Saints who lost so much after 17 October. See Anderson's argument in "Atchison's Letters," 14–15.

259. See Allen Joseph Stout, "Autobiography and Journal," 7, for testimony of an admitted Danite that the "Apostates swore to some lies and some truths against the Mormons."

260. *Correspondence and Orders*, 57–59.

261. See below.

262. Even Hyde and Marsh in their testimony before Jacobs spoke more of intentions than actual depredations. They did record that the elders stole property and drove citizens away.

263. See above, where the Danites destroyed Penniston's home and drove out armed citizens.

264. Orson Hyde to Brigham Young, 30 March 1839.

265. HC 3:180–81, where Smith denounces it and is reported to have cut Avard off from the church "when . . . [his] rascality came to the Presidency of the Church." Avard was not cut off until March 1839, while Smith was in Liberty Jail, and may have had more to do with punishing military failure than insubordination. Smith may have regretted organizing the Danites, however, because he tried to legitimize the military arm of the

church in Nauvoo, Illinois, by establishing it as part of the state militia under the Nauvoo charter.

266. Ibid., 379. Hyde was restored to church membership on 26 June 1839 but not to the Quorum of the Twelve until 5 October. Heber C. Kimball and Hyrum Smith prevailed with the prophet to restore him. See my "Historical Study of the Life of Orson Hyde, Mormon Missionary and Apostle, 1805–1852," M.A. thesis, Brigham Young University, 1955, 41.

267. Orson Hyde to Brigham Young, 30 March 1839.

268. Wilford Woodruff recorded Hyde's contrition at this time but said nothing as to his repudiation of his testimony. See Kenney, 1:340. Hyde told the elders he was motivated by fear, and at a conference on 27 June further explained his actions, but it is not recorded that he denied what he said in his testimony to Jacobs. See my "Historical Study of the Life of Orson Hyde," 40–41.

269. When Sidney Rigdon sought to be appointed guardian to the church and Smith's successor following his death, Hyde was opposed and recalled Rigdon's extremism in Missouri. He made no mention of Smith's collaboration with Rigdon in Missouri, as Hyde and Marsh had in their letter to the Abbotts and in their testimony before Jacobs. See *The Prophet*, 2 Nov. 1844.

270. Thomas B. Marsh to Heber C. Kimball, 5 May 1857, Marsh papers, LDSCA.

271. See the *Missouri Argus*, 31 Jan. and 15, 23 Feb. 1839, for repercussions from the rising protest in some circles against the way the Mormons were harassed and mistreated.

272. See below, pp. 101–102.

CHAPTER 6

"EVERYTHING GOD DOES IS TO AGGRANDIZE HIS KINGDOM"

1. HC 5:285. Smith made this statement in February 1843.

2. Thomas Gregg explains the sheer necessity of returning east to Illinois in his *History of Hancock County, Illinois* (Chicago: Charles C. Chapman & Co., 1880), 246.

3. Robert B. Flanders, *Nauvoo: Kingdom on the Mississippi* (Urbana: University of Illinois Press, 1965), 13.

4. JH, 17 March 1839; HC 3:265; and Flanders, 42.

5. Ibid.

6. Ibid., 3:260–61.

7. On Rigdon's disillusionment with gathering, see Brigham Young's remarks in JD 11:17.

8. HC 3:250–51.

9. Ibid., 251, 254–56, 261–63, 274, 284, 308–309, 319, 322–23.

10. Ibid., 283–84

11. Ibid., 319, 322–23, 327.

12. Kenney, 1:332–33.

13. HC 3:267–71; *The Return* 2 (April 1890): 243; and compare *Quincy Whig*, 22 Dec. 1838, 23 Feb. 1839, and 2 March 1839. See also "The Mormons and the Whigs," *Illinois State Register*, 20 Oct. 1843, 3. In Iowa, however, one editor greeted the coming of the Mormons with mixed feelings, pleased that they were treated with compassion but wondering if they might not be a source of future trouble. See *Iowa News* (Dubuque), 1 June 1839. I made use here of Dale Morgan, comp., "The Mormons and the Far West, Transcripts from American Newspapers," copy at Harold B. Lee Library, Brigham Young University, Provo, Utah; hereafter "The Mormons and the Far West."

14. HC 3:342, 349; and Flanders, 28–37, 44–45.

15. Ibid., 391.

16. Alanson Ripley to Joseph Smith, 10 April 1839, in "Joseph Smith Letter Book," LDSCA.

17. JH, 14 May 1839.

18. Eliza Snow to Isaac Streater, 20 Feb. 1839, Snow papers, LDSCA. Compare the apocalyptic forebodings of Smith's father that "the Sword was unsheathed & could not be sheathed again until sin was swept from the face of the Earth & Christ come to reign with his Saints. Our Prophet & Brethren are now brought before the Governor & rulers of this state & no doubt they will soon be brought before Kings and nobles for the testimony of Jesus. . . . the testimony of judgements have now commenced & a whirl-pool will sweep our inhabitants off the U. States." In P. P. Pratt to Brother Nurse, 19 Nov. 1838, Albert P. Rockwood Letters.

19. JH, 20 March 1839; and Parley P. Pratt Correspondence, 1837–48, Special Collections, Harold B. Lee Library.

20. HC 3:310–11 for a letter by Rigdon and p. 312 for further comments by Ripley.

21. Ibid., 333.

22. See ibid., 4:37, 38, 53 for evidence that Mormons would have welcomed any sort of relief. B. H. Roberts maintains, without providing any documentation, that the Saints wanted the federal government to *force* Missouri to grant them remuneration for their losses. See Brigham H. Roberts, *A Comprehensive History of the Church of Jesus Christ of Latter-day Saints*, 6 vols. (Salt Lake City: Deseret News Press, 1930), 2:28.

23. Ibid., 4:24–38, 49–73, and especially 81, where Elias Higbee states that he argued before the committee that "the whole persecution, from beginning to end, was grounded on our religious faith."

24. Ibid., 4:40.

25. This quote appears in a letter, dated 5 Dec. 1840, in Joseph Smith's Kirtland Letter Book, but not in the published history.

26. Ibid.

27. See the letters of Elias Higbee to Joseph Smith recounting the arguments of the Missourians before the Senate Judiciary Committee in HC 4:81–87, but especially 82, 83, 85–86.

28. Ibid., 88; and *Quincy Whig*, 29 Feb. 1840, 1.

29. Ibid., 4:88, 90–92, where the report of the judiciary committee is given in full. Compare Sidney Rigdon's letter to Joseph Smith, 3 April 1840, in ibid., 102.

30. Elias Smith to the Honorable E. Higbee, 7 May 1840, in Joseph Smith's Kirtland Letter Book.

31. Jackson assumed a states' rights position on most issues confronting him during his two terms. See also Richard H. Brown, "The Missouri Crisis, Slavery, and the Politics of Jacksonianism," *South Atlantic Quarterly* 55 (Winter 1966): 55–72.

32. Robert V. Remini describes Jackson's careful politicking to isolate South Carolina from other Southern states during the 1832–33 nullification crisis. See *Andrew Jackson and the Course of American Democracy, 1833–45* (New York: Harper & Row, 1984), 8–23. Ironically, Joseph Smith looked upon Jackson as the last great American president, particularly for his plan of removing the Indians to western reservations. This seemed a proper use of presidential power, and Jackson seemed the model of the powerful and just president, although in this instance he stood against the interests of a minority and their rights. See also HC 2:358–62; and Smith's *Views of the Powers and Policy of the Government of the United States*, 32, where he writes "General Jackson's administration may be denominated the acme of American glory." This essay is included in Smith's *Voice of Truth* (Nauvoo, 1844).

33. In Harold M. Hyman and William M. Wiecek, *Equal Justice Under Law* (New York: Harper & Row, 1982), 15.

34. Roberts, *Comprehensive History*, 2:35–38.

35. G. J. Adams, *A Letter to His Excellency John Tyler* (New York: C. A. Calhoun, 1844), 14.

36. HC 4:80, 89, where Joseph Smith said the desire for popularity and power controlled leaders in Washington. See also ibid 6:57, where Smith wanted the death penalty for officials who were negligent of their duties to protect citizens.

37. Ibid. 4:89.

38. Dean Jessee, "Joseph Smith's July 19, 1840 Discourse," *Brigham Young University Studies* 19 (Spring 1979): 392–94, reproduces Martha Jane Coray's notes on the prophet's address.

39. Orson Pratt repeated the prophesy as it was told to him by Parley P. Pratt. See Orson's letter to George A. Smith, 21 Jan. 1841, Orson Pratt's Letters, LDSCA.

40. "Address of Joseph Smith to the Nauvoo Saints, July 19, 1840," Joseph Smith papers, LDSCA.

41. Flanders, 48–49.

42. *Times and Seasons* 1 (June 1840): 123–24.

43. Ibid. 2 (1 Jan. 1841): 258–59.

44. According to Charlotte Haven in "A Girl's Letters from Nauvoo," *Overland Monthly* 16 (Dec. 1890): 627.

45. "A Glance at the Mormons," *Alton Telegraph*, 14 Nov. 1840.

46. *The Banner of Peace*, 2 Sept. 1842.

47. Thomas Gregg, *The Prophet of Palmyra* (New York: John B. Alden, 1890), 156. Gregg said Mormons settled most heavily in LaHarpe, Plymouth, Macedonia, Green Plains, and Montebello. Several of these towns would later become centers of anti-Mormon activity.

48. *Quincy Whig*, 7 March 1841, 2.

49. Compare the occasion where a group of ministers burned the Book of Mormon, *Illinois State Register*, 20 March 1840, in "Mormons and the Far West."

50. *Missouri Republican*, 17 Aug. 1841; *Warsaw Signal*, 29 Dec. 1841, 2; HC 4:487. The full account of affairs at Warren may be traced in HC 4:405, 407, 410, 412, 471–72, and 487.

51. *Illinois State Register*, 8 Nov. 1844, 2.

52. JH, 14 Oct. 1841, records Willard Richards's protest against high rents and high prices in general at Warsaw.

53. HC 4:487.

54. Dallin H. Oaks and Marvin Hill, *Carthage Conspiracy: The Trial of the Accused Assassins of Joseph Smith* (Urbana: University of Illinois Press, 1975), 59, 94n38, 79, 177–79, for the anti-Mormon activities of Levi Williams, Calvin Warren, Onias Skinner, and pp. 86–87, 158–59, for some of Sharp's anti-Mormon activities. Sharp and Williams, both from Warsaw, were the two most bitter anti-Mormons. Warren and Skinner defended them in the trial for the murder of Joseph Smith.

55. See *History of Lee County Iowa* (Chicago: Western Historical Co., 1879), 675, and Edward Stiles, *Recollections and Sketches of Notable Lawyers and Public Men of Early Iowa* (Des Moines: The Homestead Publishing Co., 1916), 339–40. Kilbourn had surveyed the site for the town of Montrose in 1837.

56. See "Latter-day-ism No. 3," *Hawk-Eye and Iowa Patriot*, 14 Oct. 1841, 2.

57. *Davenport Gazette*, 16 Dec. 1841, 3.

58. Joseph Smith said, "Shall Missouri Filled with Negro drivers, and white men stealers, go unwhiped of justice, for tenfold greater sins than France? No! verily, no! While I have powers of body or mind . . . I or my posterity will plead the cause of injured innocense, untill Missouri makes atonement." See Diary of Emily Dow Partridge Young, p. 20. A typewritten copy is in Special Collections, Harold B. Lee Library, Brigham Young University. The editor of the *Times and Seasons* denounced southerners in Missouri as a "cursed, infuriated inhuman set, or race of beings who are enemies to their country, to their God, to themselves, and to every principle of

righteousness and humanity." See HC 4:199. In 1844 the editor of the Mormon journal said, "We can never forget the injuries done us in Missouri. They are ever present in our minds. We feel it impossible to efface them from our memories." *Times and Seasons* 5 (15 Jan. 1844): 405.

59. "Diary of Joel Hills Johnson," 1:24–25, which indicates that the depredations continued despite his best efforts to curb them. Compare also *Times and Seasons* 1 (15 Nov. 1840): 221; *The Wasp*, 29 March 1843, 1, 3; and HC 4:219–20, 461, 469.

60. Alexander Neibaur journal, 15 April 1841, LDSCA, which records that Smith used "very strong language" against such iniquity.

61. Faulring, 346.

62. HC 4:154–60 for affidavits of those abducted and the petition to Governor Carlin.

63. See Durkee's letter to Governor Boggs of Missouri, 22 July 1840, Mormon Papers, Missouri Historical Society, St. Louis. Compare *Quincy Whig*, 18 July 1840, 2, which indicates that the Mormons were accused of secreting stolen Tully property in a river bottom.

64. HC 4:198–99.

65. Ibid.

66. *Quincy Whig*, 12 Sept. 1840, 2.

67. HC 4:205.

68. Ibid., 206, 245–48.

69. See Dallin H. Oaks, "The Suppression of the Nauvoo Expositor," *Utah Law Review* 9 (Winter 1965): 878–82, for a discussion of the rights granted the Mormons under the habeas corpus provisions in the charter and Oaks's belief that the legislature made a deliberate concession to Saints by not specifically requiring in the charter that they be bound by state or national law. But Oaks does not discuss the more difficult question: Was the legislature acting within its just powers in allowing the Saints this prerogative? This amounted to city nullification of national law.

70. HC 4:249.

71. Thomas Ford, *A History of Illinois* (Chicago: S. C. Greggs & Co., 1854), 262.

72. *Quincy Whig*, 23 Feb. 1839, 1. Only two months earlier the editor had observed that fixing fault in the Mormon versus Missouri affair "would be very difficult." See the issue of 22 Dec. 1839, 1.

73. Ibid.

74. HC 3:263, 267–71.

75. *Quincy Whig*, 2 March 1839, 2.

76. Cited by the *Quincy Whig*, 23 March 1839.

77. Ibid.

78. Ibid., 27 March 1839, 1.

79. Ibid., 11 May 1839, 2; 18 May 1839, 1; and 25 May 1839, 2, for Wight's three letters.

80. Kenney, 1:332.

81. *Quincy Whig*, 18 May 1839, 2.

82. Ibid., 25 May 1839, 1.

83. Ibid., 1 June 1839.

84. HC 4:40. The quotation is from Joseph Smith's letter to Robert D. Foster, 11 March 1840, Smith papers.

85. Jacob's letter to Van Buren, from LaHarpe, 19 March 1840, Illinois State Historical Society.

86. JH, 11 March 1840.

87. Gregg, *Prophet of Palmyra*, 166–68

88. Andrew F. Ehat and Lyndon W. Cook, eds., *The Words of Joseph Smith* (Provo, UT: Religious Studies Center, Brigham Young University, 1980), 36.

89. Unsigned letter, Montecello, Illinois, 12 Aug. 1840, James O. Broadhead papers, Missouri Historical Society, Columbia.

90. Flanders, 220.

91. *Illinois State Register*, 14 Aug. 1840.

92. *Quincy Whig*, 7 Nov. 1840.

93. See Remini, 467–71.

94. JH, 27 Dec. 1840.

95. *Quincy Whig*, 25 July 1840, 2, 12 Sept. 1840, 2, and 25 Sept. 1841, 1; *Western World* (Warsaw), 29 July 1840, 2, and 16 Sept. 1840, 2–3.

96. *Sangamo Journal*, 18 June 1841, 2.

97. *Fort Madison Patriot*, 26 Nov. 1840; *Hawk-Eye and Iowa Patriot*, 24 June and 22 July 1841.

98. Flanders, 243, explains that the Whig party was tinged with nativism and disliked Mormon immigrants from England.

99. HC 4:248, 480.

100. Ibid., 364, 369–71, 380–81.

101. *Quincy Whig*, 19 June 1841, for bitter comments on Democratic tactics for regaining the Mormon vote.

102. HC 4:479–80.

103. *Quincy Whig*, 22 Jan. 1842, 2.

104. See Thomas Ford's comments on this (p. 269). There is substantial evidence supporting his contention that the Whigs now launched a crusade against the Saints at this time. See the *Quincy Whig*, 21 May 1842, 2; 13 Aug. 1842, 2; and the *Sangamo Journal*, 21 Jan. 1842 and 10 June 1842.

105. See discussion that follows.

106. *Quincy Herald*, 3 Feb. 1842, 2.

107. *Lee County Democrat*, 1 Oct. 1842, 2–3.

108. Flanders, 213.

109. Thomas Ford, 265, and Flanders, 106.

110. *Times and Seasons* 2 (1 May 1841): 417.

111. The charter provided that the city council could "organize the inhabitants of said city subject to military duty into a body of independent military men, to be called the 'Nauvoo Legion,' the court martial of which shall be composed of the commissioned officers of said legion, and constitute the law making department, with full powers and authority to make, ordain, establish and execute all such laws and ordinances, as may be considered necessary for the benefit, government, and regulation of said legion: *Provided,* said court martial shall pass no law or act repugnant to, or inconsistent with the Constitution of the United States, or of this State." Notice that the legion is bound to the two constitutions only, not to the laws passed by Congress or the state legislature. It is later indicated that the legion should be at the disposal of the governor "for the public defense, and the execution of the laws of the State, or of the United States," but the legion is otherwise free to execute its own laws. See Illinois, *Laws, Statutes,* 12th General Assembly, 1840, 57, and compare Oaks, *Utah Law Review,* 9:881, who overlooks this omission. The charter seems intentionally ambiguous, perhaps the product of political compromise. Mormons made the most of this ambiguity.

112. HC 4:295–96.

113. Ibid., 415.

114. *Times and Seasons* 2 (July 1841): 467.

115. Flanders, 118–19.

116. From a series of undated newspaper clippings collected by C. E. McCormack in the Stanley B. Kimball Collection, Southern Illinois University.

117. The letter, dated 2 May 1841, is found in the Kimball Collection.

118. HC 4:416–17.

119. *Warsaw Signal,* 26 Jan. 1842. In a similar mode, see the *Sangamo Journal,* 21 Jan. 1842, 3. Compare the *Alton Telegraph,* 4 June 1842, 2, and *Hawk-Eye and Iowa Patriot,* 12 May 1842, 2.

120. Governor Thomas Ford noted in his history how in Nauvoo the Saints refused "to hear anything against their system" (p. 316).

121. Thus Samson Avard was held entirely responsible for the Danites, Sidney Rigdon for bringing the Gentiles down on them with his excessive pronouncements, and George Hinkle for the abrupt surrender at Far West. The charges of treason brought against the Saints were the result of the false testimonies given before Judge King by the dissenters. Smith wrote indignantly that these witnesses had "converted" the church organization into a "temporal kingdom which was to fill the whole earth, and subdue all other kingdoms," implying that no good Mormon had ever preached such doctrine. See HC 3:180–81, 192, 209–12, and the comment by Wilford Woodruff that Rigdon's "flaming speech in Far West . . . had a tendency to bring persecution upon the whole church, especially the head of it." LDSMS 5 (Dec. 1844): 109.

122. HC 3:385.

123. Orson Spencer, *Letters Exhibiting the Most Prominent Doctrines of the Church of Jesus Christ of Latter-day Saints* (Salt lake City: Deseret News Co., 1889), 186.

124. John D. Lee, *Mormonism Unveiled* (St. Louis: Bryan, Brand & Co., 1877), 287, and compare Parley P. Pratt's urging the Reverend Mr. Briggs to come to Utah where "the law of God is honored; by it we determine what is virtue and what is vice." See Alan H. Gerber, comp., "Church Manuscripts," 9:189, Harold B. Lee Library, Brigham Young University.

125. Joseph Smith informed the Saints that "all men who become heirs of God and joint-heirs with Jesus Christ will have to receive the fullness of the ordinances of his kingdom; and those who will not receive all the ordinances will fall short of the fullness of that glory, if they do not lose the whole." HC 5:424.

126. Smith told the elders that "if a man would attain to the keys of the kingdom of an endless life, he must sacrifice all things." HC 5:555.

127. JH, 15 Aug. 1840, and HC 4:231.

128. Ibid.

129. HC 5:148–53 and LDSMS 5 (May 1845): 193, where Parley Pratt records that the prophet Elijah had restored the sealing power.

130. LDSMS 23 (16 Feb. 1841): 102. This was later deleted from HC 6:253. Sons and daughters were sealed so that more than polygamy was involved.

131. See Benjamin F. Johnson's testimony that Joseph Smith taught this doctrine, page 11 of his "interesting letter," and compare his *My Life's Review* (Independence, MO: Zion's Printing and Publishing Co., 1947), 10. See also "Journal of Joseph Fielding," *Brigham Young University Studies* 19 (Winter 1979): 154, where Fielding said the "more numerous" one's "creatures" the "greater his dominion."

132. J. W. Gunnison, *The Mormons, Or Latter-day Saints, in the Valley of the Great Salt Lake* (Philadelphia: J. B. Lippincott & Co., 1856), 56.

133. William Clayton Journal, 12 Jan. 1845, LDSCA.

134. Juanita Brooks, ed., *On the Mormon Frontier: The Diary of Hosea Stout*, 1844–61, 2 vols. (Salt Lake City: University of Utah Press, 1964), 1:178.

135. "A Proclamation and Faithful Warning to all the Saints Scattered Around in Boston, Philadelphia, New York, Salem, New Bedford, Lowell, Petersborough, Gilson, St. Louis, Nauvoo and Elsewhere in the United States," in *Warsaw Signal*, 29 Oct. 1845, 1.

136. LDSMS 5:191.

137. *Times and Seasons* 5 (15 Aug. 1844): 614.

138. D. Michael Quinn, "Latter-day Saints Prayer Circles," *Brigham Young University Studies* 19 (Fall 1978): 79–105.

139. David John Buerger, "The Fullness of the Priesthood: The Second Anointing in Latter-day Saint Theology and Practice," *Dialogue: A Journal of Mormon Thought* 16 (Spring 1983): 16, 19, 21–22. Compare "Journal of

Thomas Bullock," 25 Sept. 1846, where he was adopted into the family of Willard Richards, who became a "K[ing] of K[ings] & a K[ing] & P[riest] to the most high God." Bullock's journal is in Special Collections, Harold B. Lee Library, Brigham Young University.

140. See Johnson, *My Life's Review*, 96, and JH, 1 May 1843, for the testimony of Lucy Walker Kimball.

141. See Pratt's "Celestial Marriage," an address given 29 August 1852, in JD 1:61, 65.

142. Joseph Smith to Sarah Ann Whitney, 23 March 1843, LDSCA.

143. William Clayton Journal, 16 May 1843.

144. According to Mrs. F. D. Richards, the vast majority of Saints did not learn of plural marriage until the winter of 1845–46, when they received temple ordinances prior to the exodus from Nauvoo. See "Reminiscences of Mrs. F. D. Richards," San Francisco, 1880, 19, Bancroft, University of California, Berkeley.

145. According to "An Exile from Nauvoo," *Warsaw Signal*, 25 April 1844, 2.

146. "Migration and Settlement of the Latter-day Saints," 17, Bancroft, University of California, Berkeley.

147. Johnson, *My Life's Review*, 94–95.

148. "Plurality of Wives—The Free Agency of Man," a discourse given by Brigham Young in Provo, 14 July 1855, in JD 3:266.

149. "Journal of Levi Richards," 13 May 1843, LDSCA.

150. L. John Nuttall papers, Special Collections, Harold B. Lee Library, Brigham Young University. Nuttall records John Taylor recalling these feelings 14 October 1882.

151. "Scenes in Nauvoo, *Woman's Exponent* (Oct. 1881): 65–66.

152. *The Return* 2 (June 1890): 287.

153. "Autobiographical Sketch of Phebe W. Woodruff" (Salt Lake City, 1880), 5. This is part of the Bancroft Collection.

154. "Autobiography and Diary of Eliza Marie Partridge (Smith) Lyman, 1820–1885," typewritten copy, 7, Special Collections, Harold B. Lee Library, Brigham Young University.

155. "Autobiography of Mrs. M. A. P. Hyde." The pages of this brief account are not numbered.

156. Statement of Mrs. L. W. Kimball, Huntington Library, San Marino, California.

157. Catherine Lewis, *Narrative of Some Proceedings of the Mormons* (Lynn, MA: by the author, 1848), iv.

158. "Journal of Joseph Fielding," 154.

159. HC 4:287, 295–96.

160. The Olney papers are in the Beinecke Library, Yale University. See mss. 17. Compare the "Journal of Arvet L. Hale," 27, LDSCA, where Joseph Smith also charged that Bennett "stunk of women."

161. Letter of Joseph Smith, Brigham Young, and others to the Relief Society Sisters, 12 April 1842, "Book of Records Containing the Proceedings of the Female Relief Society of Nauvoo," LDSCA.

162. HC 5:12.

163. Joseph Smith to his clerk, James Sloan, 17 May 1842, Smith papers; "Nauvoo City Council Minutes," 19 May 1842. The thanks given to Bennett was also published in *The Wasp*, 21 May 1842. Compare J. C. Bennett to James J. Strang, 23 March 1846, Strang collection, Beinecke Library, Yale University.

164. HC 5:18. Compare "Nauvoo High Council Minutes," 23 May 1842.

165. "Nauvoo High Council Minutes," 25 May 1842.

166. HC 5:18, under date 26 May.

167. See "Nauvoo High Council Minutes," 27, 28 May 1842, for further evidence of spreading sexual experimentation; and Kenney, 2:177, where Wilford Woodruff comments that the high council found after more searching that there was "much iniquity" and sought to cleanse the church. Ebenezer Robinson said public sentiment forced Bennett to resign. The same public disfavor probably forced him out of Nauvoo. See *The Return* 2 (Nov. 1890), 363.

168. *Sangamo Journal*, 8 July 1842, for Bennett's expose of the Sarah Pratt affair, and also *Quincy Whig*, 16 July 1842.

169. HC 5: 35–38 for Smith's published expose. This appeared in the *New York Herald*, 21 July 1842.

170. "Journal of Joseph Fielding," 154.

171. See the letter of Jedediah Grant to Brigham Young, 4 Sept. 1844, which reports on conditions at Philadelphia and Winchester's attitudes toward the twelve and polygamy. Winchester said he had "witnessed the sufferings of innocent females whose characters had been traduced and ruind forever." Eliza Nicholson had complained to Smith on 23 April 1843 that Winchester had slandered her. Her letter is in the Joseph Smith Collection, LDSCA. Winchester was reprimanded by Smith and the twelve after he reported that Isabella Armstrong was the "public talk in the church." See "Minutes of the Quorum of the Twelve," 27 May 1843. Winchester's general views on plurality of wives and his reasons for ultimately leaving the church are explained in his account in Charles L. Woodward, "The First Half Century of Mormonism" (1880), 195, New York Public Library.

172. The note, dated 14 July 1842, is in the Orson Pratt papers, LDSCA.

173. Oliver Olney papers, #17.

174. The entry in Young's manuscript history is dated 8 Aug. 1842. Pratt's negative vote on Smith's morality is recorded in LDSMS, Oct. 1842, 103.

175. HC 5:120, where Amasa Lyman was named to replace Pratt. Sarah's and Orson's rebaptism was recorded in Kenney, 2:212–13. See also "Minutes of the Council of the Twelve," 20 Jan. 1843. Sarah Pratt's continued bitterness is shown in her interview by W. Wyl in *Mormon Portraits* (Salt Lake City,

1886), 61–69. Sarah said that Smith taught her that "God does not care if we have a good time or not if only other people do not know it."

176. Linda King Newell and Valeen Tippetts Avery, *Mormon Enigma: Emma Hale Smith*, (Garden City, NY: Doubleday, 1984), 96, 97, 140, 152–54, 293, 298–302.

177. Ibid., 158.

178. Ibid., 136–37, 158–60, 163–65. Compare Orson Pratt's comments on Emma's vacillating behavior in Gerber, 14:62.

179. Ibid., 158. This was 6 August 1843.

180. DC 132:4, 7.

181. Ibid., v. 26, and William Clayton's Journal, 12 July 1843.

182. See several successive issues beginning 8 July 1842.

183. *Quincy Whig*, 9, 16 July 1842.

184. JH, 14 July 1842.

185. *Hawk Eye and Iowa Patriot*, 28 Sept. 1842.

186. *Missouri Republican*, 12 Oct. 1842.

187. *Peoria Register*, 13 Jan. 1843.

188. Joseph Smith papers.

189. John E. Page to Joseph Smith, 8, 15 Aug. 1842, Smith papers.

190. Joseph Smith sent missionaries out armed with affidavits against Bennett. See HC 5:132. Also for a sample of the Mormon counter attack, see *The Wasp*, published by William Smith at Nauvoo, 25 June 1842, 2; 27 July 1842, 1–3; 30 July 1842, 2; and 4 Aug. 1842, 2.

191. HC 4:585–86; and *Warsaw Signal*, 23 July 1843, 2.

192. Olney papers, #15 and #30, and Willard Richards to James A. Bennett, 20 Nov. 1842, Richards papers, LDSCA.

193. See *Times and Seasons* 4 (15 March 1843): 143, where George Adams is quoted from the *Boston Bee* that the accusation that Mormons advocate a plurality of wives is "as false as the many other ridiculous charges."

194. Sarah Scott's letter to her parents in Massachusetts is quoted in William Mulder and A. Russell Mortensen, eds., *Among the Mormons: Historic Accounts by Contemporary Observers* (New York: Alfred A. Knopf, 1958), 143–45. On the other dissenters, see the account by Horace Cummings in *The Contributor* 5 (April 1884): 252.

195. See *Quincy Whig*, 9 July 1842, 2, and 6 Aug. 1842, 2; *Sangamo Journal*, 29 July 1842; and *Alton Telegraph*, which supported Duncan in the campaign, 25 June 1842, 2, and 6 July and 9 July 1842, 2–3. The *Alton* editor urged Bennett to "come out now" and "expose Mormon corruption."

196. *Alton Telegraph and Democratic Review*, 4 June 1842.

197. Ibid., 11 June 1842. *The Wasp*, 4 July 1842, published at Nauvoo, indicates that the candidates supported by the Mormons were Mark Aldridge, a non-Mormon who later turned against the Saints when he no longer needed the political advantage, Orson Pratt, Backenstos, a so-called "jack-Mormon"

(or friendly non-Mormon), Rigdon, Daniel Wells (who converted to Mormonism later), and Hiram Kimball, so that it was a Mormon dominated ticket.

198. Flanders, 249, and compare Thomas Ford, 269. See also the *Alton Telegraph*, 4 June 1842, 2.

199. The attitudes of the editor of the *Illinois State Register* are commented on by the editor of the *Alton Telegraph*, 4 June 1842, 2, and 25 June 1842, 2, where Stephen A. Douglas is cited as affirming that he wanted to prevent mob violence against the Saints.

200. Flanders, 250–51.

201. Flanders, 251, argues that Ford's move here came from conviction, not calculation, but this ignores the fact that the *Alton Telegraph* had put great pressure on Ford three days before he came out for repeal by maintaining that the Nauvoo charter was "anti-republican" and that Ford was not offered the nomination until he had been approved by the Saints. The editor of the Whig newspaper argued that Ford would thus be dominated by the Mormons if he won. Ford could hardly ignore this allegation so near the election since it was a close race. See the *Alton Telegraph*, 6 July 1842, 2.

202. Flanders, 251. But notice that Ford's total vote was 46,507 while Duncan's was 39,020. Thus Ford's margin was large enough that the 1,038 votes which the Saints gave him in Hancock County made no difference. However, they did have the balance of power in Hancock where Ford carried the county by 1,037. See *Quincy Whig*, 6 Aug. 1842, 2, for the Mormon vote for Ford in Hancock, and compare Theodore Calvin Pease, *Illinois Election Returns, 1818–1848* (Collections of the Illinois State Historical Library, Vol. 18; Springfield: Trustees of the Illinois State Historical Library, 1923), 127, for the state results.

203. Mormons made no apologies for seeking group political power. The editor of the *Nauvoo Neighbor* said simply, "We would suggest the necessity of unanimity. It can answer no good purpose that half the citizens should disfranchise the other half, thus rendering Nauvoo powerless as far as politics are concerned." Mormon anti-pluralism was thus in part related to their desire for political power. Smith contended that this quest was due to the fact that "Mormons were driven to union in their elections by persecution." See Faulring, 286. Mormon group voting began in Kirtland prior to any strong opposition so that other considerations were involved. It should have been obvious by this time that collective voting made enemies and prompted violence, not vice versa. It is noteworthy that as early as July 1842 the editor of the *Alton Telegraph* affirmed that "the people throughout the state have become justly alarmed at the assumption on the part of the Mormons through their spiritual head, 'Joe Smith,' to decide who shall and who shall not be elected in this state." Smith then urged the people to vote against all candidates who courted Mormon favor, thus further encouraging the formation of an anti-Mormon political bloc in the state.

204. *Alton Telegraph and Democratic Review*, 6 Aug. 1842.

205. HC 5:86–87.

206. Ibid., 87.

207. Ibid., 88.

208. Ibid., 190–91

209. Ibid., 89–137.

210. *Warsaw Signal*, 13 Aug. 1842, 3, and 20 Aug. 1842, 2.

211. Bennett's letter was originally addressed to the *Louisville Journal* but was published in the *Sangamo Journal*, 19 Aug. 1842, 2. John Corrill had voiced a similar opinion in 1839, saying, "They esteem the law of God, as given through their prophet, to be vastly superior to any other law; and if they could have their privilege they would prefer to be governed by that alone." John Corrill, *A Brief History of the Church of Christ of Latter-day Saints, Including Their Doctrine and Discipline* (St. Louis: For the author, 1839), 47.

212. HC 5:154.

213. *Reports Made to the Senate and the House of Representatives of the State of Illinois at Their Session Begun at Springfield, December 5, 1842* (Springfield, 1842), 2:32. The speech is also cited in *The Wasp*, 24 Dec. 1842, 2.

214. *Quincy Whig*, 24 Dec. 1842, 2.

215. *The Wasp*, 14 Jan. 1843, 1–2, for William Smith's speech.

216. Ibid., 1 Feb. 1843, 3.

217. Ibid.

218. *Quincy Whig*, 8 Feb. 1843, 2. Charles Thompson suggests that Stephen Douglas may have been behind the effort to curb Mormon power, which could explain why the Whigs reacted against the repeal of the charter. See his *Illinois Whigs Before 1846* (Champaign: University of Illinois, 1915), 99.

219. *Illinois State Register*, 8 Nov. 1844, 2; Gregg, *History of Hancock County*, 748–49, 757.

220. *Warsaw Signal*, 9 June 1841, 2.

221. Flanders, 241.

222. *Warsaw Signal*, 25 Aug. 1841, 2. The office of county commissioner was taken by a mere fourteen votes, the school commissioner by 114.

223. *Warsaw Signal*, 4 Aug. 1841, 2.

224. Ibid., 26 Jan. 1842, 2.

225. Ibid., 23 July 1842, 2.

226. Ibid., 20 Aug. 1842, 2.

227. HC 5:55–56.

228. *Warsaw Signal*, 6 Aug. 1842, 2.

229. Gregg, *History of Hancock County*, 749. Sharp took up farming until January 1844, when he again assumed editorship of the *Signal* and leadership of the anti-Mormon movement in Hancock County.

230. *The Wasp*, 16 July 1842, 2; and compare HC 7:143, 420.

231. Ford wrote that the Saints purposely sought to get the question of Carlin's writ before the federal bench, pp. 313–14. He neglected to mention

that he had urged Smith to seek a judicial settlement. See HC 5:205–206. The events leading up to the trial at Springfield, the legal documents involved, and the substance of Pope's decision are found in HC 5:209–12, 223–31, 233–45.

232. William Weston to George C. Weston, Feb. 1843, Manuscript Collection, Newberry Library, Chicago, Illinois.

233. The editor of the *Alton Telegraph* declared that "no man whose hands are stained with blood can elude punishment, the day of visitation upon him may be far distant, but arrive it certainly will." See 11 Jan. 1843, 2.

234. *Quincy Herald*, 12 Jan. 1843, 2; *Warsaw Message*, 28 Jan. 1843, 2.

235. HC 5:232.

236. Ibid., 259.

237. Ibid., 286.

CHAPTER 7
APPEAL TO A "HIGHER POWER"

1. A typical success story for Mormon missionaries in the east is that of Benjamin C. Elsworth who baptized large numbers in New York. See JH, 18 Oct. 1840, and compare Whitney R. Cross, *The Burned-over District* (New York: Cornell University Press, 1950), 149–50. Robert Flanders estimates that by 1845 five thousand Saints, or about one fourth of the population, had come into Nauvoo from England. See *Nauvoo: Kingdom on the Mississippi* (Urbana: University of Illinois Press, 1965), 74–76, 84, 92. Compare also P. A. M. Taylor, *Expectations Westward* (Edinburgh: Oliver and Boyd, 1965), 19–20, for some comparable figures.

2. Flanders's chapter on the Nauvoo economy (155–92) is well done, and I have relied heavily upon it.

3. HC 4:93.

4. Ibid., 228, 482; Flanders, 159–60; *Times and Seasons* 2 (15 Jan. 1841): 274; and 5 (1 Jan. 1844): 391–92. See also Rita Latimer Halford, "Nauvoo—the City Beautiful," M.A. thesis, University of Utah, 1945, 291.

5. Flanders, 191–92

6. Ibid., 123–24, 168–71.

7. Ibid., 156.

8. Ibid., 157, and compare Joseph Smith's "Nauvoo Account Book" which covers 1839–40 and shows that several commercial transactions by Hyrum Smith and others were handled in kind or by personal notes. See pp. 9, 20–23, 84–87 of this ledger which is in the Rare Book Room, Harper Library, University of Chicago.

9. Ford Family Correspondence, Stanley B. Kimball Collection, Southern Illinois University.

10. Flanders, 158.

11. HC 4:303.

12. *Nauvoo Neighbor*, 13 Nov. 1844, 2.

13. Some Mormons feared the impending repeal of the charter. Flanders, 161–62, and compare HC 5:436–37.

14. See "Our City and the Present Aspect of Affairs," *Times and Seasons* 5 (15 March 1844): 471, and compare "The Trades," *Nauvoo Neighbor*, 16 Oct. 1844, 2, and 18 Dec. 1844, 3, where plans were outlined for bringing carriage and harness, cotton and stove factories to the city.

15. Flanders, 166, and *Times and Seasons* 5 (1 Jan. 1844): 391–92. Compare Rita Halford, "Nauvoo—The City Beautiful," M.A. thesis, University of Utah, 1945, 309–26.

16. Flanders writes that "the record does not indicate whether the products of the city were sold in outside markets to any extent" (166). My own research gives little evidence that they did since there are no protests against such in the Gentile literature. There seems to have been some disposition in St. Louis to shun a Mormon steamer carrying passengers to Nauvoo but not much more than this. There is no clue in the report of the Senate judiciary committee or in the account of the House debates by the *Alton Telegraph* as to why some wanted the Nauvoo Agricultural and Manufacturing Association charter repealed. It may be that there was fear of its potential rather than any concrete competition. See *Nauvoo Neighbor*, 10 May 1843, for evidence of trouble with St. Louis. Also *Reports Made to the Senate and House of Representatives of the State of Illinois . . .* , 127–30, for the views of the Senate judiciary committee. For the details of the House debate see *Alton Telegraph and Democratic Review*, 17 Dec. 1842, 3.

17. Letter from David Jenkins to Leonard Pickel, Nauvoo, 28 Sept. 1842, Pickel papers, Yale University.

18. See the complaint of "a Mechanic" and the admissions of John Taylor in *The Wasp*, 29 March 1843, 2. Taylor said there was a marked difference between goods that sold for cash and those traded by barter.

19. Hyrum Smith told those at April 1843 conference that a former Saint informed him of a secret band making bogus money in Nauvoo. See HC 5:333–34, and compare Orson Hyde's warning to Brigham Young in 1844 that "if there are not sufficient measures taken to break up a company of bogus makers and route them from this place. . . . I am apprehensive of very serious consequences" (JH, 29 Dec. 1844).

20. In the *Warsaw Signal*, 25 April 1844, Sharp noted the circulation of "Nauvoo Bogus" half-dollars dated 1828, said to be made in Nauvoo. Compare also the issue of 22 Jan. 1845.

21. *Missouri Republican*, 4 July 1844, 2.

22. The *Messenger and Advocate of the Church of Christ* 1 (1 Feb. 1845): 101.

23. Ibid. Rigdon said that many of the builders had to go as far as St. Louis to find work. Compare the predictions of a non-Mormon that the Saints

would emigrate in 1845 due to the lack of work in the city in *Quincy Whig*, 25 Dec. 1844. Some friends of George Whitaker in St. Louis told him in 1845 not to go to Nauvoo for it was a poor place to make a living. See "Life of George Whitaker, a Utah Pioneer, as Written by Himself," 7, in Kimball Collection.

24. Brigham Young and Wilford Woodruff wrote to Reuben Hedlock in England that "all things are going gloriously at Nauvoo." The whole tone of the letter is optimistic, while nothing is said of the sagging Nauvoo economy. It is significant, however, that the apostles also told Hedlock that all of the United States is Zion and the English Saints might begin to settle elsewhere than Nauvoo. See HC 6:351–54.

25. Orson Spencer, *Letters Exhibiting the Most Prominent Doctrines of the Church of Jesus Christ of Latter-day Saints* (Salt Lake City: Deseret News Co., 1889), 36, maintained that the Saints had every opportunity to become rich, despite some "deep penuary," but instead "long to behold the beauty of the Lord."

26. *The Messenger and Advocate of the Church of Christ* 1 (1 Feb. 1845): 101.

27. B. H. Roberts, *A Comprehensive History of the Church of Jesus Christ of Latter-day Saints*, 6 vols. (Salt Lake City: Deseret News Press, 1930), 2:166–71 details the developments.

28. Ibid., 166, and Thomas Ford, *A History of Illinois* (Chicago: S. C. Greggs & Co., 1854), 315, who says that Bennett was involved in the indictment.

29. HC 5:440–43.

30. Ibid., 444.

31. That Walker understood this to mean the Mormon vote as well is indicated by his comment to Stephen Markham, "I am now sure of my election, as Joseph Smith has promised me his vote, and I am going to defend him." See B. H. Roberts, *Comprehensive History*, 2:194.

32. Ibid., 168.

33. The best detail of Mormon preparations to liberate the prophet by military means is found in the papers of William Pattersen McIntyre, in a report written in 1854, LDSCA.

34. HC 5:93.

35. Thomas Ford, in his letter to Governor Thomas Reynolds, 17 Aug. 1843, declining to order out the state militia to arrest Smith, relates the charges of Reynolds that he was taken to Nauvoo "under constraint" and "against his will." Ford's letter appears in *Times and Seasons* 4 (15 Aug. 1843): 293–95.

36. HC 5:460.

37. *Quincy Herald*, 30 June 1843, 2.

38. *Times and Seasons* 4 (15 Aug. 1843): 294. Ford wrote to Governor Reynolds that Sheriff Reynolds was taken to Nauvoo "by lawful process; by

an authorized officer who acted, so far as I have any evidence, freely and voluntarily in so doing."

39. Roberts, *Comprehensive History*, 2:172–73.

40. *Quincy Herald*, 30 June 1843, 2.

41. Roberts, *Comprehensive History*, 2:170–71.

42. Smith's address of June 30, 1843, is recorded most fully by Wilford Woodruff in his journal. See Kenney, 2:248–252. Andrew F. Ehat and Lyndon W. Cook, *The Words of Joseph Smith* (Provo, UT: Religious Studies Center, Brigham Young University, 1980), 222–25, reproduce accounts of the same speech by Willard Richards and William Clayton.

43. Hall's letter appears in the *Nauvoo Neighbor*, 23 Aug. 1843.

44. HC 5:457–58.

45. Letter of George Rockwell to Thomas H. Rockwell, 3 Aug. 1843, in Kimball Collection.

46. *Warsaw Message*, 12 July 1843, 2.

47. HC 5:521 and compare Charlotte Haven's affirmation that "all summer politicians, able men of both parties, have been making speeches caressing and flattering the Saints." *Overland Monthly* 16 (Dec. 1890): 636.

48. T. Ford, 317–18. Ford held that this mission "produced a total change in the minds of the Mormon leaders."

49. Brayman's letter to the prophet is in RLDSCA.

50. Oliver Olney papers, #17, Yale University. Olney said this occurred on Saturday, 30 July, but he was wrong on his date. His general accuracy is supported by an editorial in the *Nauvoo Neighbor* which urged "the necessity of unanimity [in voting] . . . it can answer no good purpose that half the citizens should disfranchise the other half, thus rendering Nauvoo powerless as far as politics are concerned." See the issue of 2 Aug. 1843.

51. Willard Richards to Brigham Young, 5 Aug. 1843, Richards papers, LDSCA.

52. Faulring, 401–402. Compare HC 5:526.

53. Flanders, 329.

54. *Nauvoo Neighbor*, 30 Aug. 1843, 2.

55. T. Ford, 329.

56. *Davenport Gazette*, 10, 17 Aug. 1843.

57. Faulring, 405–406.

58. *Warsaw Message*, 6 Sept. 1843.

59. HC 5:528.

60. *Lee County Democrat*, 2 Sept. 1843, 2.

61. *Warsaw Message*, 13 Sept. 1843.

62. HC 5:537–38; Thomas Gregg, *History of Hancock County, Illinois* (Chicago: Charles C. Chapman & Co., 1880), 299.

63. See the charges of John Harper, a political opportunist, who out of "curiosity" attended the meeting. Harper insisted that it "was a Whig meeting" and that the "president, Secretary and leading members were all

Whigs." Thomas Gregg admitted that the president and secretary were Whigs but said that the committee which brought forward the resolutions was composed of three Whigs and three Democrats and that "several other Democrats took part." See *Warsaw Message*, 27 Sept. 1843, 2. Compare also the protest of A. Rasp who took issue with Harper but could only name three Democrats who did not fit Harper's generalization. Ibid., 4 Oct. 1843, 2.

64. Thus of twenty-two members of the committees of correspondence organized in the local precincts, Gregg's work shows that at least nine were among the earliest settlers in the county. In addition, he recounts that George Rockwell, Edward Bedell, William Grover, Jacob C. Davis, and Robert F. Smith, all of whom became leaders in the anti-Mormon campaign, were early residents. See a list of the members of the committees of correspondence in HC 6:8; compare Gregg's *History of Hancock County*, 510, 511, 578, 608, 637–38, 653, 790, 816, 819, 837, 895, and 900, for details of the lives of some of the anti-Mormons.

65. Of the ten identifiable townships represented at the meeting in September, six were located in the eastern half of the county—LaHarpe, Fountain Green, St. Mary's, Augusta, Chili, and Carthage. Appanoose, Montebello, and Warsaw were river towns, economic rivals of Nauvoo but too close to the Mormons for comfort. See a map of the townships in Gregg, at the front.

66. See also *Warsaw Message*, 6 Sept. 1843, 2, and 27 Sept. 1843, 2.

67. The resolutions are reproduced in HC 6:4–8. According to the *Davenport Gazette*, the delegates pledged that they would not obey the mandates of the newly elected officials of the county, but there is no specific clause in the resolutions to this effect. See 14 Sept. 1843, 2.

68. HC 6:31, 35. Ford promised he would protect them from invasion.

69. See "Carthage vs. Nauvoo," *Nauvoo Neighbor*, 13 Sept. 1843, 2. John Taylor and Wilford Woodruff were the editors of the Mormon paper.

70. Ibid., 25 Oct. 1843, 3.

71. Ibid., 27 Sept. 1843, 2.

72. Andrew Moore to Levi Moore, Carthage, Illinois, 15 Oct. 1843, Mormon Collection, Beinecke Library, Yale University.

73. HC 6:104.

74. Ibid., 105–106.

75. Ibid., 117–18. This is Sisson Chase's testimony.

76. Ibid., 119–20.

77. Ibid., 124; "Nauvoo City Council Minutes," 197, LDSCA.

78. *Warsaw Message Extra*, 26 Dec. 1843, Mormon Collection, Chicago Historical Society.

79. Two different accounts of the degree of resistance to the arresting officer may be seen in HC 6:171–73 and *Quincy Whig*, 24 Jan. 1844, 2.

80. *Warsaw Message*, 27 Sept. 1843, 2.

81. *Warsaw Signal*, 17 Jan. 1844, 2. Compare "Hannibal's" remarks, p. 1.

82. Smith was told on 14 December not to muster any part of the legion. HC 6:113.

83. Ibid., 119–21. After receiving Ford's "milk and water letter" of 14 December, Smith sent part of the legion to assist a justice of the peace in capturing one of the Avery kidnappers and also to guard against mobbers collecting near Warsaw. Smith's history indicates that on 19 December Hosea Stout, a colonel in the legion, returned to Nauvoo with his troops after coming within two miles of the mob. In a letter to Governor Ford on 30 December Smith said that although the legion had been put on alert no troops had been ordered to march. See HC 5:443 and 6:153, 362.

84. *Missouri Republican*, 6 Jan. 1844, 2.

85. HC 5:510–12.

86. *Times and Seasons* 4 (15 Sept. 1843): 330; compare HC 6:48–49, which has been altered form the original to cast suspicion on Rigdon again.

87. HC 6:152.

88. *Times and Seasons* 4 (15 May 1843): 204.

89. HC 6:13–14.

90. Ibid., 15–16. Pratt added that the Mormons had political and temporal ambitions like those of Joseph who was sold into Egypt. See the uncensored version, LDSMS 22 (3 March 1860): 134.

91. The plea to Pennsylvania was made by Sidney Rigdon. See HC 6:191–92.

92. Ibid., 90, 92–93.

93. Such would not have been possible without the consent of the state of Illinois.

94. HC 6:131. The legion was to be incorporated into the United States army with Joseph Smith in command.

95. LDSMS 22 (21 July 1860): 455.

96. Correspondence of Joseph Smith and John C. Calhoun, 4 Nov. 1843, in *Voice of Truth* (Nauvoo, 1844), 24.

97. Ibid., 55.

98. "Diary of George Laub," 1:30, Special Collections, Harold B. Lee Library, Brigham Young University. Compare Kenney, 2:425, for Orson Hyde's lament that had the Gentiles received Smith as their leader he "would have saved the nation from ruin and destruction."

99. *Times and Seasons* 5 (1 June 1844): 556.

100. HC 6:188.

101. *General Smith's Views of the Powers and Policy of the Government of the United States*, 86.

102. HC 6:273.

103. JH, 9 June 1844.

104. In *Times and Seasons* 5 (15 Aug. 1844): 613.

105. Ibid., 4 (1 Dec. 1842): 24.

106. HC 6:322.

107. Ibid., 322.

108. *Times and Seasons* 5 (15 March 1844): 477.

109. Flanders, 301.

110. Mormon leaders took seriously *The New York Herald*'s assertion that the Saints controlled the vote in Illinois, and hence in the entire west. It warned that they might dictate the destiny of all presidential candidates. See *Nauvoo Neighbor*, 21 Feb. 1844. Klaus Hansen, *Quest for Empire: The Political Kingdom of God and The Council of Fifty in Mormon History* (Lincoln: University of Nebraska Press, 1974), 60–61. William Clayton details the full organization between 3 and 14 March, but sources conflict as to the exact date.

111. Ibid., 78. D. Michael Quinn argues that the council was not as important as Hansen believed, especially after Smith's death. Quinn is correct that the council did not challenge the system of government in Nauvoo. Nonetheless, Hansen's generalizations stand. The council certainly was prepared to take over real governing responsibilities. See Quinn's "Council of Fifty and Its Members, 1844–1845," *Brigham Young University Studies* 20 (Winter 1980): 164.

112. Klaus Hansen, 77–79, and Flanders, 302.

113. HC 6:231–32. The letter is dated 4 March 1844.

114. Kenney, 2:357.

115. Willard Richards to Orson Hyde, 25 May 1844, Richards papers.

116. Willard Richards to Hugh Clark, 24 May 1844, Richards papers.

117. Charles C. Rich papers, LDSCA.

118. Young to Willard Richards, 8 July 1844, Young papers, LDSCA.

119. Bennett to Willard Richards, 14 April 1844, Bennett papers, LDSCA.

120. HC 6:516.

121. Paul D. Ellsworth, "Mobocracy and the Rule of Law: American Press Reaction to the Murder of Joseph Smith," *Brigham Young University Studies* 20 (Fall 1979): 71–82, notes that although Americans did not like Smith, they did not like his murder either, seeing it as mob violence. James Gordon Bennett, the editor of the *New York Herald* whom Joseph Smith considered an ally, wrote on 13 August 1842 that he had been given the freedom of the city in Nauvoo and commented, "We suppose it embraces a vast number of delicious privileges."

122. D. S. Hollister to Joseph Smith, 26, 28 June 1844, in Smith papers, LDSCA.

123. James Arlington Bennett to Willard Richards, 14 April 1844.

124. The "Minutes of the Quorum of the Twelve," 20 Feb. 1844, indicate that a committee was to be formed to appoint a company to explore Oregon and California and to "select a site for a new city for the Saints." Smith's diary kept by Willard Richards has Smith saying, "I instructed the 12 [apostles] to send out a delegation and investigate the locations of California and Oregon and find a good location where we can remove after the

Temple is completed and build a city in a day and have a government of
our own in a healthy climate" (Faulring, 447). Thus it does not sound as
though the prophet was abandoning the idea of a central gathering place, a
city, where he would preside. However, for a counter argument, see Flanders,
289–91.

125. Faulring, 458.

126. *Correspondence of Bishop George Miller with the Northern Islander From
His Acquaintance with Mormonism Up to Near the Close of His Life, 1855* (Burlington,
WI: W. Watson, 1916), 20.

127. Ehat and Cook, 367.

128. *Times and Seasons* 5 (15 March 1844): 470.

129. Flanders, 87–88; HC 6:274–77.

130. T. Ford, 321.

131. The letter, written from Springfield sometime in January 1844, is
in the John J. Hardin Collection, Chicago Historical Society.

132. William D. Abernethy to John J. Hardin, Augusta, Illinois, 19 March
1844, John J. Hardin Collection.

133. *Warsaw Signal*, 31 Jan. 1844, 3, and 28 Feb. 1844, 2.

134. Ibid.

135. Ibid., 14 Feb. 1844, 2, and 21 Feb. 1844, 2.

136. See "Buckeye's Lamentation for the Want of More Wives," *Warsaw
Signal*, 7 Feb. 1844, 1. Smith indicated that this piece may have been written
by Wilson Law who had recently been at odds with the church leader. See
HC 6:210.

137. *Warsaw Signal*, 21 Feb. 1844, 2.

138. HC 6:212. Smith said afterward that he thought if the Gentiles
desired peace this should satisfy them. But the bitterness between the two
communities had become too deep for a token compromise to satisfy them.
See p. 219.

139. *Warsaw Signal*, 28 Feb. 1844, 2.

140. Ibid., 25 April 1844, 2. Compare HC 6:278–80.

141. HC 4:286.

142. Law recalled this disagreement with Hyrum and Joseph during
an interview in the 1880s. See Charles Woodward, "The First Half Century
of Mormonism" (1880), 288, New York Public Library. Compare Francis M.
Higbee's denunciation of the revelation to Hyrum in the *Nauvoo Expositor*, 7
June 1844, 3.

143. HC 5:84. Law had replaced John C. Bennett as Major-General.

144. Ibid., 6:355 and 7:57.

145. Ibid., 6:417 and 7:57.

146. The quotation is from the account by Dennison L. Harris and
Robert Scott in *The Contributor* 5 (April 1884): 254. Francis M. Higbee wrote
to Smith on 10 January 1844, saying that "he is still of the same opinion fixed
and determined as the pol[ar] star that any revelation commanding in any

wise suffering sexual intercourse, under any other form than that prescribed by the laws of our country, which has been ratified by Special revelation through you is of *HELL*; and I [say] defiance to any or all such." Higbee's letter is in the Joseph Smith Collection, LDSCA. William Law's difficulties with the prophet over plural marriage are detailed in Richard S. Van Wagoner, *Mormon Polygamy: A History* (Salt Lake City: Signature Books, 1986), 63–65.

147. HC 6:436.

148. Ibid., 287–96, and "William Law Diary," 6. A typed copy of this diary is in my possession.

149. Compare Woodruff's journal with the original manuscript of the HC, E1, p. 1,977, where Hyrum's remarks, deleted in the published work, 6:300, were recorded.

150. HC 6:341.

151. Alexander Neibaur in his diary in 1844 said he understood that Jane Law had attempted to be sealed to Smith.

152. See "Minutes of the Council of the Twelve," 18 April 1844, and "William Law Diary," 7. Law dated this 19 April.

153. HC 6:354, and Kenney, 2:393.

154. "William Law Diary," 9.

155. *Warsaw Signal*, 15 May 1844, 2.

156. The letter, written in May, is located in the Mormon Manuscript Collection, Chicago Historical Society.

157. "William Law Diary," 8–9.

158. *Warsaw Signal*, 29 May 1844, 2; compare *Nauvoo Neighbor*, 7 June 1844, 3, which shows that several charges were brought simultaneously by the dissenters. The charge of perjury was brought by Alex Sympson. See HC 6:464–65; *Warsaw Signal*, 25 April 1844, 3.

159. Ibid.

160. *Upper Mississippian*, 25 May 1844.

161. Robert D. Foster to Joseph Smith, 7 June 1844, Smith papers. In HC 6:437. Smith, or those who compiled his history, argued at length that Foster initiated the attempt at reconciliation and that Smith knew nothing of Dimick Huntington's visit to Foster (pp. 436–40). It seems that when Foster turned down his offer Smith was humiliated and did not wish to acknowledge that he had made the effort. See Law's diary, 13 May and 7 June 1844.

162. *Nauvoo Expositor*, 7 June 1844.

163. HC 6:438.

164. Ibid., 445–46. Dallin H. Oaks has argued that Smith and the city council had legal precedent for declaring the newspaper a nuisance but that this did not justify their destroying the press itself. See Oaks, *Utah Law Review*, 862–903.

165. Ibid., 446–48.

166. Ibid., 432, and Oaks, 876.

167. *Quincy Whig*, 19 June 1844, 2.

168. *Alton Telegraph*, 15 June 1844, 2.

169. *Lee County Democrat*, 22 June 1844, 2.

170. *Quincy Herald*, 14 June 1844.

171. H. H. Bliss to Franklin Bliss, 8 June 1844, Indiana University Library. The press was destroyed on 10 June, so the letter is misdated.

172. *Warsaw Signal*, 12 June 1844, 2.

173. "William Law Diary," 10 June 1844.

174. HC 6:453–54.

175. Ibid., 454, 485–91. Smith claimed later that his trial before Daniel H. Wells satisfied the demands of the law on the riot charge. See pp. 498–582. Oaks, 865n17, seems to err in maintaining that the trial to which Smith referred was the preliminary hearing described on pp. 456–58 of the *History*. Smith's remarks refer to the trial before Wells, not the hearing before John P. Greene.

176. The letter, dated from Warsaw, 18 June 1844, is in the *Missouri Republican*, 21 June 1844, 2.

177. H. H. Bliss to Franklin Bliss, 8 July 1844.

178. Samuel O. Williams to John A. Prickett, 10 July 1844, Mormon Manuscript Collection, Chicago Historical Society.

179. George Rockwell to his father, 22 June 1844.

180. *North Western Gazette & Galena Advertizer*, 21 June 1844, 2.

181. Ibid.

182. *Warsaw Signal*, 19 June 1844, 2.

183. HC 6:466–67.

184. Ibid., 497, 499–500.

185. Ibid., 518.

186. Ibid., 528.

187. Ibid., 533.

188. Oaks, 862–903.

189. Broad powers were conceded to other Illinois cities, including the right granted to Alton to issue legal writs within its jurisdiction. But it is not likely that Alton took advantage of this to the degree that Nauvoo did. James L. Kimball details the special privileges granted to Nauvoo, and those that were not unique, in "The Nauvoo Charter: A Reinterpretation," *Journal of the Illinois Historical Society* 64 (Spring 1971): 66–78.

190. HC 6:533–37.

191. *Warsaw Signal*, 29 May 1844, 2, and 18 June 1844.

192. At one point Smith planned to go east to appeal to President Tyler but afterward may have decided to flee westward. See HC 6:540, 545.

193. *Quincy Whig*, 19 June 1844. The editor reported threats at Carthage that if Smith were not surrendered it would lead to a war of extermination. Governor Ford warned Smith on 22 June that Nauvoo stood on a "powder

keg which a very small spark may explode" if Smith did not submit to Carthage authorities. HC 6:536. Minor Deming wrote to his parents on 20 June 1844 that he feared that once the troops were in Nauvoo they would "demolish the city." The Deming papers are in the Illinois Historical Survey, University of Illinois Library, Urbana.

194. HC 6:547–48.

195. Wilford Woodruff said it was Emma who persuaded Joseph by letter that he must return to Nauvoo; but she maintained that the urgings of certain elders who accused him of cowardice caused the return. See ibid., 549–52; and Emma's interview in Edmund C. Briggs, "A Visit to Nauvoo in 1856," *The Journal History* 9 (Oct. 1916): 453–54.

196. HC 6:555–56.

197. *Times and Seasons* 5 (15 July 1844): 585.

198. HC 6:550.

199. In "Recollections of Joseph Smith," *Juvenile Instructor*, 15 Aug. 1892, 490.

200. HC 6:563–64; Samual O. Williams to John A. Pricket, 10 July 1844.

201. Dallin H. Oaks and Marvin S. Hill, *Carthage Conspiracy: The Trial of the Accused Assassins of Joseph Smith* (Urbana: University of Illinois Press, 1975), 18.

202. Georqe T. M. Davis, *An Authentic Account of the Massacre of Joseph Smith* (St. Louis: Chambers and Knapp, 1844), 17.

203. Edward H. Stiles, *Recollection and Sketches of Notable Lawyers and Public Men of Early Iowa* (Des Moines: The Homestead Publishing Co., 1916), 269–70.

204. PW, 611.

205. See William Clayton's letter, written for Joseph Smith, 26 June 1844, to Judge Thomas telling him to come to Nauvoo for "the Governor is coming with Genl Smith tomorrow, and the case is to be tried before your honor in this place." Clayton's letter is in the Joseph Smith papers.

206. HC, manuscript E1, 27 June 1844. The quotation was deleted from the printed version, 6:605.

207. PW, 612.

208. *Warsaw Signal*, 10 July 1844, 2.

209. Thomas Sharp in the *Warsaw Signal*, 10 July 1844, identified the troops from Warsaw and Green Plains who "thought Ford had trifled with them." George Rockwell, a druggist from Warsaw and a member of the militia, wrote on 3 August 1844 that the Warsaw troops, "feeling unwilling to be trifled with any longer they determined to take the matter into their own hands." Rockwell said he regretted the necessity of the murder.

210. Oaks and Hill, 19, 87, 119, 125–26, 130–31, 145, 152. Some of this comes from the testimony at the trial of the accused murderers.

211. Ibid., 21.

212. I tended to discount the reports that Smith was stabbed when Oaks and I wrote *Carthage Conspiracy*, but I now think that there were too many testimonies to that effect to ignore. See Kenney, 2:423–28; Samuel O. Williams to John A. Pickett, 10 July 1844, Mormon Manuscript Collection, Chicago Historical Society. Williams was at the jail. Also the testimony of Colonel M. B. Darnell, who said he was a few feet from the body, in N. B. Lundwall, *The Fate of the Persecutors of the Prophet Joseph Smith* (Salt Lake City: n.p., 1952), 212–13.

213. See the letter by "Hancock" in the *Warsaw Signal*, 31 July 1844, 1. Hancock said the Mormon leaders "set the laws at defiance, and openly declared themselves above them."

214. *Warsaw Signal*, 10 July 1844, 2.

215. "Diary of William Law," 12–13.

216. Willard Richards was told that Law knew of the impending murder early in the day, 27 June. See "Journal of Willard Richards," 11 July 1844, LDSCA. An unnamed witness said he saw Law, Higbee, and Foster at the jail. *Naked Truths About Mormonism* 1 (April 1888). Willard Richards included Law on his list of murderers, HC 7:146. J. B. Backenstos, however, listed Francis Higbee as one of the mobbers, not Law, ibid., 144.

217. "Diary of William Law," 13–14.

CHAPTER 8
"TO THE WILDERNESS FOR SAFETY AND REFUGE"

1. "Diary of Job Smith," 28 June 1844, Huntington Library, San Marino, California.

2. Linda King Newell and Valeen Tippetts Avery, *Mormon Enigma: Emma Hale Smith* (Garden City, NY: Doubleday, 1984), 197.

3. Sarah M. Kimball to Sister Heywood, n.d., Kimball papers, LDSCA.

4. *Times and Seasons* 5 (15 Dec. 1844): 743.

5. "Autobiography of George Morris," 22, typescript, Special Collections, Harold B. Lee Library, Brigham Young University, Provo, Utah.

6. Henry W. Bigler, "Diary of a Mormon in California," 14, Bancroft Library, University of California, Berkeley.

7. Jacob Gibson to James J. Strang, 25 June 1846, Strang papers, Beinecke Library, Yale University.

8. HC 7:147–48.

9. Kenney, 2:419.

10. Stanley B. Kimball, ed., *On the Potter's Wheel: The Diaries of Heber C. Kimball* (Salt Lake City: Signature Books and Smith Research Associates, 1988), 73.

11. HC 7:197. I have followed Heber C. Kimball's dating here, in contrast to the published history.

12. Ronald K. Esplin, "Joseph, Brigham and the Twelve: A Succession of Continuity," *Brigham Young University Studies* 21 (Summer 1981): 319–20. Esplin's argument does not carry its point because his sources date from August 1844 and after, thus relying on recollections after the apostles had assumed the succession. A better indication of what church leaders in Nauvoo thought after the assassinations is found in William Clayton's diary, 12 July 1844, LDSCA, where he indicates that Joseph Smith had said "that if he and Hyrum were taken away Samuel H. Smith would be his successor." If Joseph Smith ordained the twelve to succeed him, Bishop Newell K. Whitney and William Clayton knew nothing about it in July, as Clayton's diary makes clear. But when Samuel died on 30 July everything changed, and the twelve's claims were as good as any at this time.

13. HC 7:198.

14. In D. Michael Quinn, "Joseph Smith III's 1844 Blessing and the Mormons of Utah," *Dialogue: A Journal of Mormon Thought* 15 (Summer 1982): 77.

15. S. Kimball, 74.

16. Quinn, 80.

17. Jedediah M. Grant, *A Collection of Facts, Relative to the Course Taken by Elder Sidney Rigdon, in the States of Ohio, Missouri, Illinois and Pennsylvania* (Philadelphia: Brown, Bicking & Guilbert, 1844), 22.

18. *Times and Seasons* 5 (1 July 1844): 568. The italics are mine.

19. Newell and Avery, 201–202.

20. Quinn, 78; Klaus Hansen, *Quest for Empire: The Political Kingdom of God and the Council of Fifty* (Lincoln: University of Nebraska Press, 1974), 94.

21. See Grant, 22–23, for Orson Hyde's testimony.

22. Richard S. Van Wagoner, *Mormon Polygamy: A History* (Salt Lake City: Signature Books, 1986), 30–32, 35, 71–73.

23. Newell and Avery, 201.

24. Grant, 34, 36, for the recollections of Heber Kimball and Brigham Young.

25. Newell and Avery, 202.

26. Quinn, 80.

27. Ibid., 81.

28. Ibid., 70.

29. HC 3:17–19.

30. Roger Van Noord, *King of Beaver Island* (Urbana: University of Illinois Press, 1988), 8.

31. Klaus J. Hansen, "The Making of King Strang: A Reexamination," *Michigan History* 46 (Sept. 1962), 201–219; and Roger D. Launius, *Joseph Smith III: Pragmatic Prophet* (Urbana: University of Illinois Press, 1988), 79.

32. Grant, 25.

33. Kenney, 2:434.

34. Grant, 26.

35. Kenney, 2:435–36.

36. Ibid., 436.

37. Ibid.

38. Ibid., 437.

39. Ibid. 439; William Clayton Diary, 4 Sept. 1844, says that Rigdon had converted Edward Hunter, Leonard Soby, William Cottier, and B. Coles.

40. Quinn, 79.

41. *Times and Seasons* 5 (15 Aug. 1844): 618.

42. HC 5:521.

43. Ibid., 7:240.

44. JD 6:319.

45. *Times and Seasons* 5 (15 Sept. 1844): 655; *The Prophet*, 9 Nov. 1844, for the remarks of Orson Hyde; Brigham Young Journal, 1 Sept. 1844; and Newell and Avery, 202–203.

46. Brigham Young Journal, 3 Sept. 1844.

47. William Clayton Diary, 4 Sept. 1844; Grant, 31, for the testimony of John Taylor.

48. Ibid., 5 Sept. 1844.

49. Ibid., 8 Sept. 1844.

50. *Messenger and Advocate of the Church of Christ* 1 (1 Jan. 1845): 75. Compare Kirtland Council Minute Book, 18 March 1833, LDSCA, where Rigdon and Williams are said to be equal with Joseph Smith in holding the keys of the kingdom and in the presidency of the high priesthood of the church.

51. Ibid.

52. Ibid. 1 (15 Feb. 1845): 113–14.

53. *The Ensign*, 15 July 1844, 13.

54. Ibid., 2 Aug. 1844, 29.

55. Ibid., 1 Oct. 1844, 136.

56. *Messenger and Advocate of the Church of Christ* 1 (15 April 1845): 168, and (1 May 1845): 190.

57. John A. Forgeus to Samual Forgeus, 25 Sept. 1844, in *Messenger and Advocate of the Church of Christ* 1 (15 Oct. 1844): 1–2.

58. See ibid. 1 (1 Jan. 1845): 75; 1 (15 Feb. 1845): 126; 1 (15 March 1845): 145–46; and 2 (1 Dec. 1845): 401.

59. Ibid. 1 (15 July 1845): 267; 2 (1 Nov. 1845): 397; 2 (1 Jan. 1846): 427; 2 (1 June 1846): 480; and 2 (1 March 1846): 460.

60. Winchester had been recalled to Nauvoo and had his license temporarily revoked. See *Times and Seasons* 5 (1 Nov. 1844): 701.

61. William Smith to Brigham Young, 16 Oct. 1844, Smith papers, LDSCA.

62. David J. Whittaker, "Early Mormon Pamphleteering," Ph.D. diss., Brigham Young University, 1982, 181–83, 188, 191.

63. William Smith to Brigham Young, 21 Aug. 1844, Smith papers.

64. Ibid., 26 Dec. 1844.

65. Whittaker, 185–86.

66. *Times and Seasons* 6 (1 Dec. 1844): 727.

67. William Smith to Heber C. Kimball, 21 Dec. 1844, Smith papers.

68. Wilford Woodruff to Brigham Young, 9 Oct. 1844, Young papers.

69. Whittaker, 187.

70. *Ensign of the Church of Christ* 1 (March 1847): 17.

71. Ibid., 2–11, 17.

72. Ibid., (May 1848): 93.

73. See "Manuscript History of the Church," Book A-1, 5 Dec. 1834, LDSCA, for Cowdery's early standing.

74. *Warsaw Signal*, 10 July 1844.

75. *Times and Seasons* 6 (15 April 1845): 869.

76. Newell and Avery, 215.

77. Ibid.

78. See Quorum of the Twelve Folder, Nauvoo Box Meetings and Conferences, 27 May 1843, LDSCA, for Joseph Smith's announcement.

79. A transcript of William's ordination, dated 24 May 1845, is in the Brigham Young papers and shows that William was set apart as patriarch "to the whole church."

80. *Times and Seasons* 6 (15 May 1845): 905.

81. Ibid., (1 June 1845): 920–22.

82. William Clayton Diary, 23 May 1845.

83. "Journal of James Monroe," 27 May 1845, microfilm copy at Utah State Historical Society.

84. William Clayton Diary, 28 May 1845.

85. HC 7:420.

86. William Smith to Brigham Young, 25 June 1845; HC 7:429.

87. HC 7:428–29.

88. Mary B. Smith to Ina Smith Coolbrith, 24 April 1908, Smith papers, LDSCA.

89. HC 7:429.

90. Lucy's revelations, dated 27 June 1845, are among her papers, LDSCA.

91. Brigham Young to Wilford Woodruff, 27 June 1845, Young papers.

92. JH, 28 June 1845.

93. Ibid., 30 June 1845.

94. Newell and Avery, 217.

95. William Clayton Diary, 30 June 1845.

96. Brigham Young to William Smith, 10 Aug. 1845, Young papers.

97. Notes of the meeting were kept by George Watt and are in the William Smith papers.

98. William Smith to Jesse Carter Little, 20 Aug. 1845, Smith papers.

99. Willard Richards to William Smith, 27 Aug. 1845, Richards papers, LDSCA.

100. William Smith to Brigham Young, 25 Sept. 1845, Smith papers.

101. William Smith to Brother Robbins, 15 Oct. 1845, Smith papers.

102. William Smith to James J. Strang, 2 Dec. 1846, Strang papers; and Van Noord, 45.

103. *Melchizedek and Aaronic Herald* 1 (1 May 1849): 2. Shelah Lane (Sheen) provides an account of William's revelation of 13 March 1849; compare Launius, 82–85, for some of William's subsequent activities leading to the rise of the Reorganized Church of Jesus Christ of Latter Day Saints in the 1860s.

104. Unpublished sermon of Brigham Young, 7 Oct. 1863, Young papers.

105. HC 7:288.

106. Richard E. Bennett, *Mormons at the Missouri, 1846–1852* (Norman, OK: University of Oklahoma Press, 1987), 210–11.

107. JD 6:319.

108. Ibid. 10:339.

109. Juanita Brooks, ed., *On the Mormon Frontier: The Diary of Hosea Stout, 1844–1861*, 2 vols. (Salt Lake City: University of Utah Press, 1964), 1:221.

110. *Northern Islander*, 13 Sept. 1855, 1.

111. Lyman Wight did not claim to be a prophet but waited for Joseph Smith III to be. See *Gospel Herald*, 31 Aug. 1848, 105.

112. William R. Dixon, who joined the church in 1842, asked James J. Strang in 1846 if he was such a prophet. His letter to Strang is dated 15 June and is in the Strang papers.

113. Ford's proclamation was published in the *Times and Seasons* 5 (1 July 1844): 565–66.

114. Ibid., 565.

115. Ibid., 566–67.

116. *Quincy Whig*, 3 July 1844.

117. *Illinois State Register*, 5 July 1844.

118. *Alton Telegraph*, 13 July 1844.

119. HC 7:159.

120. *Quincy Whig*, 3 July 1844.

121. *Missouri Republican*, 3 July 1844.

122. *Quincy Herald*, 5 July 1844.

123. Ibid.

124. HC 7:160–62.

125. *Warsaw Signal*, 10 July 1844.

126. William Hickman, *Brigham's Destroying Angel* (Salt Lake City: Shepard Publishing Company, 1904), 39.

127. *Quincy Whig*, 28 July 1844.

128. HC 7:203–204.

129. Ibid., 214–15.

130. Minor Deming to his parents, 22 Aug. 1844, Deming papers, Illinois Historical Society, Springfield.

131. *Warsaw Signal*, 4 Sept. 1844.

132. Thomas Ford to W. W. Phelps, 8 Sept. 1844, JH, under date. Also *Illinois State Register*, 20 Sept. 1844.

133. *Warsaw Signal*, 7 Aug. 1844.

134. Deming's letter to Ford was published in the *Warsaw Signal*, 4 Sept. 1844.

135. Dallin H. Oaks and Marvin S. Hill, *Carthage Conspiracy: The Trial of the Accused Assassins of Joseph Smith* (Urbana: University of Illinois Press, 1975), 124.

136. Franklin Worrell to Thomas Gregg, 8 Aug. 1844, Thomas C. Sharp papers, Beinecke Library, Yale University.

137. Thomas Ford to W. W. Phelps, 8 Sept. 1844, JH, under this date.

138. Oaks and Hill, 36.

139. Ibid.

140. Ibid., 36–37.

141. Ibid., 37–59.

142. Dean Jessee, ed., "The John Taylor Journal," *Brigham Young University Studies* 23 (Summer 1983): 41, 49.

143. Oaks and Hill, 97–185, for the full details of these events.

144. In HC 7:422.

145. Brigham Young to Wilford Woodruff, 27 June 1845, Young papers.

146. *Warsaw Signal*, 14 May 1845.

147. Ibid., 4 June 1845.

148. Ibid., 11 June 1845.

149. Ibid., 18 June 1845.

150. *Illinois State Register*, 4 July 845; Brigham Young to Wilford Woodruff, 27 July 1845, Young papers.

151. Minor Deming to his parents, 24 June, 1 July 1845.

152. *Quincy Whig*, 2 July 1845.

153. *Warsaw Signal*, 16 July 1845.

154. In *Chicago History*, 1 (Winter, 1948–49):58–59.

155. *Quincy Whig*, 15 Oct. 1845.

156. A former resident of Hancock County, the Reverend B. F. Morris, wrote of the situation in a letter to the editor of the *Indiana Blade*, which Sharp reprinted. Morris reported that the older citizens were "only waiting for some attrocious and lawless act of the Mormons to raise en masse, and expel them." He said the Saints were aware of this feeling and "just now are more quiet and orderly." But Morris complained of the deplorable state of society, saying that nearly every man was armed, "not knowing when or by whom he may be attacked." One older citizen told him that "every tie that binds man to his fellows, seems to be broken." Morris concluded that "the

influence on social life, on education, morals, and the interests, of pure Christianity is deeply withering" (*Warsaw Signal*, 13 Aug. 1845).

157. Ibid.; *Quincy Whig*, 13, 20 Aug. 1845.

158. Ibid., 3 Sept. 1845.

159. JH, 25, 26 June 1845.

160. Brigham Young to Wilford Woodruff, 21 Aug. 1845, Young papers.

161. JH, 28 Aug. 1845.

162. "Manuscript History of the Anti-Mormon Disturbances in Illinois, 1845," Thomas Sharp papers.

163. *Nauvoo Neighbor*, 10 Sept. 1845, 1–2.

164. JH, 9 Sept. 1845.

165. William Clayton Diary, 11 Sept. 1845.

166. *Nauvoo Neighbor*, 10 Sept. 1845.

167. William Clayton Diary, 11 Sept. 1845.

168. Brigham Young to Solomon Hancock, 11 Sept. 1845, Young papers.

169. Brigham Young to J. B. Backenstos, 11 Sept. 1845, Young papers.

170. Her letter of 30 Sept. 1845 is in the Deming papers, Illinois Historical Society, Springfield.

171. JH, 12 Sept. 1845.

172. Ibid., 14 Sept. 1845.

173. Ibid., 15 Sept. 1845.

174. HC 7:444.

175. William Clayton Diary, 16 Sept. 1845.

176. For Backenstos's account, see JH, 16 Sept. 1845; for Sharp's version, see *Warsaw Signal*, 24 Sept. 1845. See also "Journal of Thomas Bullock," 5 Sept. 1845, Special Collections, Harold B. Lee Library, Brigham Young University.

177. *Quincy Signal*, 17 Sept. 1845.

178. S. Kimball, 134.

179. *Missouri Republican*, 20 Sept. 1845. The editor's letter is dated 17 Sept.

180. William Clayton Diary, 16 Sept. 1845.

181. JH, 18, 19 Sept. 1845.

182. William Clayton Diary, 19 Sept. 1845.

183. Thomas Ford, *A History of Illinois* (Chicago: S. C. Greggs & Co., 1854), 410; Thomas Ford to J. B. Backenstos, 21 Sept. 1845, Ford papers, LDSCA.

184. Young's statement of 22 Sept. 1845 is in his papers at LDSCA.

185. *Missouri Republican*, 26 Sept. 1845; Henry Asbury, 160.

186. Oaks and Hill, 197.

187. Young to Wilford Woodruff, 16 Oct. 1845, Young papers; JH, 22 Sept. 1845.

188. A typescript of the Carthage Resolutions, dated 1 Oct. 1845, is in Special Collections, Harold B. Lee Library, Brigham Young University.

189. William Clayton Diary, 6 Oct. 1845.

190. Minutes of LDS General Conference, 6–8 Oct. 1845, in Mormon Broadsides, Chicago Historical Society.

191. *Times and Seasons* 6 (1 Nov. 1845): 1010, for Pratt's remarks of 6 Oct.

192. William Clayton Diary, 10 Oct. 1845.

193. *Illinois State Register*, 10 Oct. 1845.

194. Young to Woodruff, 16 Oct. 1845.

195. Thomas Ford to John J. Hardin, 13 Oct. 1845, Hardin Collection, Chicago Historical Society.

196. JH, 25 Oct. 1845.

197. Brooks, *Diary of Hosea Stout*, 2:83. Stout wrote this on 25 Oct.

198. Orson Spencer to Thomas Ford, 23 Oct. 1845, Ford papers.

199. JH, 30 Oct. 1845.

200. Thomas Ford to J. B. Backenstos, 29 Oct. 1845, Ford papers.

201. Pierpont Sperry to Anson Sperry, 27 Oct. 1845, Mormon Collection, Chicago Historical Society.

202. Ford to Backenstos, 29 Oct. 1845.

203. *Quincy Whig*, 5 Nov. 1845.

204. JH, 15 Nov. 1845; T. Ford, 432.

205. JH, 15, 18, 21 Nov. 1845.

206. *Quincy Whig*, 19 Nov. 1845.

207. *Times and Seasons* 6 (15 Nov. 1845): 1031.

208. Ibid. (1 Dec. 1845): 1042–43. Compare Eugene Campbell, "Pioneers and Patriotism: Conflicting Loyalties," in Davis Bitton and Maureen Ursenbach Beecher, eds., *New Views of Mormon History* (Salt Lake City: University of Utah Press, 1987), 307–22, for a balanced assessment of Mormon attitudes toward the United States at this time.

209. Brigham Young to Wilford Woodruff, 19 Nov. 1845, Young papers.

210. JH, 29 Nov. 1845.

211. Willard Richards to Benjamin Wiley, 11 Dec. 1845, Richards papers.

212. Brooks, *Diary of Hosea Stout*, 1:99; JH, 23 Dec. 1845.

213. "Journal of Heber C. Kimball," 2 Jan. 1846, in handwriting of William Clayton, LDSCA.

214. "Journal of John D. Lee," 10 Jan. 1846, LDSCA.

215. JH, 29 Jan. 1846.

216. Ibid., 2 Feb. 1846. Thomas Bullock in his journal for 17 Feb. 1846 recorded, however, that Senator Hoge in Washington, D.C., wrote that Congress said the Mormons had a right to leave the U.S. "if they pleased." But by this time the exodus was underway.

217. Ibid., 4 Feb. 1846.

218. This was reported by Thomas Sharp in the *Warsaw Signal*, 11 Feb. 1846.

219. Brooks, *Diary of Hosea Stout*, 1:123–24.

220. T. Ford, 412.

221. *Warsaw Signal*, 10 June 1846.

222. Ibid., 24 July 1846.

223. T. Ford, 413–14; *Hancock County Eagle*, 12 July 1846.

224. Ibid.

225. *Warsaw Signal*, 11 Aug. 1846.

226. Ford's address was printed in the *Illinois State Register*, 11 Dec. 1846.

227. Alexis de Tocqueville, *Democracy in America* (New York: Vintage Books, 1955), 1:271.

Index

A

Aaronic priesthood: elder as office in, 26

Abbott, Brother and Sister: receive letter from T. B. Marsh, 96

Adam-ondi-Ahman: established, 74; formed into stake of Zion, 74; Saints on defensive, 87

Adams, George: perceives congressional insult, 102–103

Adams County (IL): citizens warn Mormons away, 131

Ahlstrom, Sidney, viii

Albrecht, Stanley, ix

Aldrich, Mark: indicted for murder, 170; politico siding with Joseph Smith, 124–25

Alexander, Thomas, viii

Alger, Fanny: alleged plural wife of Joseph Smith, 62

Allen, James, viii

Alton Telegraph: disapproves Mormon political ticket, 121; complains of anti-Republican tendencies of Mormonism, 122; on destruction of *Nauvoo Expositor*, 145; dislikes murderers taking law into own hands, 166

America: social disintegration, xi

American Constitution: pluralism in, xiii–xiv; appeal to by Thomas Ford, 147–48

American Home Missionary Society, 7

American Indians: Kirtland Saints believe Indians will crush Roman Catholics, 67

American revolutionary tradition: appeals to higher law discussed, 81

Ancient of Days: to visit Adam-ondi-Ahman, 74

Andrews, Benjamin: sees prophet as national deliverer, 137

antagonism: against Smith family, 3

anti-Mormons: convention at Warsaw (IL), 124; indictment of Mormon kingdom, 133–34; appeal to natural rights, 134; call for military support, 134; hurry Mormon exodus from Illinois by threats of violence, 180

anti-pluralism: in Missouri brings trouble, 97; voiced by Joseph Smith, 138

anti-sectarianism: in Ohio, 32

apocalyptic: Mormons rely on, 136

apostles, dissenting: believe wicked, 96

appeal to higher law: in Missouri, 80

Armies of Israel: organized, 75; siege at house of Adam Black, 84; reach house of Lyman Wight, 85

Army of Israel: organization of, 53

Arrington, Leonard J., ix; Law of Consecration, 37

Atchison, David R.: protection of Mormon witnesses in Independence (MO), 42; finds Missourians marshalled for war, 87; orders militants to disband, 87; reports situation stable, Mormons not to be feared, 88; writes governor on lawless troops, 90; pleads for Boggs's intervention, 90; leads Missouri militia against Far West, 94

Palmyra (NY), 20; objection to Mormon militarism, 47; criticizes Kirtland bank failure, 57

Harrison, William Henry: Mormons vote for, 109

Haun's Mill: attacked by Missouri militia, 94; attack embitters Mormons, 94; extermination talk encourages attack on, 94

Hawkins, Uriah and Lydia: practiced unlawful matrimony, 51

Hayden, Amos: on millennialism among Campbellites, xx

Heath, Harvard, viii

Henry, A. G.: sees Mormons worth political courting, 141

Heywood, Joseph C.: urges Brigham Young to flee, 179–80

Hickman, Martin, ix

Higbee, Chauncey: excommunicated for teaching unchaste principles, 116; Nauvoo dissenter, 142

Higbee, Elias: goes to Washington, 101; hopes for redress, 102

Higbee, Francis: Nauvoo dissenter, 142; describes plans for anti-Mormon newspaper, 143

Hill, Donna, viii
Hill, Leslie, ix
Hill, Lila, ix
Hill, Robert, ix
Hill, Steven, ix

Hinkle, George: leads Mormon forces, 91; support Sidney Rigdon, 159; leads splinter group, 159

Hiram (OH): LDS reject Law of Consecration, 37

History of the Church: Melchizedek priesthood restoration, 25–26

Hoge, Joseph P.: political candidate visits Nauvoo, 131

Hollister, D. S.: on lack of political support, 140

Horne, Mrs. Joseph: on opposition to polygamy among Saints, 115

Houston, Sam: Lyman Wight hopes to covert, 140

Houston (IL): Mormons warned at, 105

Howard, Richard P., vii

Howe, Daniel, viii

Howe, E. D.: *Mormonism Unvailed*, 24; first Mormon missionaries, 26; Mormon missionaries, 32; City of Joseph, description of establishment of, 32; Zion's Camp preparations, 42–43; would investigate Book of Mormon, 64; criticizes Mormon excesses, 64; policy to report on Mormons, 64; warns of impostors, 64

Hubble: Mormon prophetess, 34

Hughes, Richard, viii

Hunter, Edward: sectarian strife, 15

Huntington, Oliver B.: calls Danites a divine brotherly union, 76; sent to Robert Foster, 144

Hurlbut, Philastus: collaborates with E. D. Howe, 23–24; collection of documents for E. D. Howe, 24; exposes Book of Mormon, 24

Hyde, Orson: sent to England on mission, 59; knew of Danites, 76; leaves church for conscience's sake, 96; would take no part with Danites, 96; war causes him to flee, 97; shows support for law, 97; relies on stories told him, 97; inclined to blame Sidney Rigdon, 98; does not deny published testimony, 98; advocates Law of Adoption, 114; reacts to polygamy, 115; wife resists polygamy, 115; says prophet will execute justice, 138; Willard Richards writes regarding election, 139; writes to Sidney Rigdon, 155

I

Illinois: early anti-Mormonism in, 105; state legislature demands repeal of Nauvoo charter, 123; state legislature charges misuse of habeas corpus by Mormons, 123; citizens respond to Smith murders, 166–67; Mormonism in reveals democratic limitations, 181–82

Illinois State Register: criticizes Mormons, 109; calls Smith murders cowardly, 166; describes anti-Mormon feelings, 177

Independence (MO): central gathering place of Saints, 40

seeks economic self-sufficiency, 127; taken into custody, 129; accused of attempted murder, 129; pledges vote to Walker, 129; instructs Wilson Law, 129; appeals to higher law, 130; pledges use of military force, 130, 131; defends chartered rights, 130; warns against mobs, 131; announces vote for Walker, 132; endorse Hyrum Smith's political revelation, 132; blames Democrats, 132–33; consequences of political policies, 133; fears kidnapping of Mormons, 135; seeks city ordinance, 135; conspiracy against, 135; aware of dissenters, 136; calls out Nauvoo Legion, 136; calls on volunteers, 136; pleads for justice against Missouri, 137; petitions Congress, 137; sees fall of nation, 137; candidate for president, 137; wants to deal with wicked, 137–38; seeks national political power, 139; on establishing political kingdom, 140–41; issues writ to offset Carthage warrant, 144; seeks rapprochement with dissenters, 144; denounces *Nauvoo Expositor*, 145; released under Nauvoo writ, 146; calls for volunteers, 146–47; declares martial law, 146; defends actions to Governor Ford, 146; raises new national standard, 147; dilemma of, 148; returns to Nauvoo, 148; flees to Iowa, 148; surrenders to state authorities, 148; returns to Nauvoo, 148; charged with treason, 149; taken to Carthage, 149; hopes to survive Carthage, 149–50; murdered, 150; murderers of appeal to revolutionary tradition, 150; funeral, 153; Mormons react to murder, 153–54; uncertainty regarding mantle, 155

Smith, Joseph, Sr.: ginseng operation, defrauded in, 1; financial difficulties, 1, 19; crop failures, 1; excessive drinking, 1; farming and merchandising, 1; owns a farm, 1; tenancy, 1; loses farm, 2; get-rich-quick schemes, 2; emigrates to western New York, 1, 2; attracted by rich farm land, 2; moves to Manchester, 2; builds small house, 2; buys 100-acre farm, 2; settles in Palmyra, 2; takes odd jobs, 2; money digging, 3, 12; religious seekers, 4; joins

Universalists, 5; religious differences with wife, 5; Universalism and conflict with neighbors, 5; church meetings, 5; concern for religion, 6; Methodism and family dissension, 6; religious dreams, 6; fears for salvation, 6; funeral of Alvin Smith, 10; imprisoned for debt, 27

Smith, Joseph, III: no initial support as successor to father, 156

Smith, Lucy Mack: socially disinherited, 1; financial difficulties, 1, 19; tenancy, 1; emigrates to western New York, 1, 2; leads family westward, 2; settles in Palmyra, 2; takes odd jobs, 2; moves to Manchester, 2; eight children, 2; Presbyterian church, 3, 5; folk magic, 3; religious seekers, 4; studies word of God, 5; promises to get religion, 5; baptism, 5; religious differences with husband, 5, 6; promises to God, 5; anguish over religion, 6; first vision, 10; grieves for Alvin Smith, 10; revival, 10; Presbyterians, 11; dilemma regarding church membership, 11; conversion experience rejects Calvinism, 13; sell copies of Book of Mormon to buy food, 20; reports secret meeting at Kirtland, 60; on death of sons, 153; supports twelve apostles at first, 156; supports William Smith, 162, 163; says Smith family founded church, 163; fears for William, 163; has revelation for William, 163

Smith, M. J.: says things improve in Kirtland with dissenters confession, 61

Smith, Sylvester: criticizes Kirtland bank failure, 57

Smith, William: recalls hard work, 2; says Smiths respected at first, 3; father's Universalism, 5; Melchizedek priesthood restored, 25–26; reports on Law of Adoption, 114; fights with Benjamin Winchester, 117, 159, 160; opposes repeal of Nauvoo charter, 123; no support as successor to Joseph Smith, 156; supports James J. Strang, 156; supports twelve apostles in east, 160; demands rights in east, 160; on office of patriarch, 160–63; named patriarch to the

Warren, Catherine: charged with affair
with John C. Bennett, 116; reports on
spreading illicit sex, 117
Warren (IL): Mormon plans, 105
Warsaw (IL): land speculators oppose Mormon settlement, 105; citizens charge
high rents, 105; anti-Mormon feelings
in, 133; militia seeks opportunity to kill
Joseph Smith, 150; Committee of
Safety tells Ford why they will drive
Mormons out, 167; citizens call for military encampment, 170; citizens cele-
brate Deming death, 173
Warsaw Message: praises Pope decision, 125;
laments harassment of Mormon
prophet, 131
Warsaw Signal: announces victory of anti-
Mormons, 124; Thomas Sharp returns
as editor, 141; reports on military activities, 146
Wayne Sentinel, 7
Western Star: reports Adam Black misrep-
resentations, 87; editor says land speculators oppose Mormons, 87
Weston, William: protests Mormon legal
exemption, 125
Whigs: block bank charters, 56–57; seek
Mormon vote, 106; press favors Mormons, 109; oppose repeal of city charters, 123; lead anti-Mormons at Carthage, 133; give up on Mormons as
political allies, 141
Whitlock, Harvey: supports Sidney
Rigdon, 159
Whitmer, David: organization of church
by 1829, 20; chooses twelve disciples,
25; Melchizedek priesthood, date of
restoration, 25–26; captain of Lord's
host, 53; says Joseph Smith lost humility, 60; dissatisfied at Far West, 62;
meets with dissenters, 62; rejected as
leader in Zion, 69; excommunication,
69, 71; protests church action, 72;
refuses to take oath, 77; assumes new
church leadership, 161;
Whitmer family: opposition to Smith revelation, 27; meeting in secret with
Hiram Page, 27; included in Law of
Stewardship, 38
Whitmer, Jacob: meets with dissenters at
Far West, 62

Whitmer, John: dates restoration of
Melchizedek priesthood, 25; says leaders lust after forbidden things, 60; criticizes Joseph Smith, 60; controls land
sales in Missouri, 61; meets with dissenters at Far West, 62; dissatisfied at
Far West, 62; sells Missouri land, 69;
rejected as president in Zion, 69;
excommunication, 69; claims funds
donated to church, 69–70; reports on
Danites, 75
Whitney, Helen Mar: recalls father's
response to polygamy, 115
Whitney, Newell K.: administers Law of
Consecration, 38
Whitney, Sarah Ann: promised eternal
glory, 115
Whitaker, George: rejects concept of endless hell, 13
Whittaker, David, viii
Wight, Lyman: lower-class origin, 16; fight
at Gallatin, 84; refusal of Missouri custody, 86; surrenders at Far West, 94;
blames Democrats of Missouri, 107;
writes to *Quincy Whig*, 108; seeks Texas
alliance, 140; wants Council of Fifty to
lead church, 155
Wild, Asa, 8
Willey, Jeremiah: anxious to move out of
U.S.A., 179
Williams, Frederick G.: criticizes Kirtland
bank failure, 57
Williams, Levi: friends would protect, 135;
charged with kidnapping, 135; says
anti-Mormon motives were political,
167; indicted for murder, 170; burns
Mormon houses, 173; calls out Warsaw
militia, 174
Williams, S. O.: describes hysteria at
Carthage, 146
Wills, John: indicted for murder, 170
Wilson, General: Whig candidate visits
Far West, 83
Winchester, Benjamin: on Kingdom of
God, xviii; Zion's Camp meant to wage
war, 44; comments on Kirtland as cen-
ter of world, 55; criticizes Joseph
Smith, 60; opposes William Smith, 117;
supports Sidney Rigdon, 159
Wingate, E. B.: supports Sidney Rigdon,
159

Woodruff, Phoebe: opposes polygamy, 115
Woodruff, Wilford: lower-class origin, 16;
    optimistic for Kirtland, 55; condemns
    Hyde and Marsh, 96; says apostles bore
    false witness, 97; resolves to build a
    city, 100; records Hyrum Smith's com-
    ment on dissenters, 143; reports on
    Sidney Rigdon's vision, 156; credits
    Jedediah Grant with saving eastern
    church, 160; discredits William Smith,
    160
Word of Wisdom: to be obeyed, 69
Worrell, Franklin: laments political losses,
    169; warns of violence if Deming
    arrests mob, 169

Y

Young, Brigham: on establishment of
    political kingdom of God, xv; lower-
    class origin, 16; conversion to Book of
    Mormon, 23; dates restoration of
    Melchizedek priesthood, 25–26; says
    Peter, James, and John restored priest-
    hood, 26; recalls Joseph Smith as store-
    keeper, 39; opposes replacing Joseph
    Smith, 59; no protest from, 96; hurries
    gathering to Illinois, 99–100; practices
    Law of Adoption, 114; learns of polyg-
    amy, 115; labors with Orson Pratt, 117;
    wants economic independence at
    Nauvoo, 128; kingdom to be
    established, 136; says government
    belongs to God, 138; pledges all out
    political campaign, 139; reaction to
    death of Joseph Smith, 154–55;
    responds to Sidney Rigdon's offer to
    lead church, 157; says church has no
    prophet, 157; on calling as church lead-
    ers, 158; fears church divisions, 158;
    sees self as people's choice to succeed,
    158; gains loyalty of church majority,
    161; seeks to appease William Smith,
    162; expects Smith family to assume

church leadership, 164–65; sees self as
    successor to Joseph Smith, 165; stresses
    apostleship as key to authority, 165;
    reorganizes First Presidency, 165;
    reluctance to assume mantle of Joseph
    Smith, 165–66; angry at trial verdict,
    171; acknowledges consecrating thieves
    at Nauvoo, 172–73; plans for exodus,
    173; lets sheriff worry about the mob,
    173–74; shows restraint on retaliation
    for burnings, 174; calls J. B.
    Backenstos's forces home, 175; seeks
    peace with Levi Williams, 175; wants
    mob dealt with by laws of God, 175;
    states Mormon terms for exodus, 175;
    tells Quincy committee Mormons will
    leave in spring, 176; describes house
    burnings, 177; relishes exodus, 179; to
    ban secularism and pluralism in val-
    ley, 179; avoids arrest, 179; longs for
    Kingdom of God, 179; tells Saints they
    must flee Nauvoo, 180; makes right
    decision, 182
Young, Joseph: predicts Kirtland growth,
    55
Young, Lorenzo Dow, 13

Z

Zion: redemption of, 53; elders prepare
    for, 53; Saints divided in, 61
Zion's Camp, 39; described by E. D. Howe,
    42–43; march to redeem promised
    land, 43; armed force as last resort, 43;
    local newspapers announce coming of,
    43; Joseph Smith belief in result of, 44;
    warned of approaching armed Missou-
    rians, 45; reaches Fishing River, 45;
    peace conference in Missouri, 45; chol-
    era epidemic, 46; disbanded, 46; Mor-
    mon anger concerning, 47; leaders
    criticize Kirtland bank, 57; influence
    on militarism, 69